A fan sent in enough four-leaf
clover key chains for the whole
Blank Page Brigade. Yessss! Now
my workplace will be lucky!!
Thank you very much.

—*Yūki Tabata, 2015*

YŪKI TABATA

was born in Fukuoka Prefecture
and got his big break in the 2011
Shonen Jump Golden Future Cup
with his winning entry, *Hungry
Joker*. He started the magical fantasy
series *Black Clover* in 2015.

BLACK CLOVER
VOLUME 4
SHONEN JUMP Manga Edition

Story and Art by YŪKI TABATA

Translation ✽ TAYLOR ENGEL,
HC LANGUAGE SOLUTIONS, INC.

Touch-Up Art & Lettering ✽ ANNALIESE CHRISTMAN

Design ✽ FAWN LAU

Editor ✽ ALEXIS KIRSCH

Printed in Italy

Published by VIZ Media, LLC
P.O. Box 77010
San Francisco, CA 94107

10 9 8 7 6 5
First printing, December 2016
Fifth printing, March 2024

RATED T TEEN ratings.viz.com

PARENTAL ADVISORY
BLACK CLOVER is rated T for Teen and is recommended for ages 13 and up. This volume contains realistic and fantasy violence.

VIZ MEDIA
viz.com

SHONEN JUMP

Fuegoleon

Asta

Leopold

Black✦Clover

4

YŪKI TABATA

THE CRIMSON
LION KING

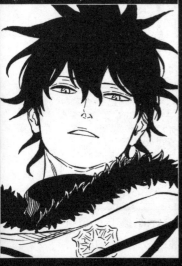

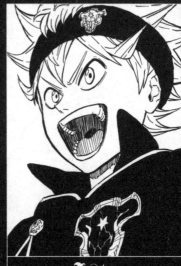

Asta

Squad: The Black Bulls
Magic: None (Anti-Magic)

He has no magic, but he's working to become the Wizard King through sheer guts and his well-trained body.

Yuno

Squad: The Golden Dawn
Magic: Wind

Asta's best friend, and a good rival who's been working to become the Wizard King right alongside him since they were little.

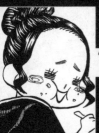

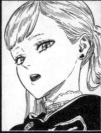

Noelle Silva

Squad: The Black Bulls
Magic: Water

A royal. She's really impudent, but can be kind too.

Charmy Pappitson

Squad: The Black Bulls
Magic: Cotton

She's small, but she eats like a maniac.

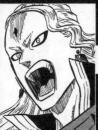

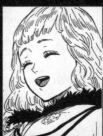

Mimosa Vermillion

Squad: The Golden Dawn
Magic: Plant

Noelle's cousin. She's calm, gentle and a bit of an airhead.

Fuegoleon Vermillion

Squad: The Crimson Lion Kings
Magic: Flame

A captain with a strong sense of justice. He's Mimosa's cousin and Leopold's older brother.

Noxel Silva

Squad:
The Silver Eagles
Magic: Mercury

A proud captain. Noelle's older brother.

Leopold Vermillion

Squad: The Crimson Lion Kings
Magic: Flame

An innocent, self-confident guy. Mimosa's cousin and Fuegoleon's younger brother.

Solid Silva

Squad:
The Silver Eagles
Magic: Water

Noelle's older brother.

Nebra Silva

Squad:
The Silver Eagles
Magic: Mist

Noelle's older sister.

???

Squad: ?
Magic: ?

A mystery man who's launched a surprise attack on the capital. He has a bitter grudge against the Clover Kingdom…

Sol Marron

Squad: The Blue Rose Knights
Magic: Earth

She's a carefree Amazon, but she adores her captain.

STORY

In a world where magic is everything, Asta and Yuno are both found abandoned on the same day at a church in the remote village of Hage. Both dream of becoming the Wizard King, the highest of all mages, and they spend their days working toward that dream.

The year they turn 15, both receive grimoires, magic books that amplify their bearer's magic. They take the entrance exam for the Magic Knights, nine groups of mages under the direct control of the Wizard King. Yuno, whose magic is strong, joins the Golden Dawn, an elite group, while Asta, who has no magic at all, joins the Black Bulls, a group of misfits. With this, the two finally take their first step toward becoming the Wizard King…

In light of their conquest of the dungeon, Asta and the others are invited to be guests at the distinguished service ceremony, held for Magic Knights who achieve great things. However, they find themselves in a tense standoff with the assembled veterans from each brigade! They then receive word that the royal capital is under attack. Asta and the others leap into action to save the country from peril!

BLACK ✦ CLOVER

CONTENTS

BLACK ❀ CLOVER

4

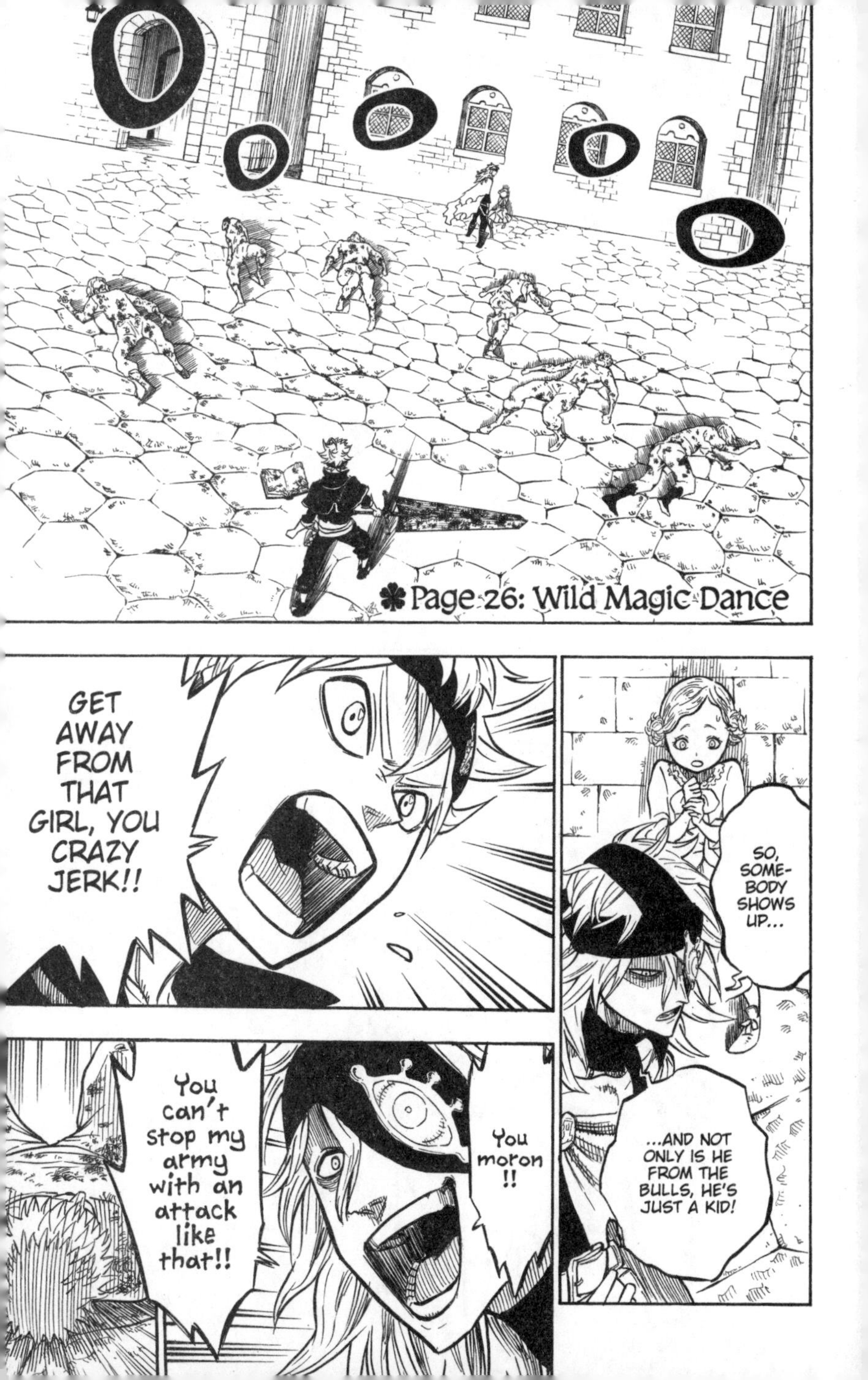

Page 26: Wild Magic Dance
SO, SOME-BODY SHOWS UP...
...AND NOT ONLY IS HE FROM THE BULLS, HE'S JUST A KID!
GET AWAY FROM THAT GIRL, YOU CRAZY JERK!!
You moron!!
You can't stop my army with an attack like that!!

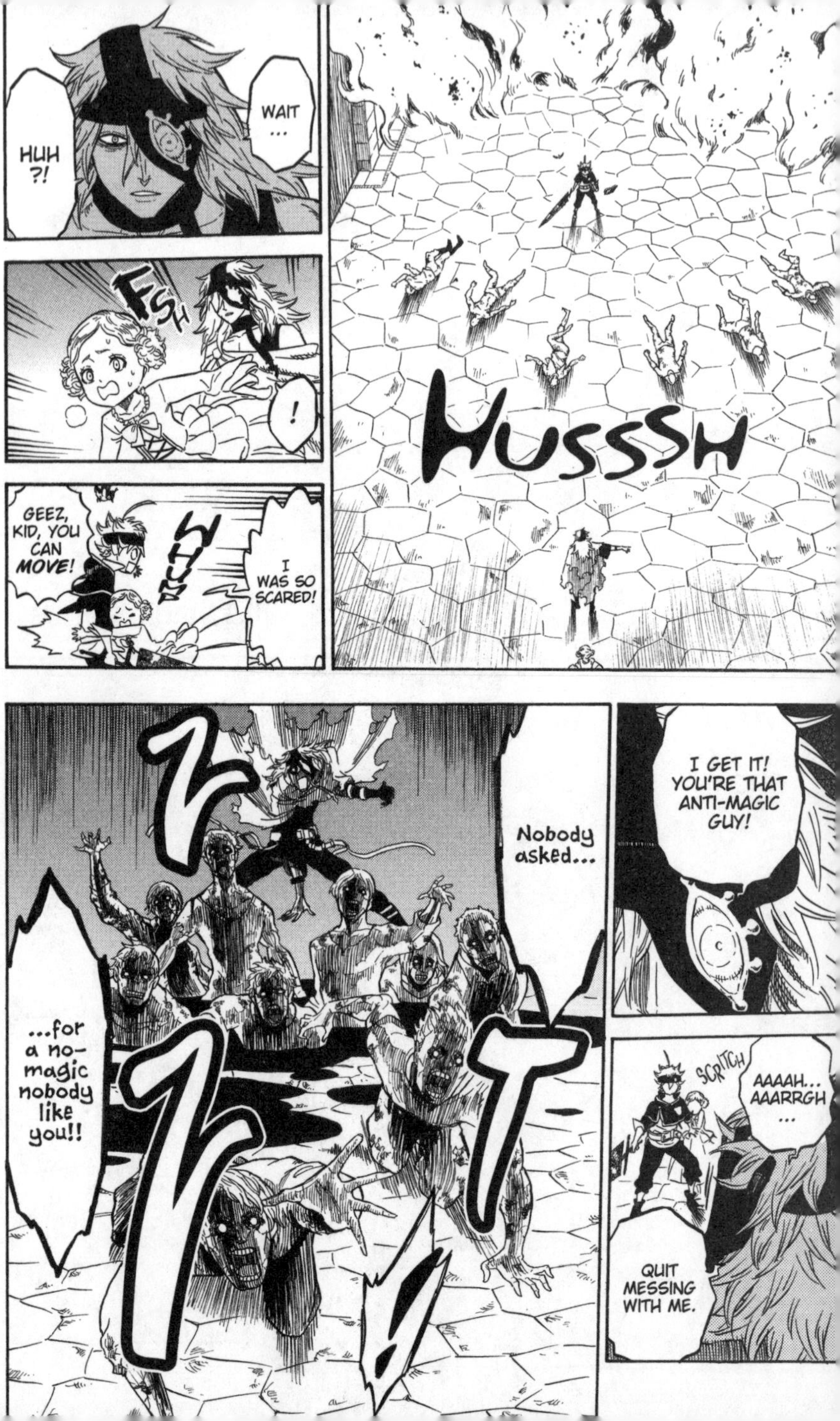
HUSSSH
WAIT ...
HUH ?!
FSH
!
I WAS SO SCARED!
WHUM
GEEZ, KID, YOU CAN MOVE!
I GET IT! YOU'RE THAT ANTI-MAGIC GUY!
AAAAH... AAARRGH ...
SCRITCH
QUIT MESSING WITH ME.
Nobody asked...
...for a no-magic nobody like you!!

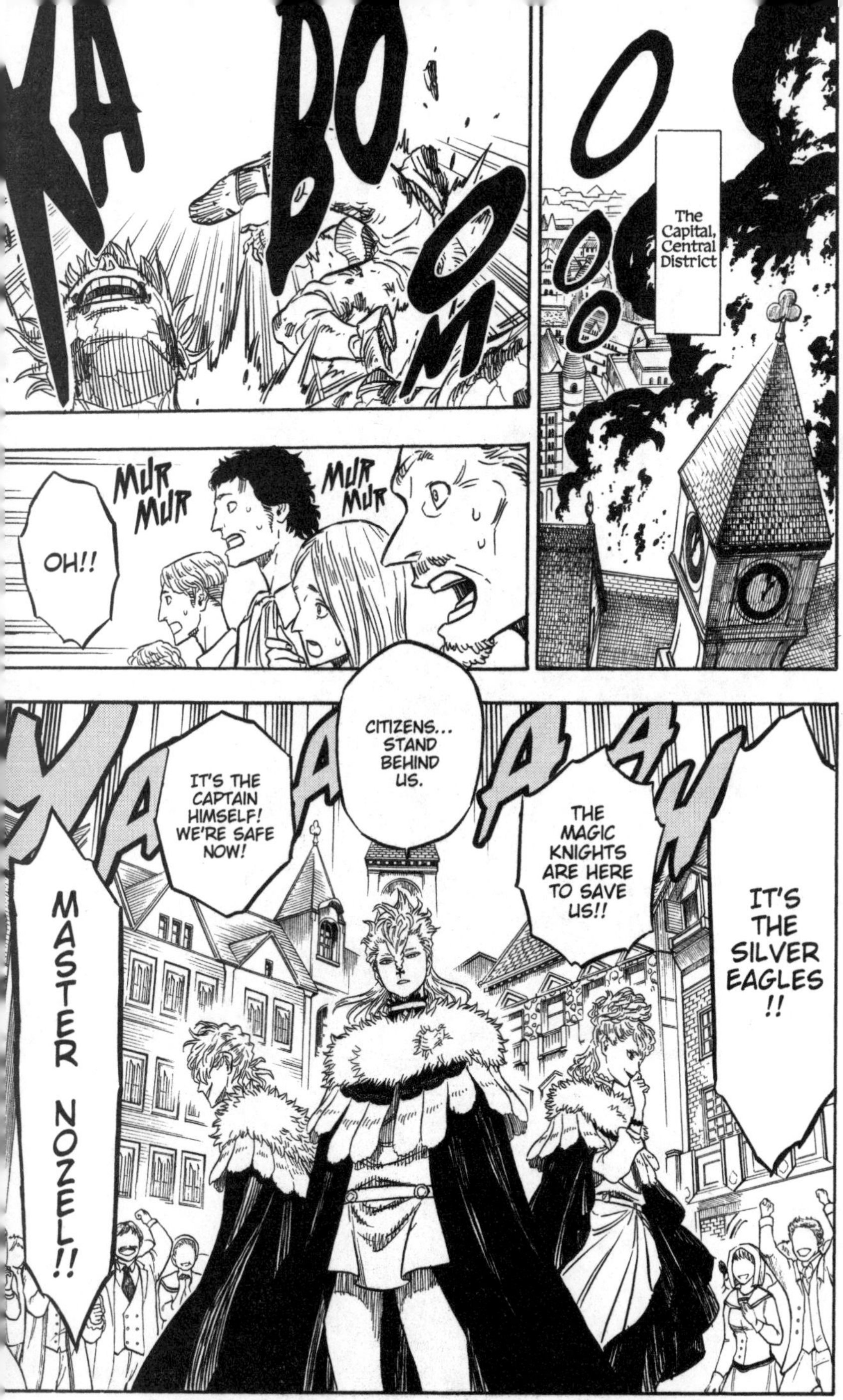
The Capital, Central District
KA BOOOOOM
MUR MUR
MUR MUR
OH!!
KAAAAH
IT'S THE SILVER EAGLES!!
THE MAGIC KNIGHTS ARE HERE TO SAVE US!!
CITIZENS... STAND BEHIND US.
IT'S THE CAPTAIN HIMSELF! WE'RE SAFE NOW!
MASTER NOZEL!!

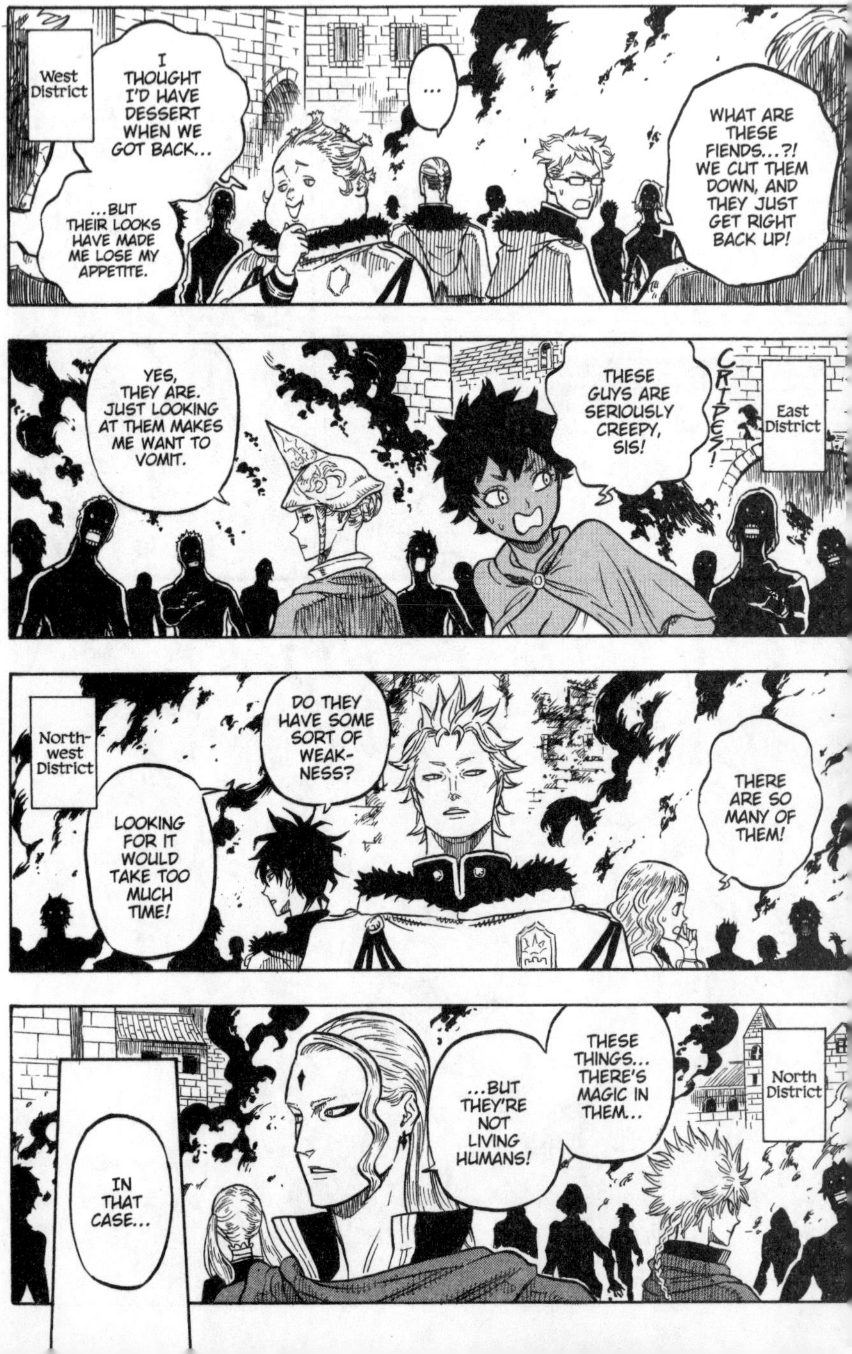
WHAT ARE THESE FIENDS...?! WE CUT THEM DOWN, AND THEY JUST GET RIGHT BACK UP!
...
West District
I THOUGHT I'D HAVE DESSERT WHEN WE GOT BACK...
...BUT THEIR LOOKS HAVE MADE ME LOSE MY APPETITE.
East District
CRIPES!
THESE GUYS ARE SERIOUSLY CREEPY, SIS!
YES, THEY ARE. JUST LOOKING AT THEM MAKES ME WANT TO VOMIT.
THERE ARE SO MANY OF THEM!
DO THEY HAVE SOME SORT OF WEAK-NESS?
North-west District
LOOKING FOR IT WOULD TAKE TOO MUCH TIME!
North District
THESE THINGS... THERE'S MAGIC IN THEM...
...BUT THEY'RE NOT LIVING HUMANS!
IN THAT CASE...

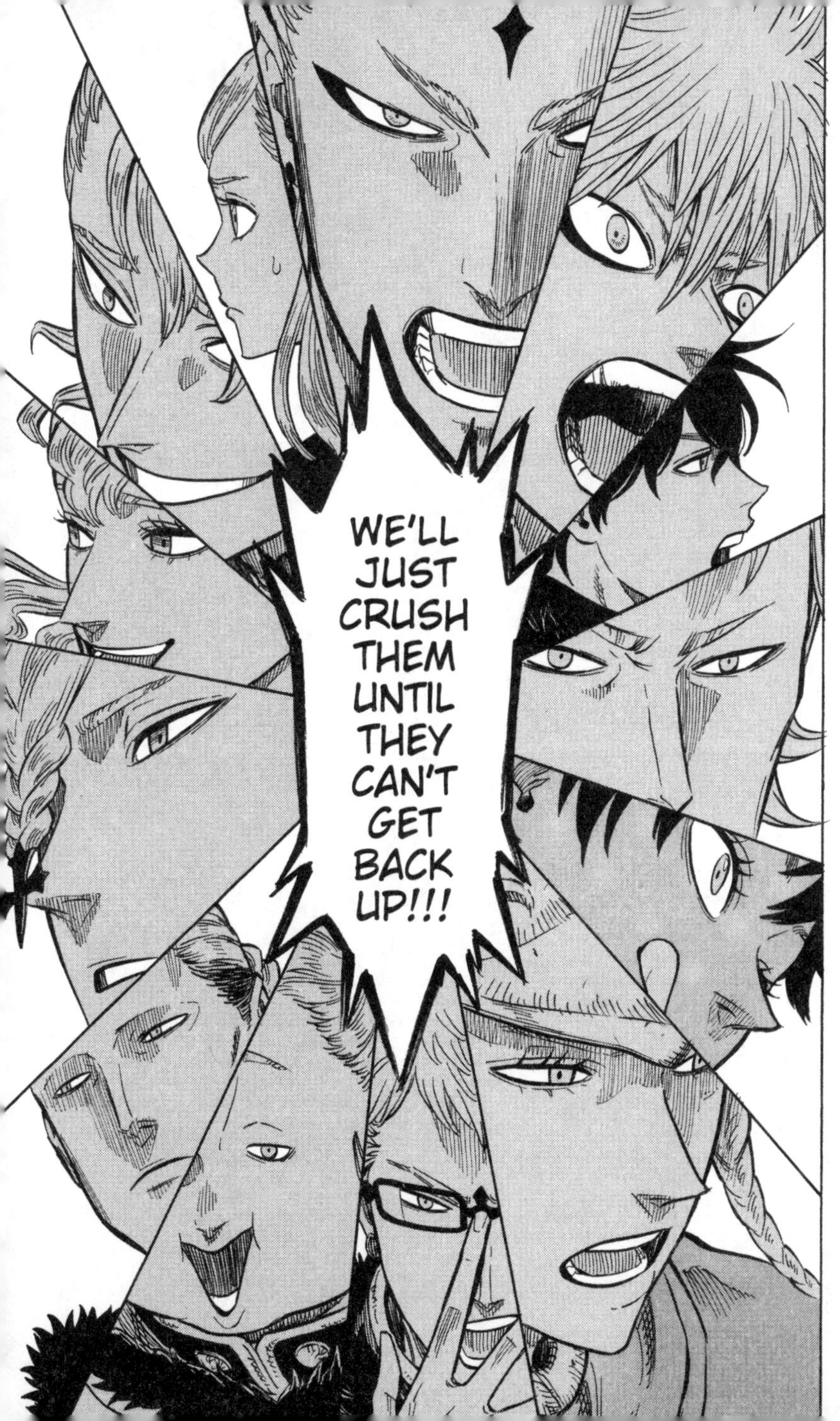
WE'LL JUST CRUSH THEM UNTIL THEY CAN'T GET BACK UP!!!

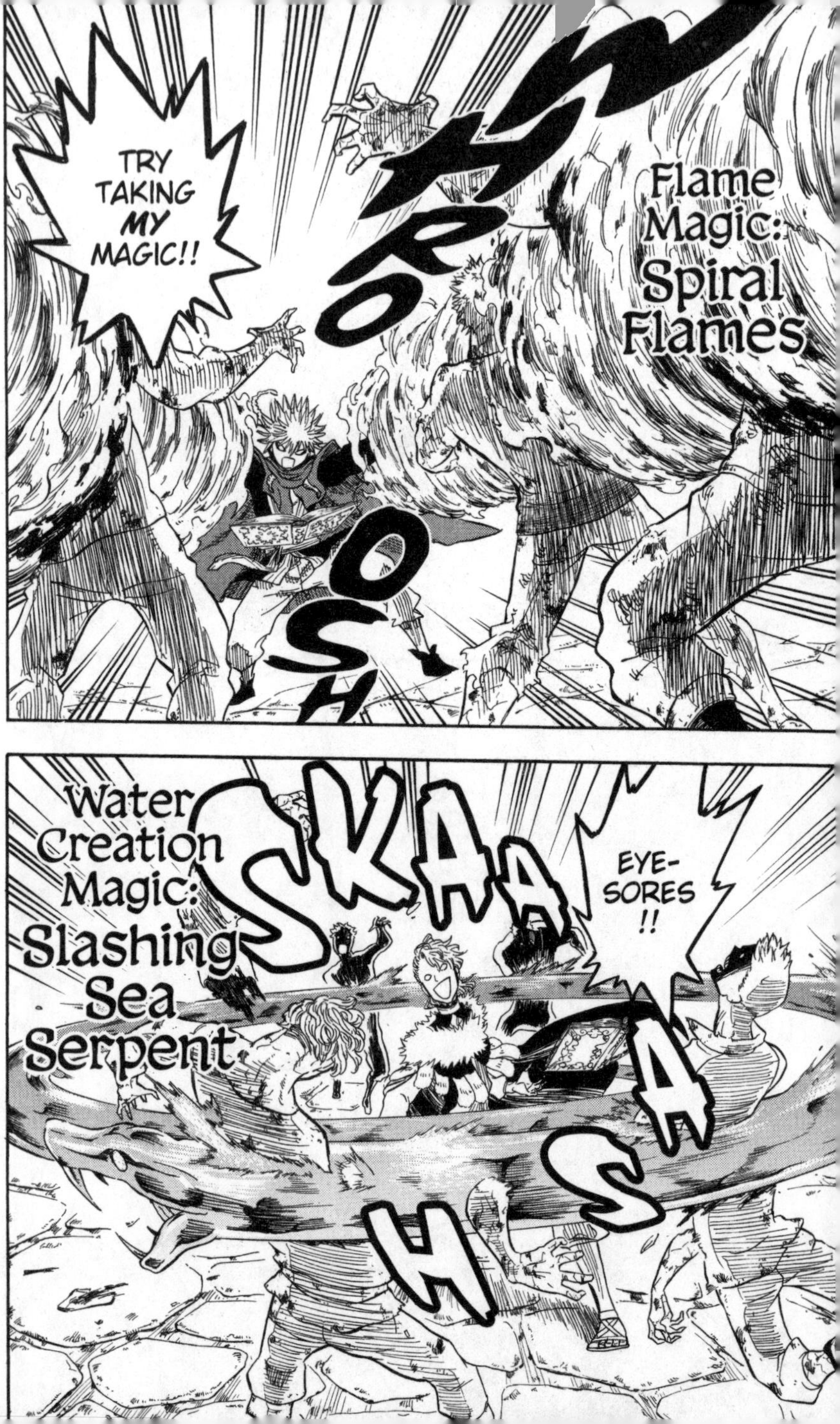
Flame Magic: Spiral Flames
TRY TAKING MY MAGIC!!
EYE-SORES!!
SKAAAASH
Water Creation Magic: Slashing Sea Serpent

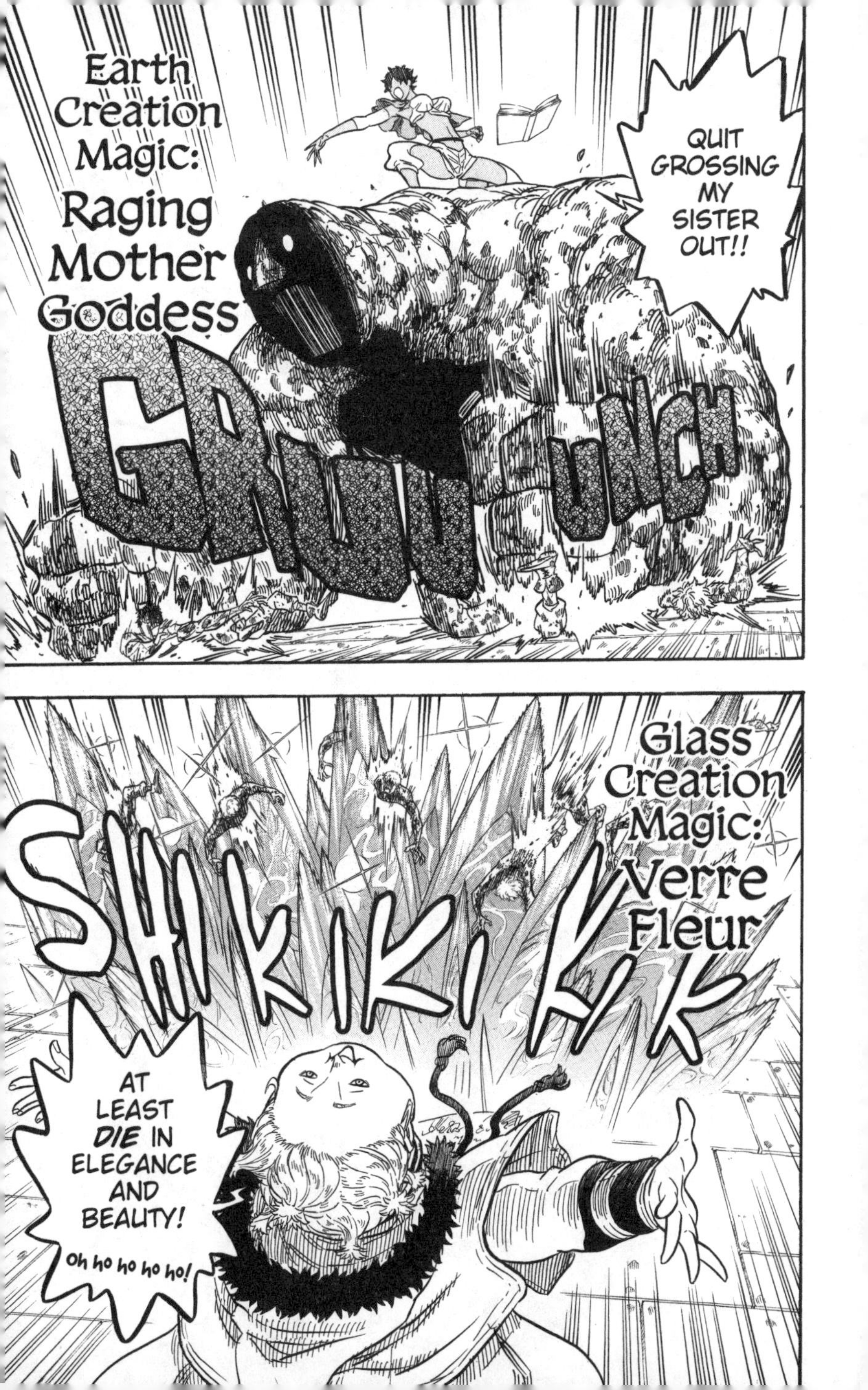
QUIT GROSSING MY SISTER OUT!!
Earth Creation Magic: Raging Mother Goddess
Glass Creation Magic: Verre Fleur
AT LEAST *DIE* IN ELEGANCE AND BEAUTY!
Oh ho ho ho ho!

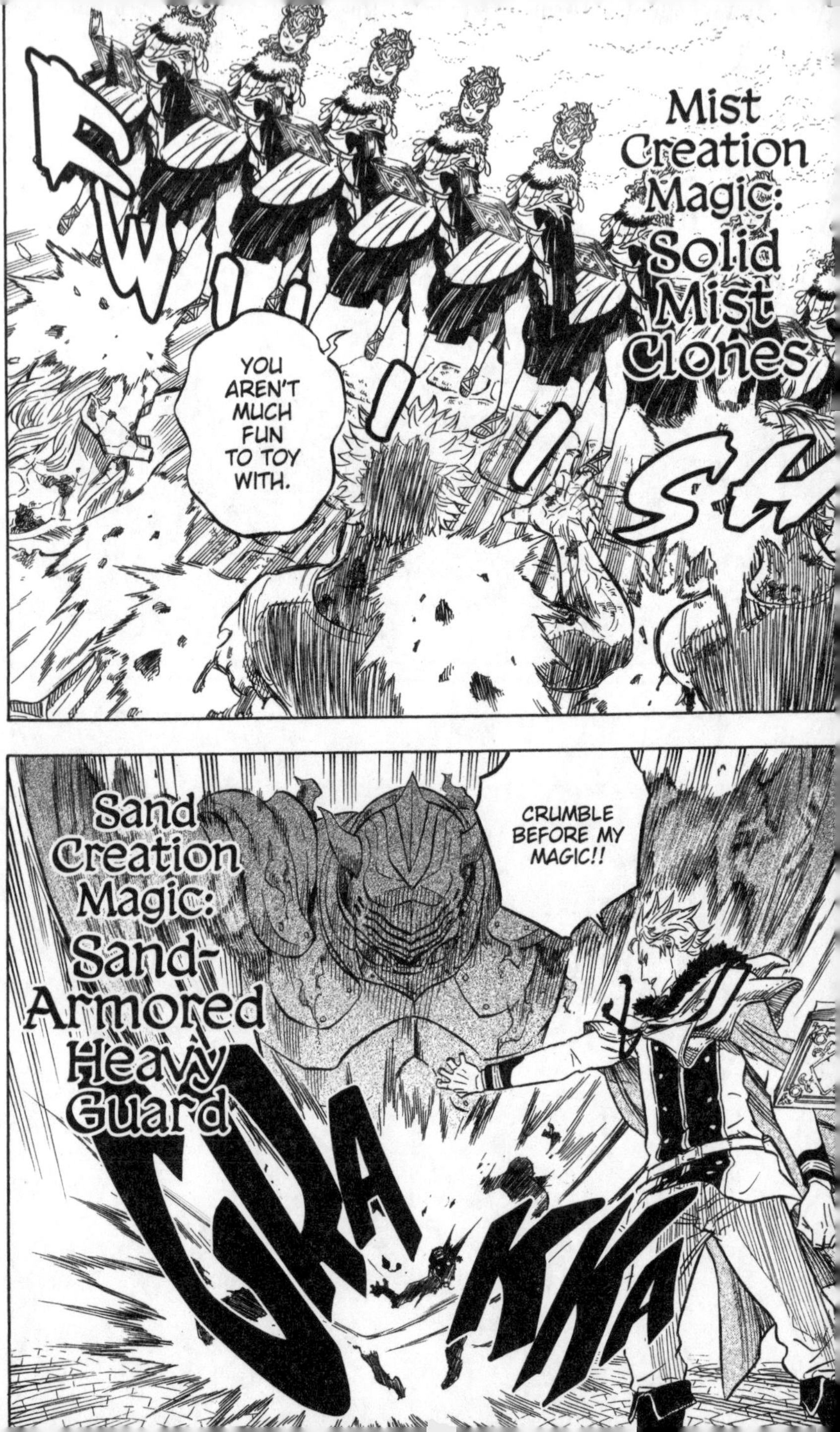
Mist Creation Magic: Solid Mist Clones
YOU AREN'T MUCH FUN TO TOY WITH.
CRUMBLE BEFORE MY MAGIC!!
Sand Creation Magic: Sand-Armored Heavy Guard

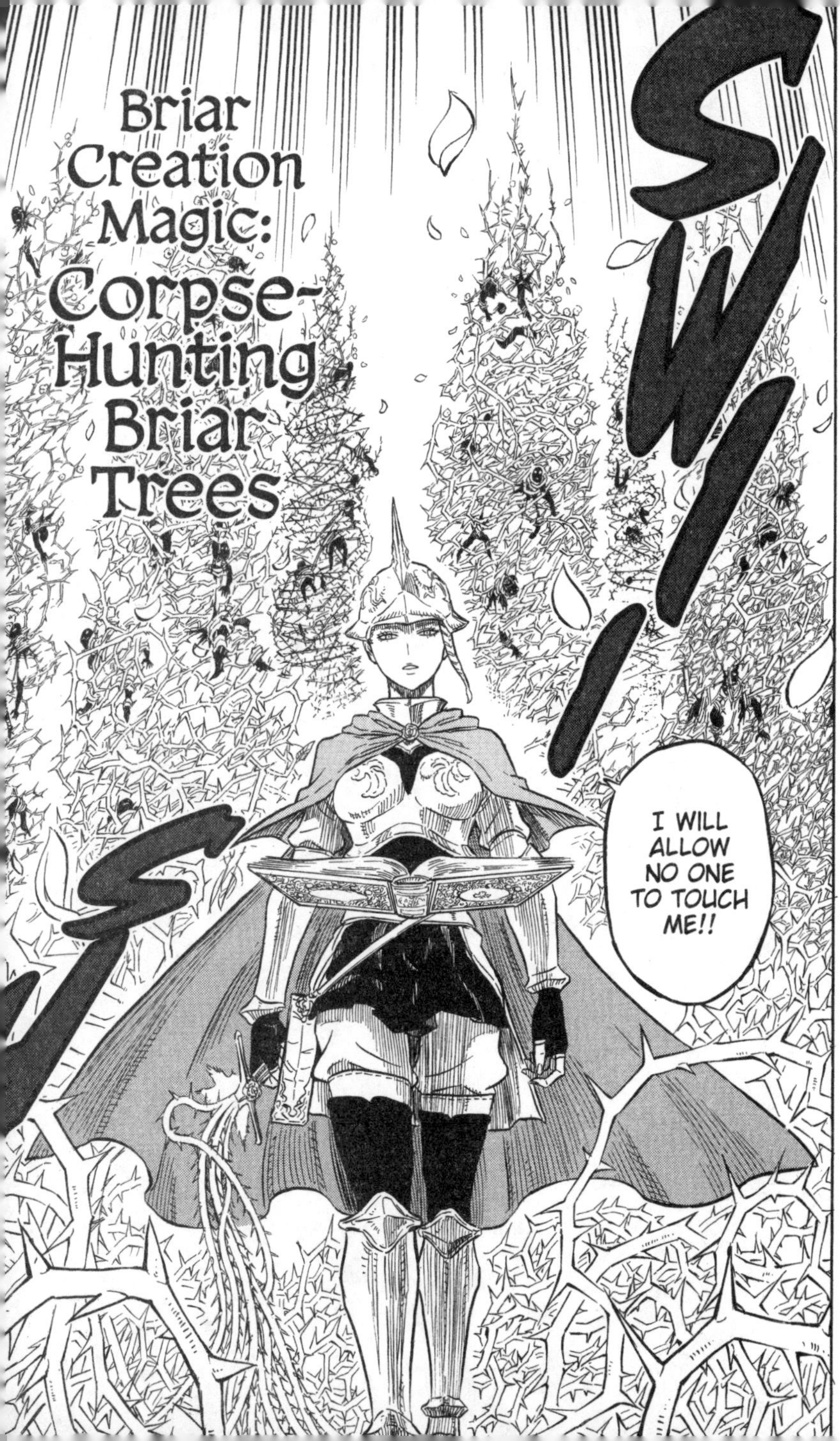
Briar Creation Magic: Corpse-Hunting Briar Trees
SWISH!!
I WILL ALLOW NO ONE TO TOUCH ME!!

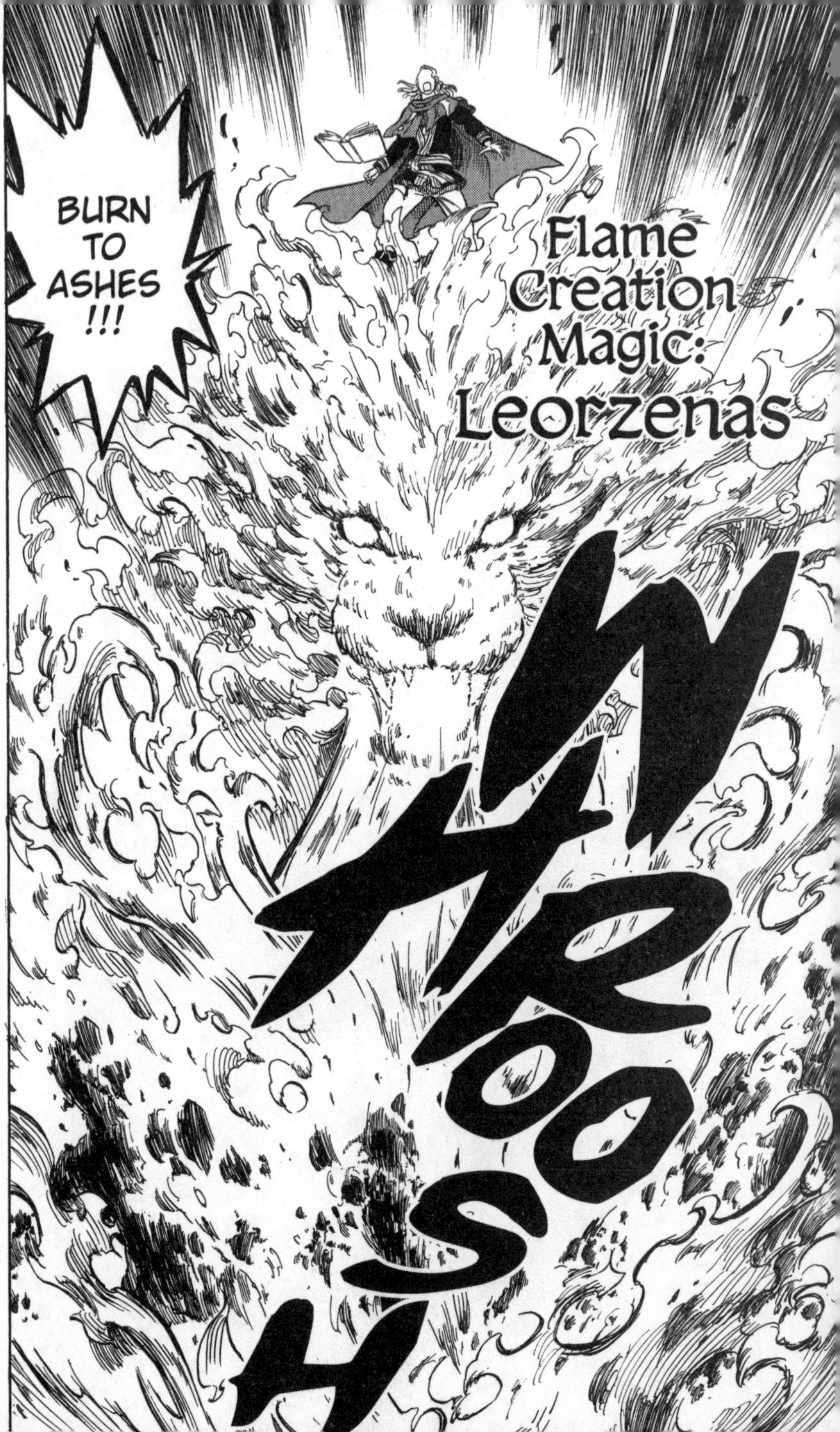
Flame Creation Magic: Leorzenas
BURN TO ASHES!!!
WHROOSH

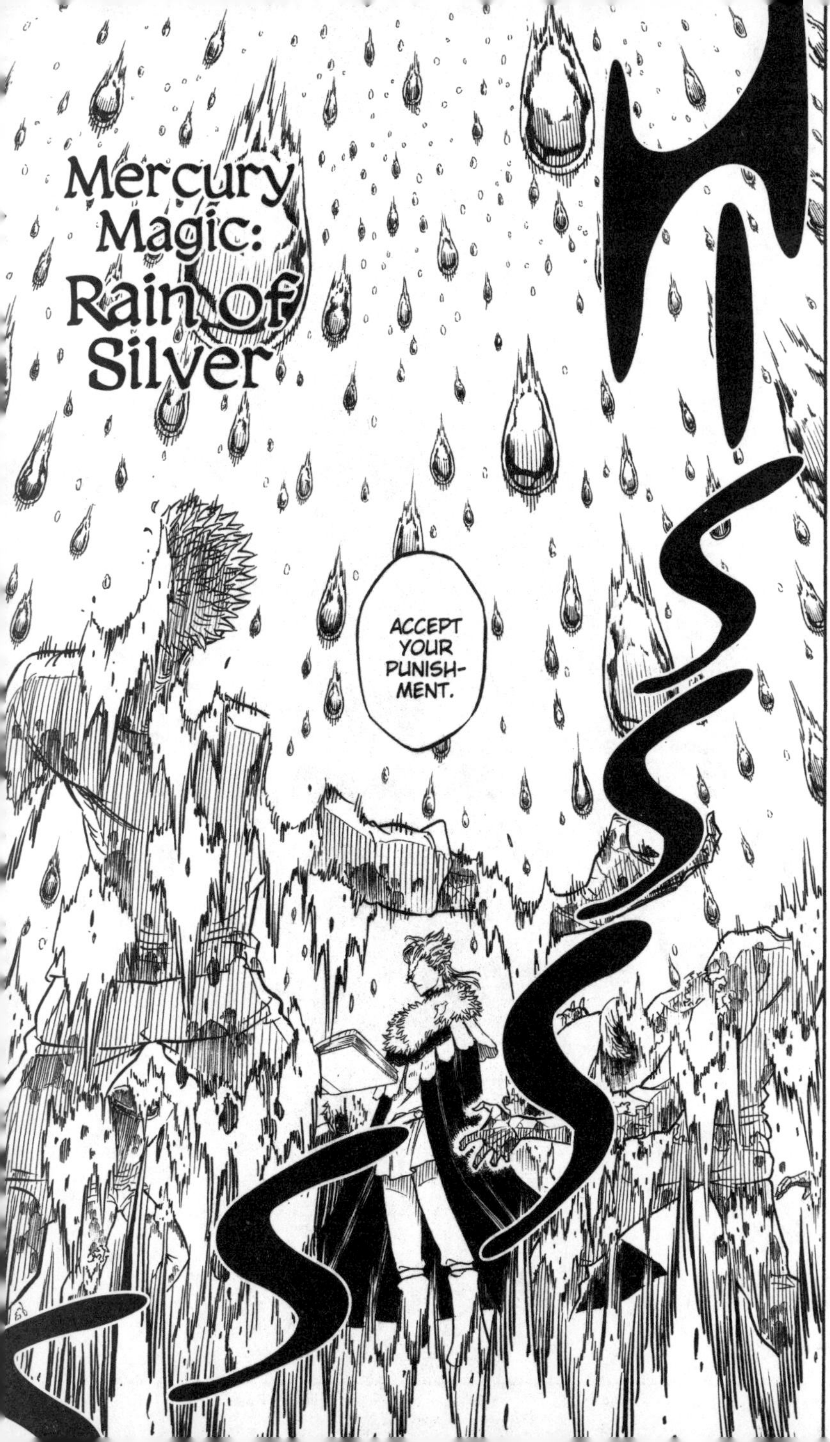
Mercury Magic: Rain of Silver
ACCEPT YOUR PUNISH-MENT.

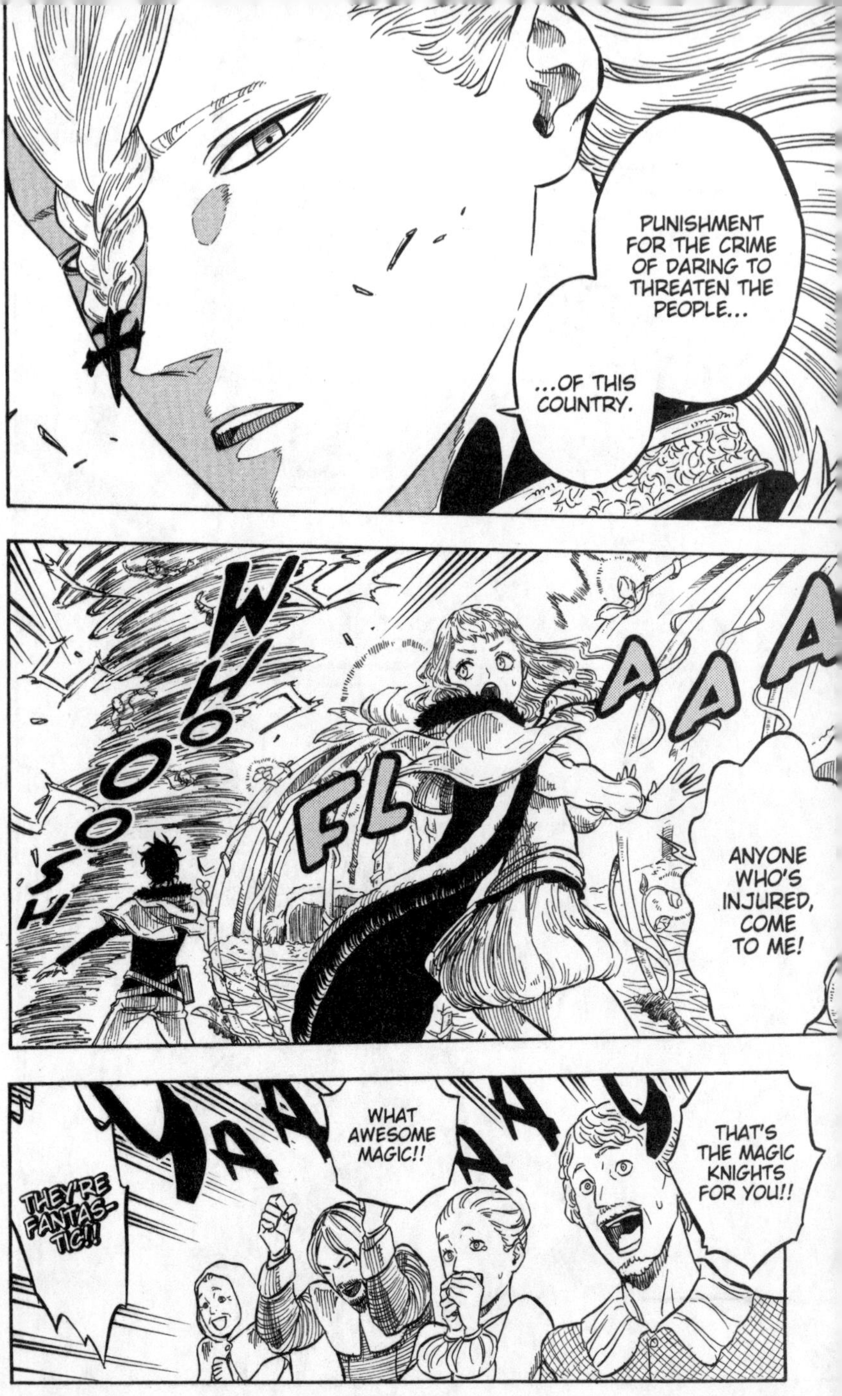
PUNISHMENT FOR THE CRIME OF DARING TO THREATEN THE PEOPLE...
...OF THIS COUNTRY.
FLAAAA
ANYONE WHO'S INJURED, COME TO ME!
WHOOOSH
YAAAAY
THAT'S THE MAGIC KNIGHTS FOR YOU!!
WHAT AWESOME MAGIC!!
THEY'RE FANTAS-TIC!!

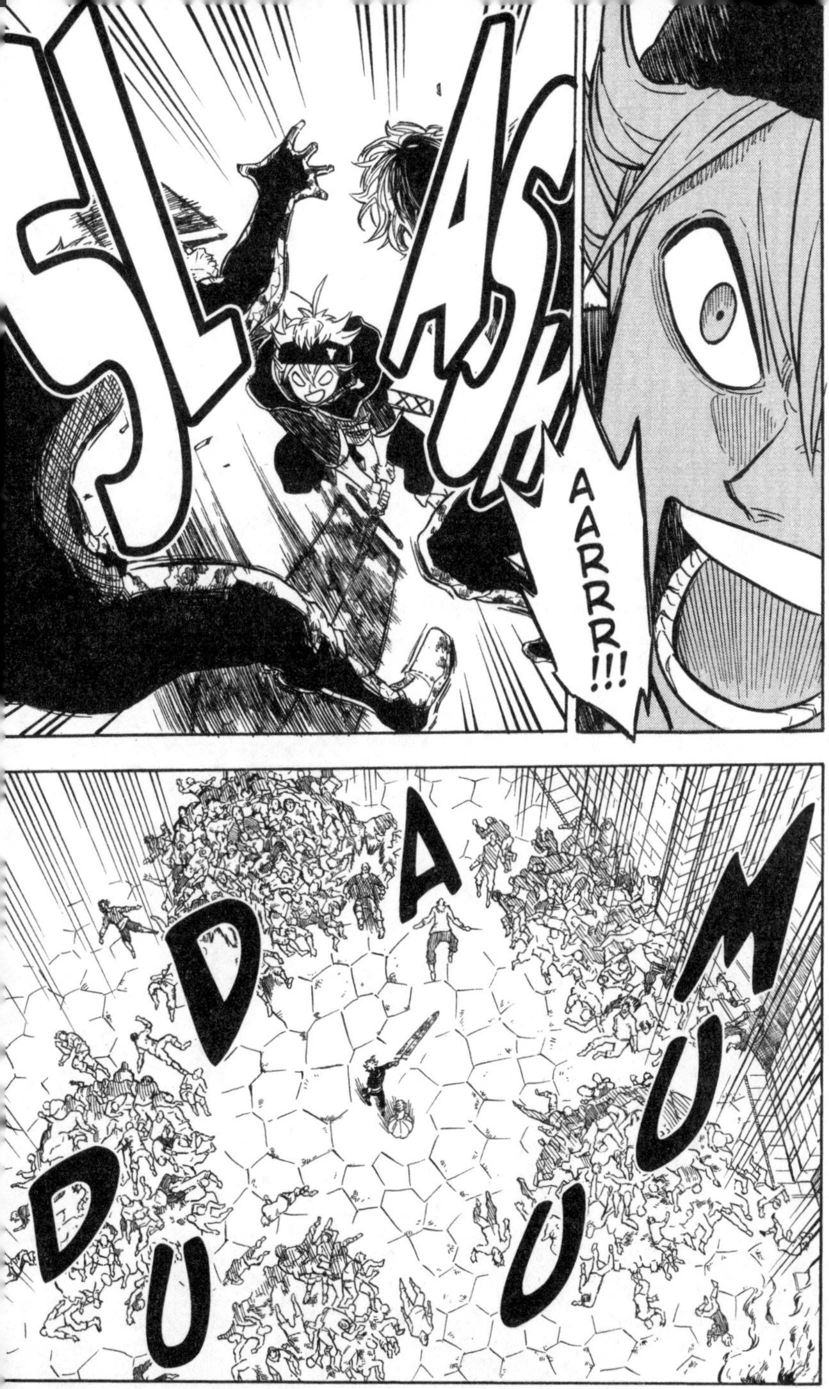
AARRRR!!!
SLASH

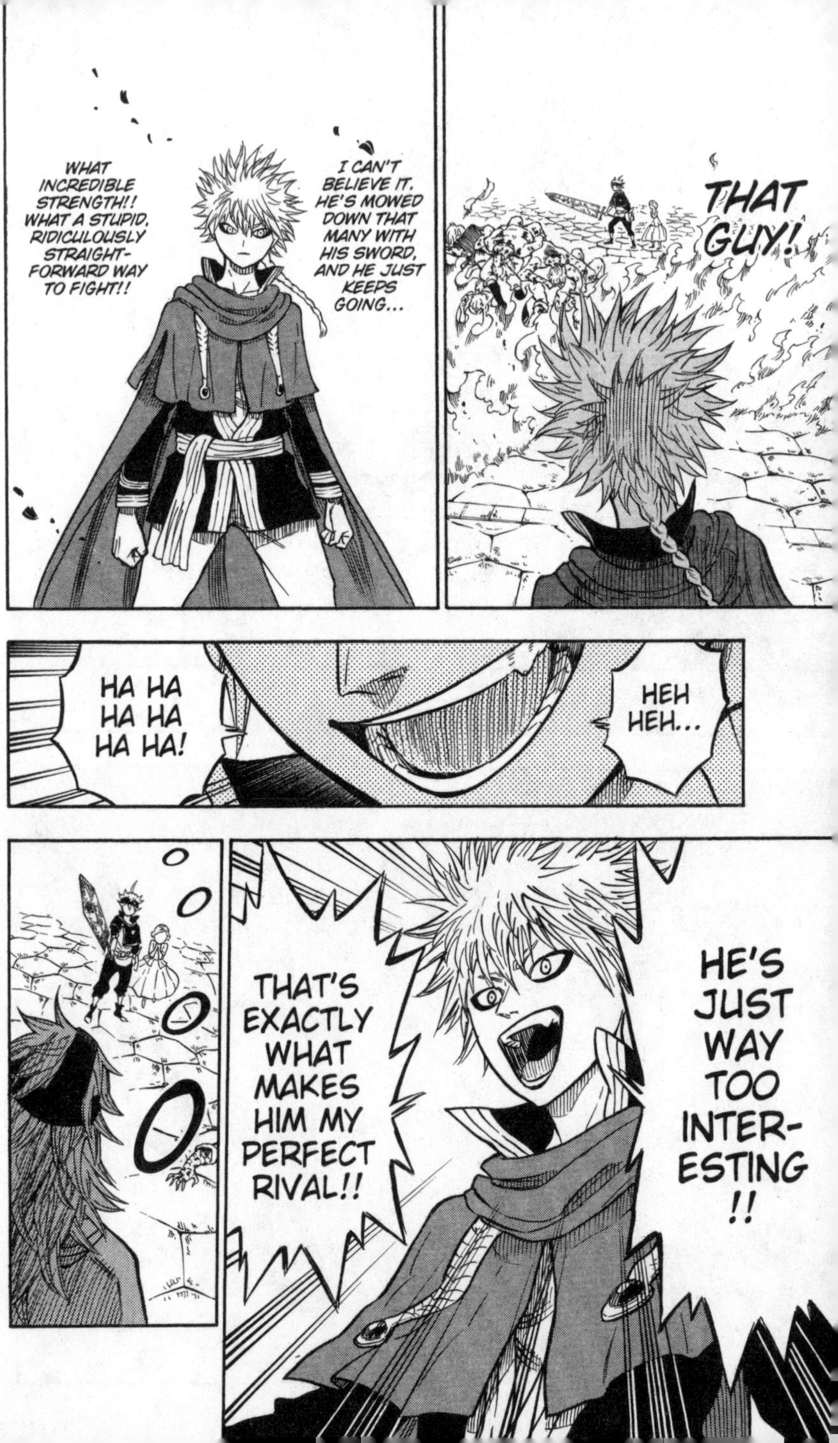
THAT GUY!
I CAN'T BELIEVE IT. HE'S MOWED DOWN THAT MANY WITH HIS SWORD, AND HE JUST KEEPS GOING...
WHAT INCREDIBLE STRENGTH!! WHAT A STUPID, RIDICULOUSLY STRAIGHT-FORWARD WAY TO FIGHT!!
HEH HEH...
HA HA HA HA HA HA!
HE'S JUST WAY TOO INTER-ESTING!!
THAT'S EXACTLY WHAT MAKES HIM MY PERFECT RIVAL!!

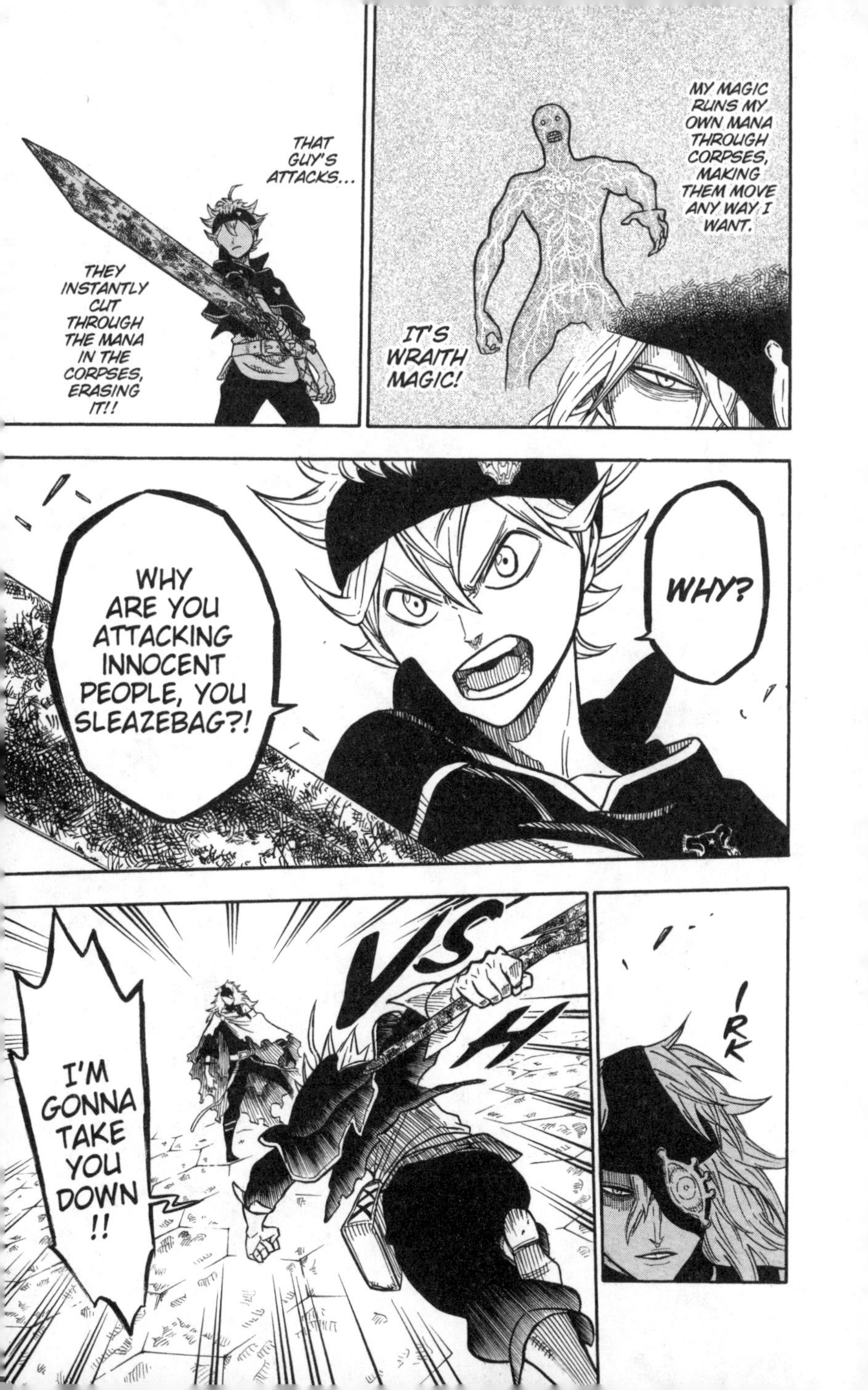
MY MAGIC RUNS MY OWN MANA THROUGH CORPSES, MAKING THEM MOVE ANY WAY I WANT.
IT'S WRAITH MAGIC!
THAT GUY'S ATTACKS...
THEY INSTANTLY CUT THROUGH THE MANA IN THE CORPSES, ERASING IT!!
WHY?
WHY ARE YOU ATTACKING INNOCENT PEOPLE, YOU SLEAZEBAG?!
IRK
VSH
I'M GONNA TAKE YOU DOWN!!

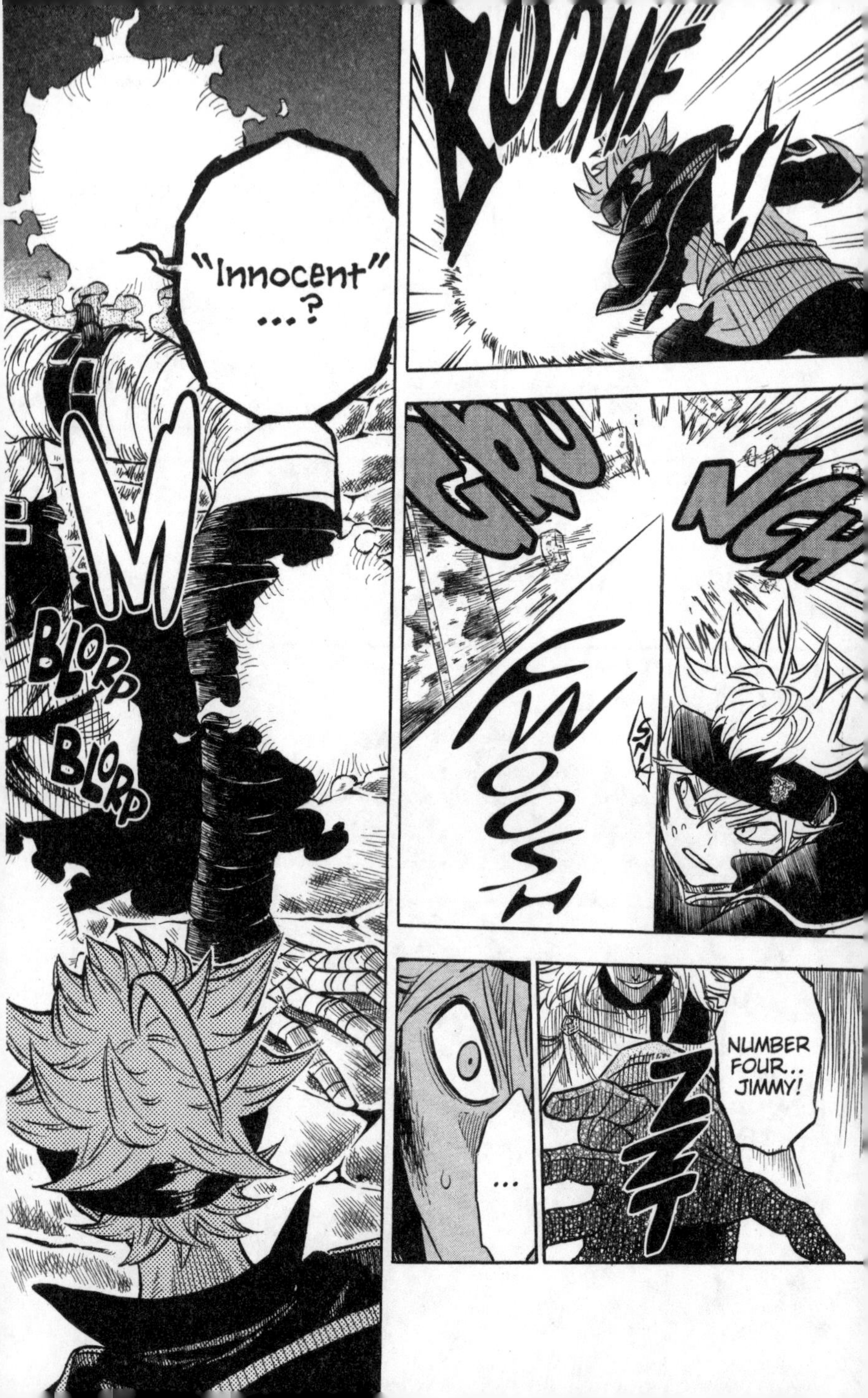
BOOMF
CRUNCH
KWOOSH
SNK
NUMBER FOUR... JIMMY!
ZZZT
...
"Innocent" ...?
M
BLORP
BLORP

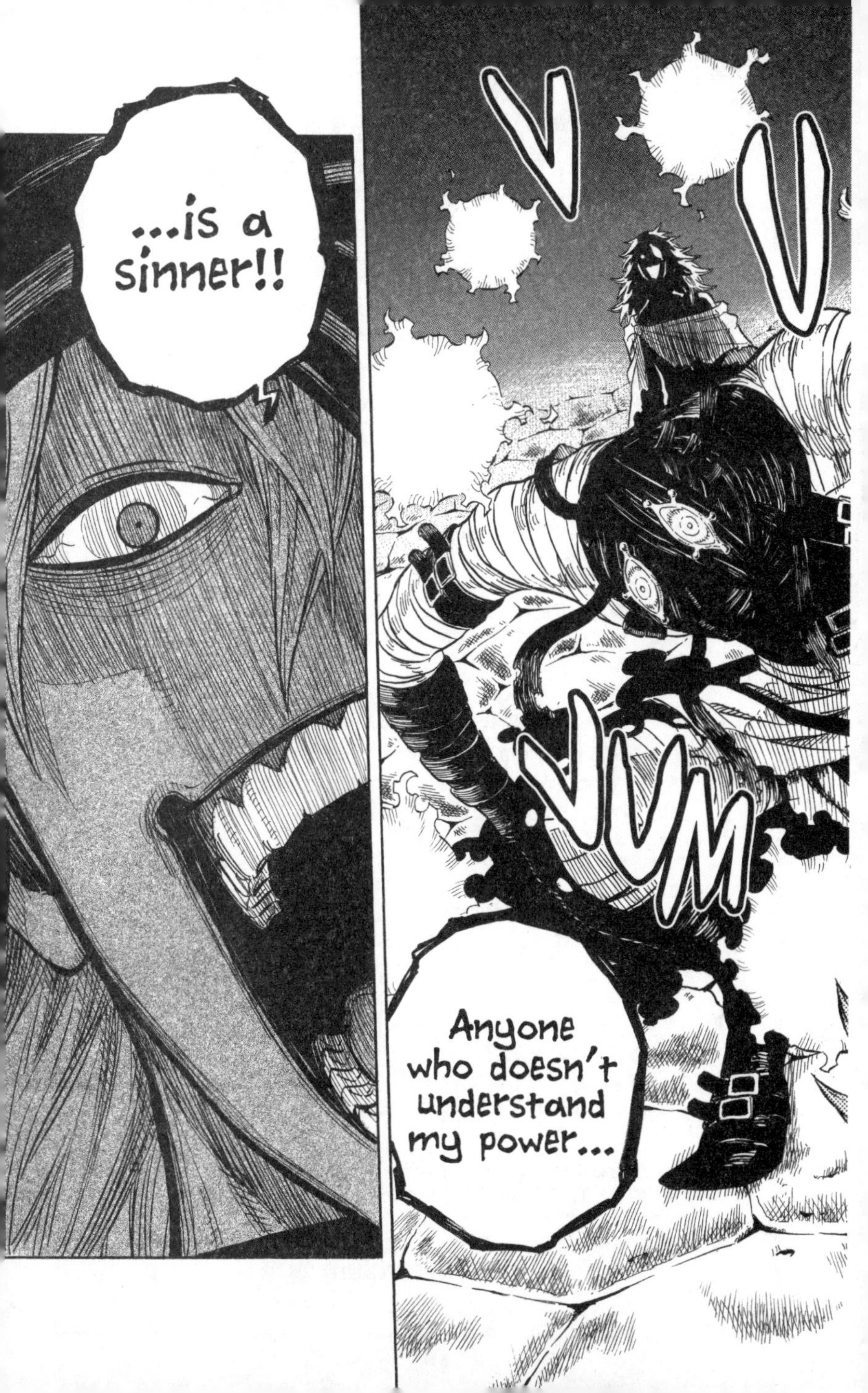
V
V
VUM
Anyone who doesn't understand my power...
...is a sinner!!

The Assorted Questions Brigade

Good day! Good evening! Good morning!
Here it is, the first question corner.
I'm so relieved we got lots of letters.
Please keep giving us your support!!

✤

Q: Which character do you have the most fun drawing? (Dragon, Tokyo)

A: The one who's most fun to draw is Charmy! She moves around in fun ways. So I guess Asta's fun too.

Q: What's the difference between magic power and mana? (Human with Absolutely No Magic, Kanagawa)

A: Mana is something fundamental and invisible that floats in the air. When mana makes its home in a living creature, it turns into power that can influence other substances, and that's magic power. When magic power is refined even further, it becomes magic... I think that's how it goes. I'm sorry I can't explain it better.

Q: How many members are in the Black Bulls? Also, is the Black Bulls member who says "FSSHHH" TV personality Matsuko Deluxe? (Kouhei Yamada, Fukushima)

A: They've got about a dozen members, I think. Lots of them are free spirits, so I'm not really sure...
The "FSSHHH" person is... There might be a hint in the back of this volume!!

Page 27: We Can Get Stronger

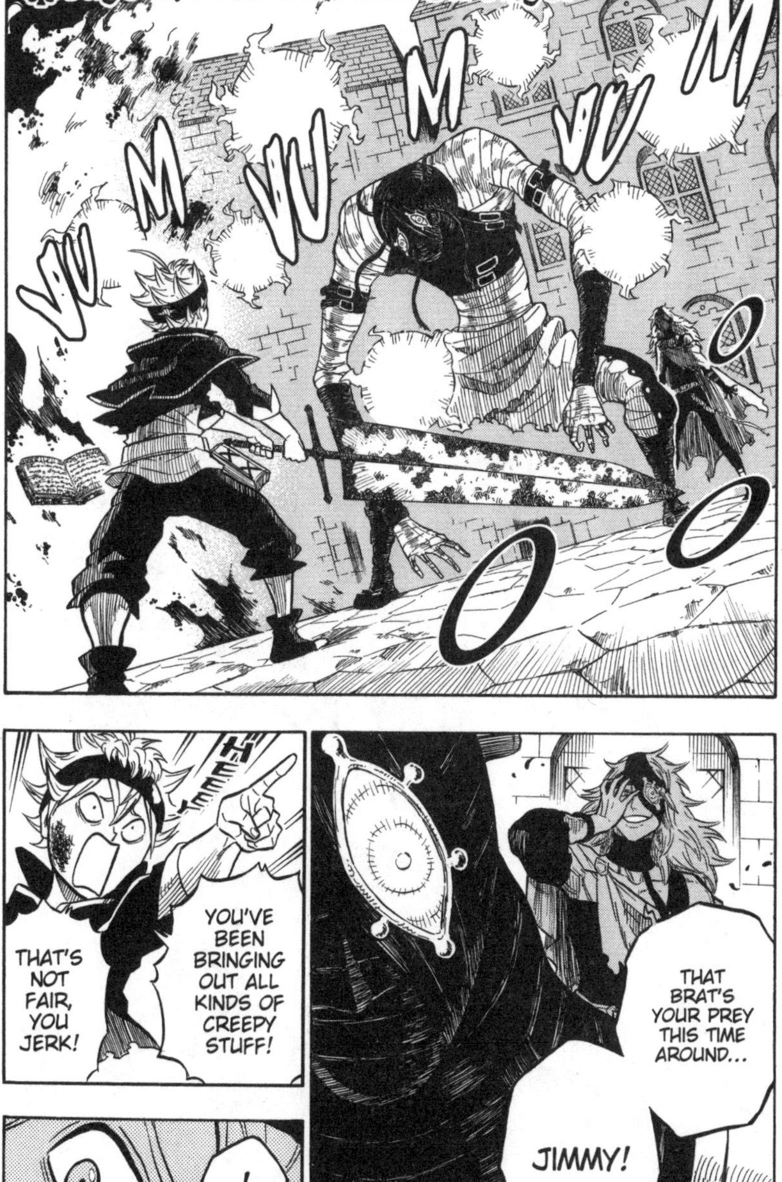
VUMVUMVUM
THAT BRAT'S YOUR PREY THIS TIME AROUND...
JIMMY!
HEY
YOU'VE BEEN BRINGING OUT ALL KINDS OF CREEPY STUFF!
THAT'S NOT FAIR, YOU JERK!
!

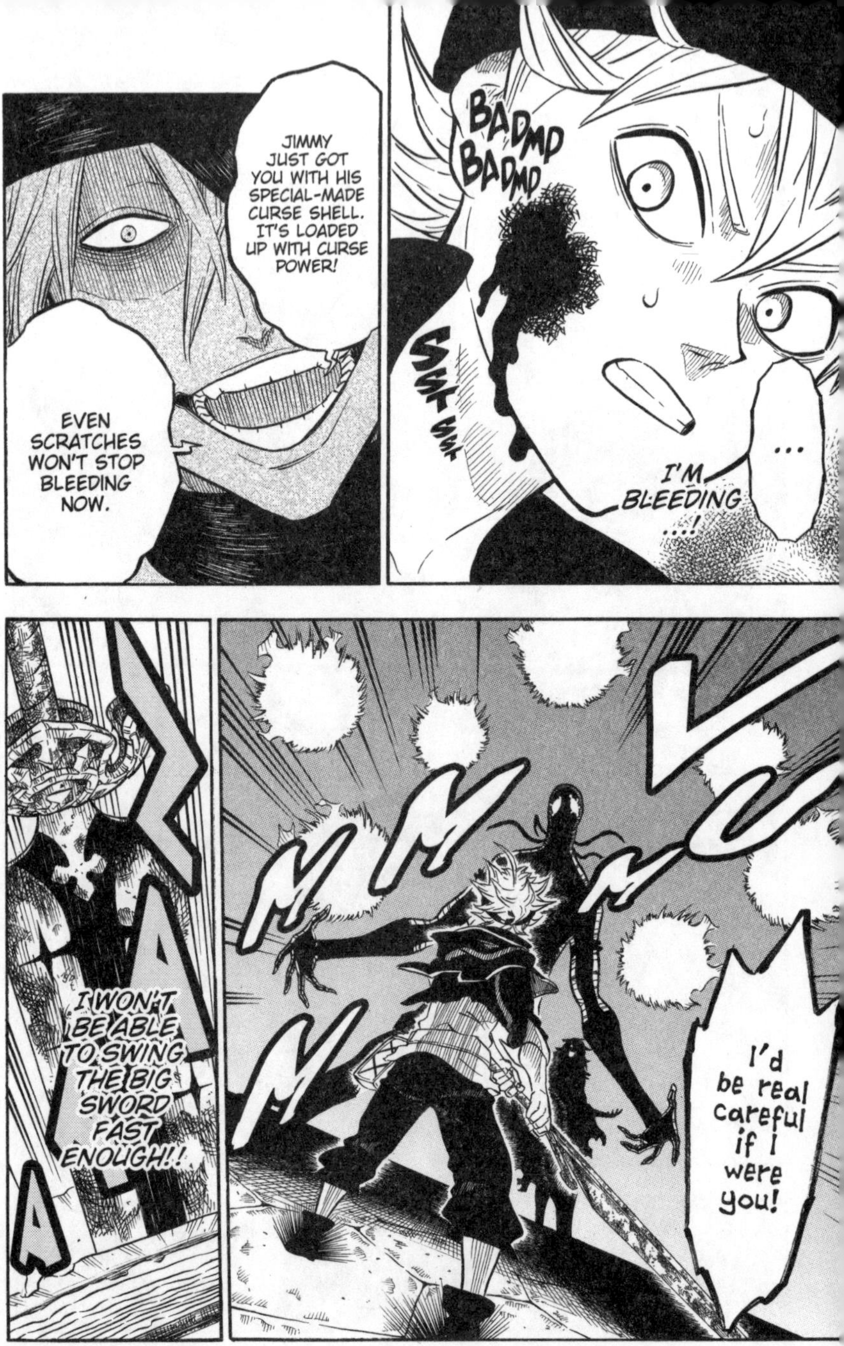
BADMP BADMP
SSST SSST
...
I'M BLEEDING ...!
JIMMY JUST GOT YOU WITH HIS SPECIAL-MADE CURSE SHELL. IT'S LOADED UP WITH CURSE POWER!
EVEN SCRATCHES WON'T STOP BLEEDING NOW.
I'd be real careful if I were you!
I WON'T BE ABLE TO SWING THE BIG SWORD FAST ENOUGH!!

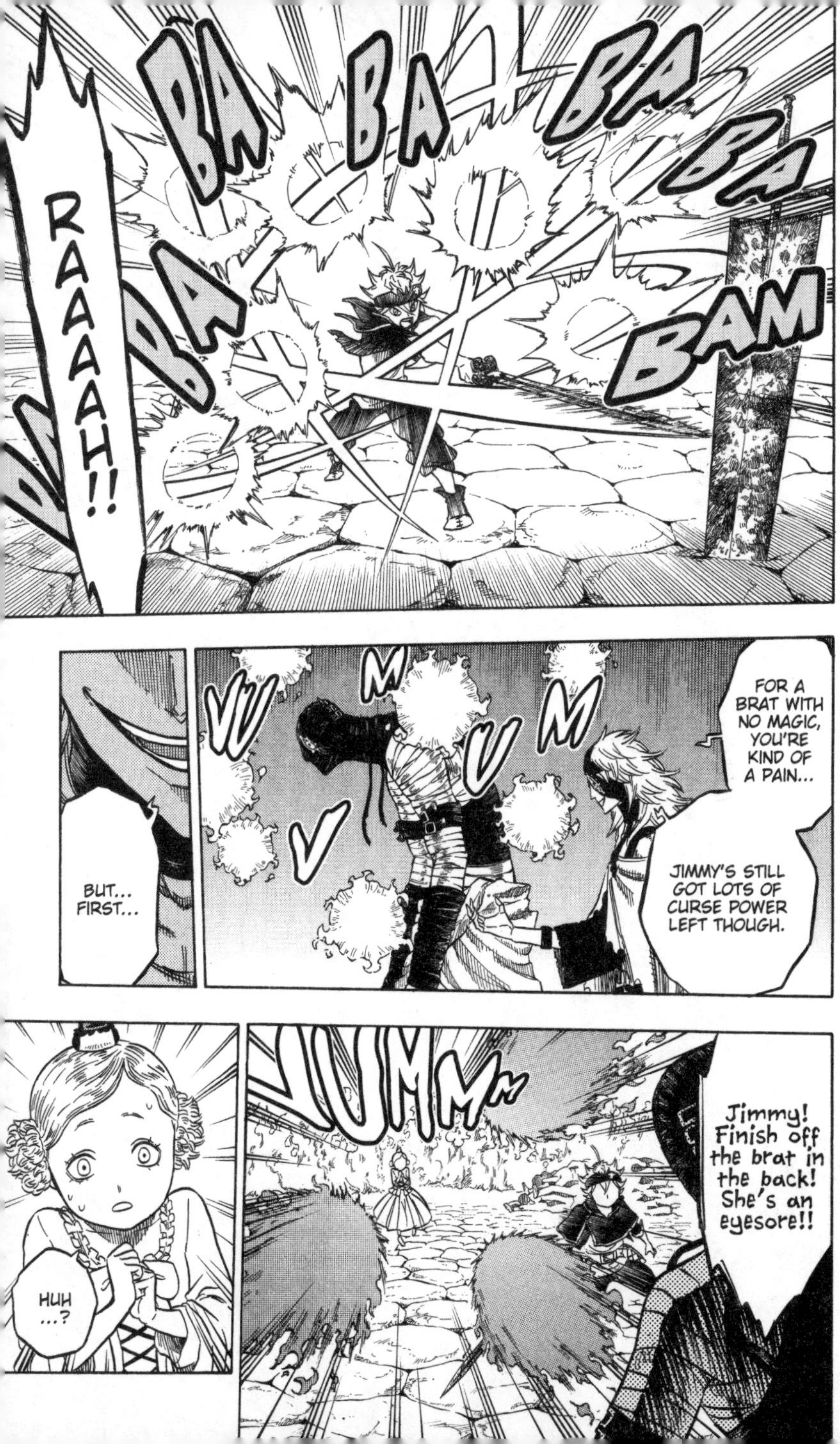
BA
BA
BA
BAM
BA
BA
BA
RAAAAAH!!
FOR A BRAT WITH NO MAGIC, YOU'RE KIND OF A PAIN...
JIMMY'S STILL GOT LOTS OF CURSE POWER LEFT THOUGH.
BUT... FIRST...
Jimmy! Finish off the brat in the back! She's an eyesore!!
VUMMM
HUH ...?

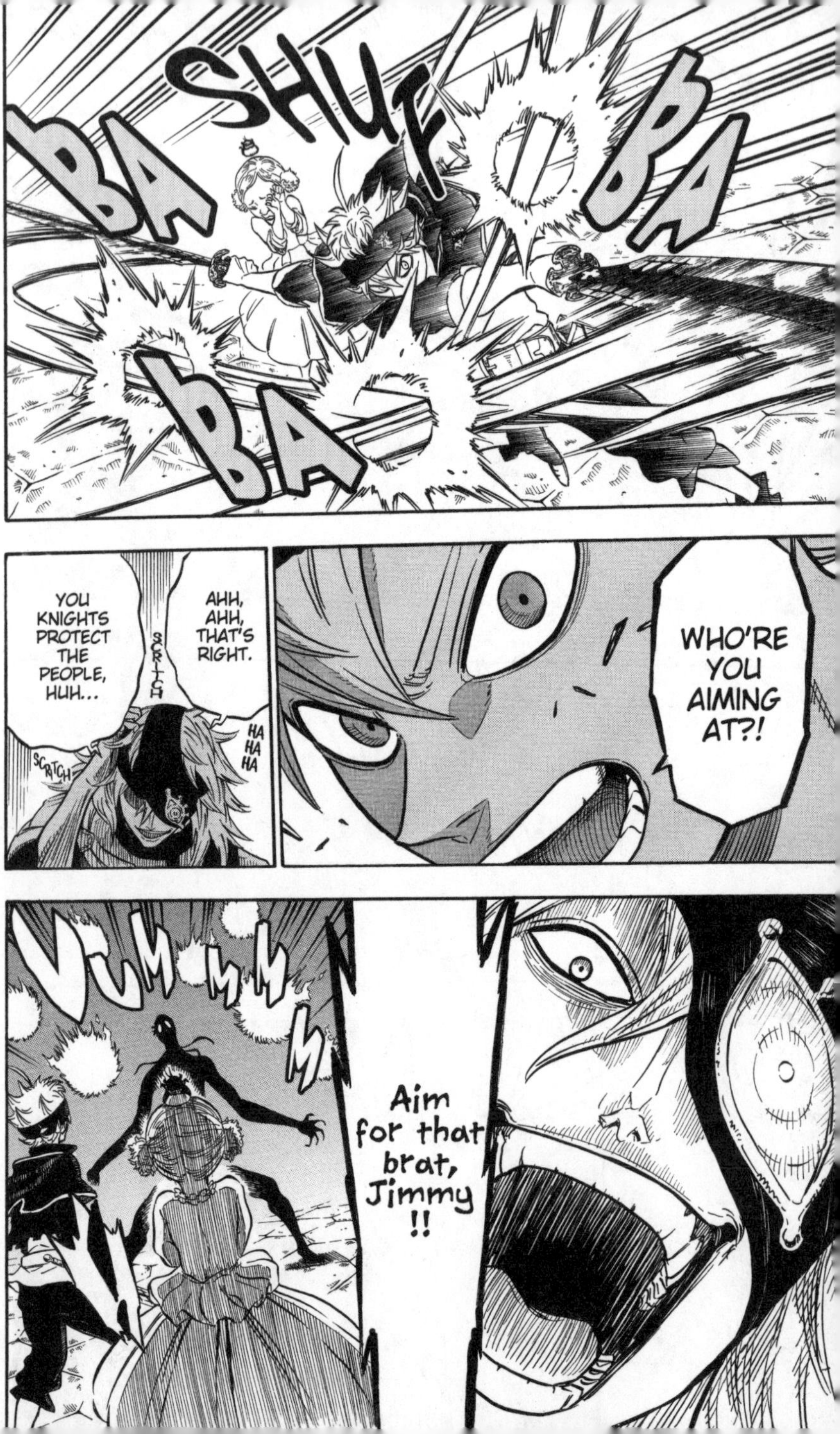
BA
SHUF
BA
BA
WHO'RE YOU AIMING AT?!
AHH, AHH, THAT'S RIGHT.
SCRITCH
YOU KNIGHTS PROTECT THE PEOPLE, HUH...
HA HA HA
SCRITCH
Aim for that brat, Jimmy!!
VUMMMMMM

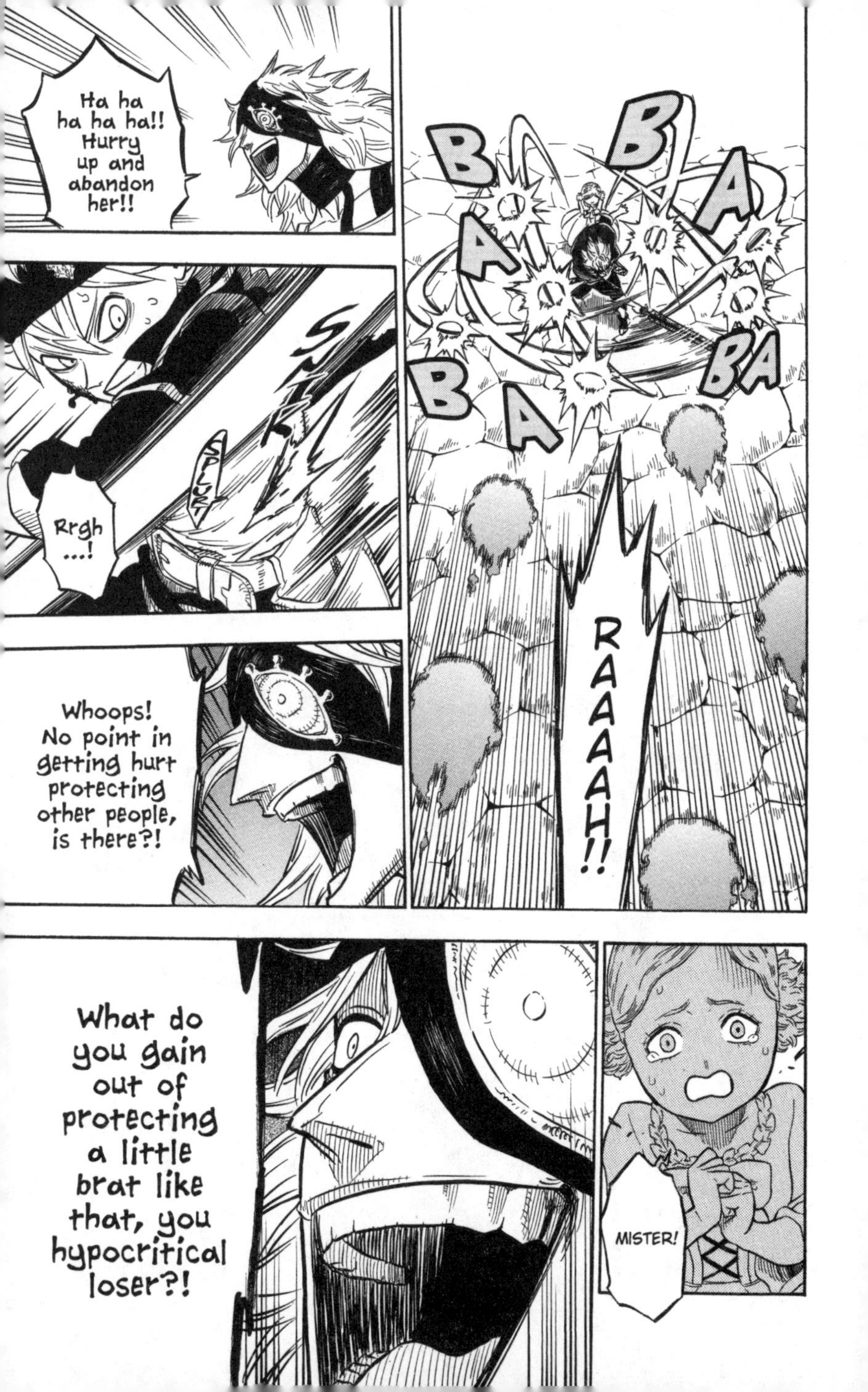
BA
BA
BA
BA
RAAAAAH!!
Ha ha ha ha ha!! Hurry up and abandon her!!
SPLURT
Rrgh ...!
Whoops! No point in getting hurt protecting other people, is there?!
MISTER!
What do you gain out of protecting a little brat like that, you hypocritical loser?!

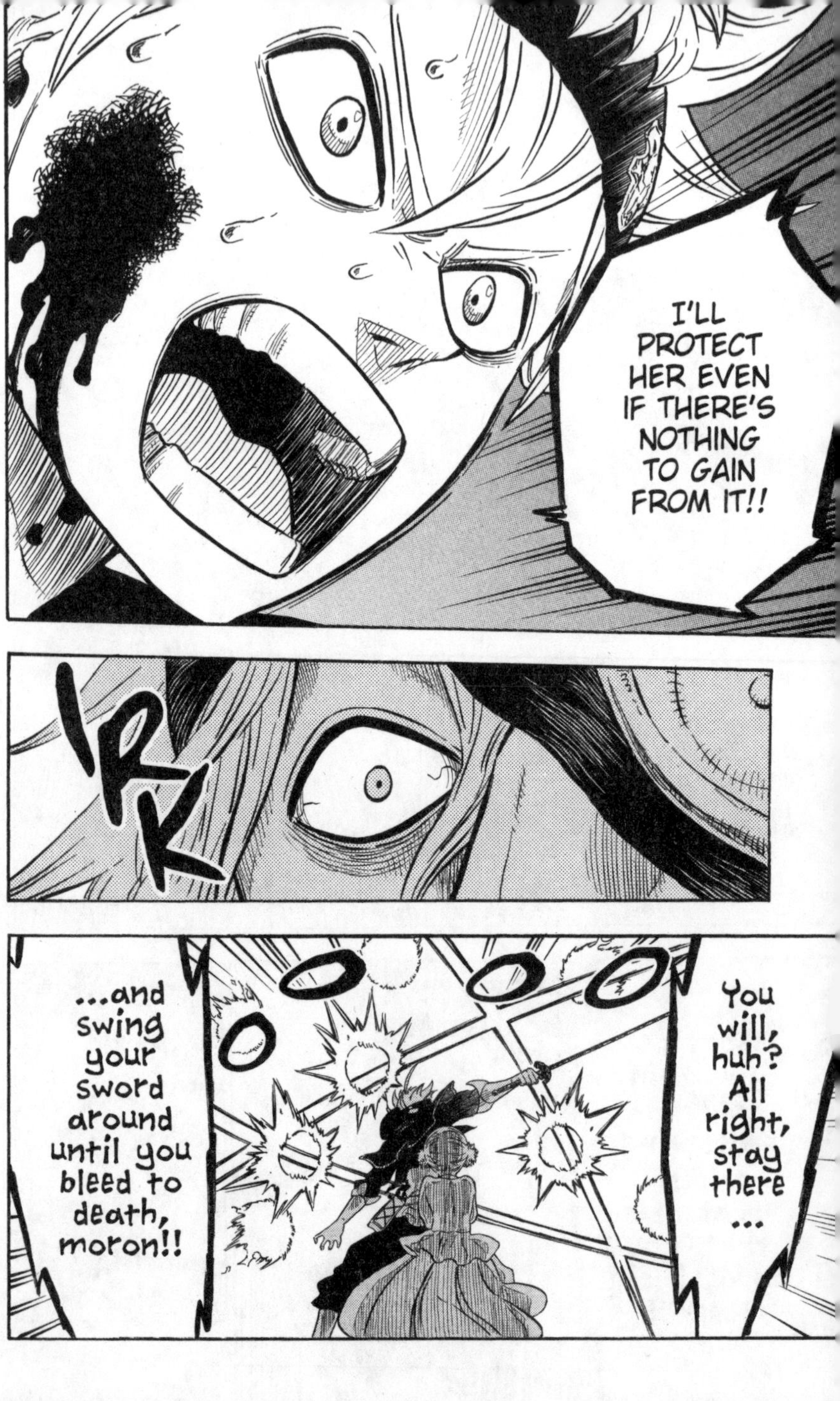
I'LL PROTECT HER EVEN IF THERE'S NOTHING TO GAIN FROM IT!!
IRK
You will, huh? All right, stay there...
...and swing your sword around until you bleed to death, moron!!

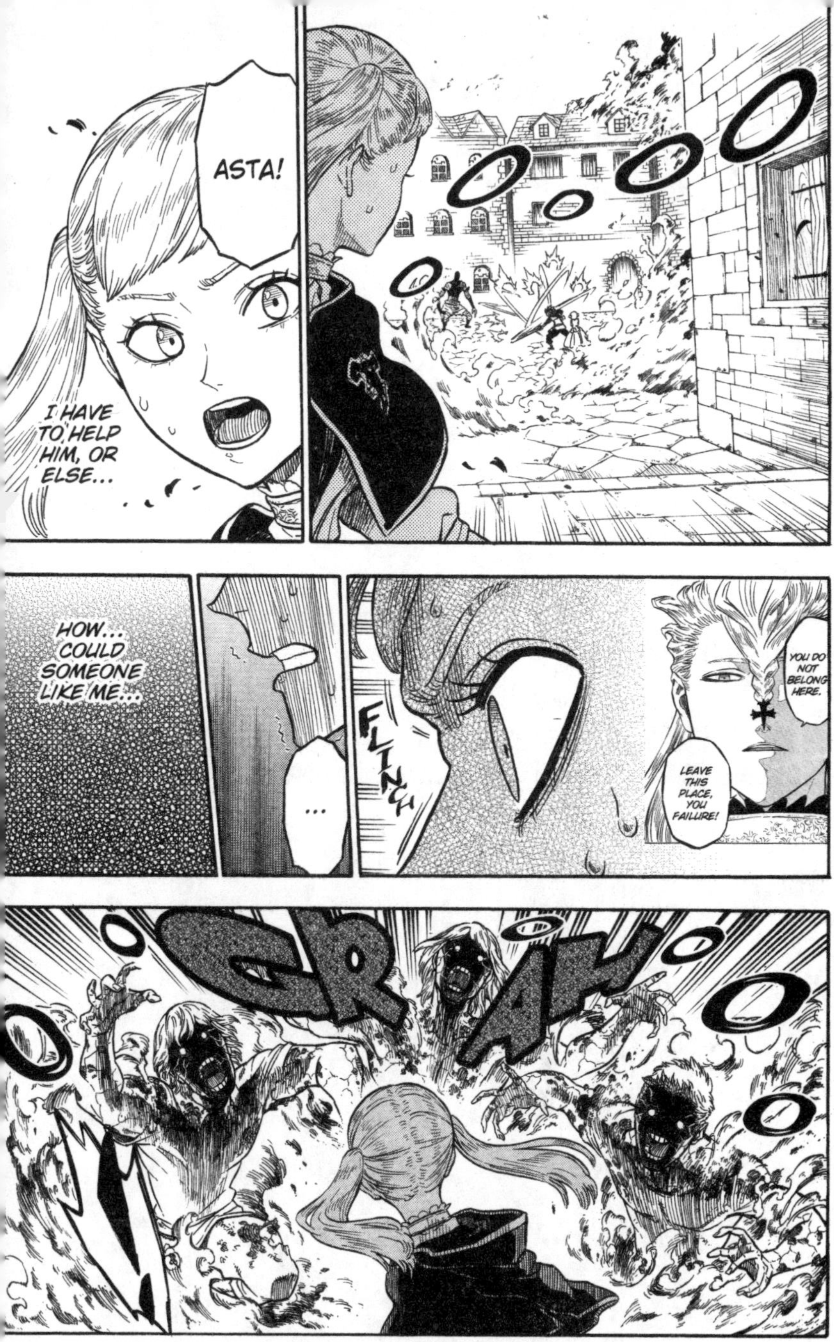
ASTA!
I HAVE TO HELP HIM, OR ELSE...
YOU DO NOT BELONG HERE.
LEAVE THIS PLACE, YOU FAILURE!
FLINCH
...
HOW... COULD SOMEONE LIKE ME...
GRAAH

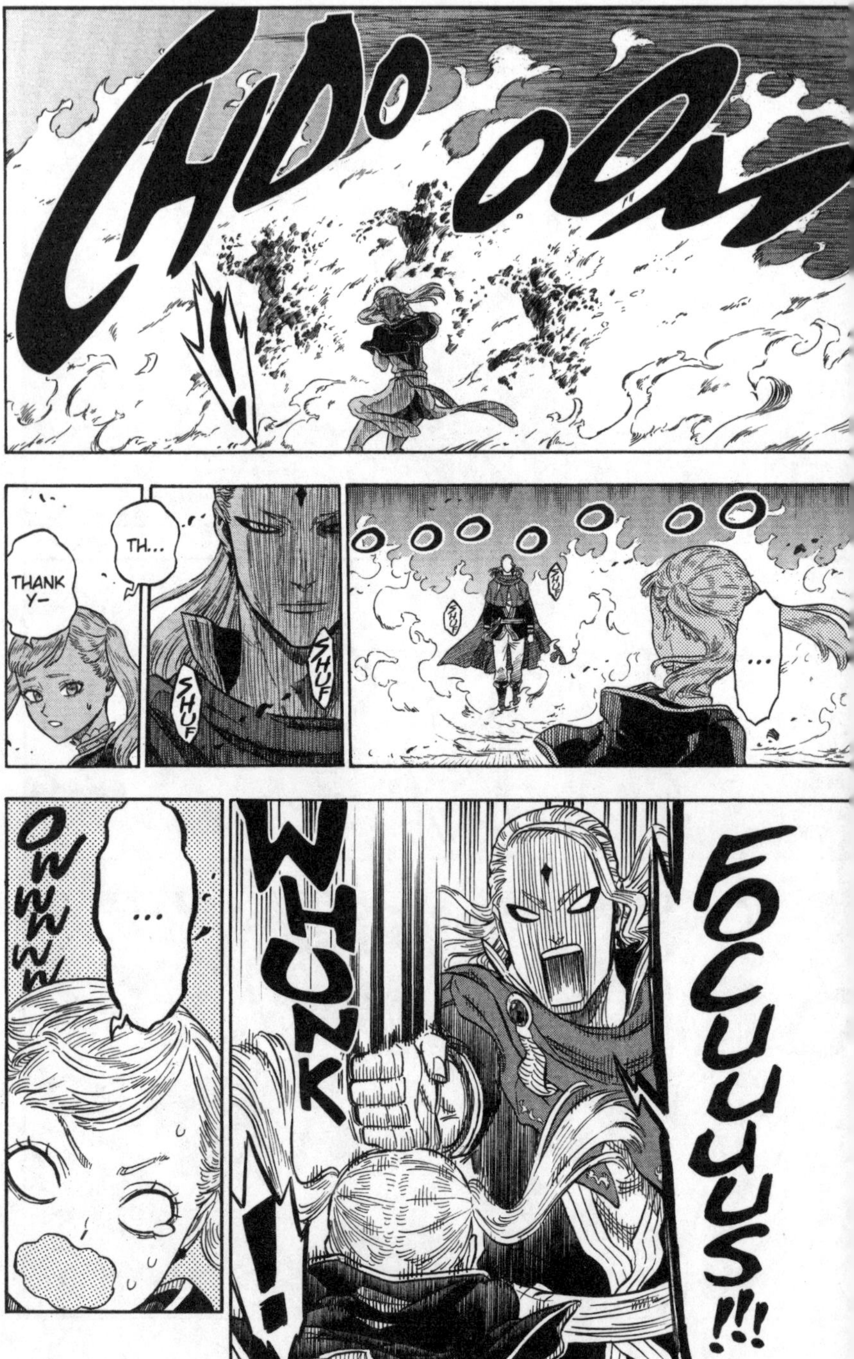
CHDOOOM
...
SHUF
SHUF
TH...
SHUF
SHUF
THANK Y—
FOCUUUUS!!!
WHUNK!
...
OWWWWW

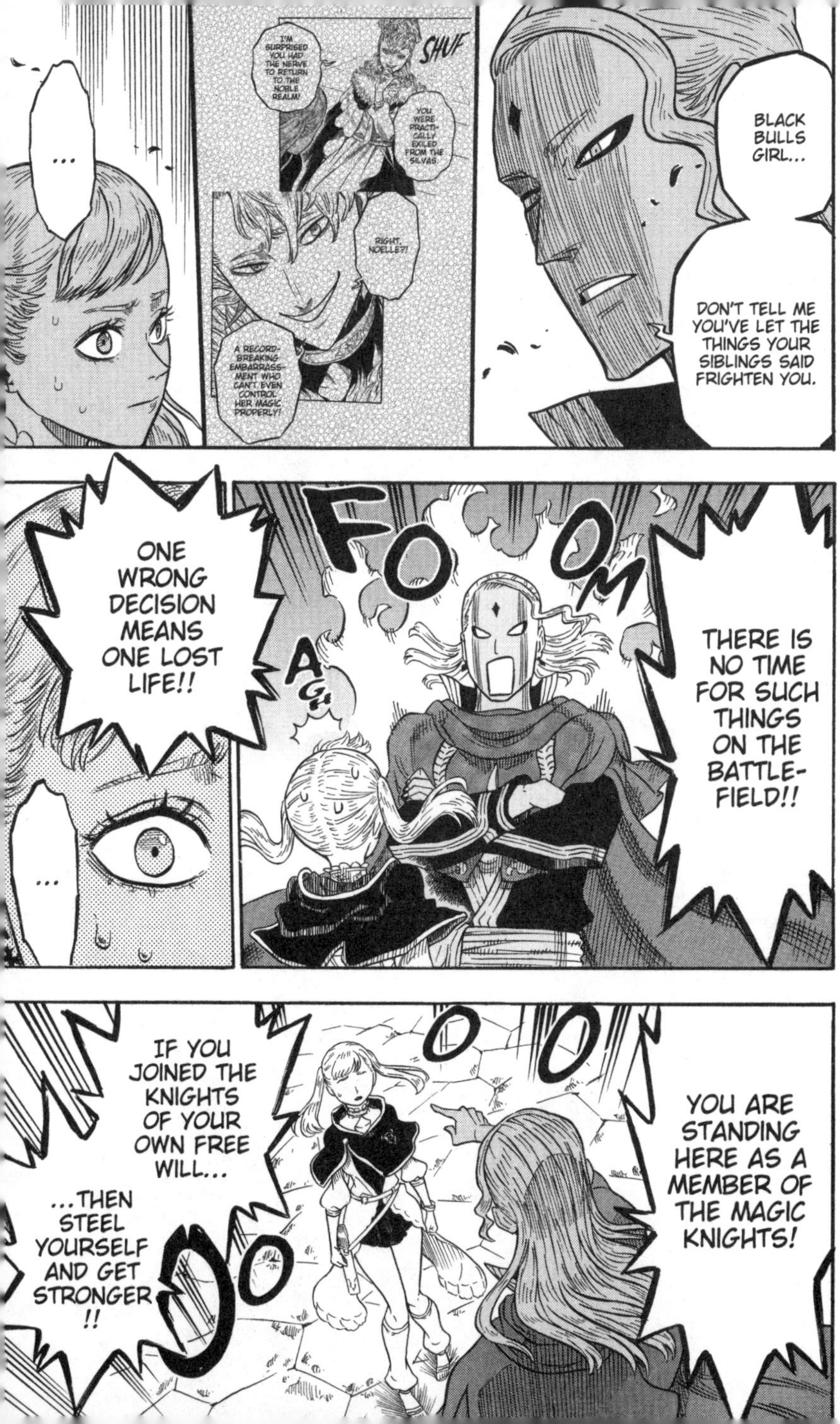
BLACK BULLS GIRL...
DON'T TELL ME YOU'VE LET THE THINGS YOUR SIBLINGS SAID FRIGHTEN YOU.
SHUF
I'M SURPRISED YOU HAD THE NERVE TO RETURN TO THE NOBLE REALM!
YOU WERE PRACTI-CALLY EXILED FROM THE SILVAS.
RIGHT, NOELLE?!
A RECORD-BREAKING EMBARRASS-MENT WHO CAN'T EVEN CONTROL HER MAGIC PROPERLY!
...
FOOM
THERE IS NO TIME FOR SUCH THINGS ON THE BATTLE-FIELD!!
AGH
ONE WRONG DECISION MEANS ONE LOST LIFE!!
...
YOU ARE STANDING HERE AS A MEMBER OF THE MAGIC KNIGHTS!
IF YOU JOINED THE KNIGHTS OF YOUR OWN FREE WILL...
...THEN STEEL YOURSELF AND GET STRONGER!!

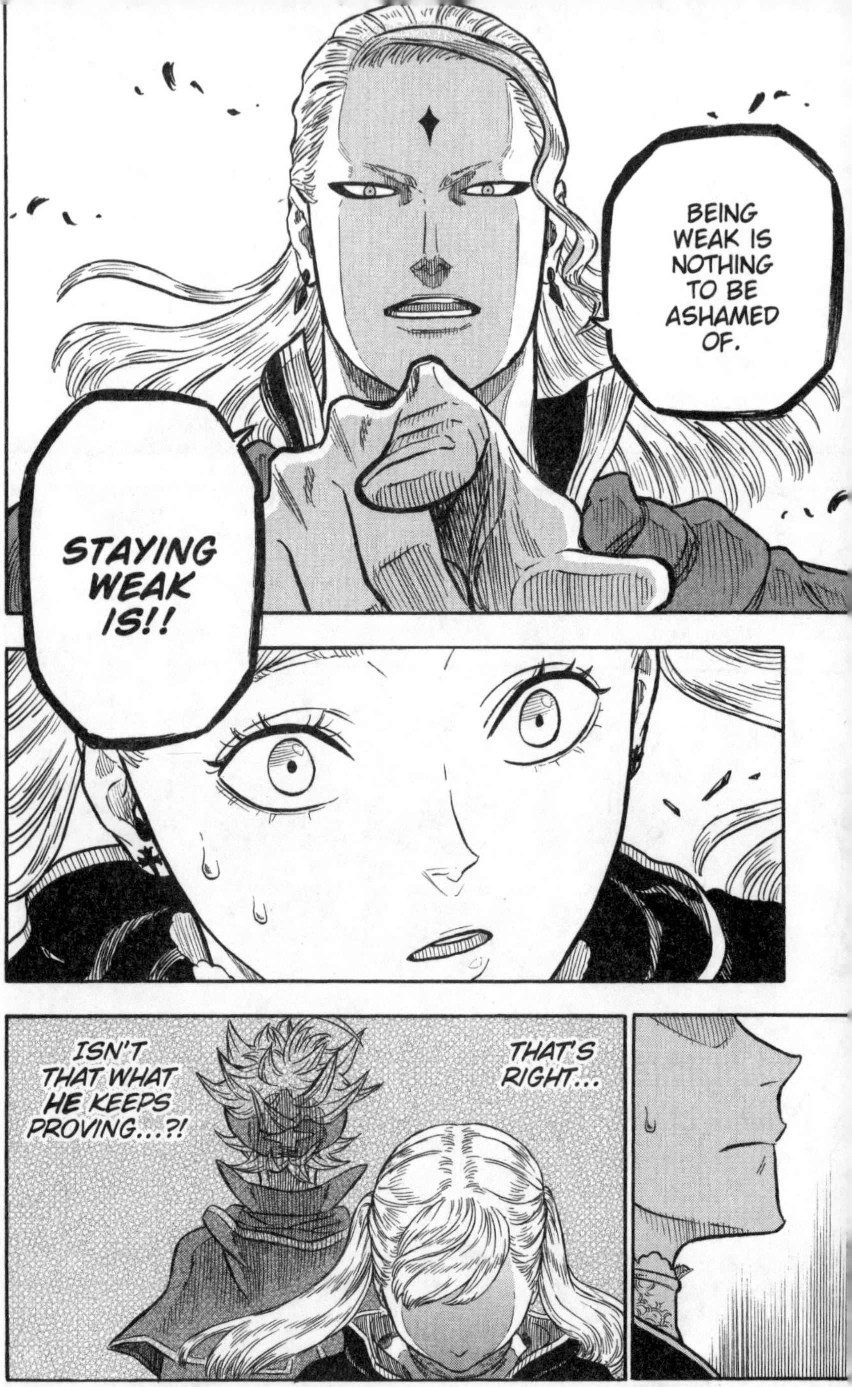
BEING WEAK IS NOTHING TO BE ASHAMED OF.
STAYING WEAK IS!!
THAT'S RIGHT...
ISN'T THAT WHAT HE KEEPS PROVING...?!

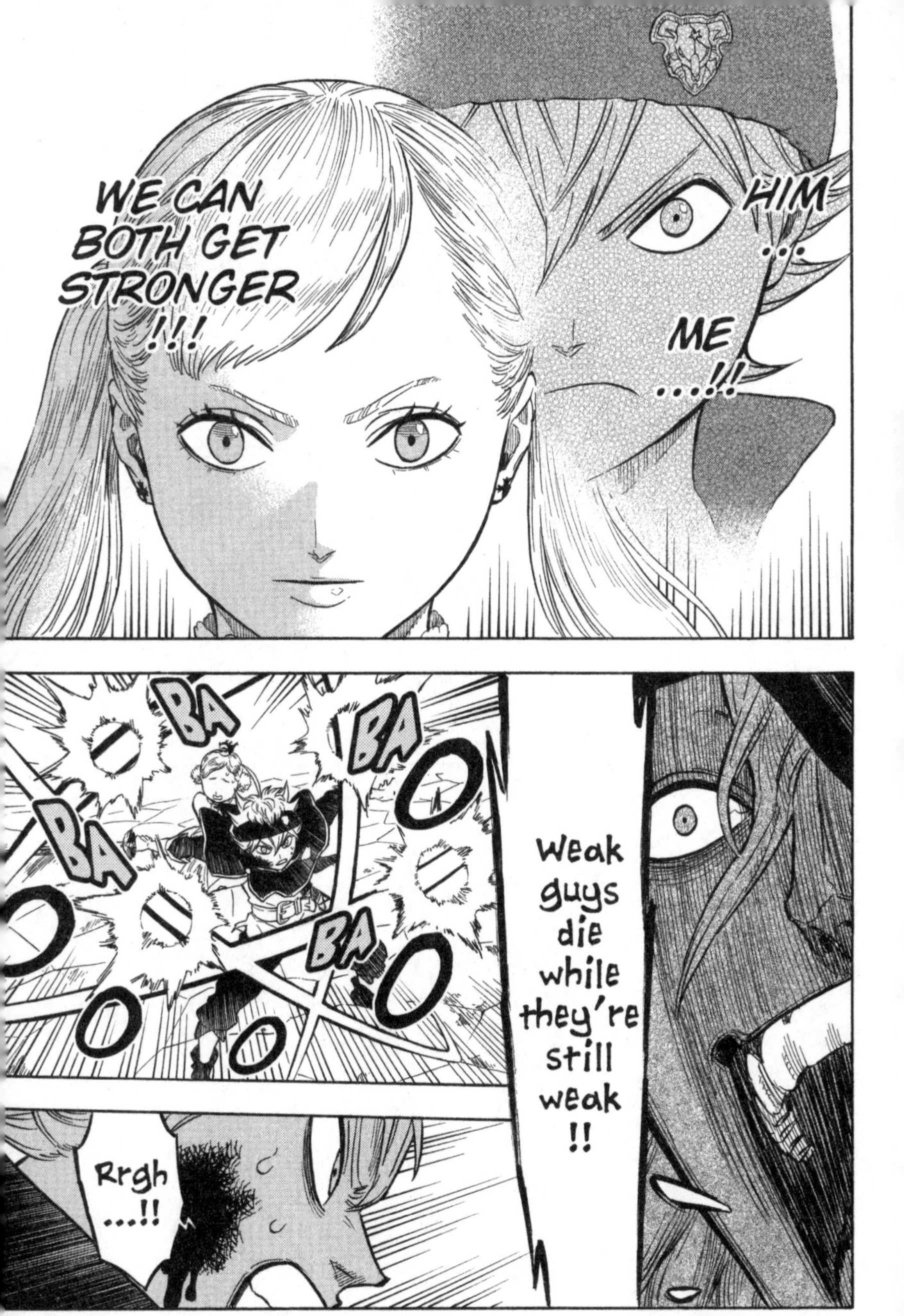
HIM...
ME...!!
WE CAN BOTH GET STRONGER!!!
Weak guys die while they're still weak!!
BAO
BA
BABA
BAO
Rrgh...!!

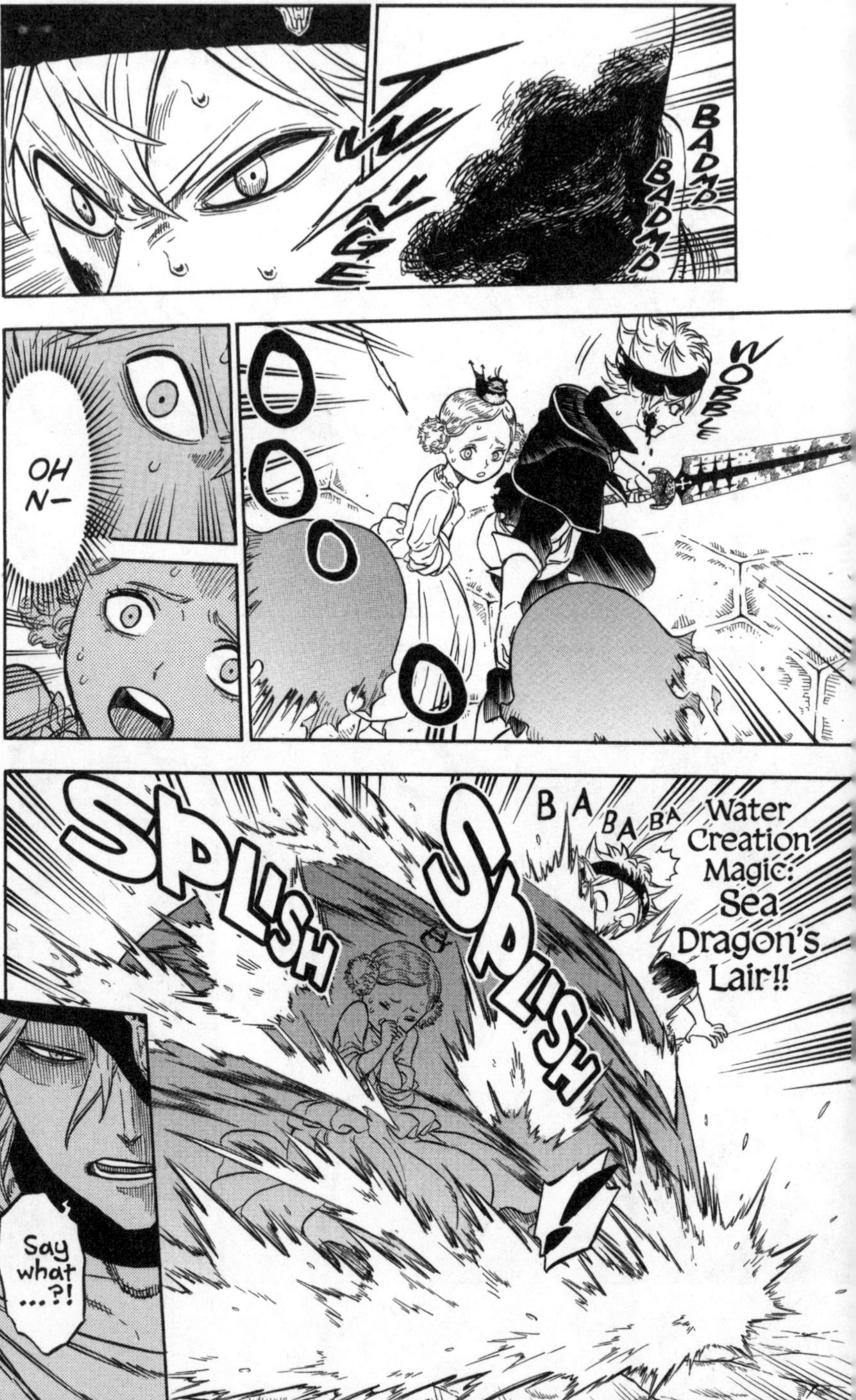
BADMP
BADMP
TWINGE
WOBBLE
OOOOO
OH N—
SPLISH
SPLISH
BA BA BA BA
Water Creation Magic: Sea Dragon's Lair!!
Say what...?!

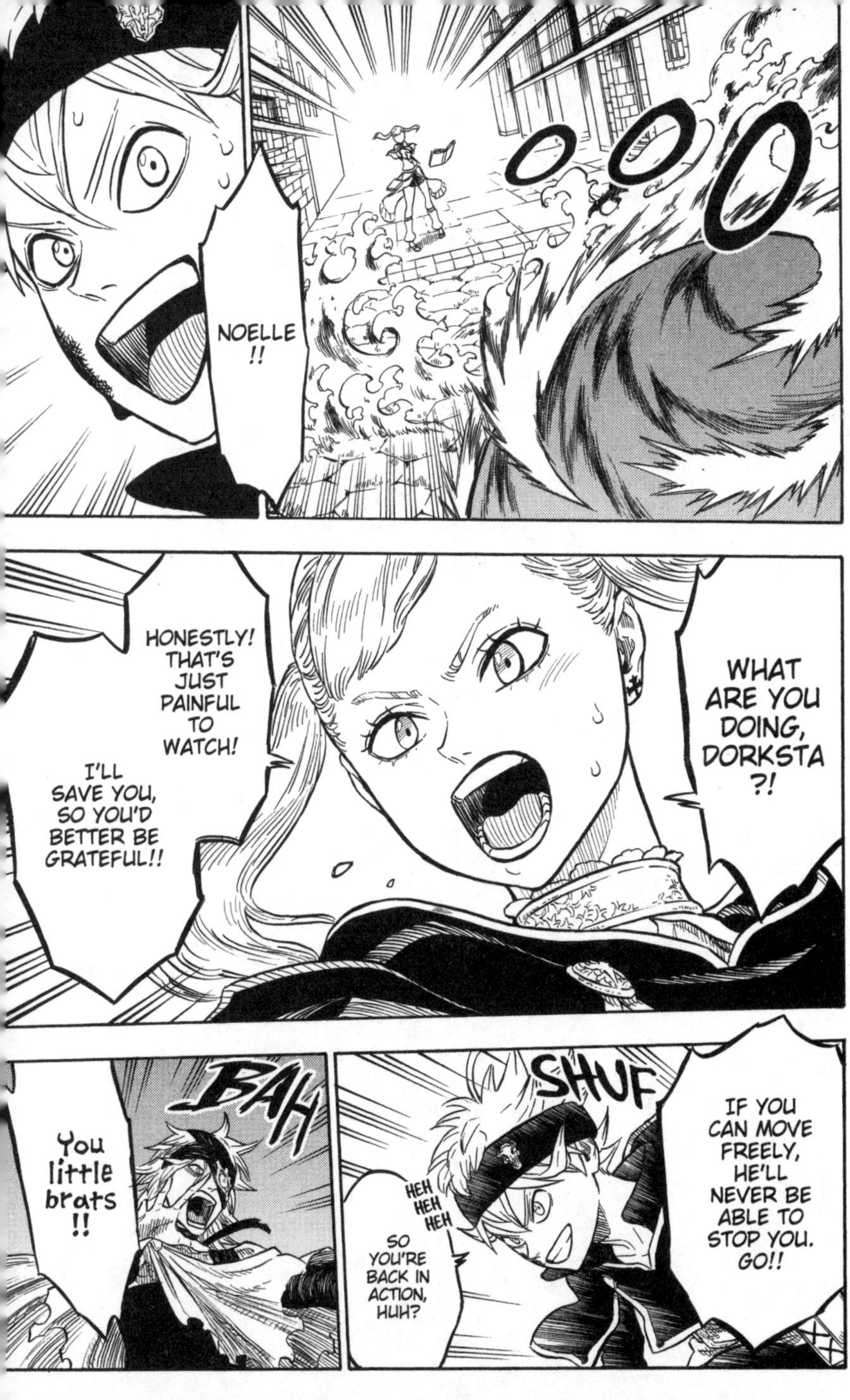
NOELLE!!
WHAT ARE YOU DOING, DORKSTA?!
HONESTLY! THAT'S JUST PAINFUL TO WATCH!
I'LL SAVE YOU, SO YOU'D BETTER BE GRATEFUL!!
SHUF
IF YOU CAN MOVE FREELY, HE'LL NEVER BE ABLE TO STOP YOU. GO!!
HEH HEH HEH
SO YOU'RE BACK IN ACTION, HUH?
BAH
You little brats!!

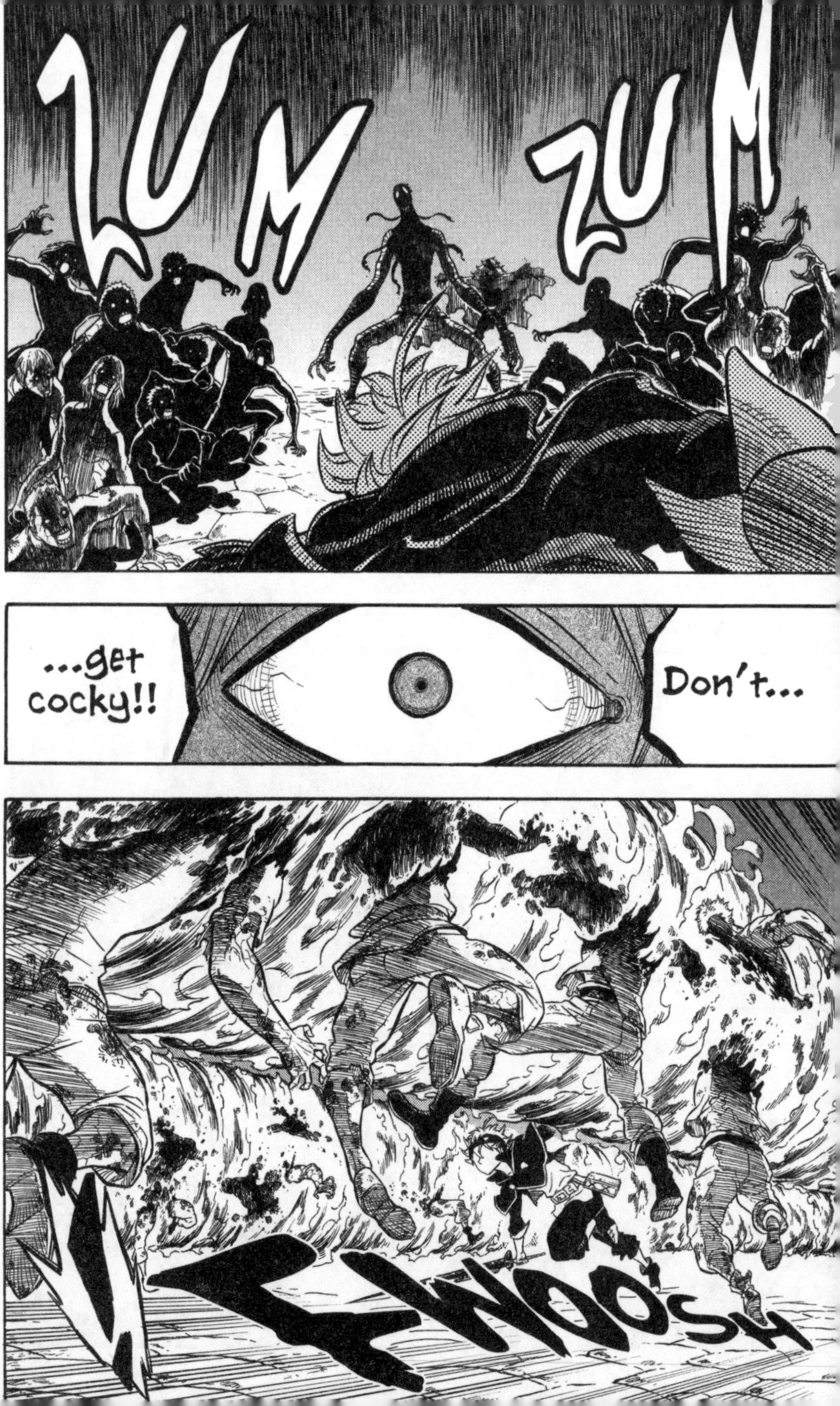
ZUM ZUM
Don't...
...get cocky!!
WHOOSH

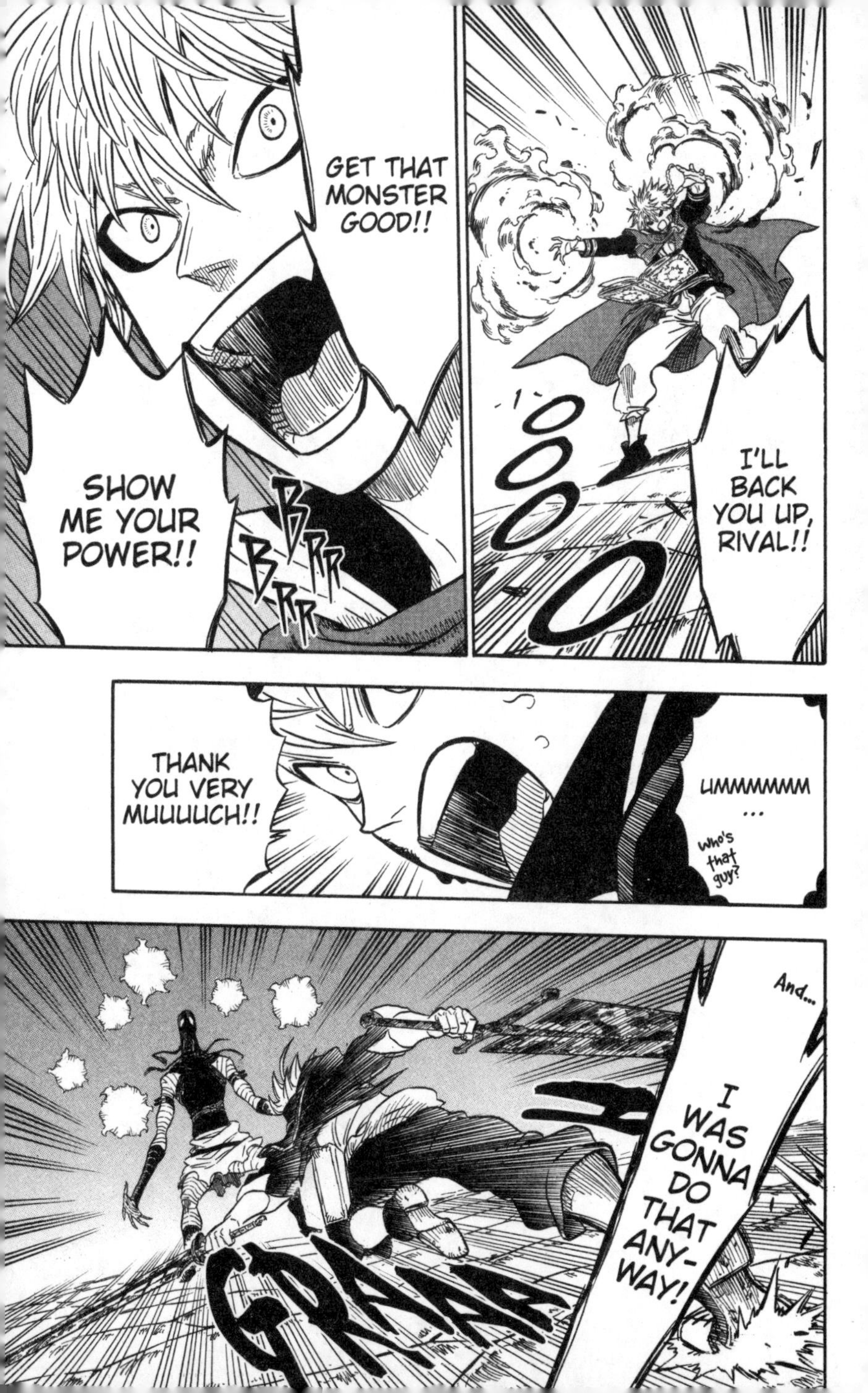
I'LL BACK YOU UP, RIVAL!!
GET THAT MONSTER GOOD!!
SHOW ME YOUR POWER!!
BRRR BRRR
UMMMMMMM ...
who's that guy?
THANK YOU VERY MUUUUCH!!
And...
I WAS GONNA DO THAT ANY-WAY!
HA
GRAAA

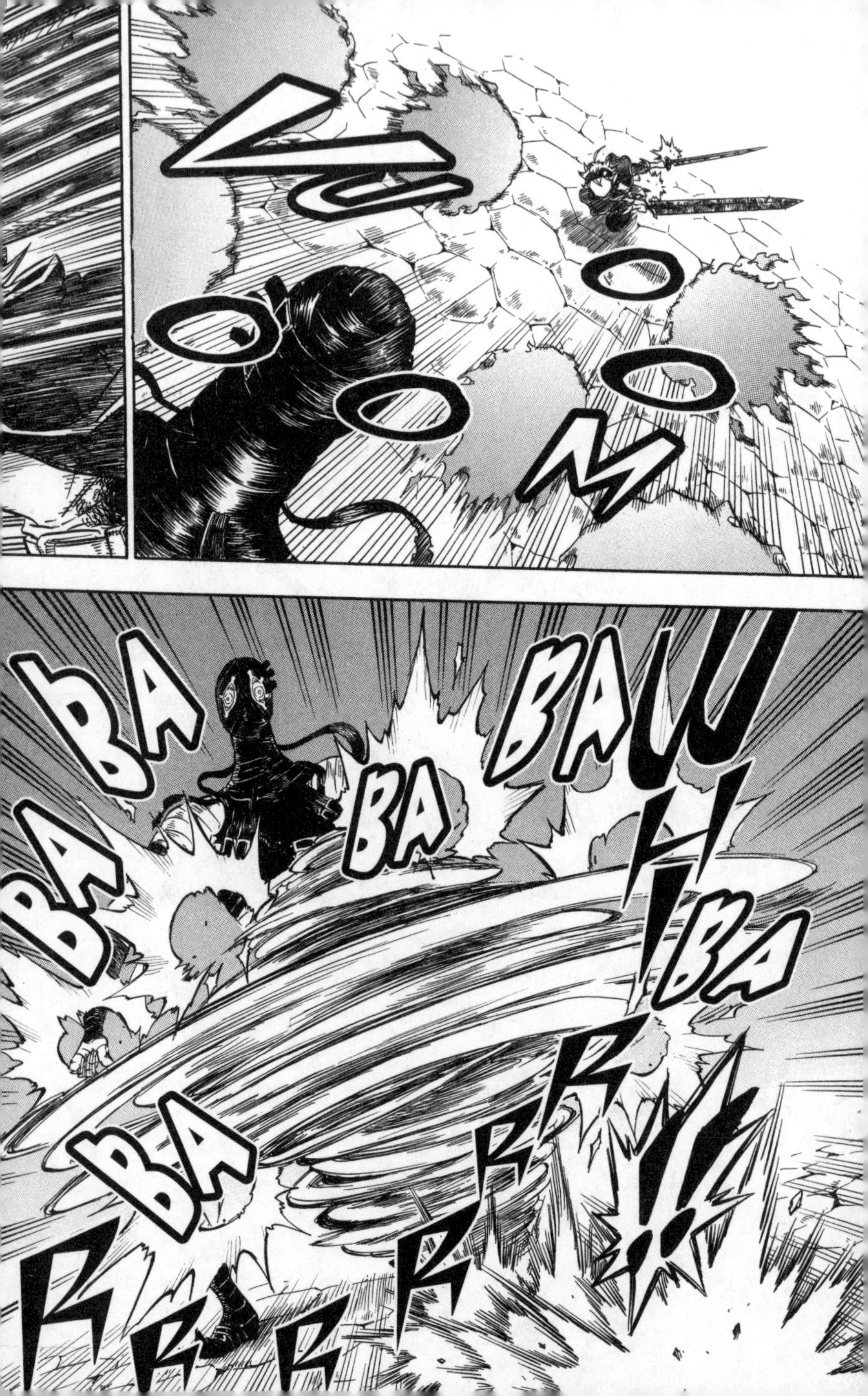

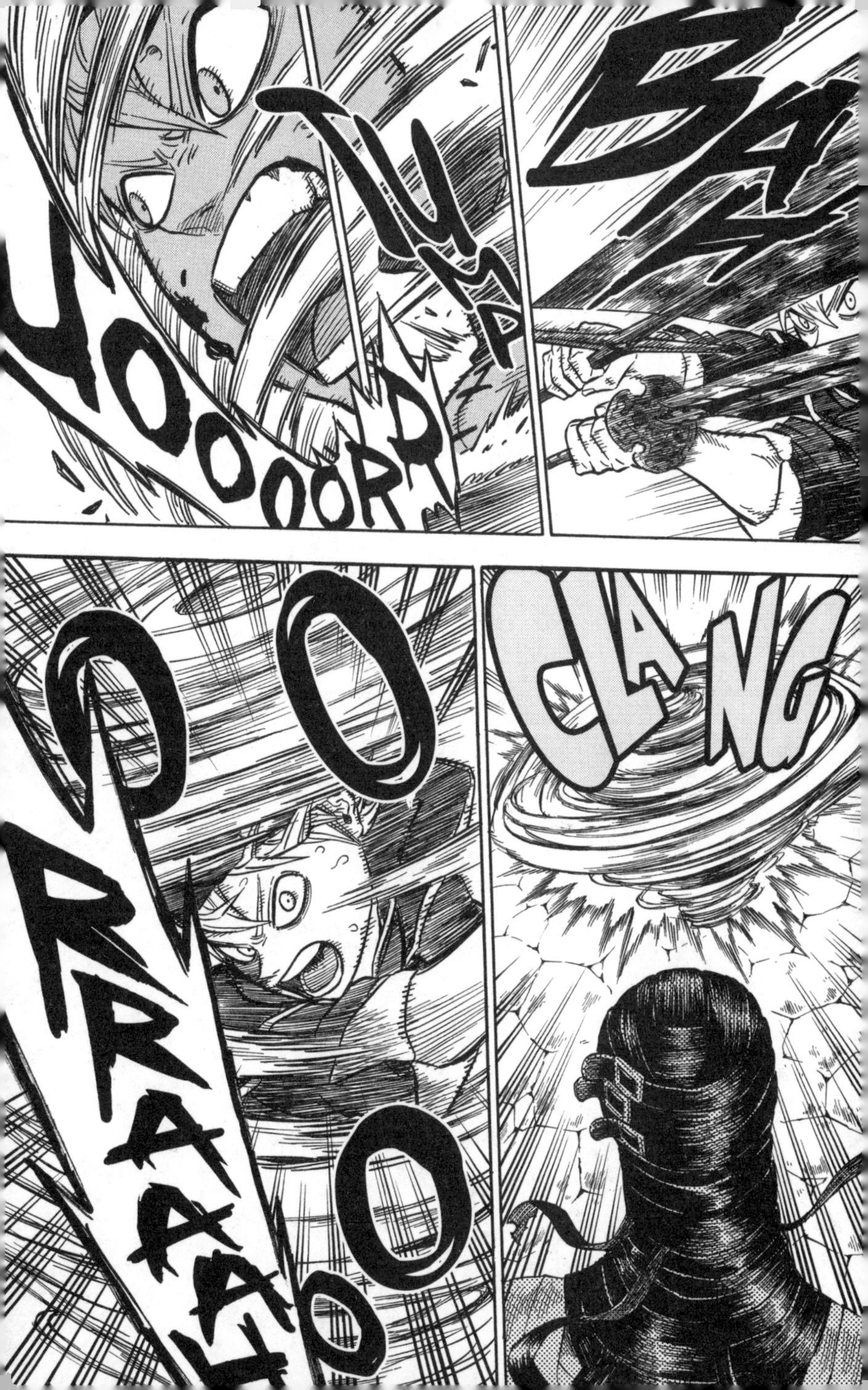
BA
JUMP
YOOOORR
CLANG
OOO

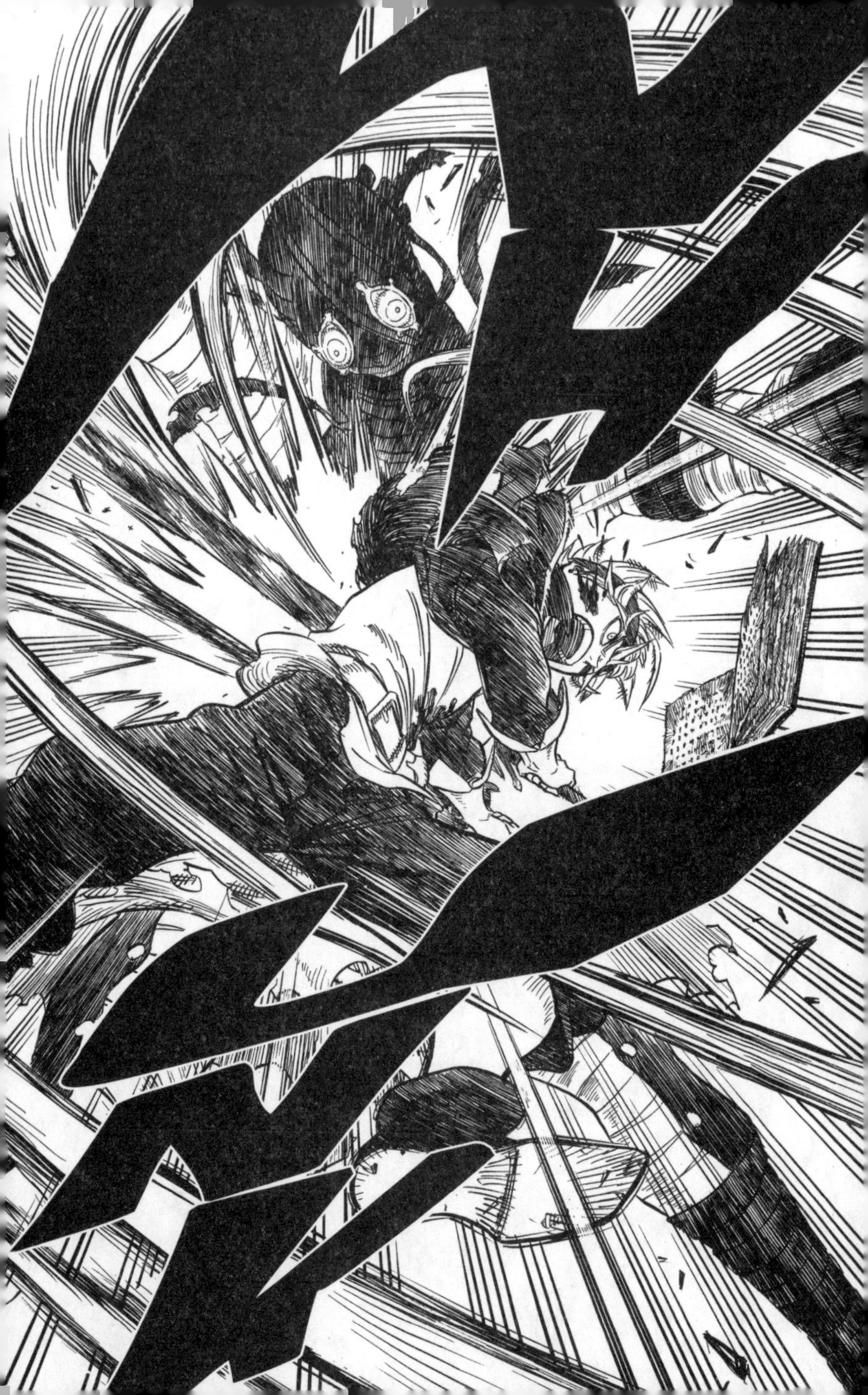

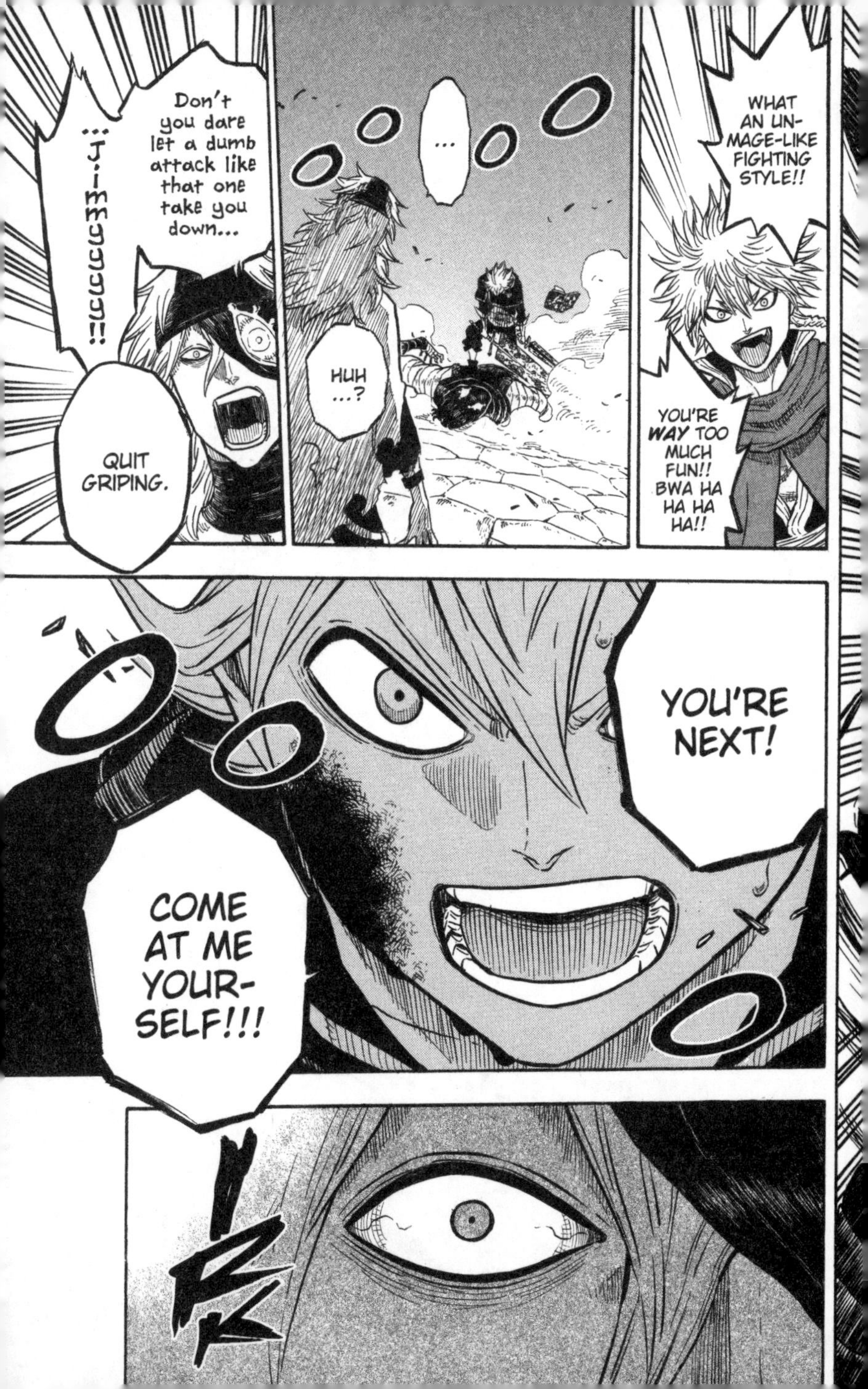
WHAT AN UN-MAGE-LIKE FIGHTING STYLE!!
YOU'RE WAY TOO MUCH FUN!! BWA HA HA HA HA!!
...
HUH ...?
Don't you dare let a dumb attack like that one take you down...
...Jimmyyyyy!!
QUIT GRIPING.
YOU'RE NEXT!
COME AT ME YOURSELF!!!

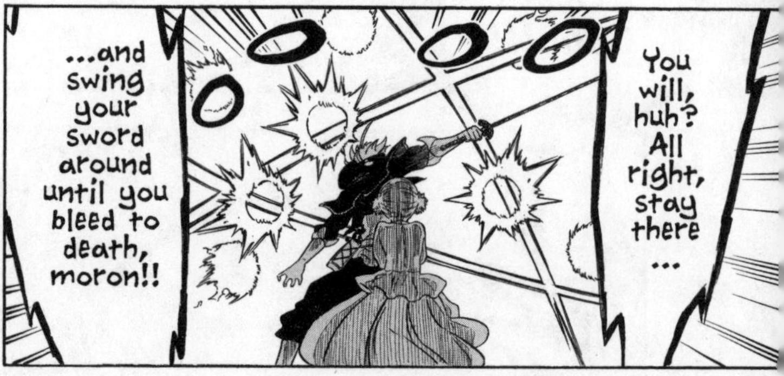
You will, huh? All right, stay there...
...and swing your sword around until you bleed to death, moron!!

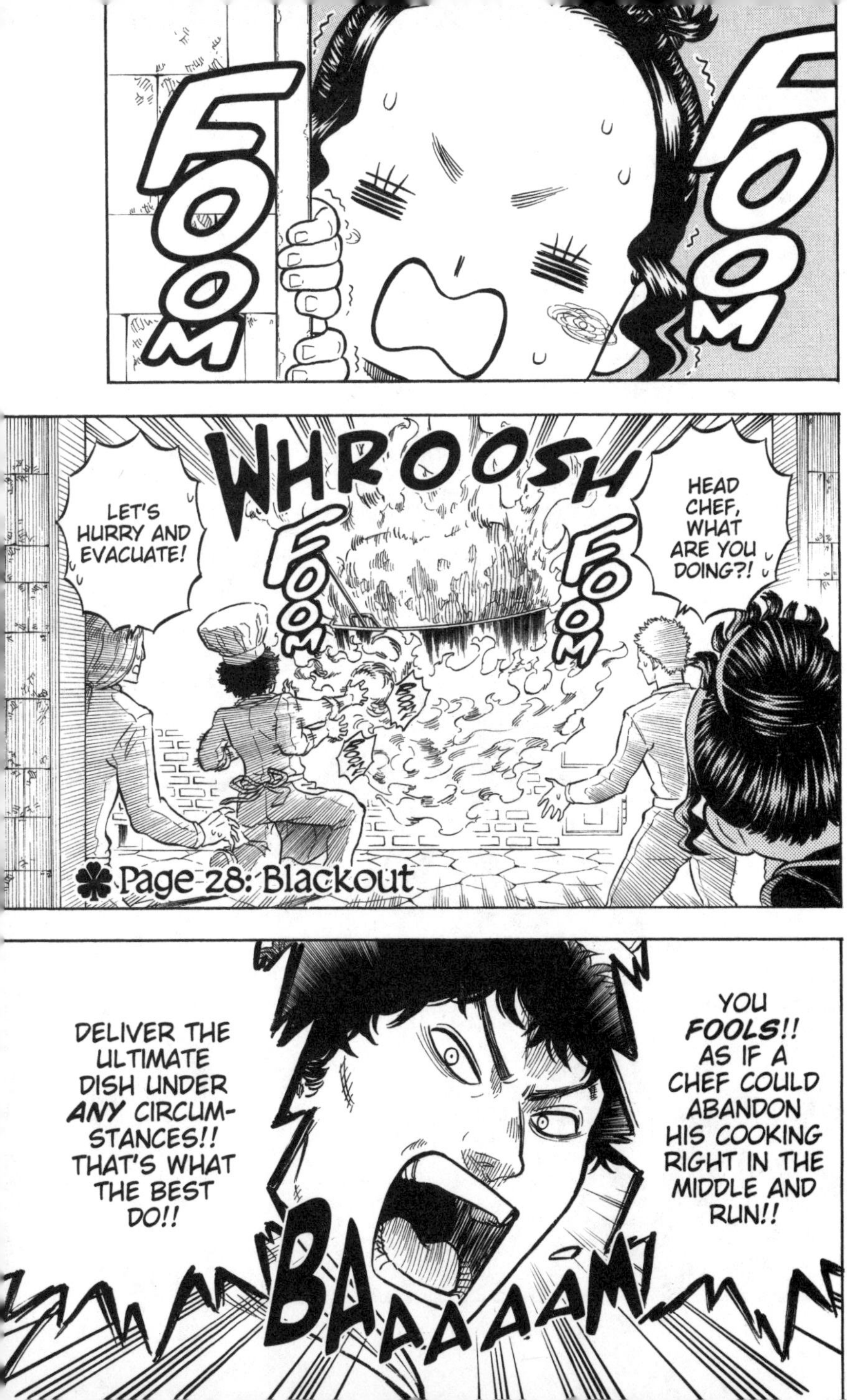
FOOOM
FOOOM
WHROOSH
FOOOM
FOOOM
HEAD CHEF, WHAT ARE YOU DOING?!
LET'S HURRY AND EVACUATE!
Page 28: Blackout
YOU *FOOLS*!! AS IF A CHEF COULD ABANDON HIS COOKING RIGHT IN THE MIDDLE AND RUN!!
DELIVER THE ULTIMATE DISH UNDER *ANY* CIRCUM-STANCES!! THAT'S WHAT THE BEST DO!!
BAAAAAM

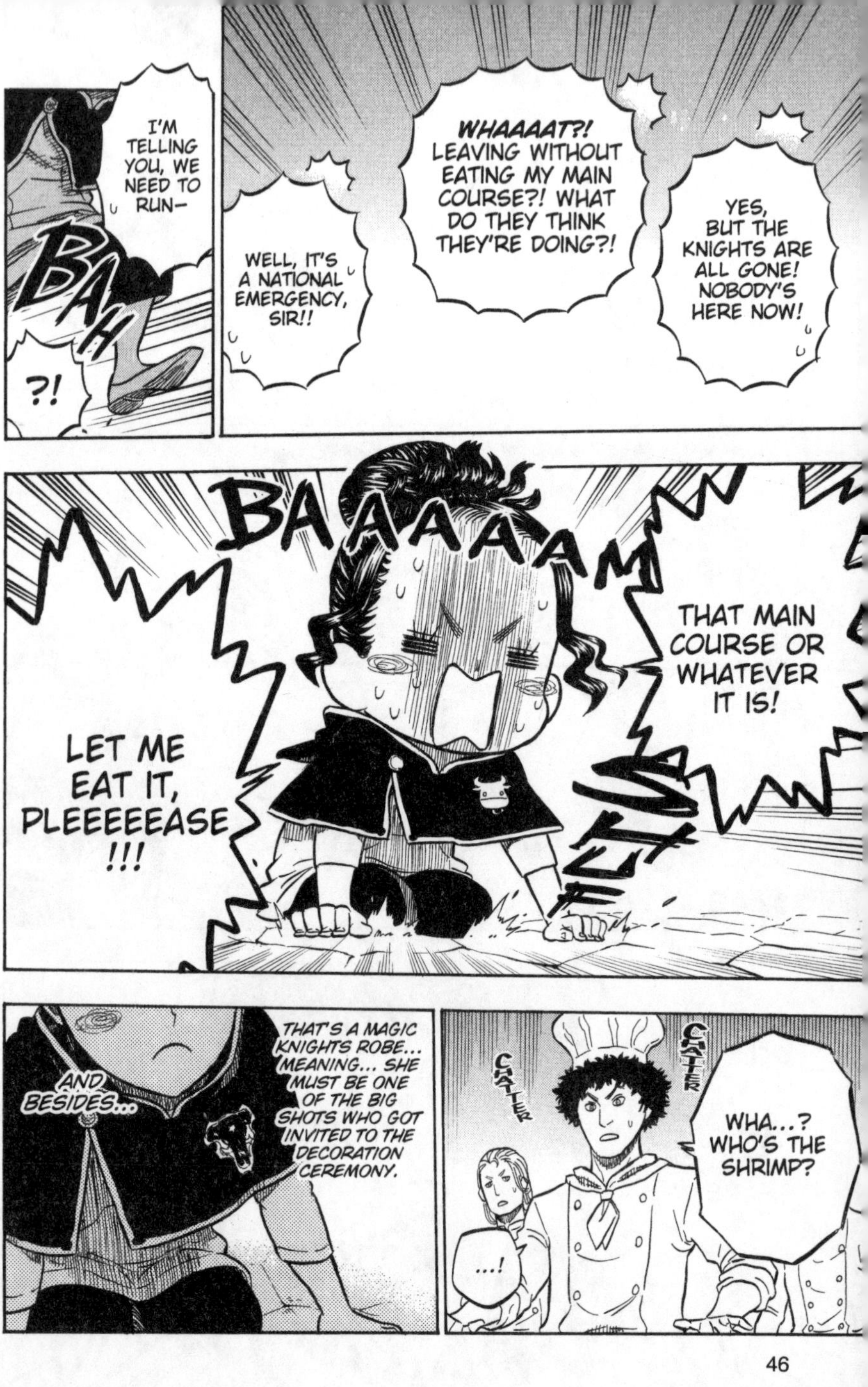
YES, BUT THE KNIGHTS ARE ALL GONE! NOBODY'S HERE NOW!
WHAAAAT?! LEAVING WITHOUT EATING MY MAIN COURSE?! WHAT DO THEY THINK THEY'RE DOING?!
WELL, IT'S A NATIONAL EMERGENCY, SIR!!
I'M TELLING YOU, WE NEED TO RUN–
BAH
?!
BAAAAAM
THAT MAIN COURSE OR WHATEVER IT IS!
LET ME EAT IT, PLEEEEEEASE!!!
SHUF
CHATTER
CHATTER
WHA...? WHO'S THE SHRIMP?
...!
THAT'S A MAGIC KNIGHTS ROBE... MEANING... SHE MUST BE ONE OF THE BIG SHOTS WHO GOT INVITED TO THE DECORATION CEREMONY.
AND BESIDES...

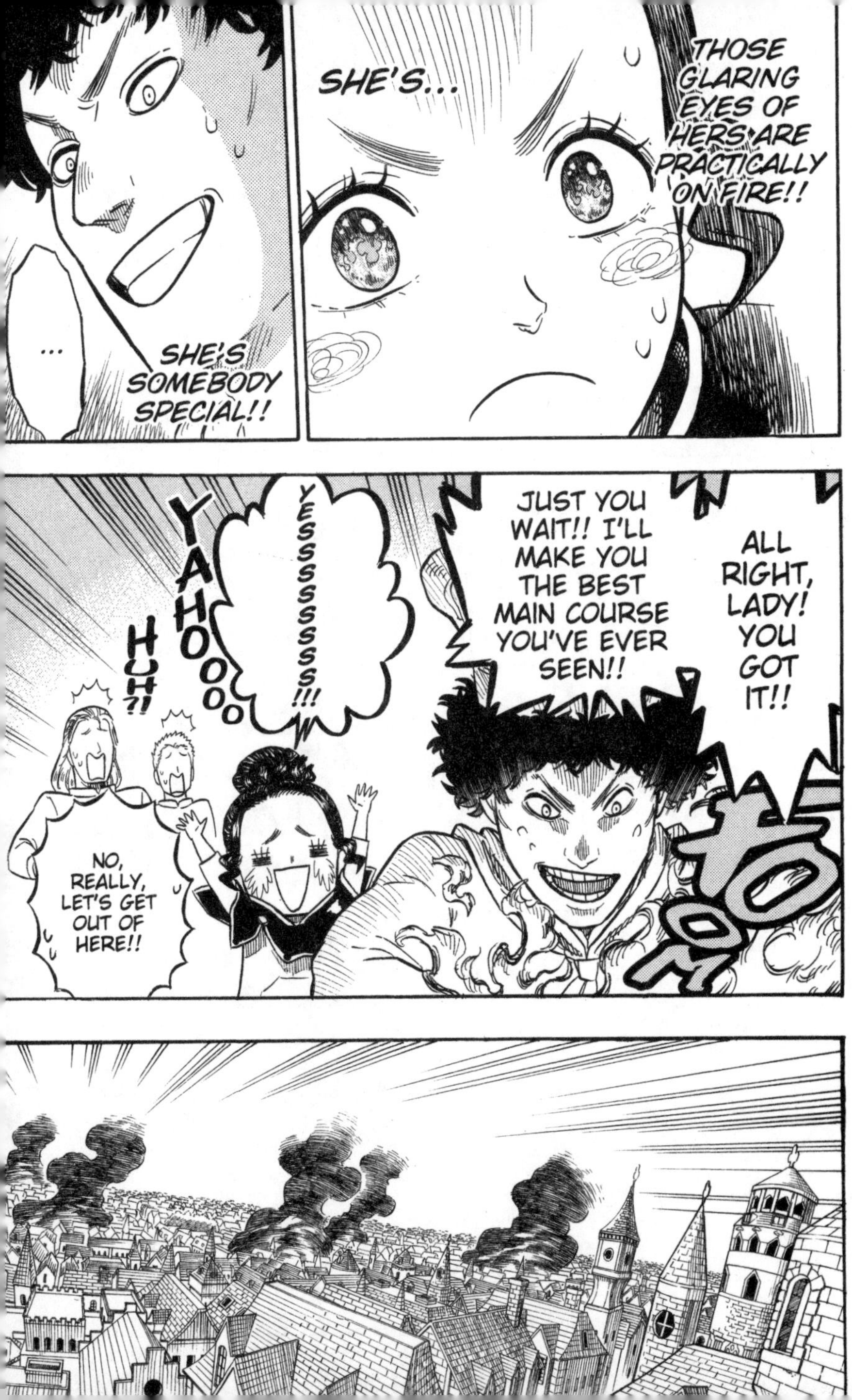
THOSE GLARING EYES OF HERS ARE PRACTICALLY ON FIRE!!
SHE'S...
...
SHE'S SOMEBODY SPECIAL!!
ALL RIGHT, LADY! YOU GOT IT!!
JUST YOU WAIT!! I'LL MAKE YOU THE BEST MAIN COURSE YOU'VE EVER SEEN!!
YESSSSSSSS!!!
YAHOOOOO
HUH?!
NO, REALLY, LET'S GET OUT OF HERE!!

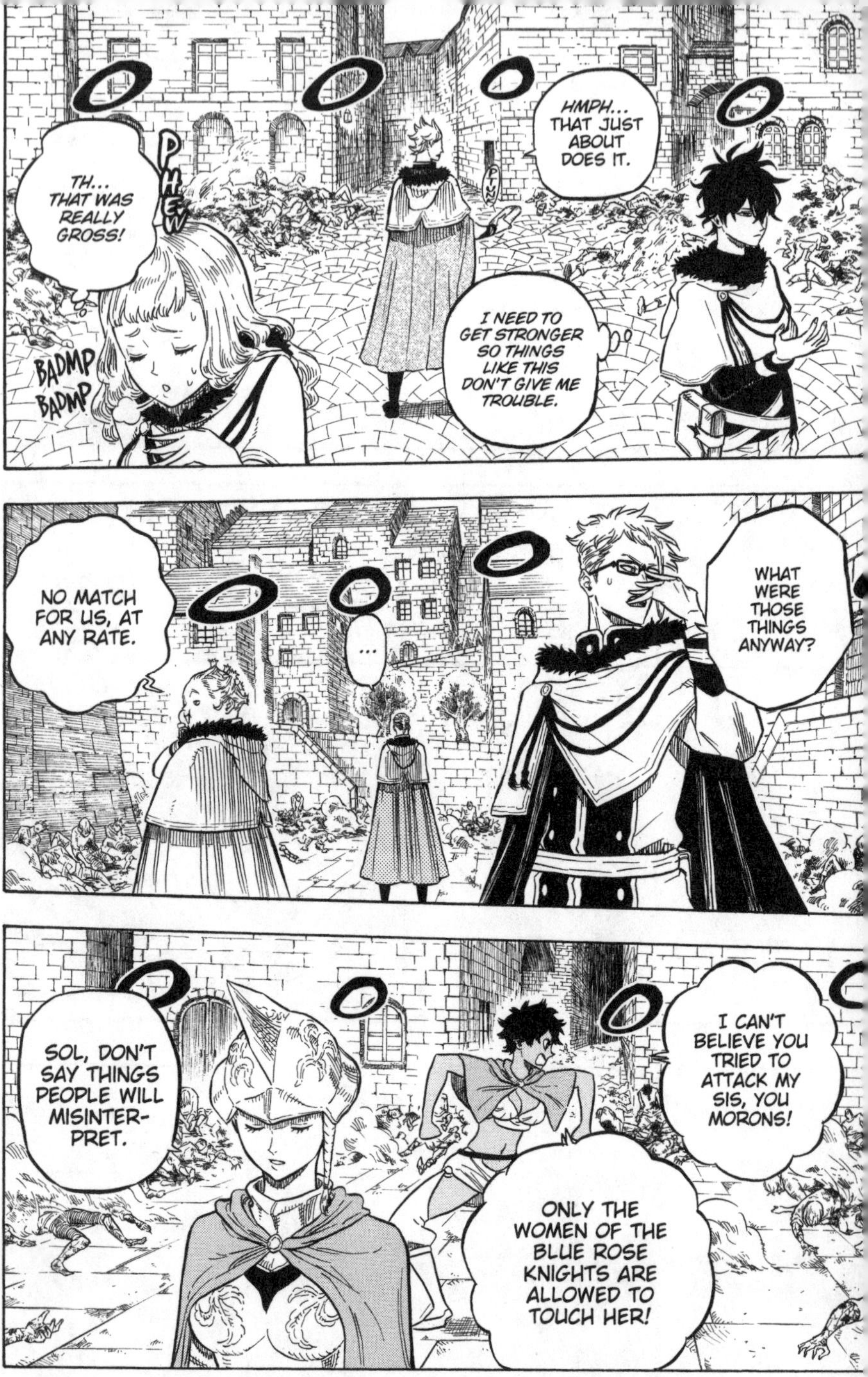
HMPH... THAT JUST ABOUT DOES IT.
I NEED TO GET STRONGER SO THINGS LIKE THIS DON'T GIVE ME TROUBLE.
TH... THAT WAS REALLY GROSS!
PHEW
BADMP BADMP
WHAT WERE THOSE THINGS ANYWAY?
...
NO MATCH FOR US, AT ANY RATE.
I CAN'T BELIEVE YOU TRIED TO ATTACK MY SIS, YOU MORONS!
ONLY THE WOMEN OF THE BLUE ROSE KNIGHTS ARE ALLOWED TO TOUCH HER!
SOL, DON'T SAY THINGS PEOPLE WILL MISINTER-PRET.

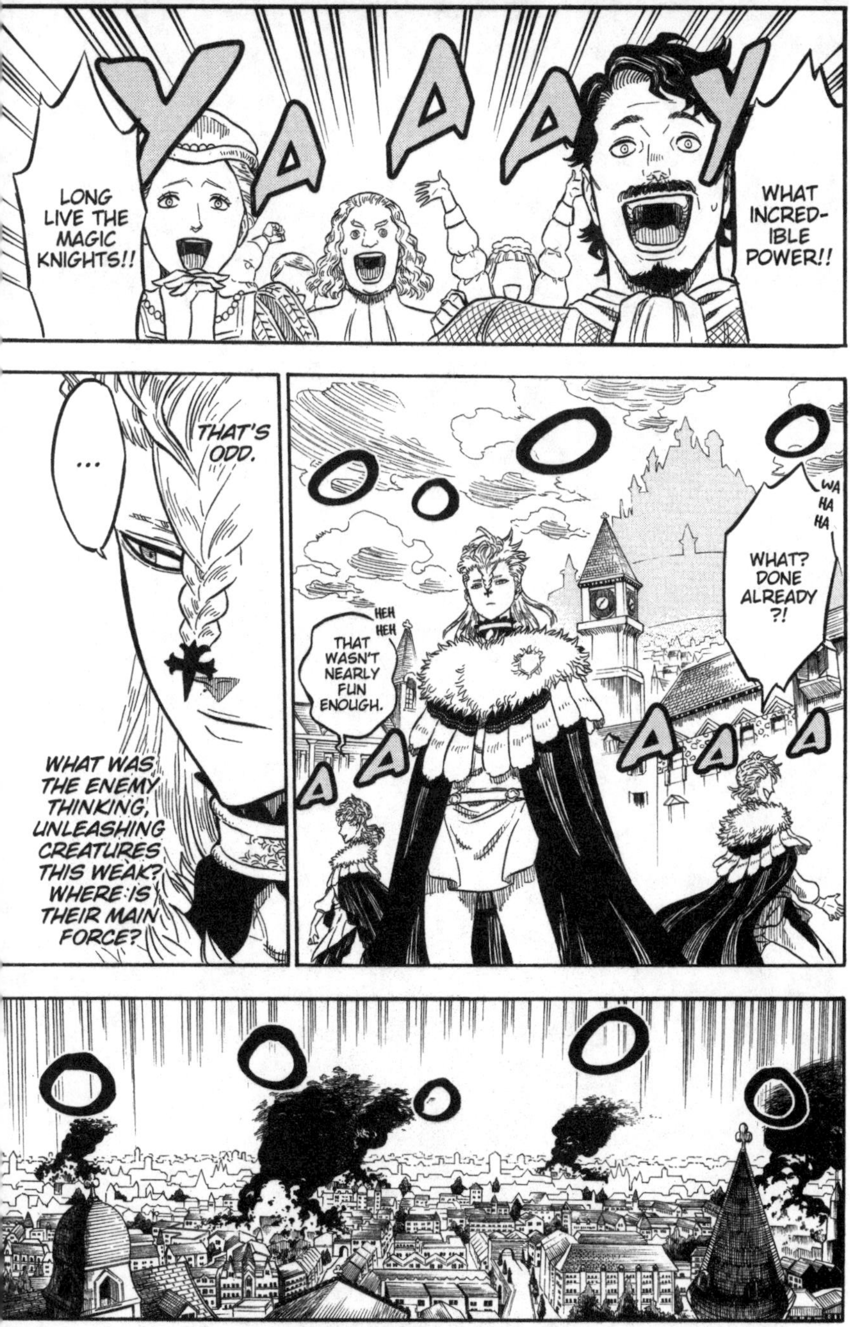
WHAT INCREDIBLE POWER!!
YAAAY
LONG LIVE THE MAGIC KNIGHTS!!
WA HA HA
WHAT? DONE ALREADY?!
OOOOO
HEH HEH
THAT WASN'T NEARLY FUN ENOUGH.
AAAAA
THAT'S ODD.
...
WHAT WAS THE ENEMY THINKING, UNLEASHING CREATURES THIS WEAK? WHERE IS THEIR MAIN FORCE?
OOOOO

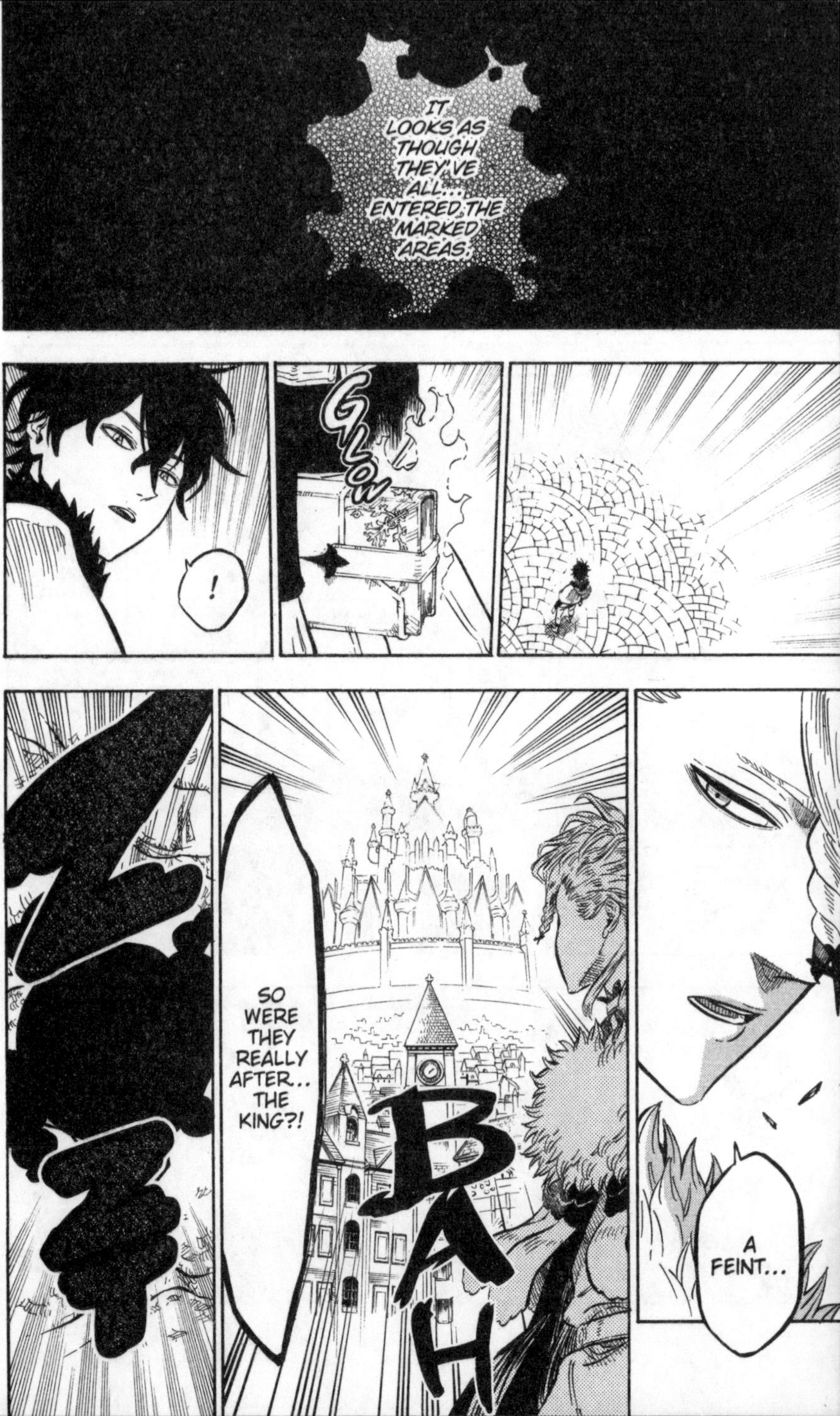
IT LOOKS AS THOUGH THEY'VE ALL... ENTERED THE MARKED AREAS.
GLOW
!
A FEINT...
SO WERE THEY REALLY AFTER... THE KING?!
BAH

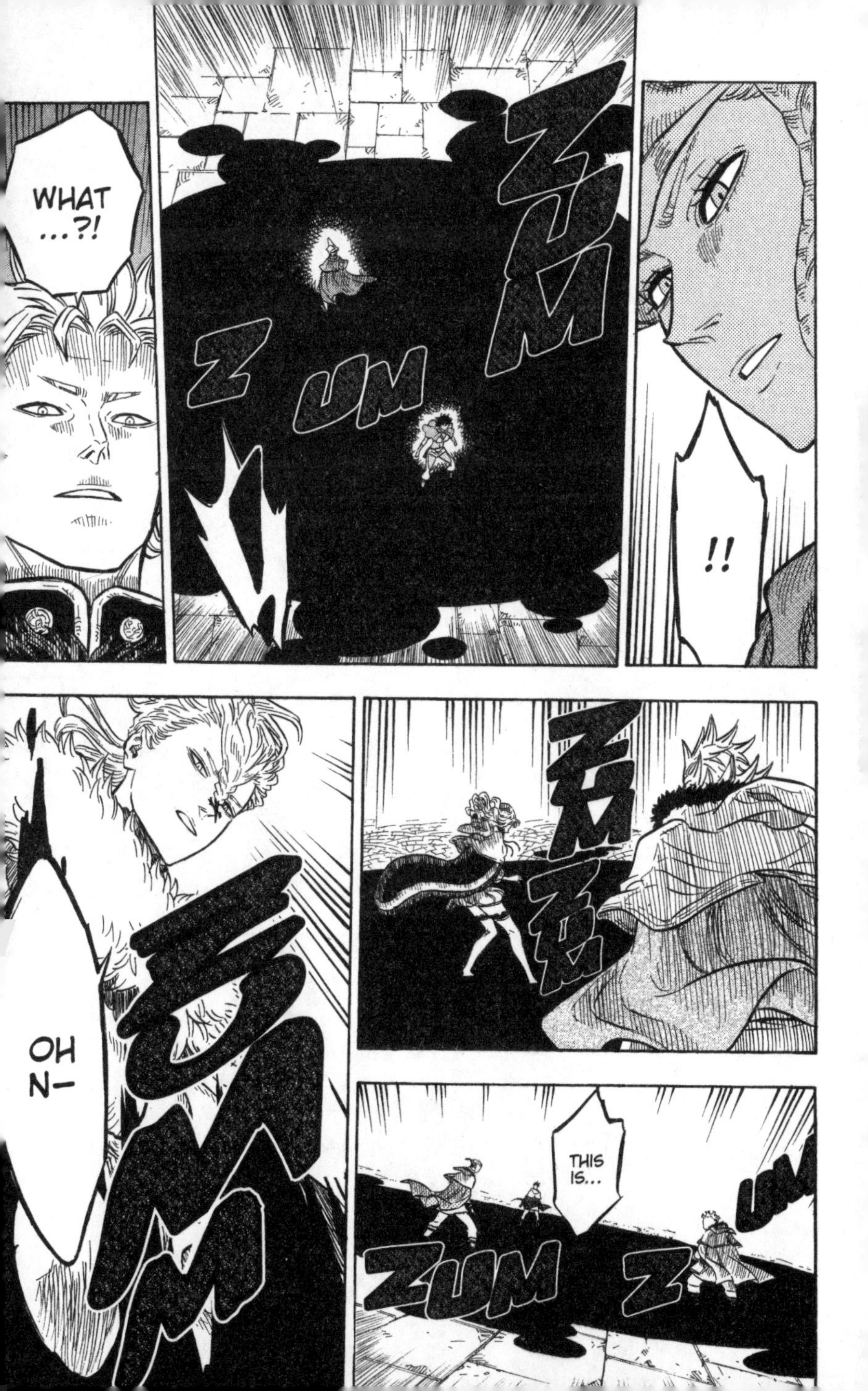
!!
Z UM
WHAT ...?!
THIS IS...
ZUM Z UM
OH N—

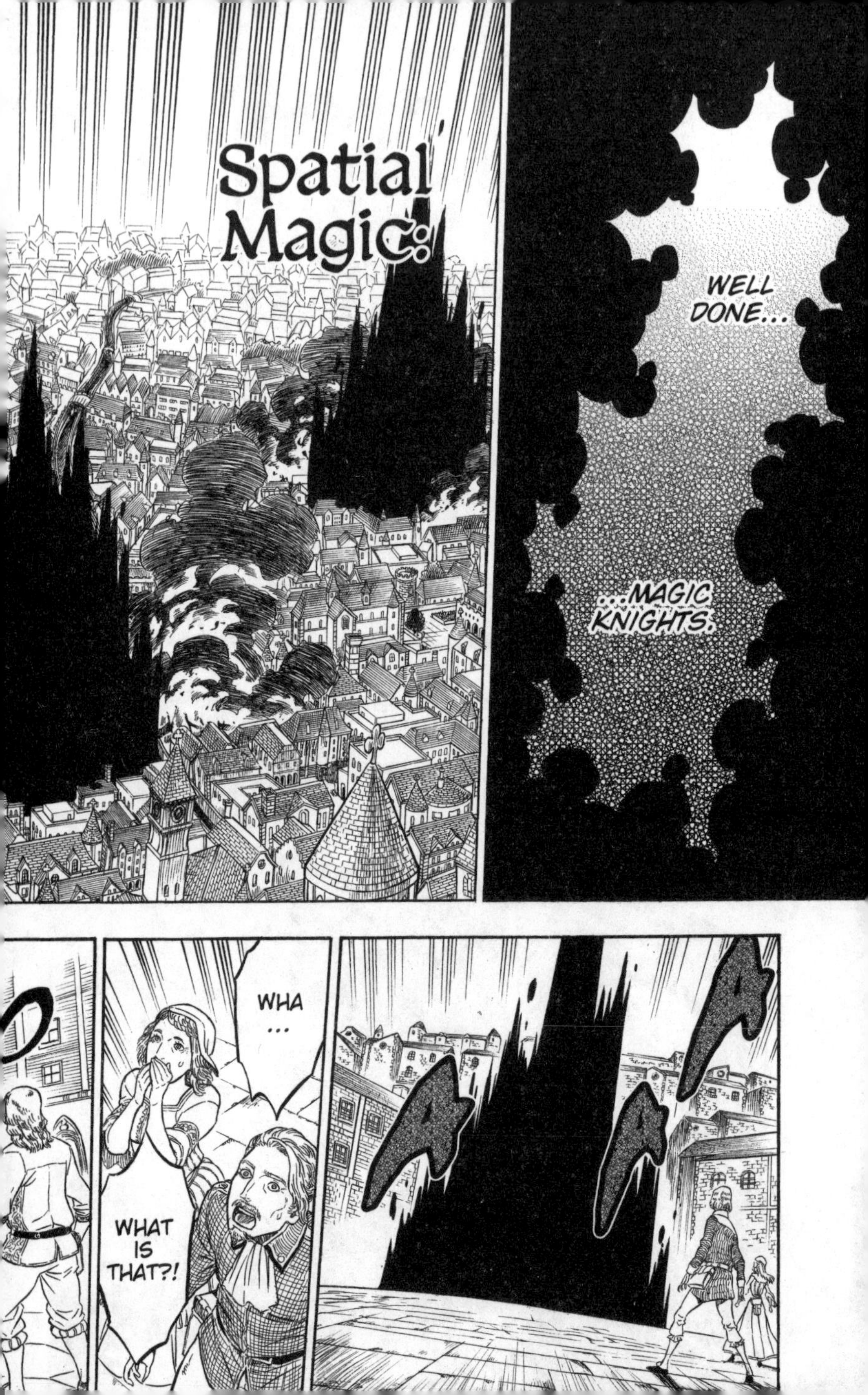
WELL DONE...
...MAGIC KNIGHTS.
Spatial Magic!
WHA...
WHAT IS THAT?!

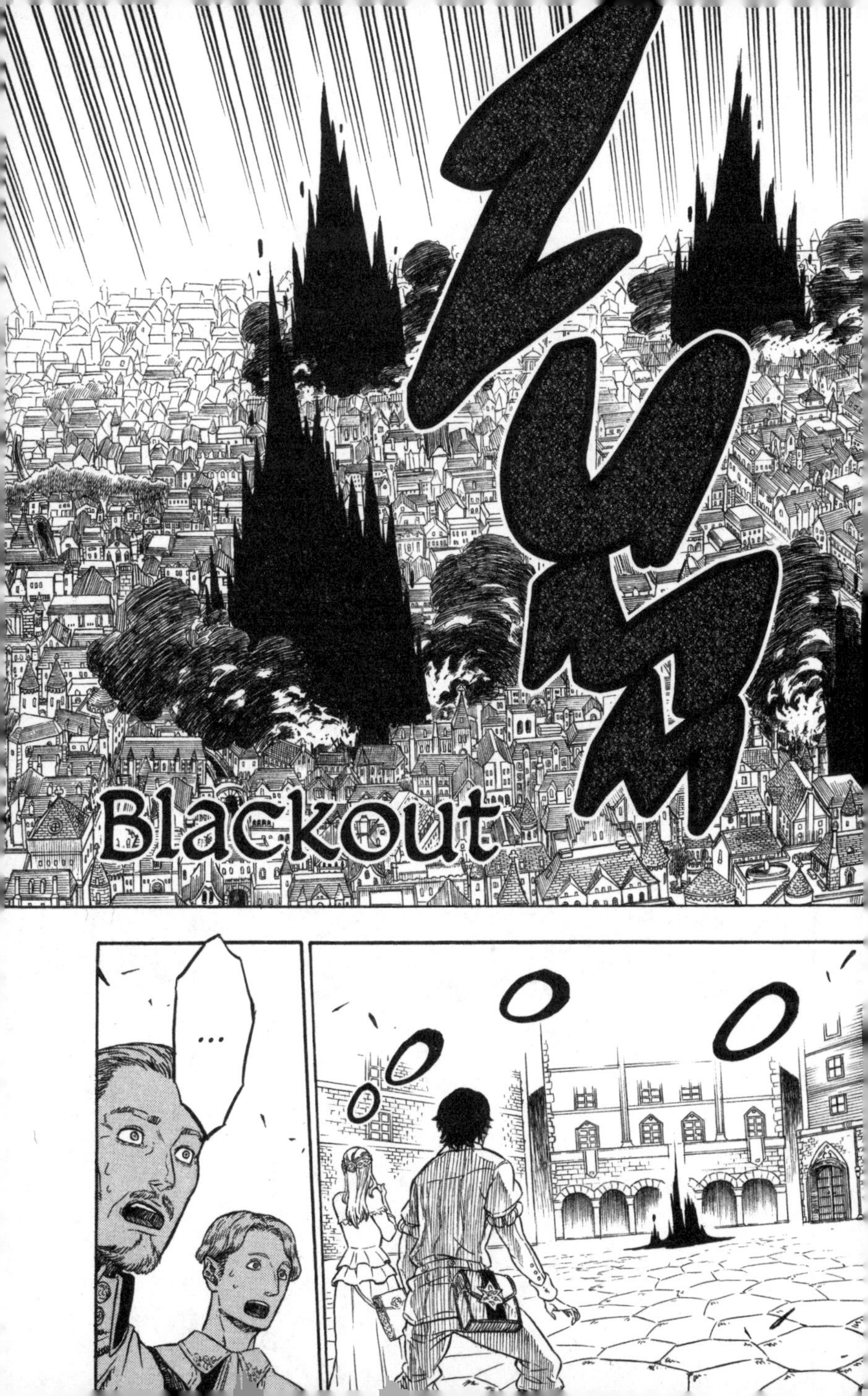
Blackout
...

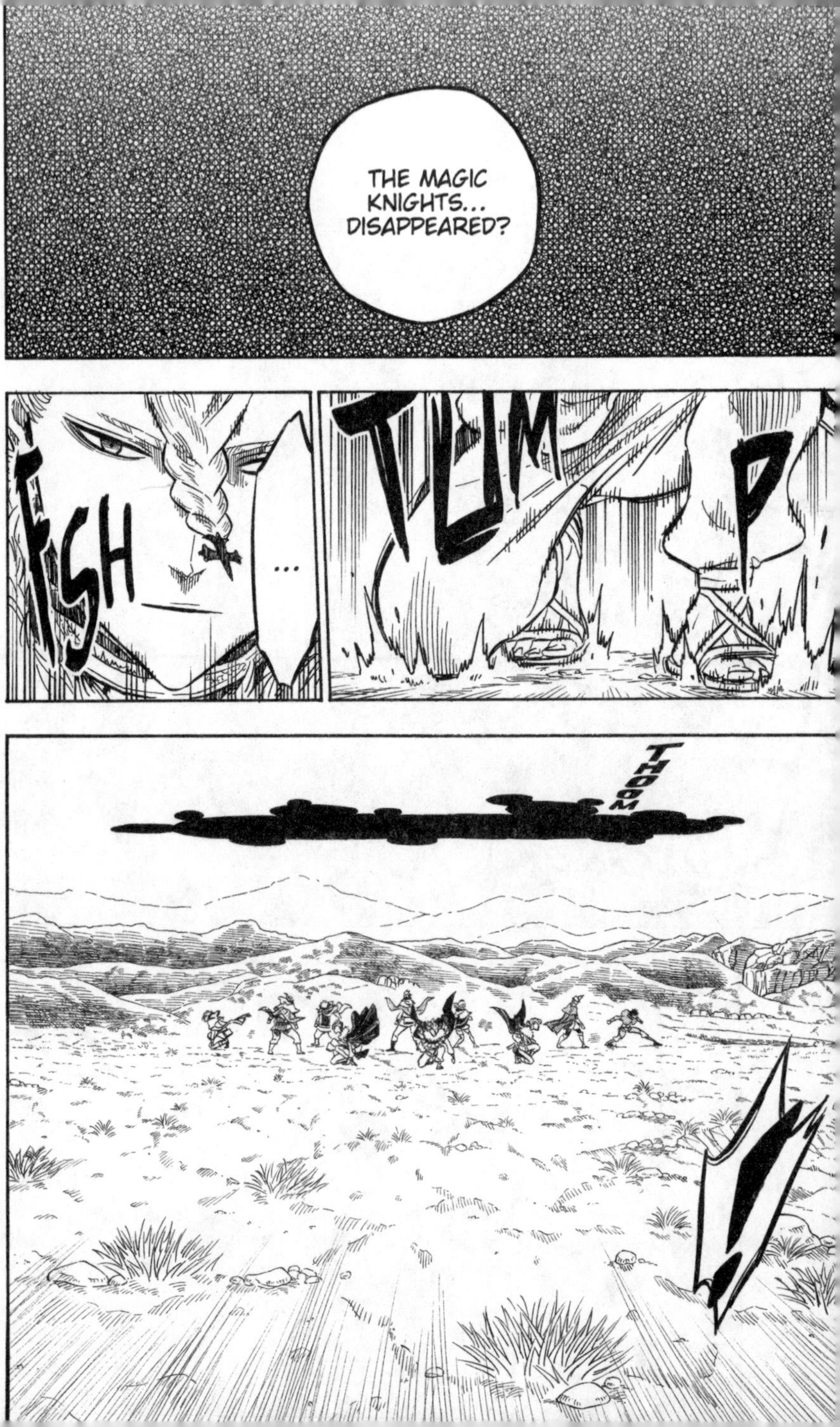
THE MAGIC KNIGHTS... DISAPPEARED?
TUMP
FSH
...
THOOM

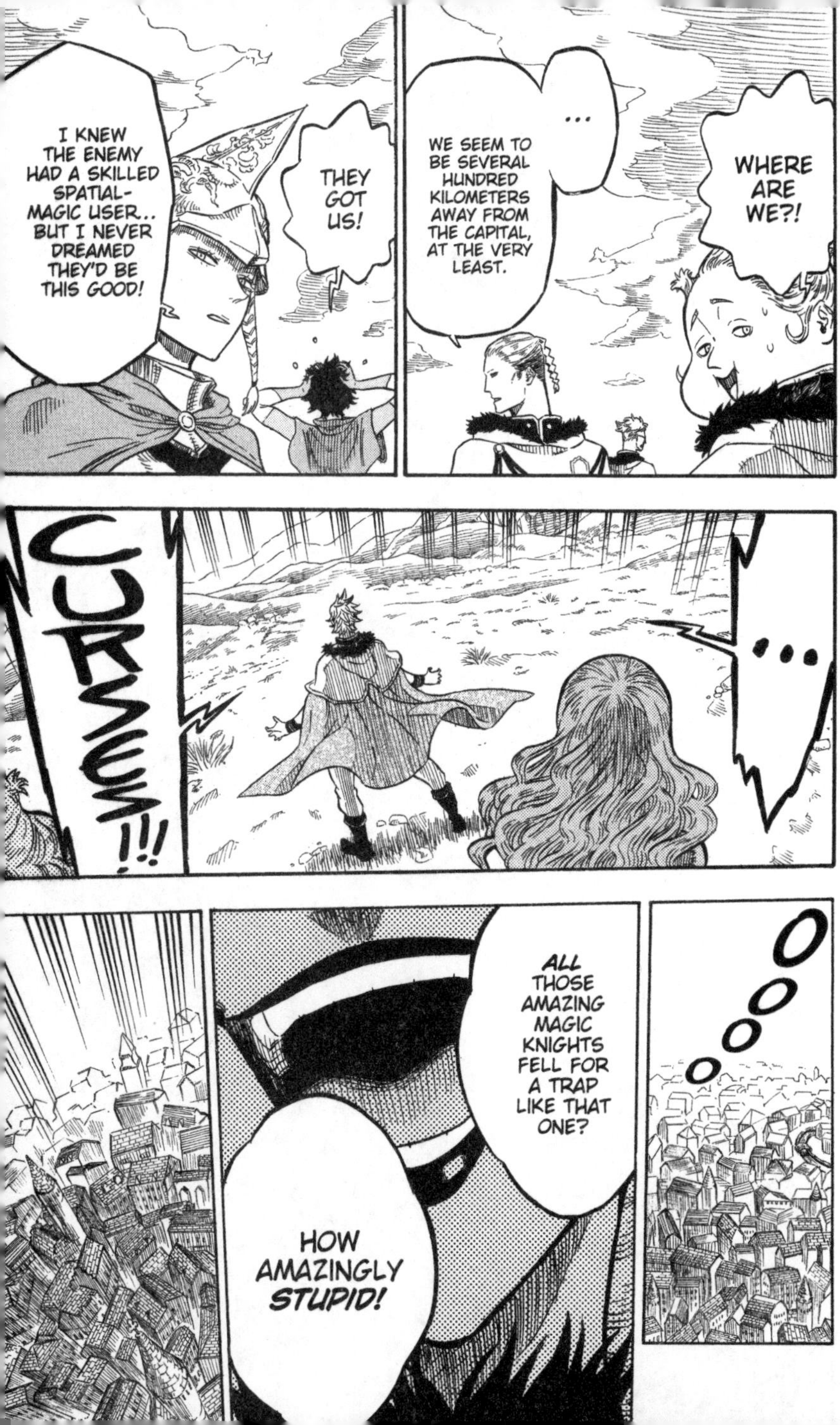
WHERE ARE WE?!
...
WE SEEM TO BE SEVERAL HUNDRED KILOMETERS AWAY FROM THE CAPITAL, AT THE VERY LEAST.
THEY GOT US!
I KNEW THE ENEMY HAD A SKILLED SPATIAL-MAGIC USER.. BUT I NEVER DREAMED THEY'D BE THIS GOOD!
...
CURSES!!!
OOOO
ALL THOSE AMAZING MAGIC KNIGHTS FELL FOR A TRAP LIKE THAT ONE?
HOW AMAZINGLY STUPID!

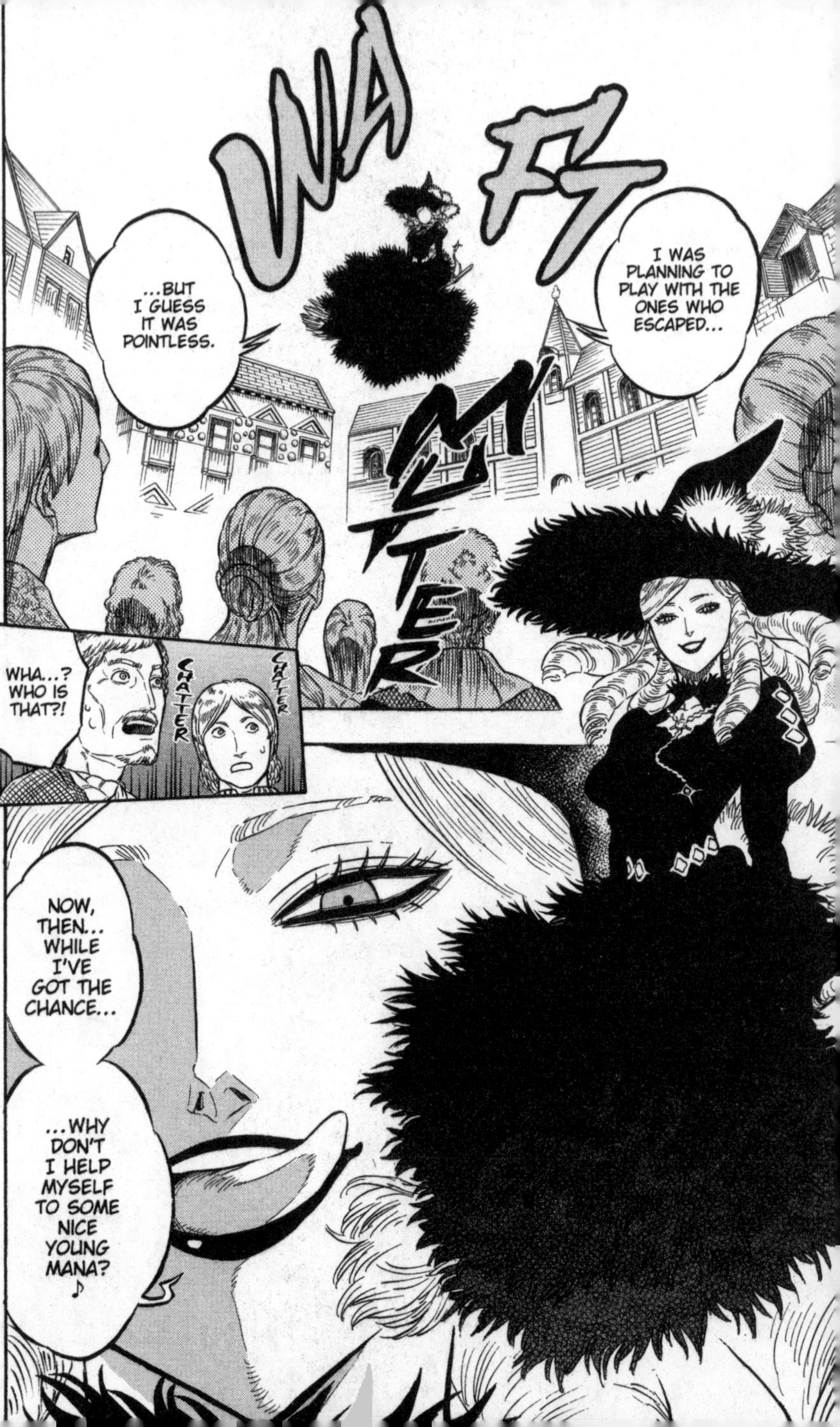
WAFT
I WAS PLANNING TO PLAY WITH THE ONES WHO ESCAPED...
...BUT I GUESS IT WAS POINTLESS.
MUTTER
CHATTER
CHATTER
WHA...? WHO IS THAT?!
NOW, THEN... WHILE I'VE GOT THE CHANCE...
...WHY DON'T I HELP MYSELF TO SOME NICE YOUNG MANA? ♪

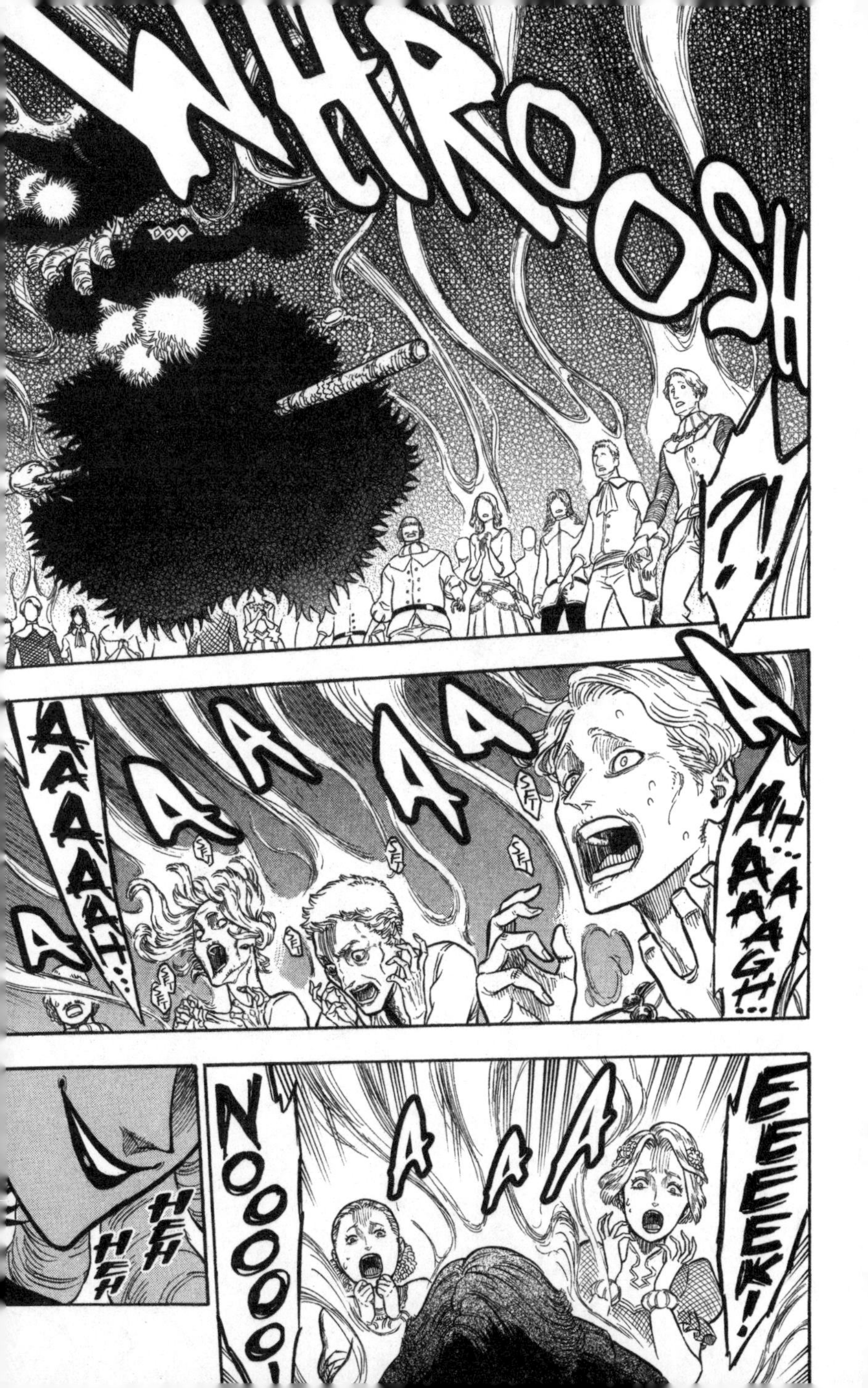
WHROOOSH
?!
AH... AAAAGH...
AAAAAAA
SFT
SFT
SFT
SFT
AAAAAAH...
EEEEEK!
AAAA
NOOOOO!
HEH HEH

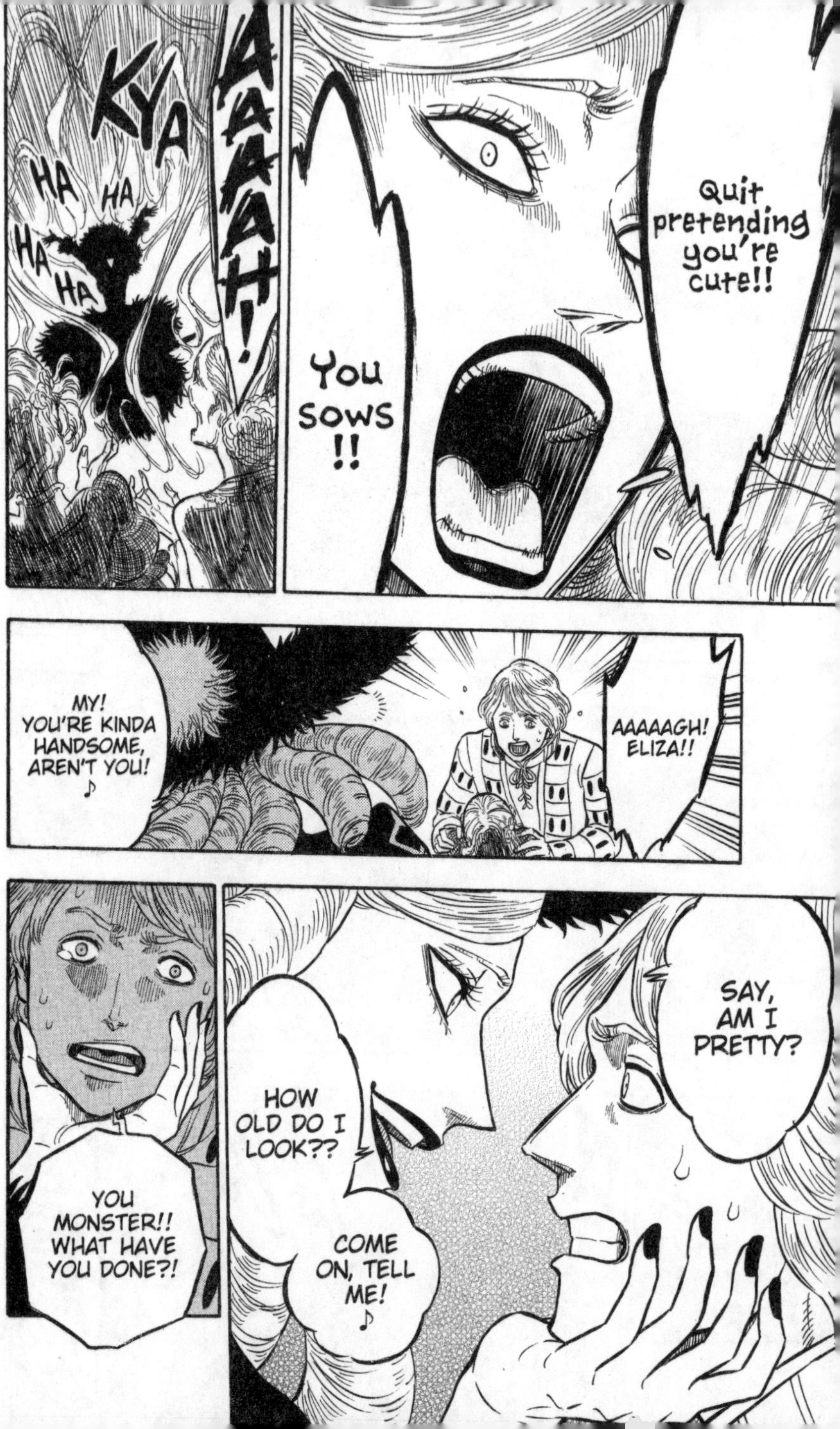
Quit pretending you're cute!!
You sows!!
KYA
AAAAAAH!
HA HA HA HA
AAAAAGH! ELIZA!!
MY! YOU'RE KINDA HANDSOME, AREN'T YOU! ♪
SAY, AM I PRETTY?
HOW OLD DO I LOOK??
COME ON, TELL ME! ♪
YOU MONSTER!! WHAT HAVE YOU DONE?!

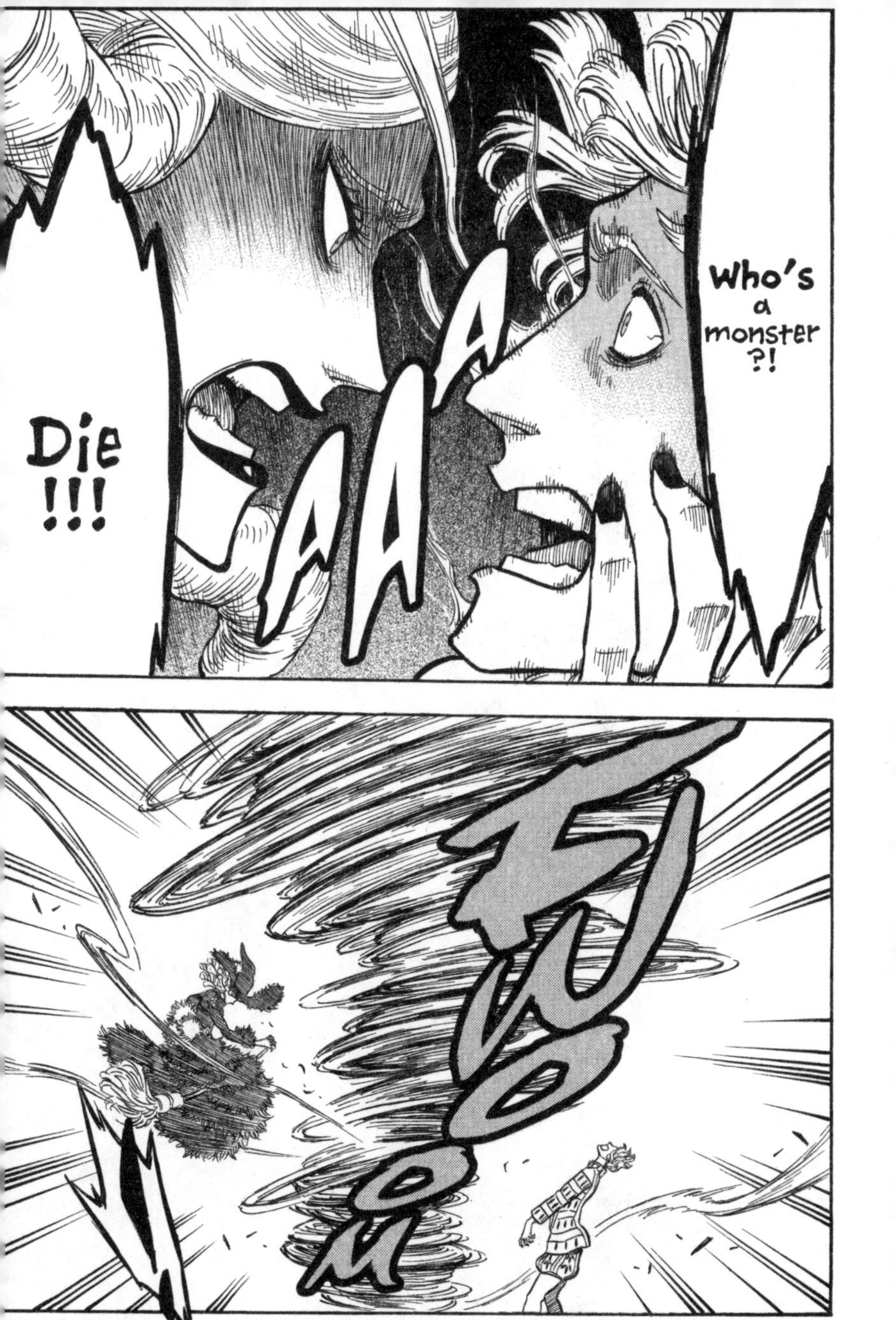
Who's a monster?!
AAAA
Die!!!

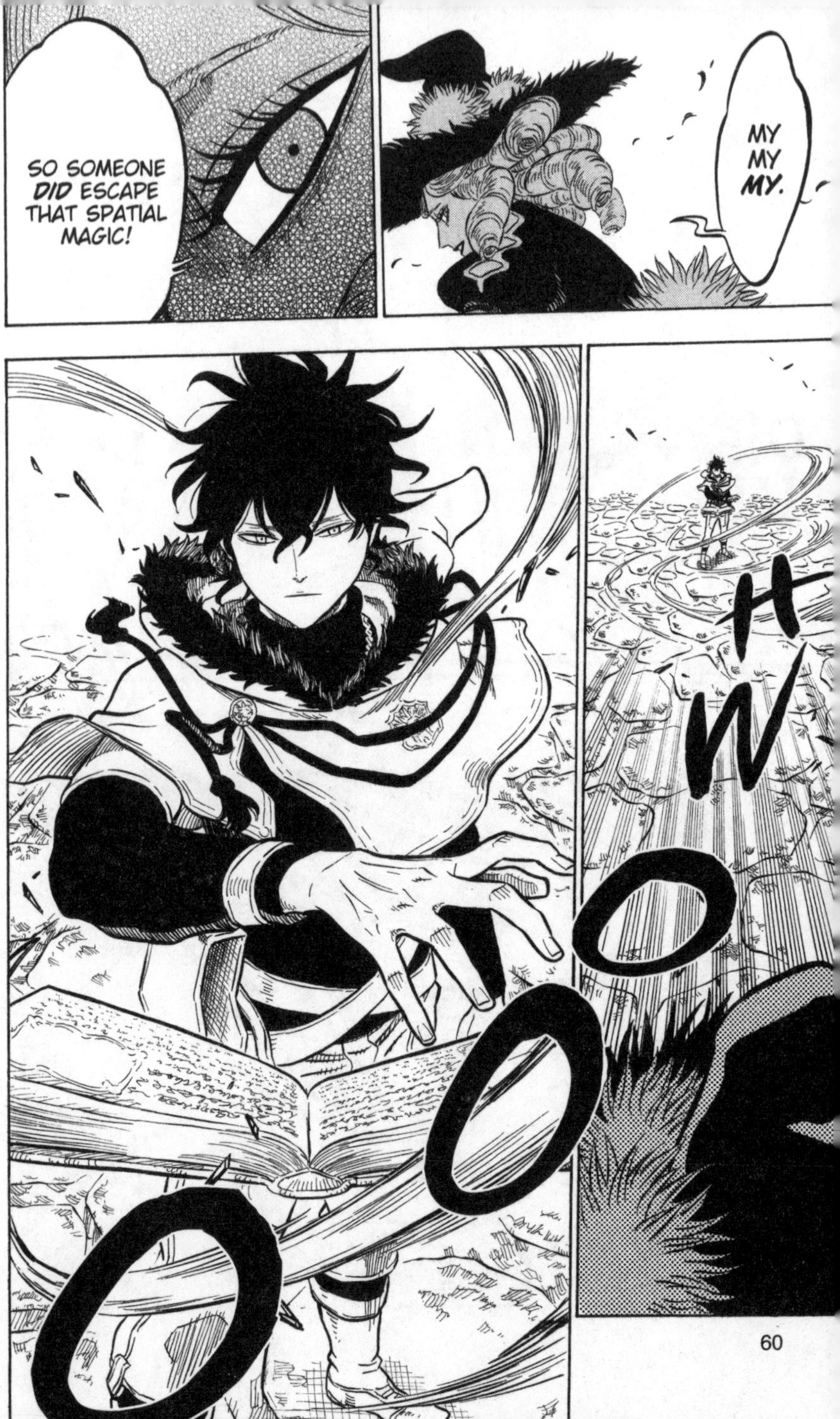
MY MY *MY.*
SO SOMEONE *DID* ESCAPE THAT SPATIAL MAGIC!
HWOOOO

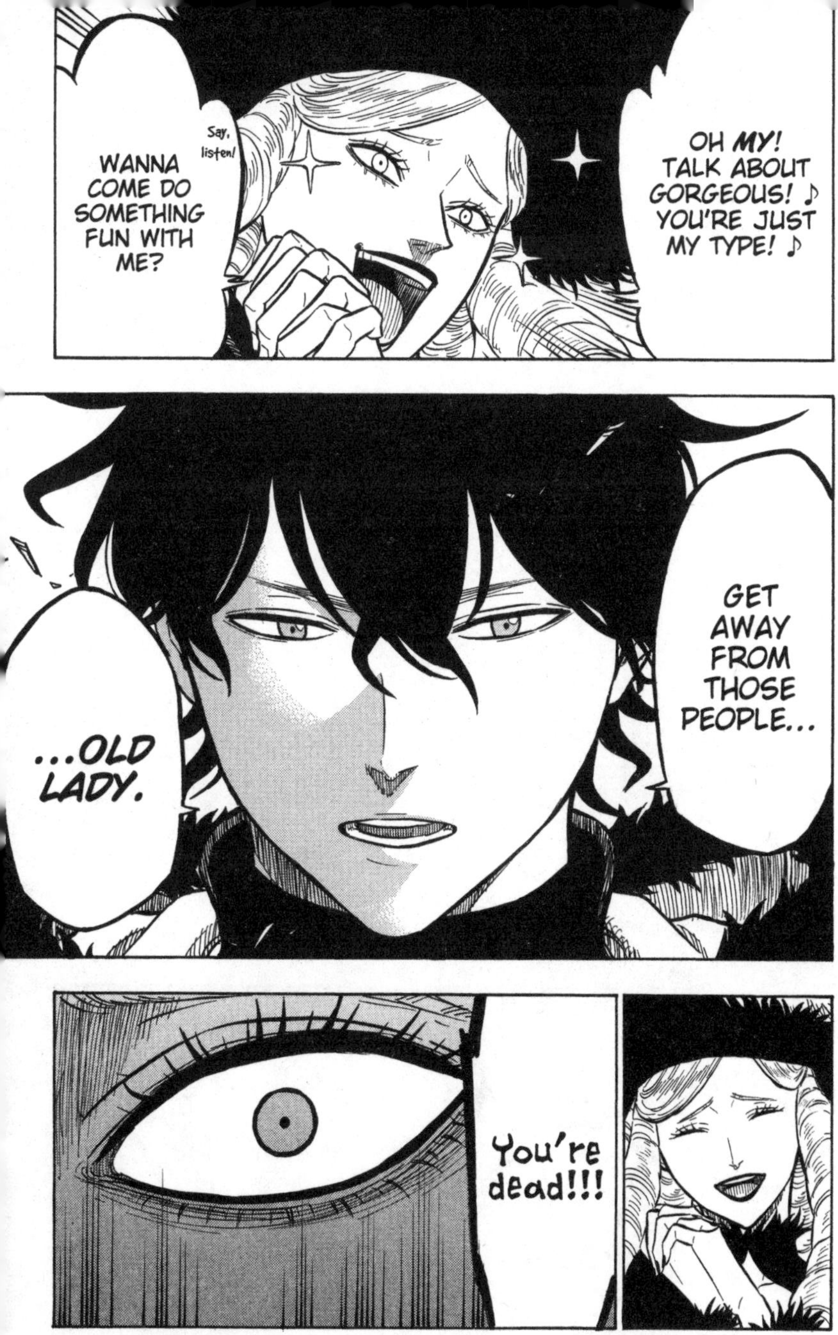
OH MY! TALK ABOUT GORGEOUS! ♪ YOU'RE JUST MY TYPE! ♪
Say, listen!
WANNA COME DO SOMETHING FUN WITH ME?
GET AWAY FROM THOSE PEOPLE...
...OLD LADY.
You're dead!!!

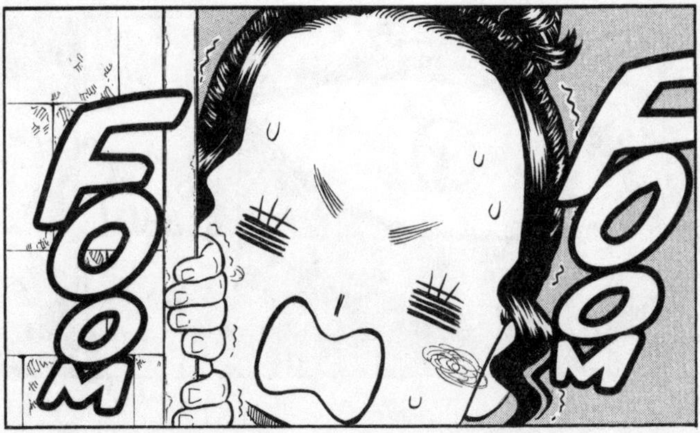
FOOOM
FOOOM

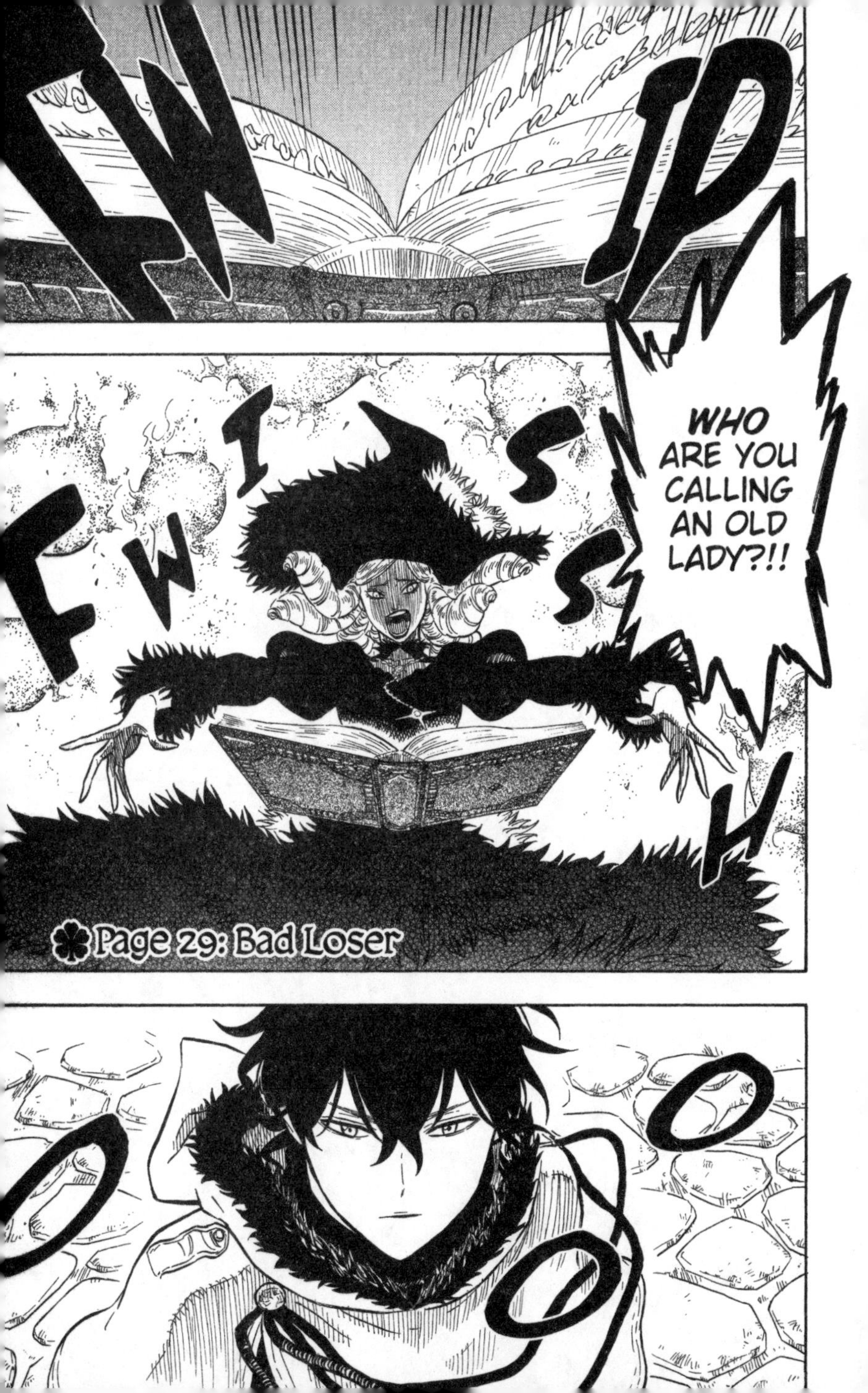
FWIP
WHO ARE YOU CALLING AN OLD LADY?!!
FWISSH
Page 29: Bad Loser

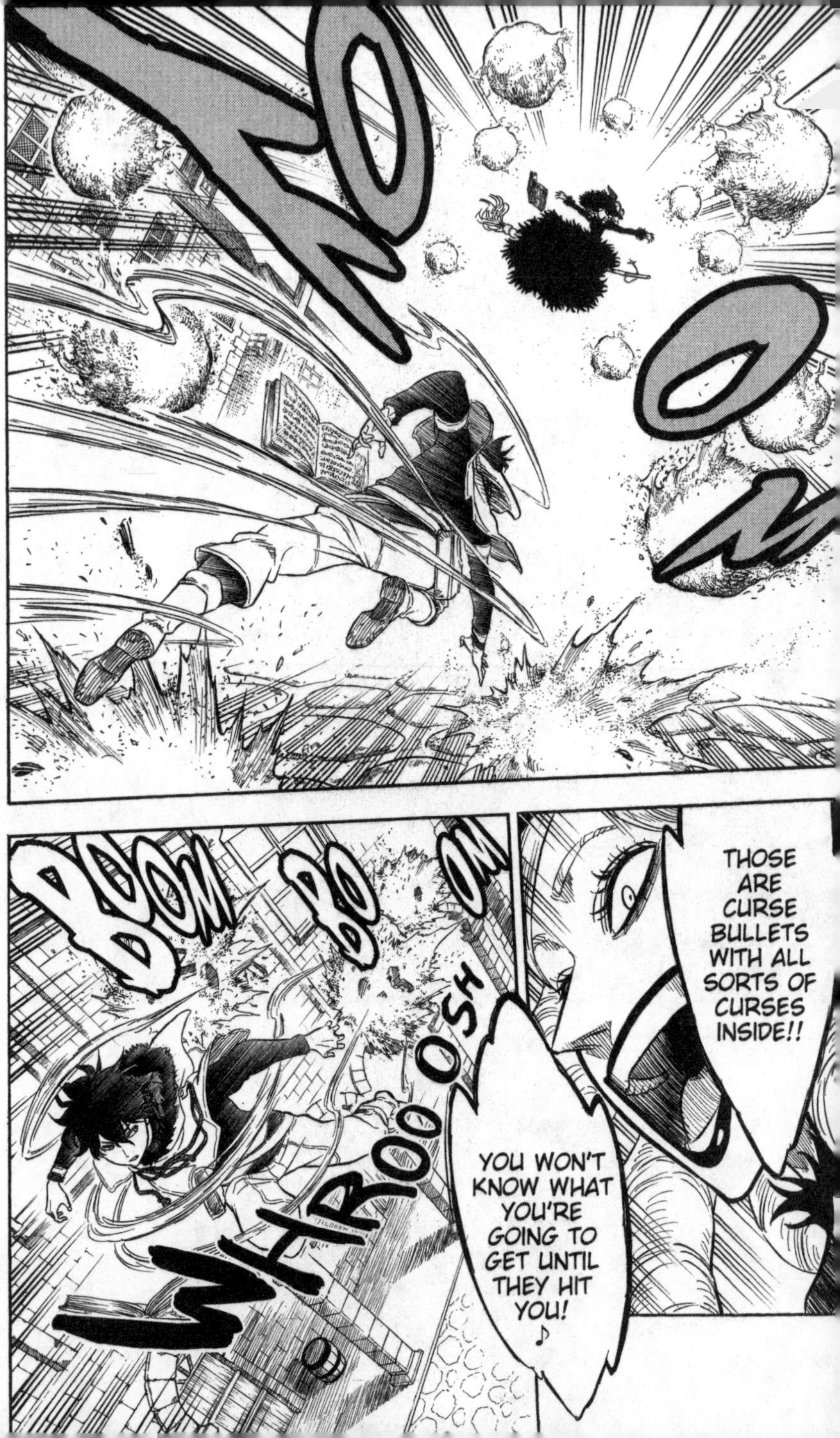
ZOOM
THOSE ARE CURSE BULLETS WITH ALL SORTS OF CURSES INSIDE!!
YOU WON'T KNOW WHAT YOU'RE GOING TO GET UNTIL THEY HIT YOU! ♪
BOOM BOOM
WHROOOSH

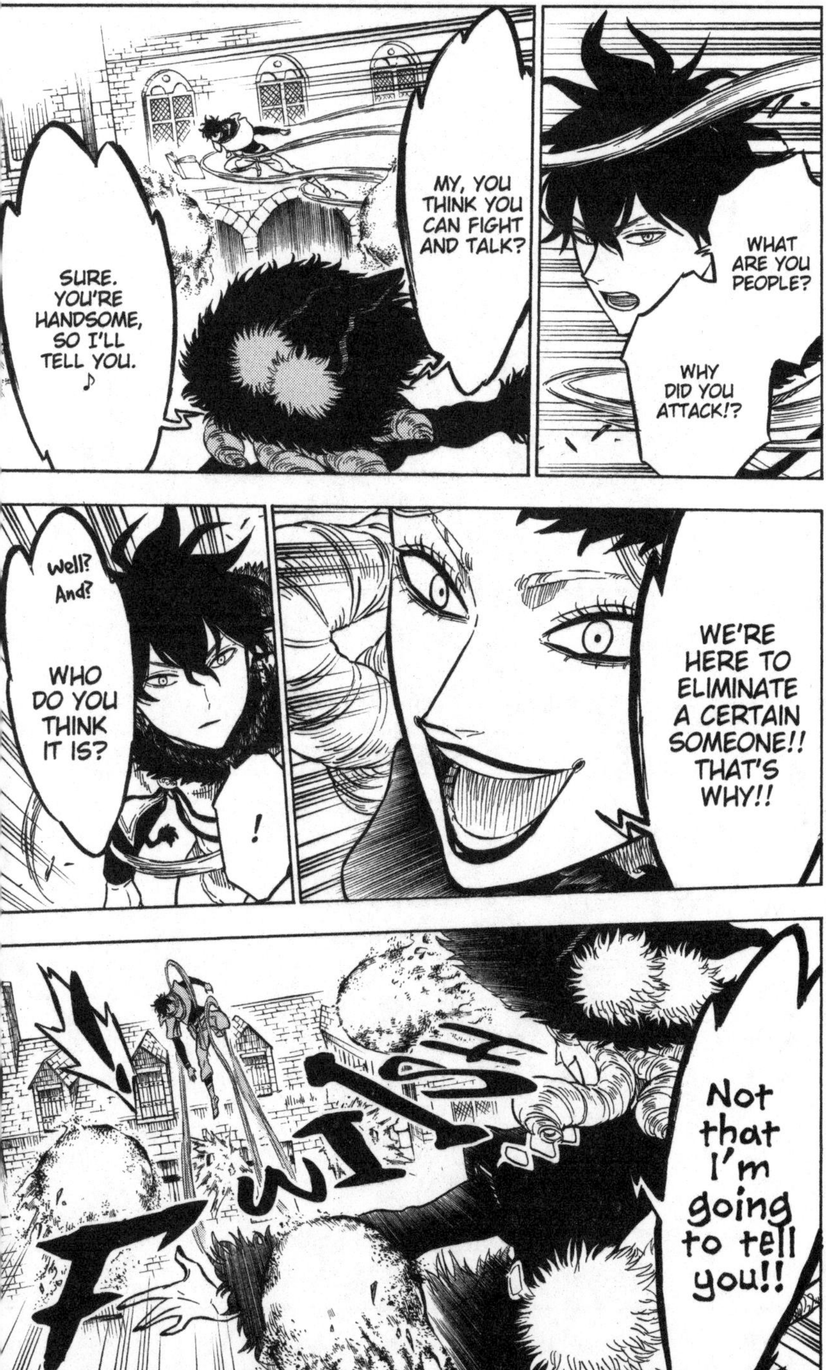

WHAT ARE YOU PEOPLE?
WHY DID YOU ATTACK!?
MY, YOU THINK YOU CAN FIGHT AND TALK?
SURE. YOU'RE HANDSOME, SO I'LL TELL YOU. ♪
WE'RE HERE TO ELIMINATE A CERTAIN SOMEONE!! THAT'S WHY!!
Well? And?
WHO DO YOU THINK IT IS?
!
Not that I'm going to tell you!!
FWISH

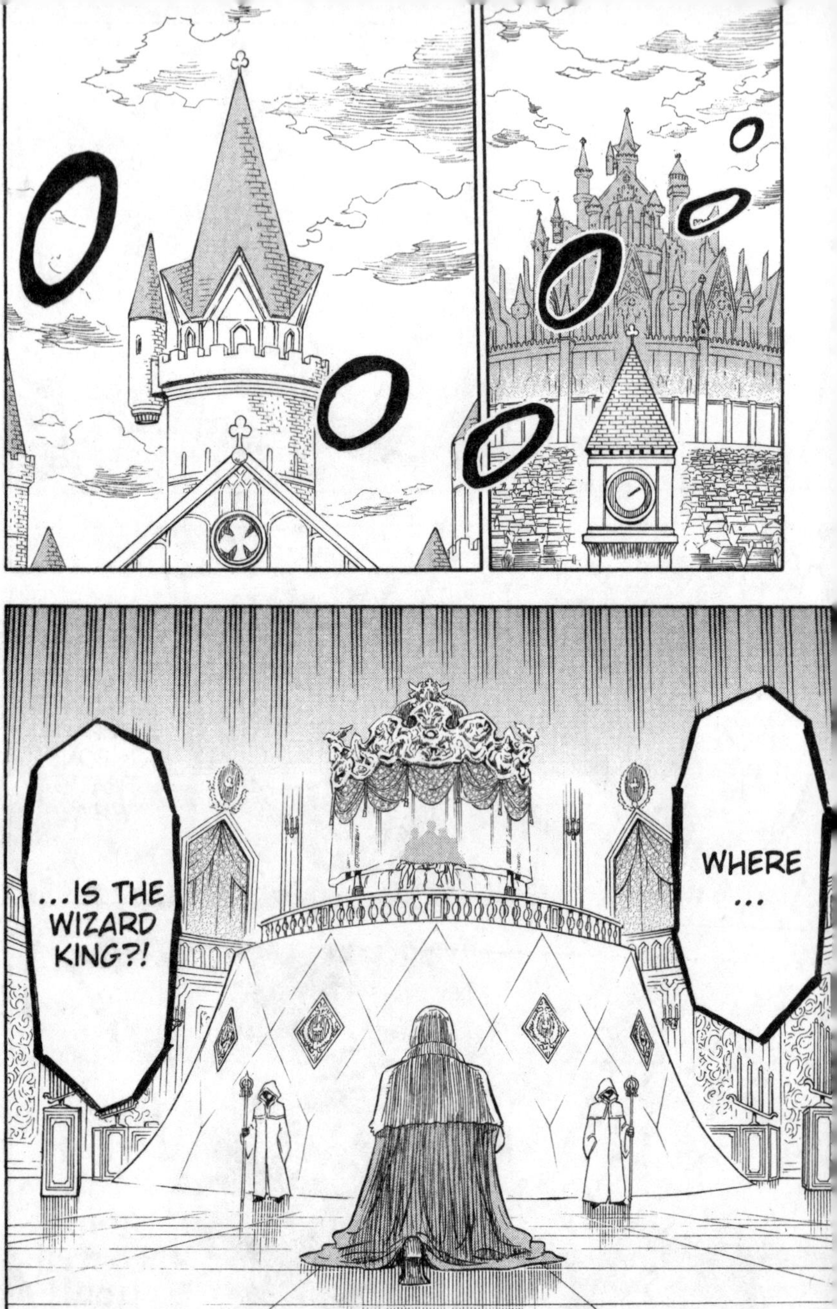
WHERE ...
...IS THE WIZARD KING?!

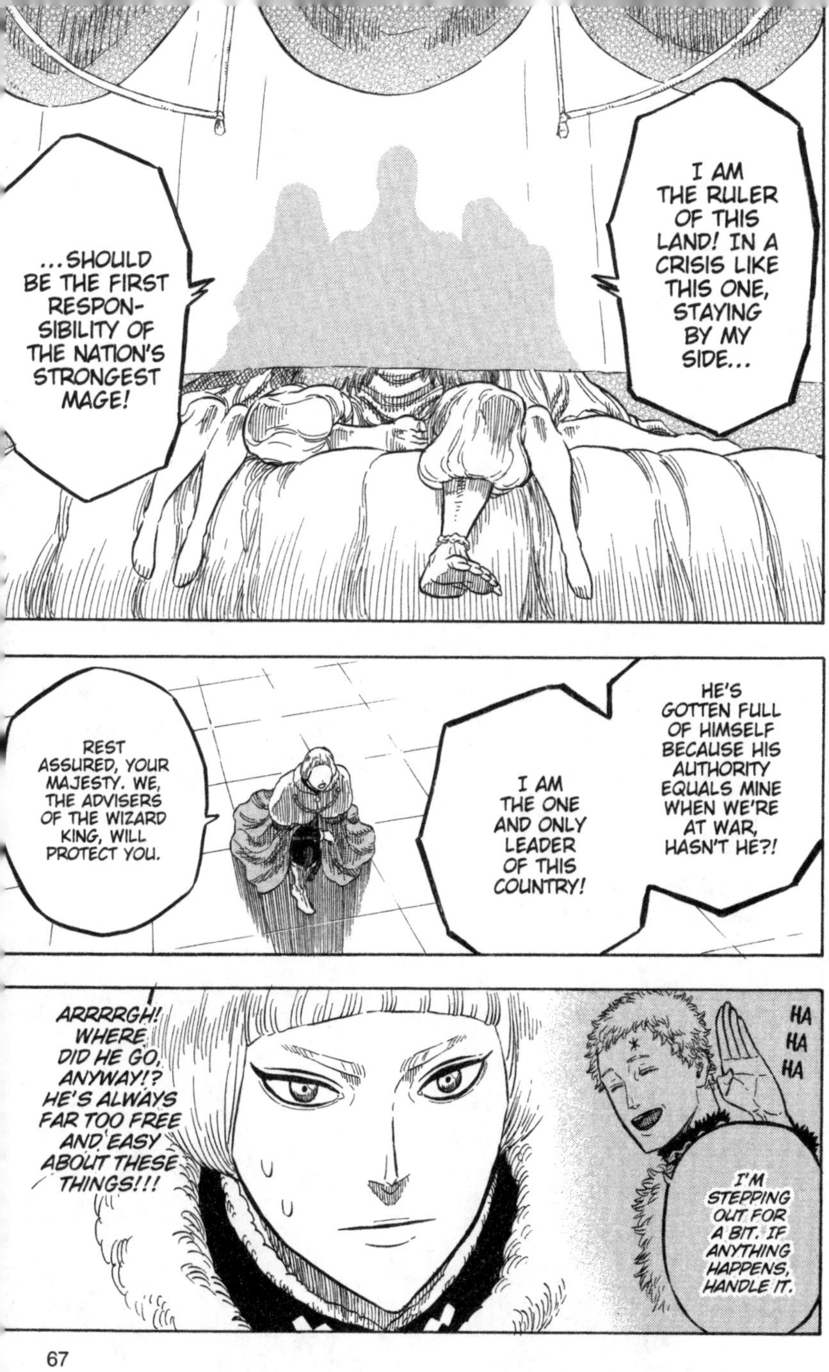
I AM THE RULER OF THIS LAND! IN A CRISIS LIKE THIS ONE, STAYING BY MY SIDE...
...SHOULD BE THE FIRST RESPON-SIBILITY OF THE NATION'S STRONGEST MAGE!
HE'S GOTTEN FULL OF HIMSELF BECAUSE HIS AUTHORITY EQUALS MINE WHEN WE'RE AT WAR, HASN'T HE?!
I AM THE ONE AND ONLY LEADER OF THIS COUNTRY!
REST ASSURED, YOUR MAJESTY. WE, THE ADVISERS OF THE WIZARD KING, WILL PROTECT YOU.
HA HA HA
I'M STEPPING OUT FOR A BIT. IF ANYTHING HAPPENS, HANDLE IT.
ARRRRGH! WHERE DID HE GO, ANYWAY!? HE'S ALWAYS FAR TOO FREE AND EASY ABOUT THESE THINGS!!!

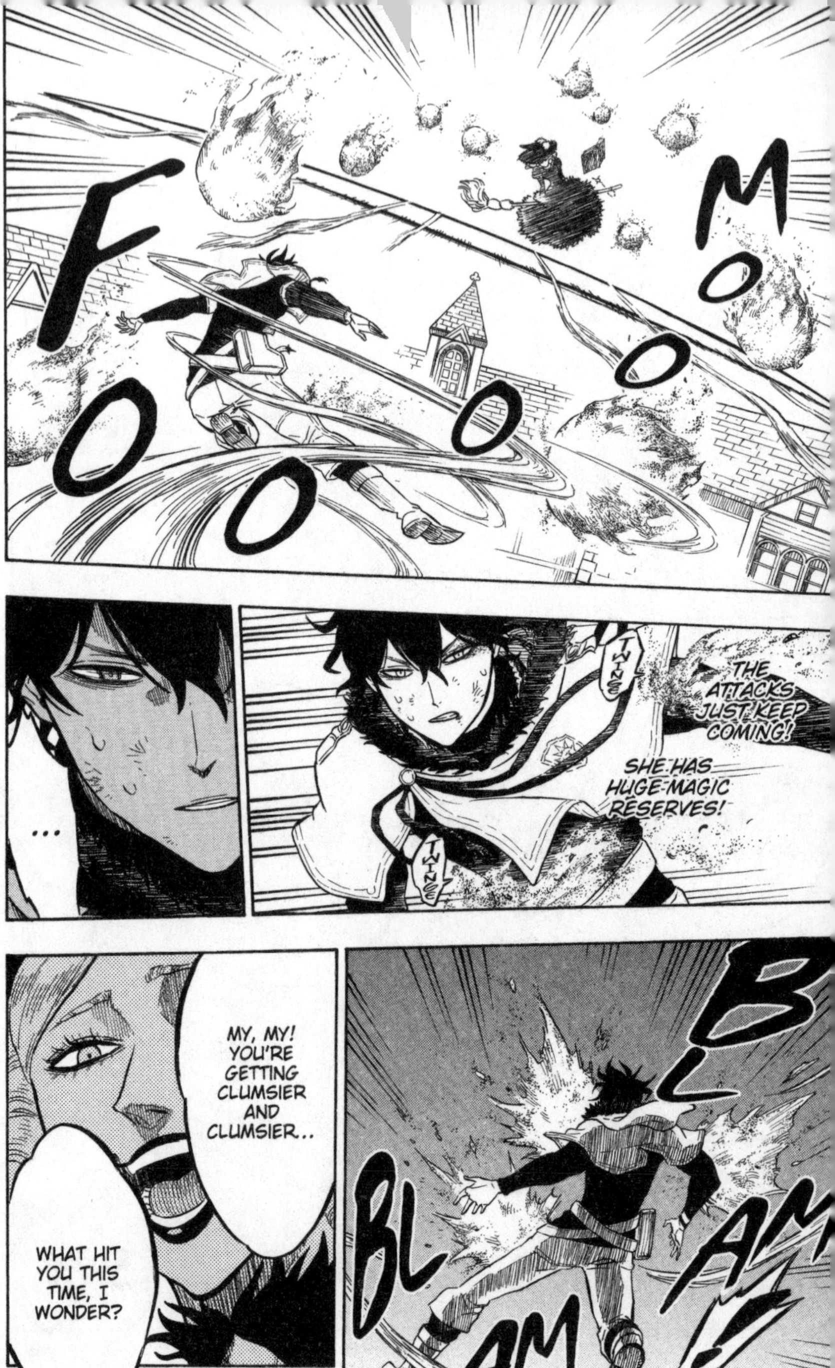
FOOOOOOM
TWINGE
THE ATTACKS JUST KEEP COMING!
SHE HAS HUGE MAGIC RESERVES!
TWINGE
...
BLAM
BLAM!
MY, MY! YOU'RE GETTING CLUMSIER AND CLUMSIER...
WHAT HIT YOU THIS TIME, I WONDER?

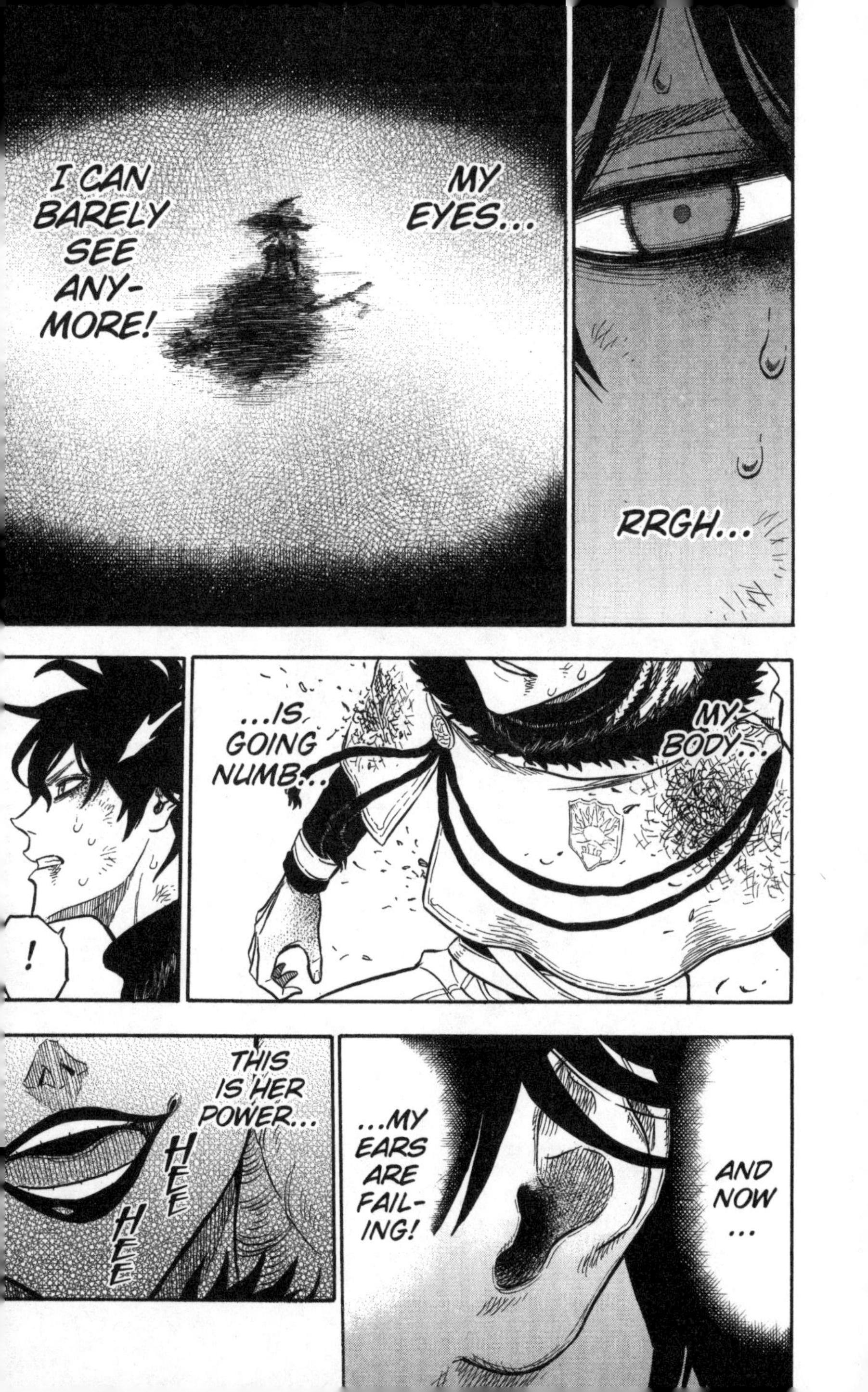
RRGH...
MY EYES...
I CAN BARELY SEE ANY-MORE!
MY BODY...
...IS GOING NUMB...
!
AND NOW...
...MY EARS ARE FAIL-ING!
THIS IS HER POWER...
HEE HEE

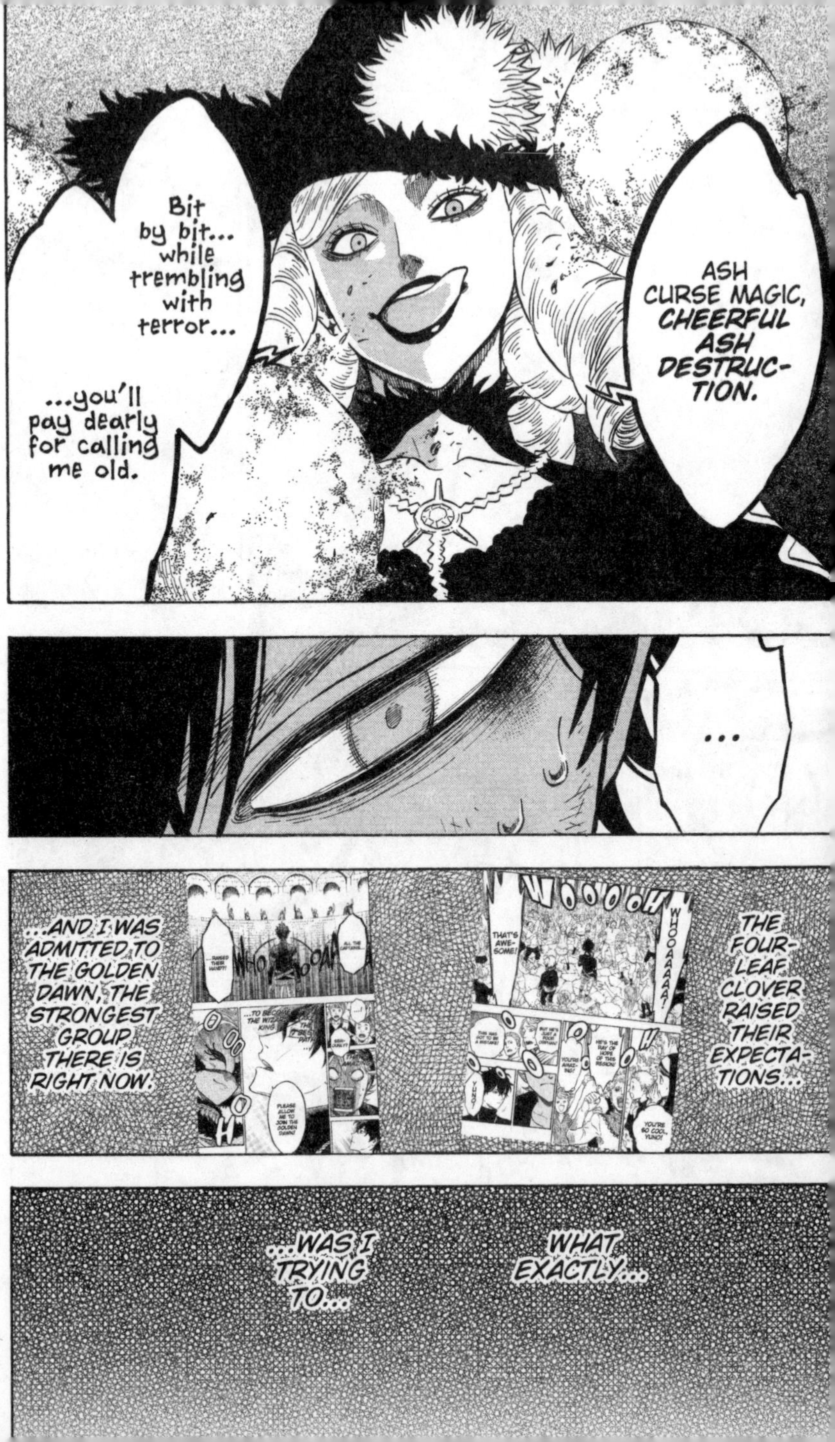
ASH CURSE MAGIC, CHEERFUL ASH DESTRUCTION.
Bit by bit... while trembling with terror...
...you'll pay dearly for calling me old.
...
THE FOUR-LEAF CLOVER RAISED THEIR EXPECTATIONS...
...AND I WAS ADMITTED TO THE GOLDEN DAWN, THE STRONGEST GROUP THERE IS RIGHT NOW.
WHAT EXACTLY...
...WAS I TRYING TO...

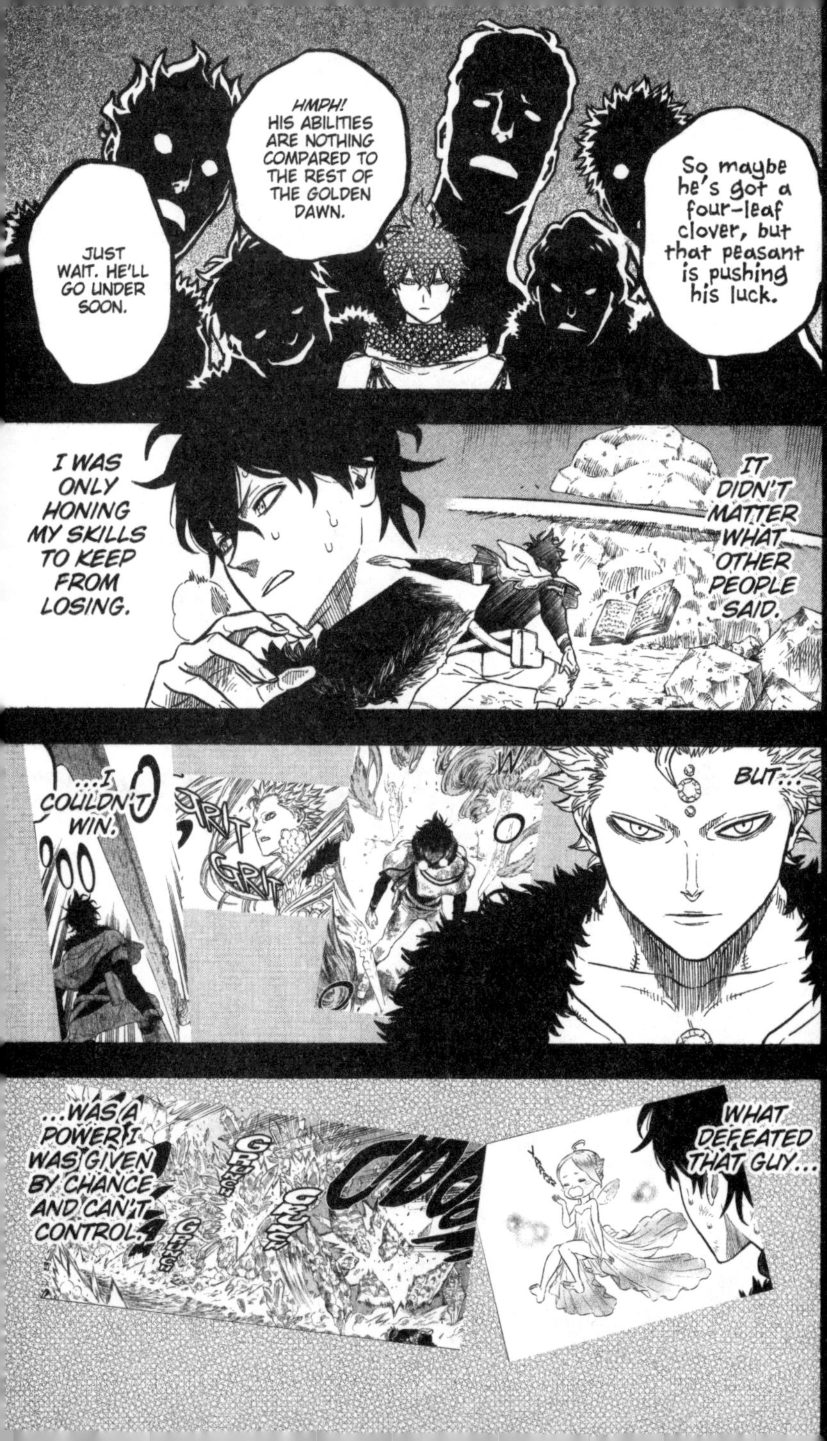
So maybe he's got a four-leaf clover, but that peasant is pushing his luck.
HMPH! HIS ABILITIES ARE NOTHING COMPARED TO THE REST OF THE GOLDEN DAWN.
JUST WAIT. HE'LL GO UNDER SOON.
IT DIDN'T MATTER WHAT OTHER PEOPLE SAID.
I WAS ONLY HONING MY SKILLS TO KEEP FROM LOSING.
BUT...
GRIT
GRIT
...I COULDN'T WIN.
WHAT DEFEATED THAT GUY...
...WAS A POWER I WAS GIVEN BY CHANCE AND CAN'T CONTROL.

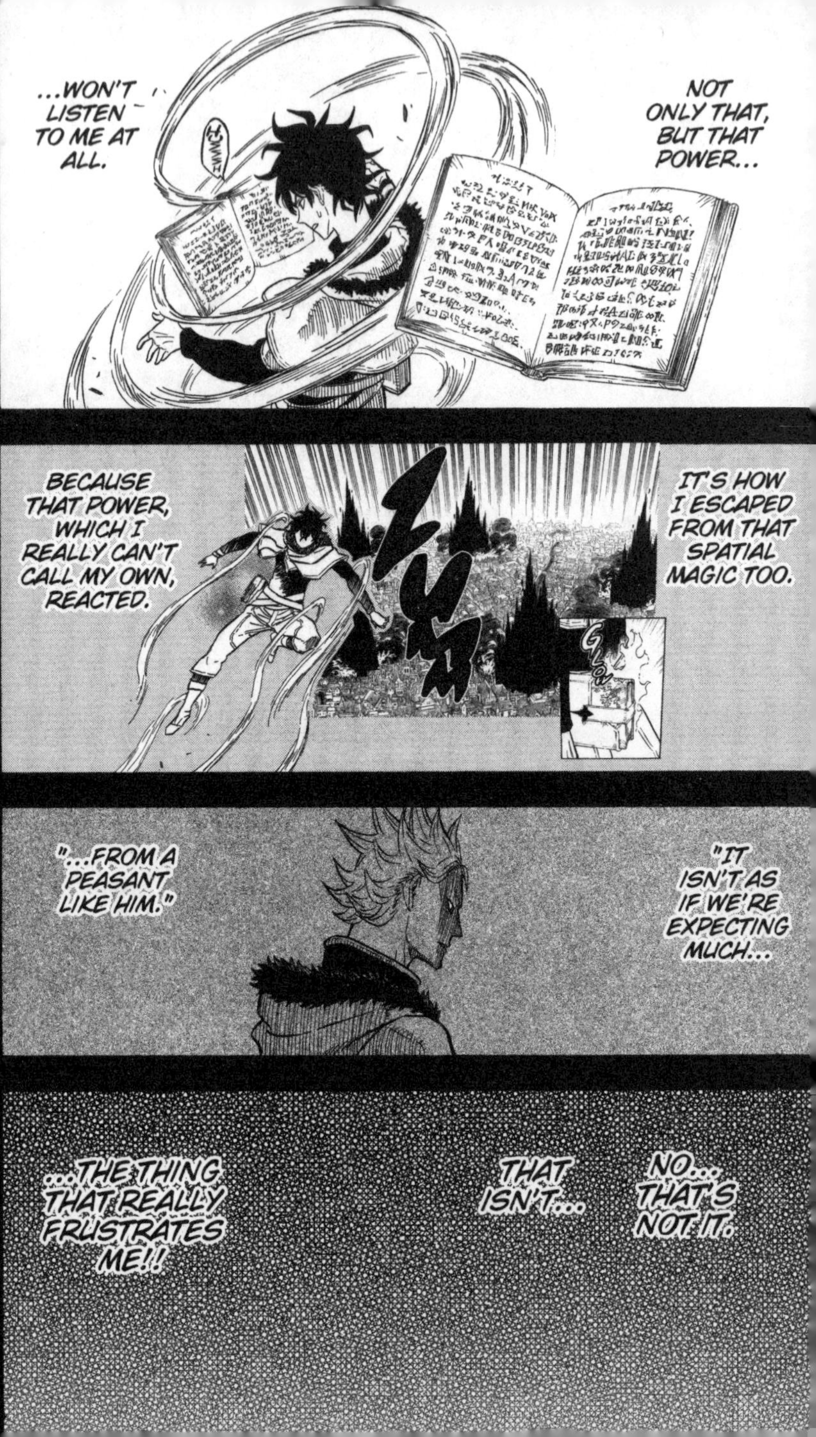
NOT ONLY THAT, BUT THAT POWER...
...WON'T LISTEN TO ME AT ALL.
IT'S HOW I ESCAPED FROM THAT SPATIAL MAGIC TOO.
GLOW
BECAUSE THAT POWER, WHICH I REALLY CAN'T CALL MY OWN, REACTED.
"IT ISN'T AS IF WE'RE EXPECTING MUCH...
"...FROM A PEASANT LIKE HIM."
NO... THAT'S NOT IT.
THAT ISN'T...
...THE THING THAT REALLY FRUSTRATES ME!!

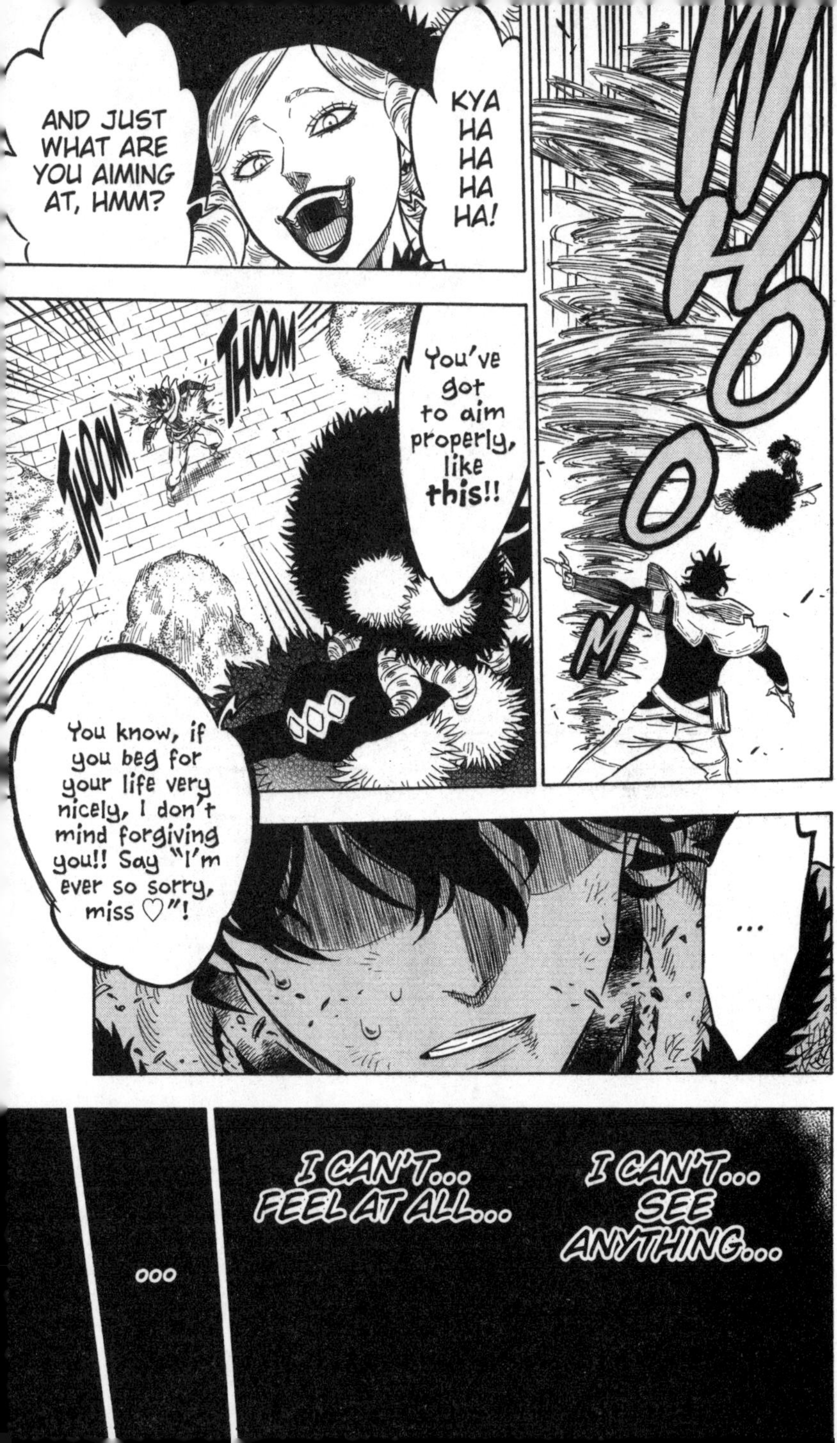
WHOOOM
KYA HA HA HA HA HA!
AND JUST WHAT ARE YOU AIMING AT, HMM?
You've got to aim properly, like **this**!!
THOOM
THOOM
You know, if you beg for your life very nicely, I don't mind forgiving you!! Say "I'm ever so sorry, miss ♡"!
...
I CAN'T... SEE ANYTHING...
I CAN'T... FEEL AT ALL...
ooo

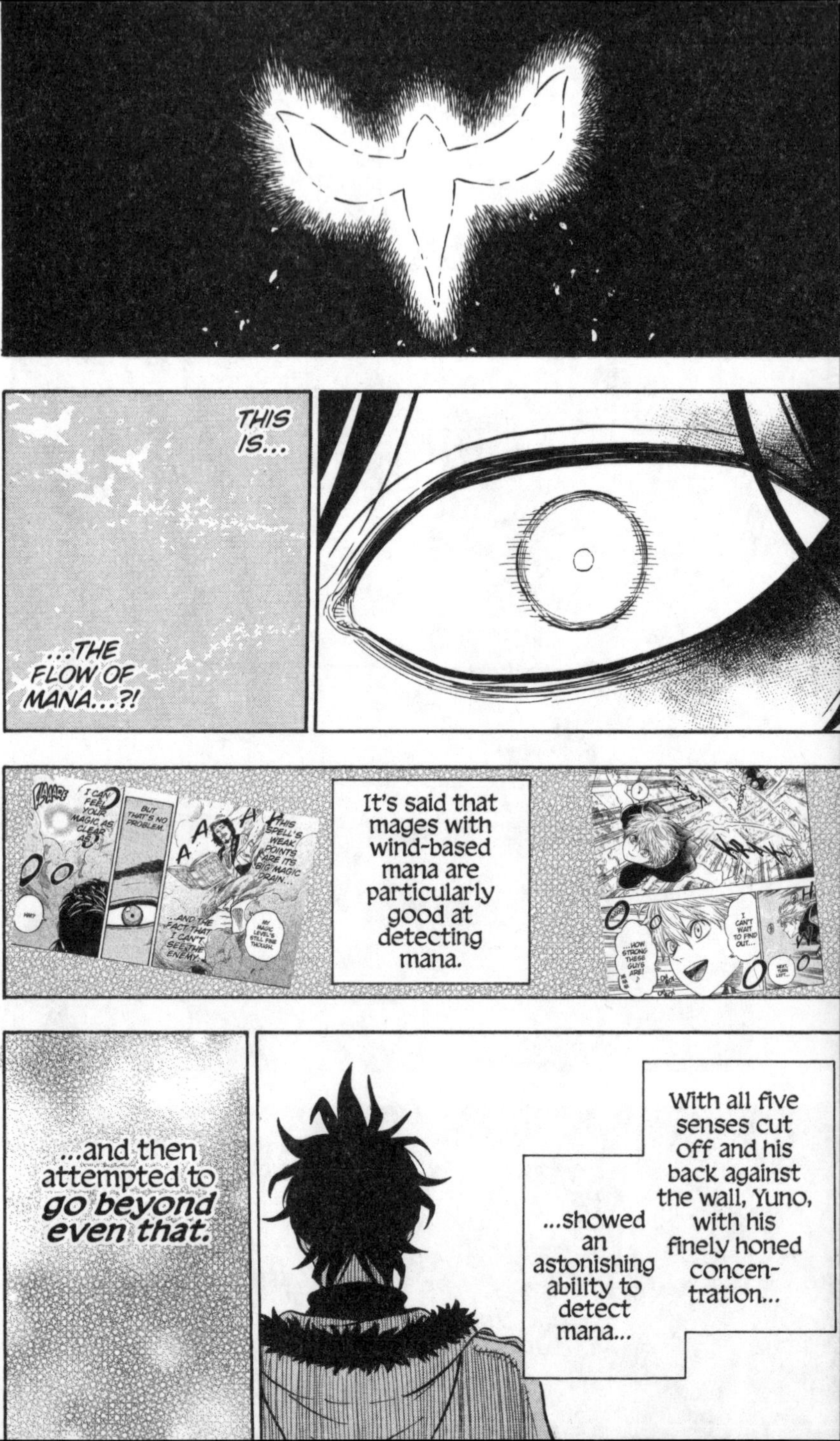
THIS IS...
...THE FLOW OF MANA...?!
NEXT, TURN LEFT...
I CAN'T WAIT TO FIND OUT...
...HOW STRONG THESE GUYS ARE! ♪
OH BOY OH BOY
It's said that mages with wind-based mana are particularly good at detecting mana.
THIS SPELL'S WEAK POINTS ARE ITS BIG MAGIC DRAIN...
MY MAGIC LEVEL'S STILL FINE THOUGH.
...AND THE FACT THAT I CAN'T SEE THE ENEMY.
AAAAH
BUT THAT'S NO PROBLEM.
I CAN FEEL YOUR MAGIC AS CLEAR AS...
FLAAARE
HM?
With all five senses cut off and his back against the wall, Yuno, with his finely honed concen-tration...
...showed an astonishing ability to detect mana...
...and then attempted to go beyond even that.

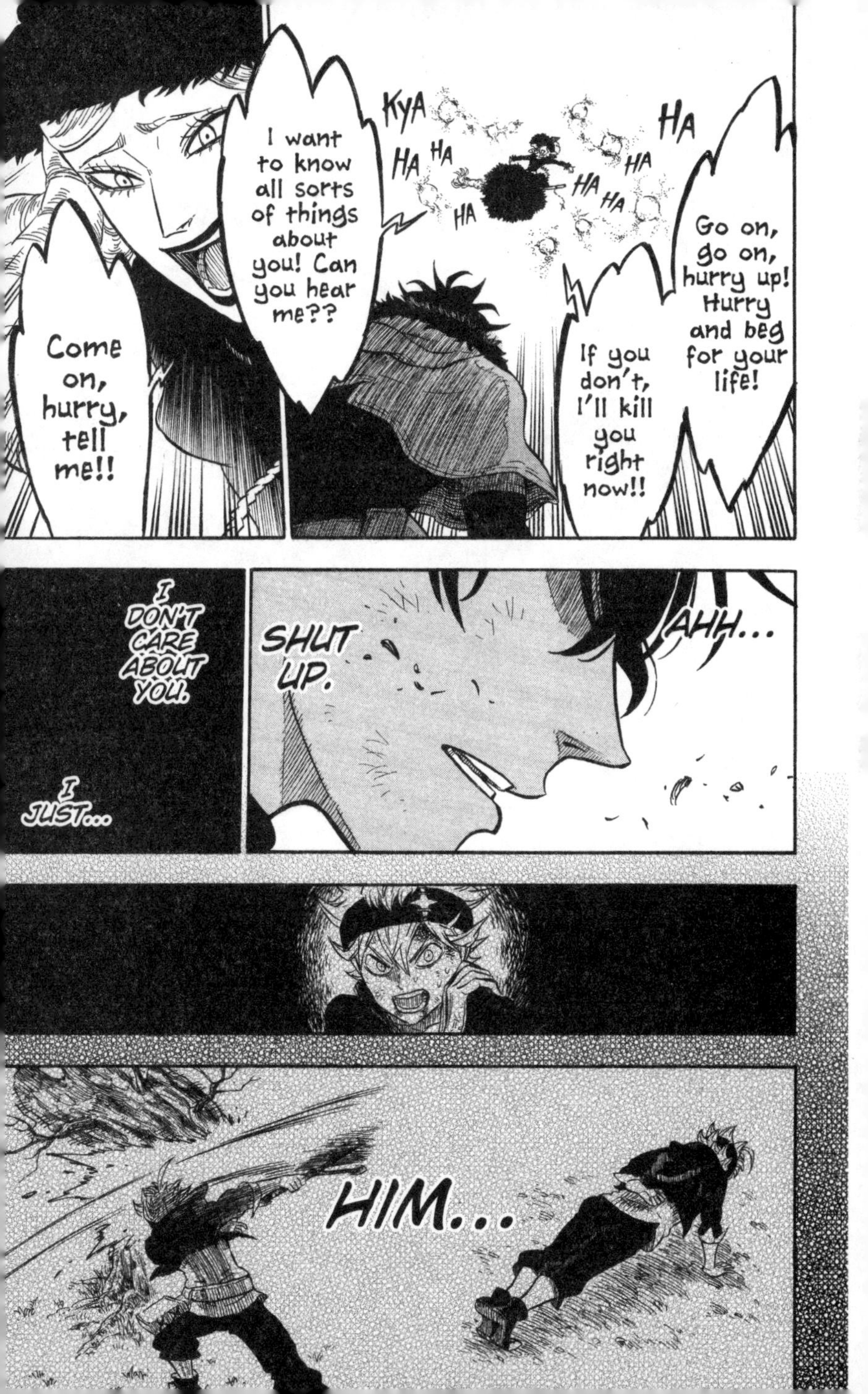
KYA HA HA HA HA HA HA HA HA HA
Go on, go on, hurry up! Hurry and beg for your life!
If you don't, I'll kill you right now!!
I want to know all sorts of things about you! Can you hear me??
Come on, hurry, tell me!!
AHH...
SHUT UP.
I DON'T CARE ABOUT YOU.
I JUST...
HIM...

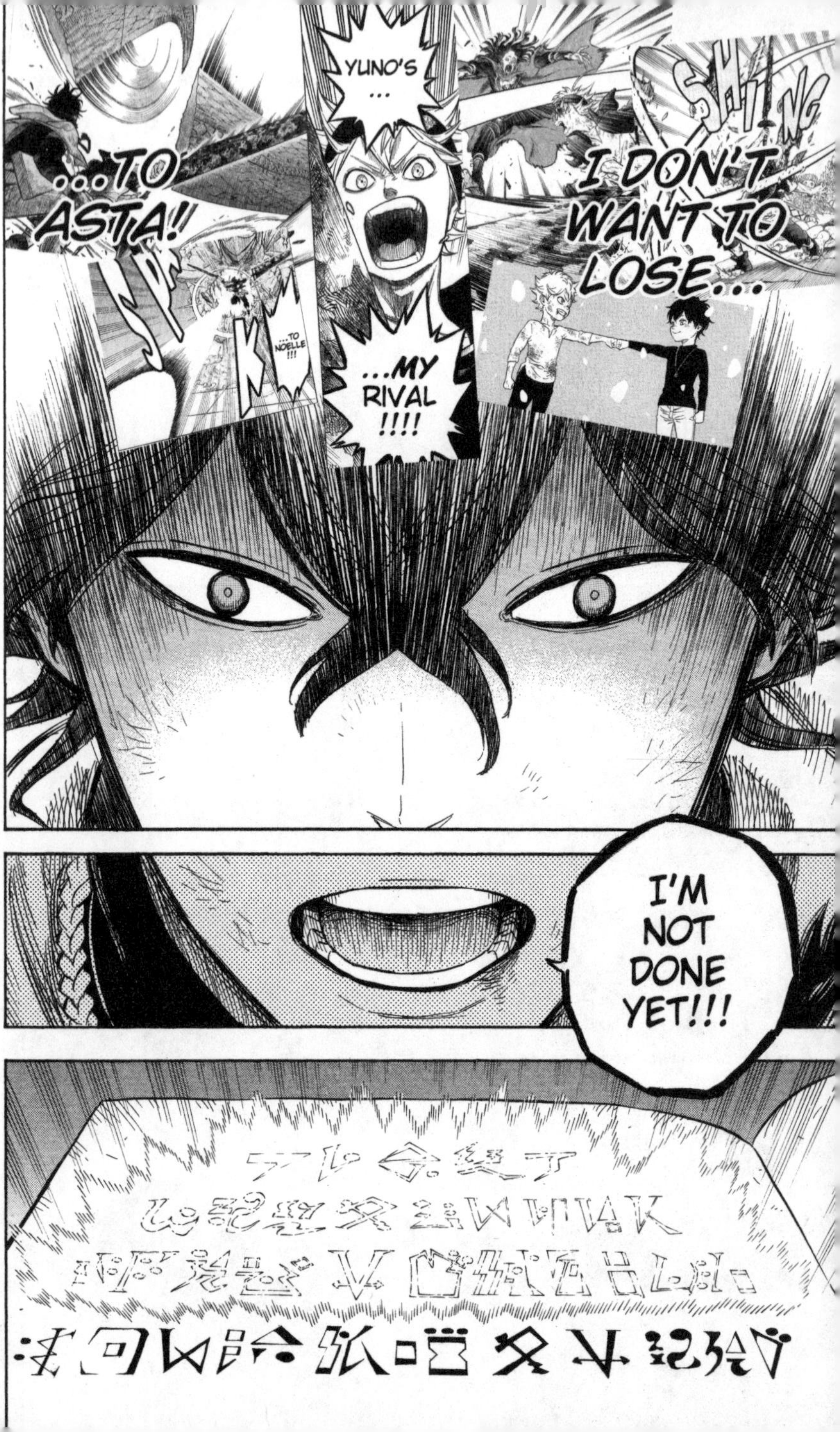
SHING
I DON'T WANT TO LOSE...
YUNO'S ...
...MY RIVAL !!!!
...TO ASTA!!
...TO NOELLE !!!
I'M NOT DONE YET!!!

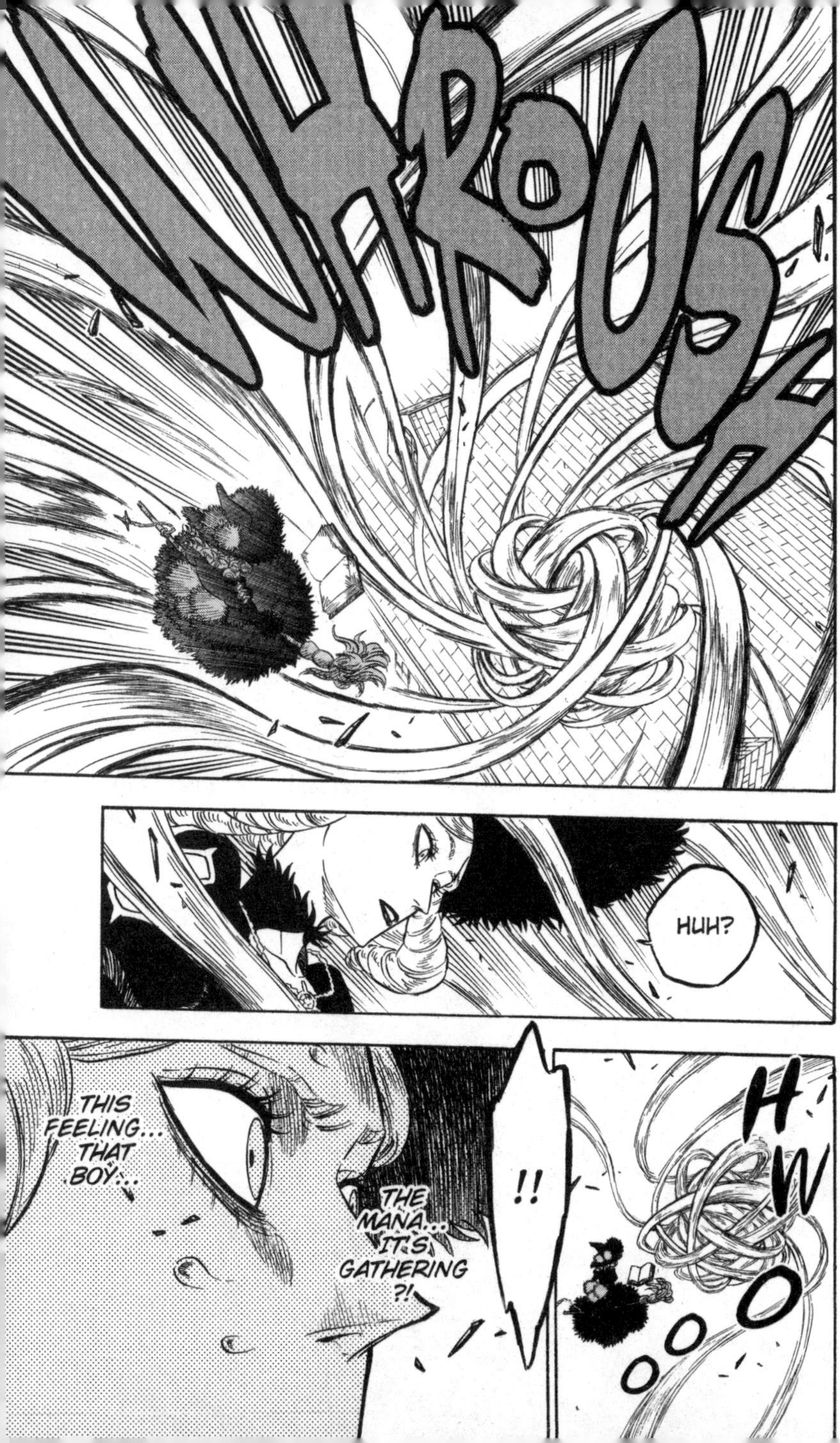
WHROOSH
HUH?
HWOOOO
!!
THE MANA... IT'S GATHERING?!
THIS FEELING... THAT BOY...

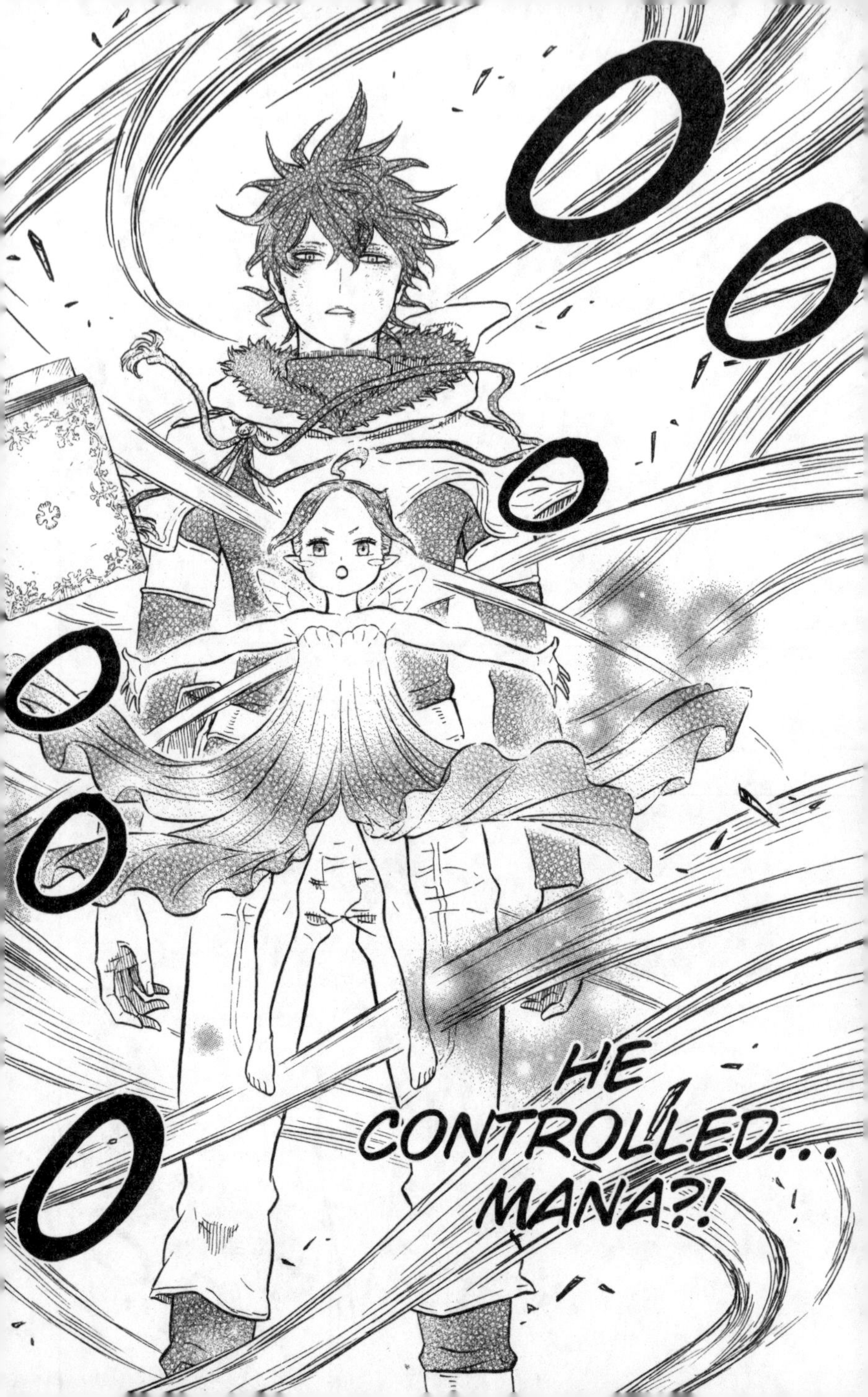
HE CONTROLLED... MANA?!

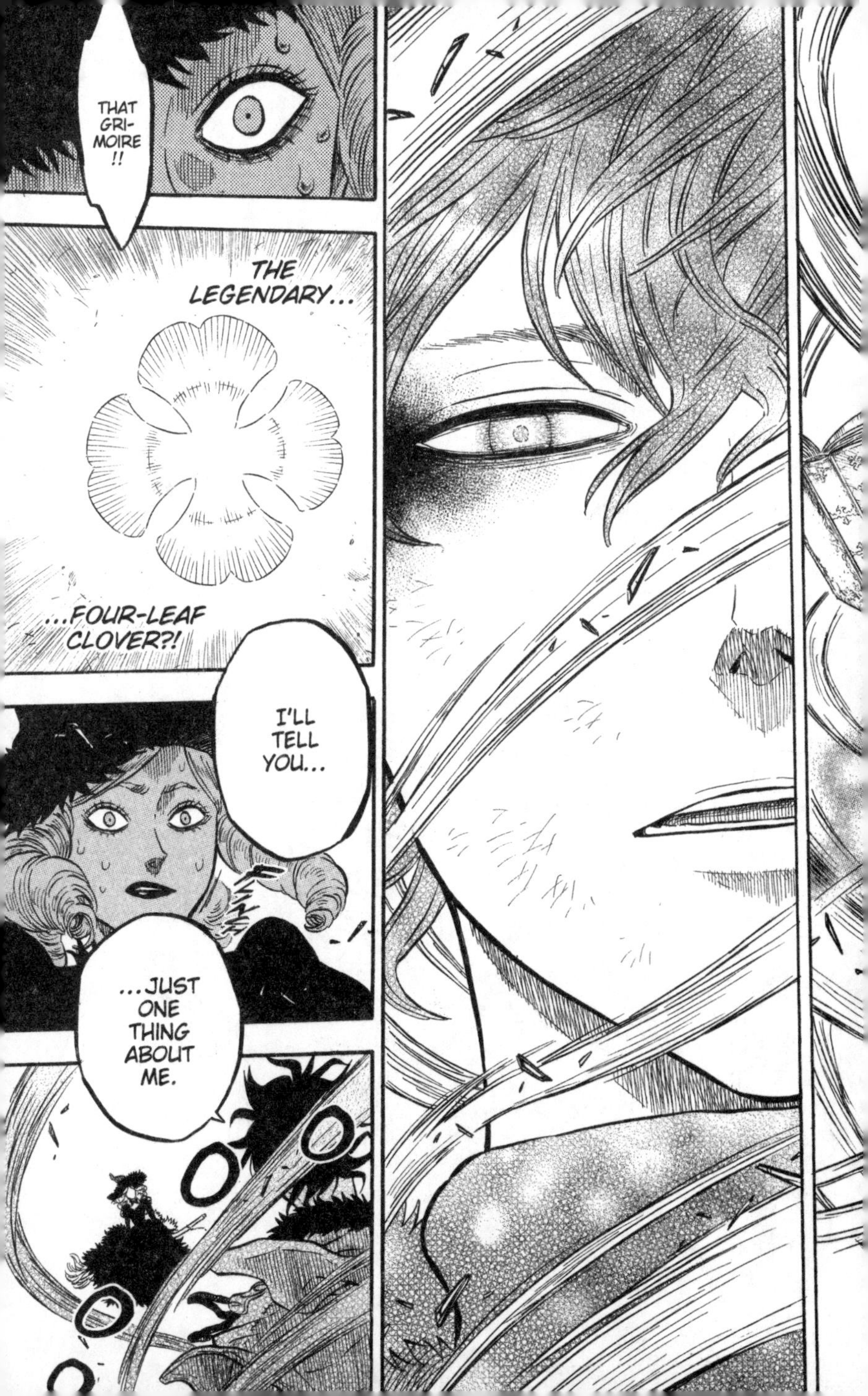
THAT GRI-MOIRE!!
THE LEGENDARY...
...FOUR-LEAF CLOVER?!
I'LL TELL YOU...
...JUST ONE THING ABOUT ME.

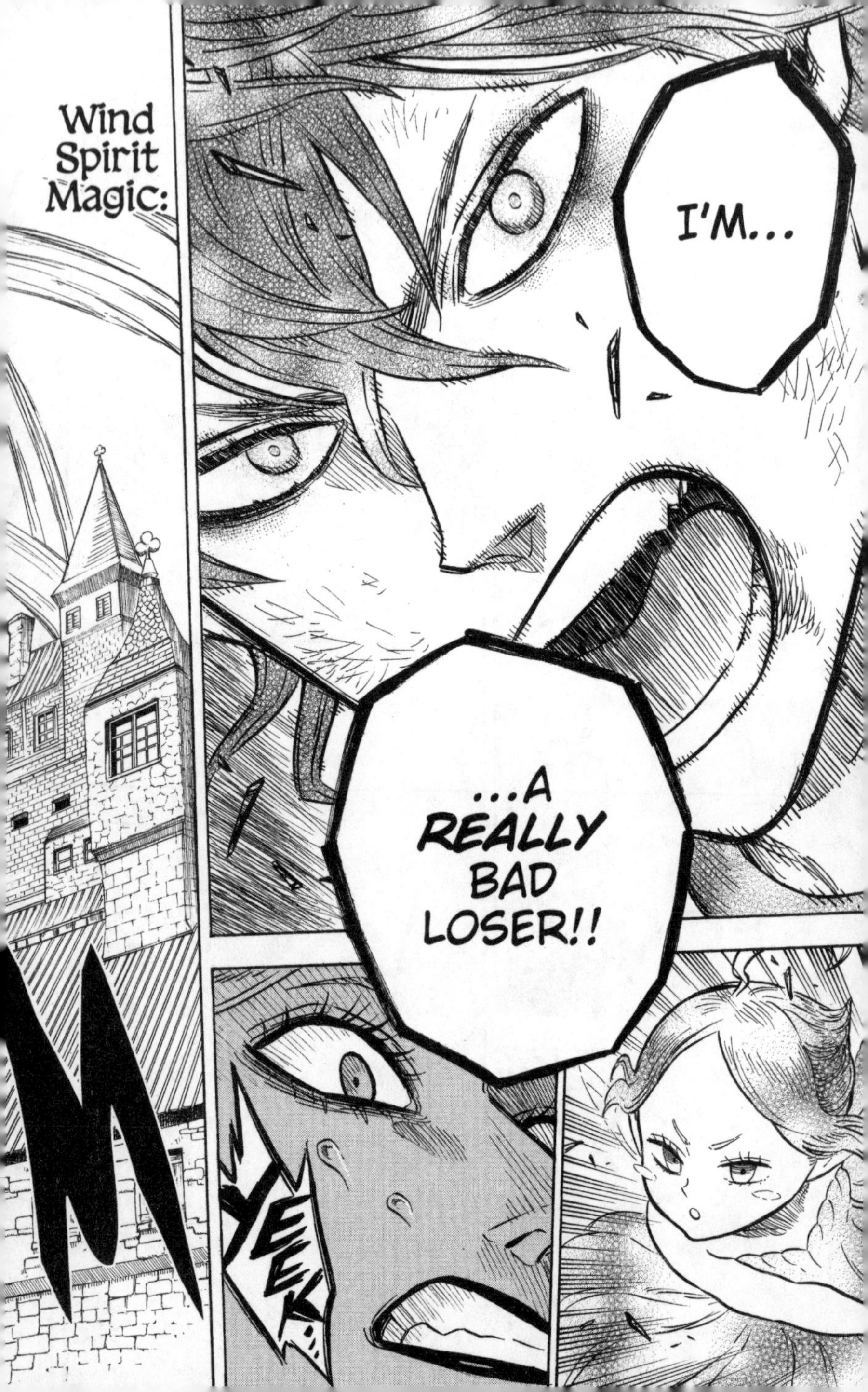
I'M...
...A *REALLY* BAD LOSER!!
YEEK
Wind Spirit Magic:
M

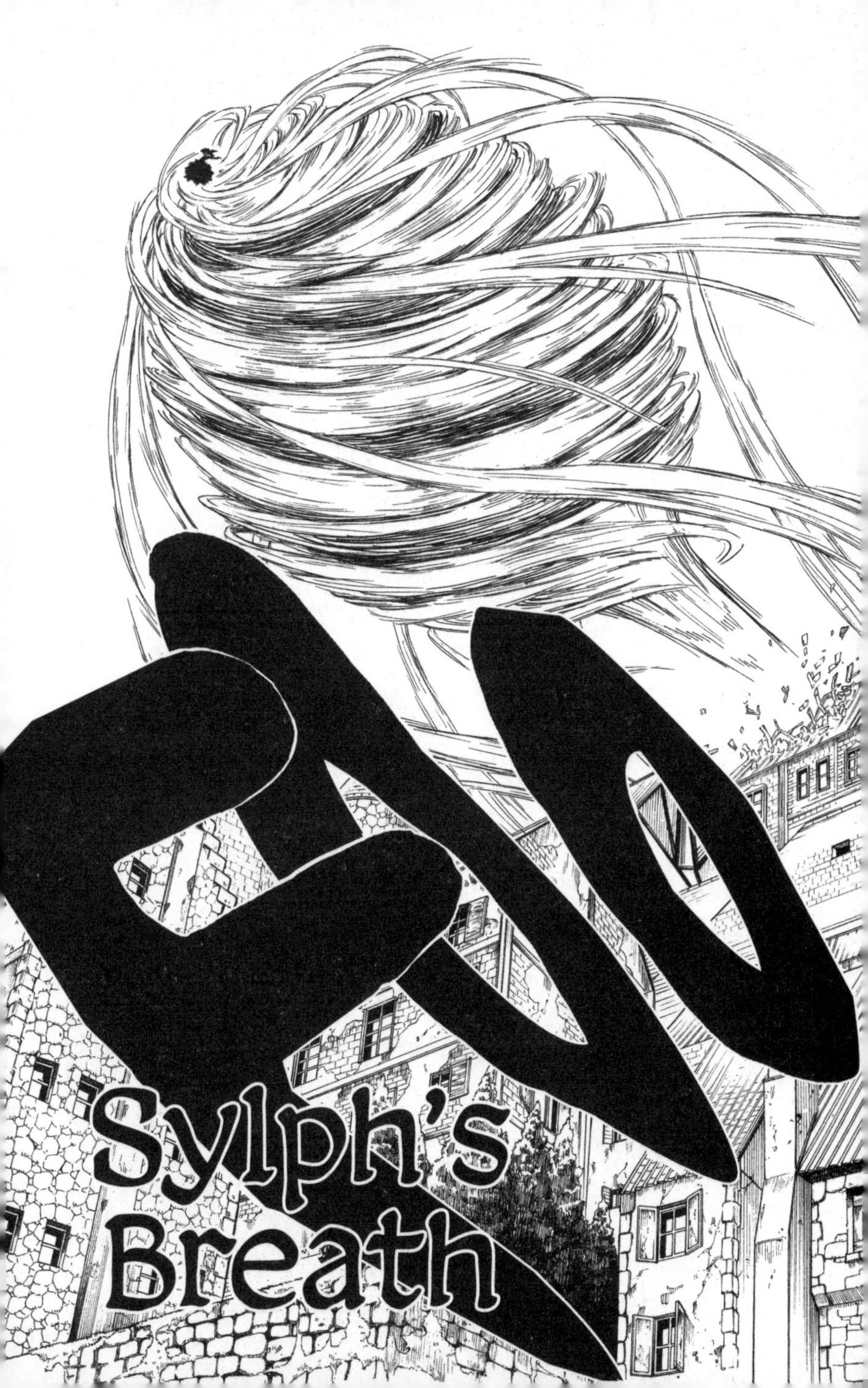
Sylph's Breath

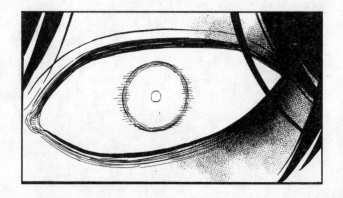

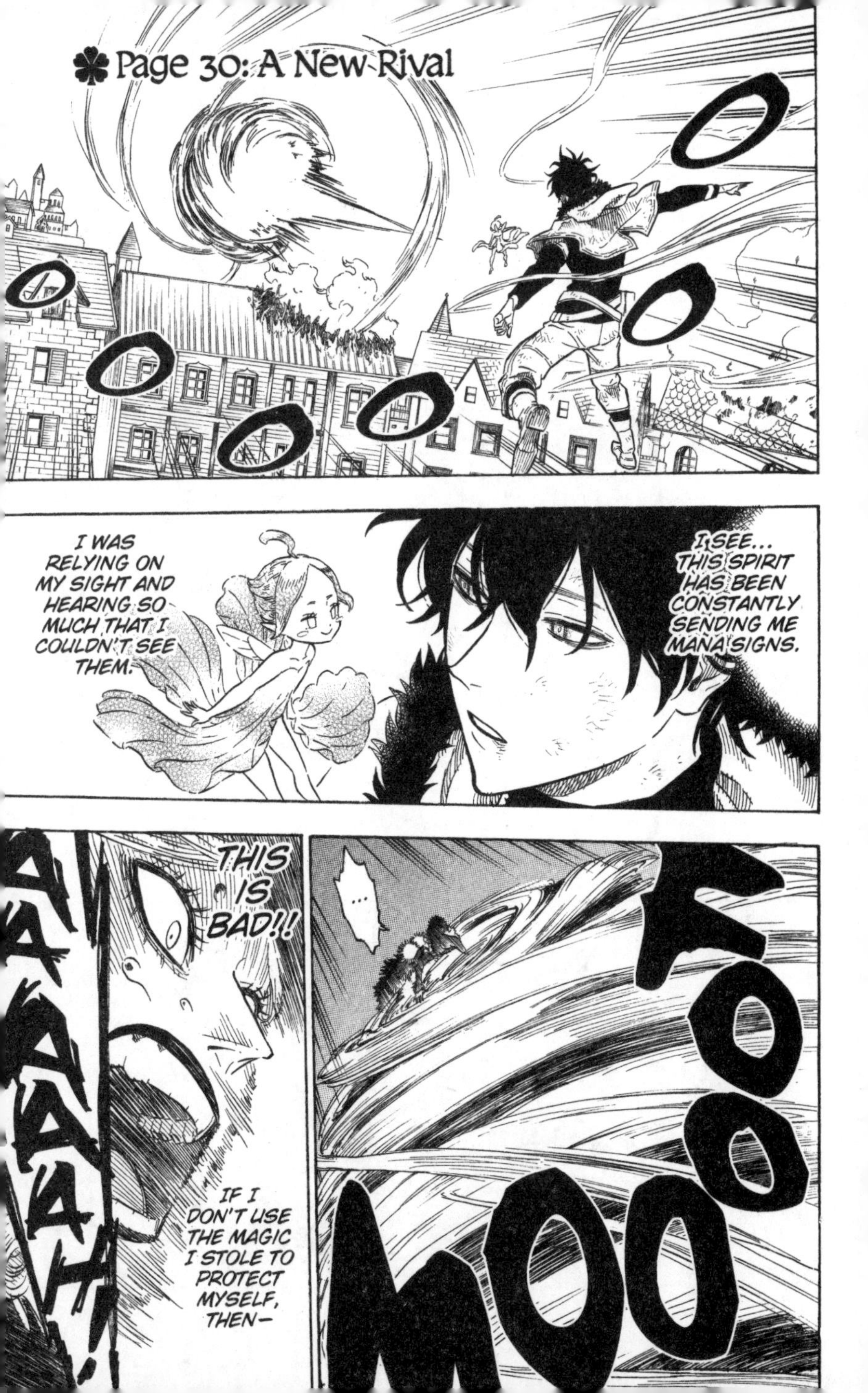
Page 30: A New Rival
I SEE... THIS SPIRIT HAS BEEN CONSTANTLY SENDING ME MANA SIGNS.
I WAS RELYING ON MY SIGHT AND HEARING SO MUCH THAT I COULDN'T SEE THEM.
...
THIS IS BAD!!
IF I DON'T USE THE MAGIC I STOLE TO PROTECT MYSELF, THEN—
AAAAAAAH!

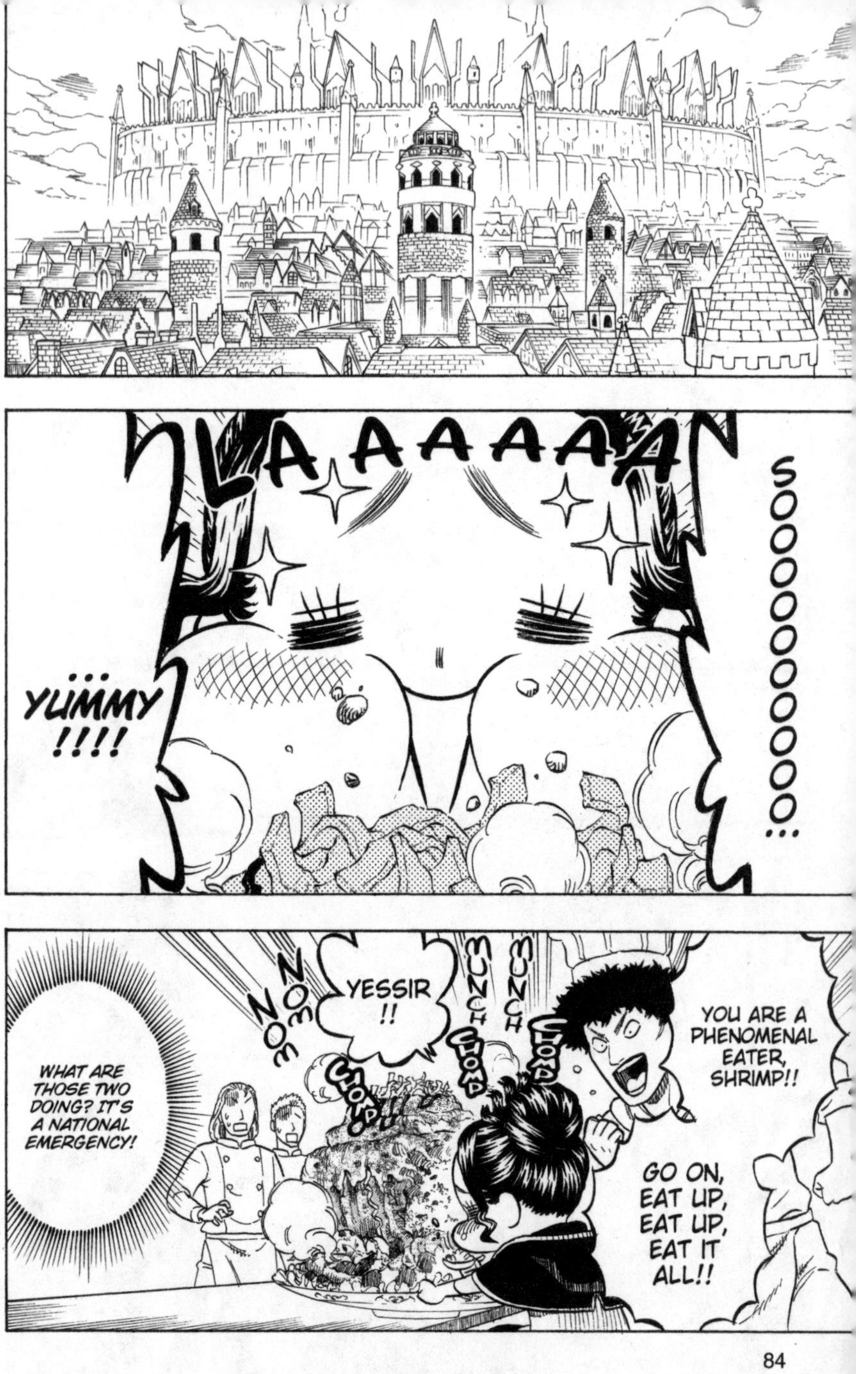
SOOOOOOOOOO...
LAAAAAA
...YUMMY!!!!
YOU ARE A PHENOMENAL EATER, SHRIMP!!
GO ON, EAT UP, EAT UP, EAT IT ALL!!
CHOMP
MUNCH
MUNCH
CHOMP
YESSIR!!
CHOMP!!
NOM NOM
WHAT ARE THOSE TWO DOING? IT'S A NATIONAL EMERGENCY!

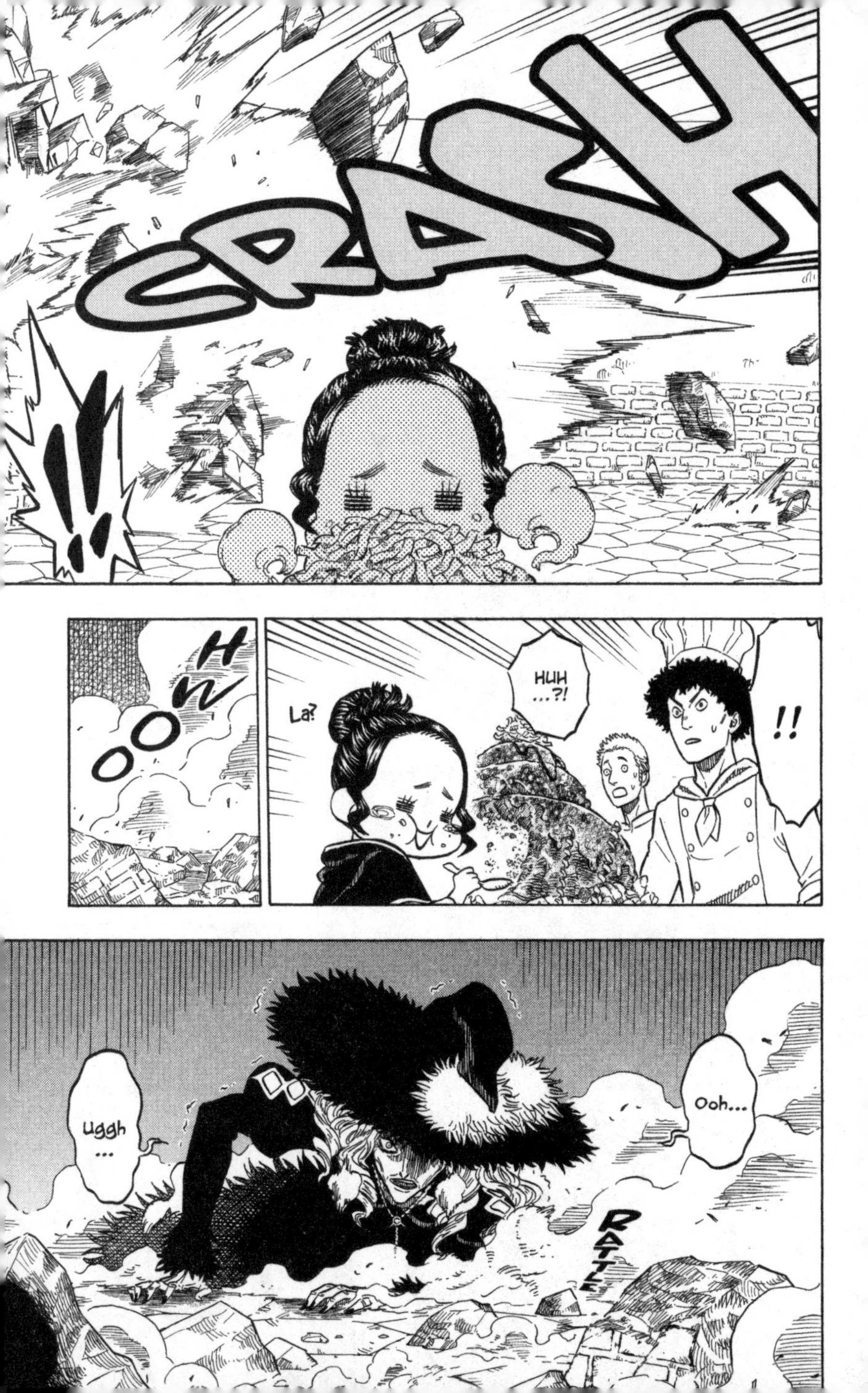
CRASH
!!
!!
HUH ...?!
La?
OOOMPH
Ooh...
RATTLE
uggh ...

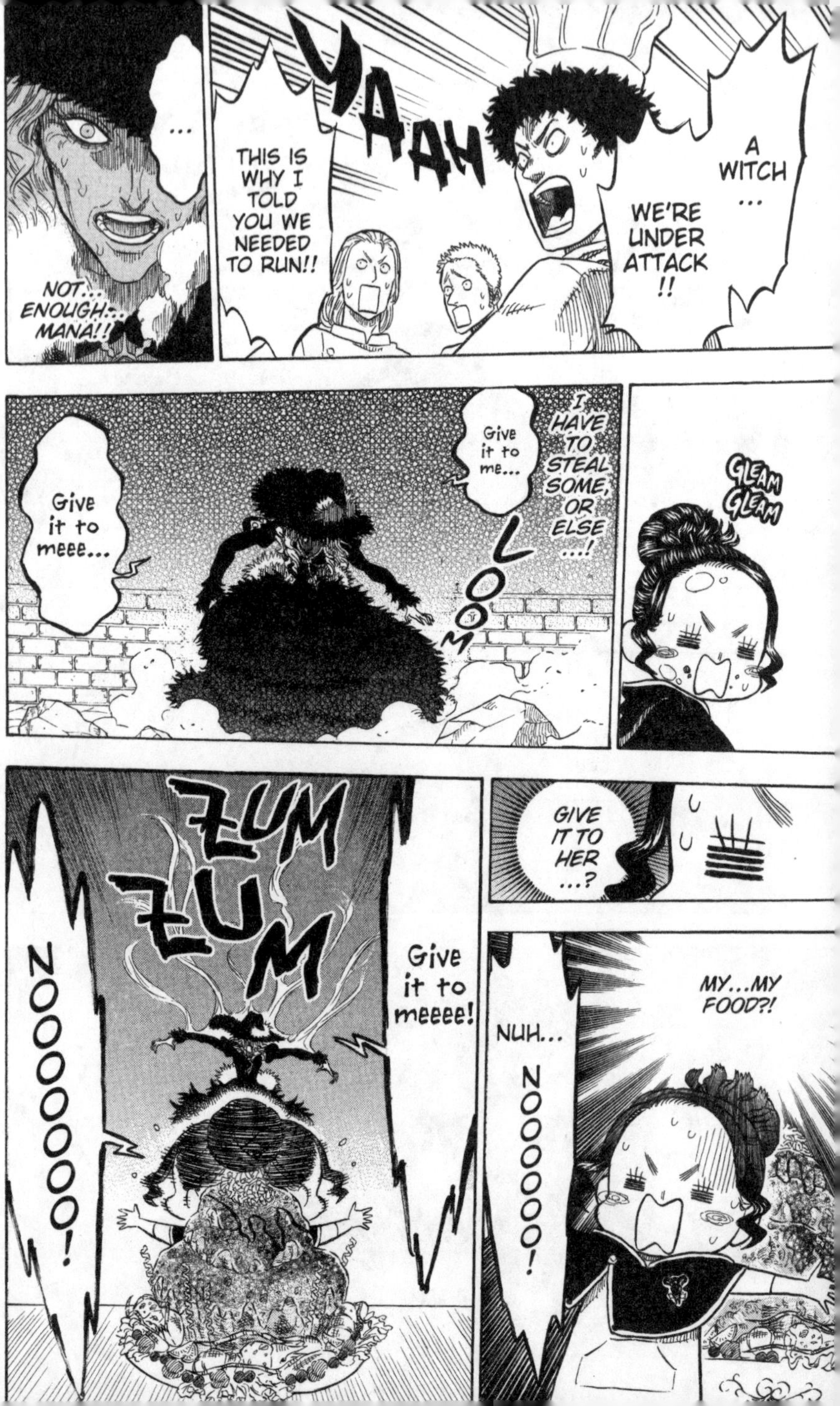
A WITCH...
WE'RE UNDER ATTACK!!
YAAAH
THIS IS WHY I TOLD YOU WE NEEDED TO RUN!!
...
NOT... ENOUGH... MANA!!
GLEAM GLEAM
I HAVE TO STEAL SOME, OR ELSE...!
Give it to me...
LOOOM
Give it to meee...
GIVE IT TO HER...?
MY...MY FOOD?!
NUH... NOOOOOOO!
Give it to meeee!
ZUM ZUM
NOOOOOOOO!

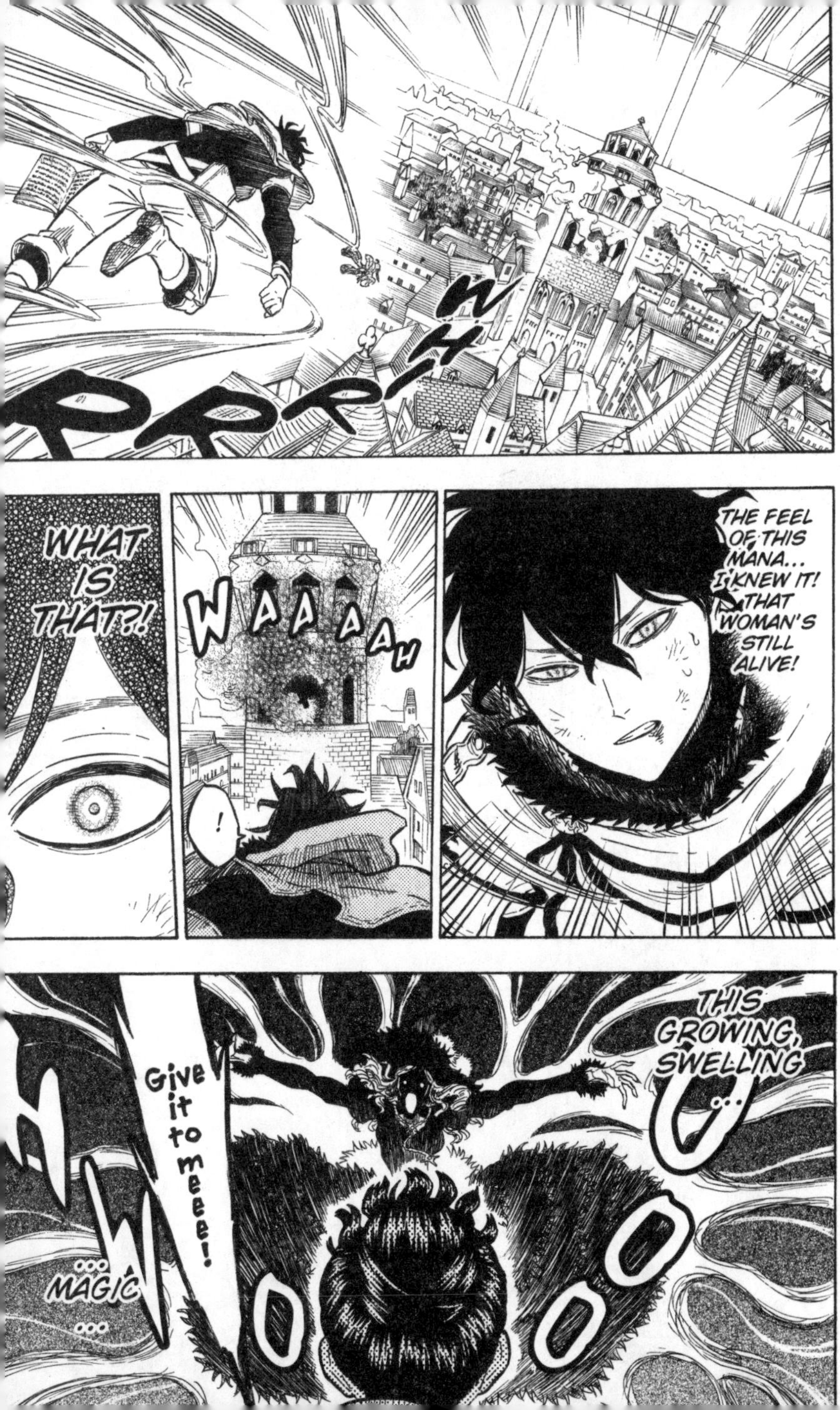
WHIRRR
THE FEEL OF THIS MANA... I KNEW IT! THAT WOMAN'S STILL ALIVE!
WAAAAAH
!
WHAT IS THAT?!
THIS GROWING, SWELLING...
Give it to meee!
...MAGIC...

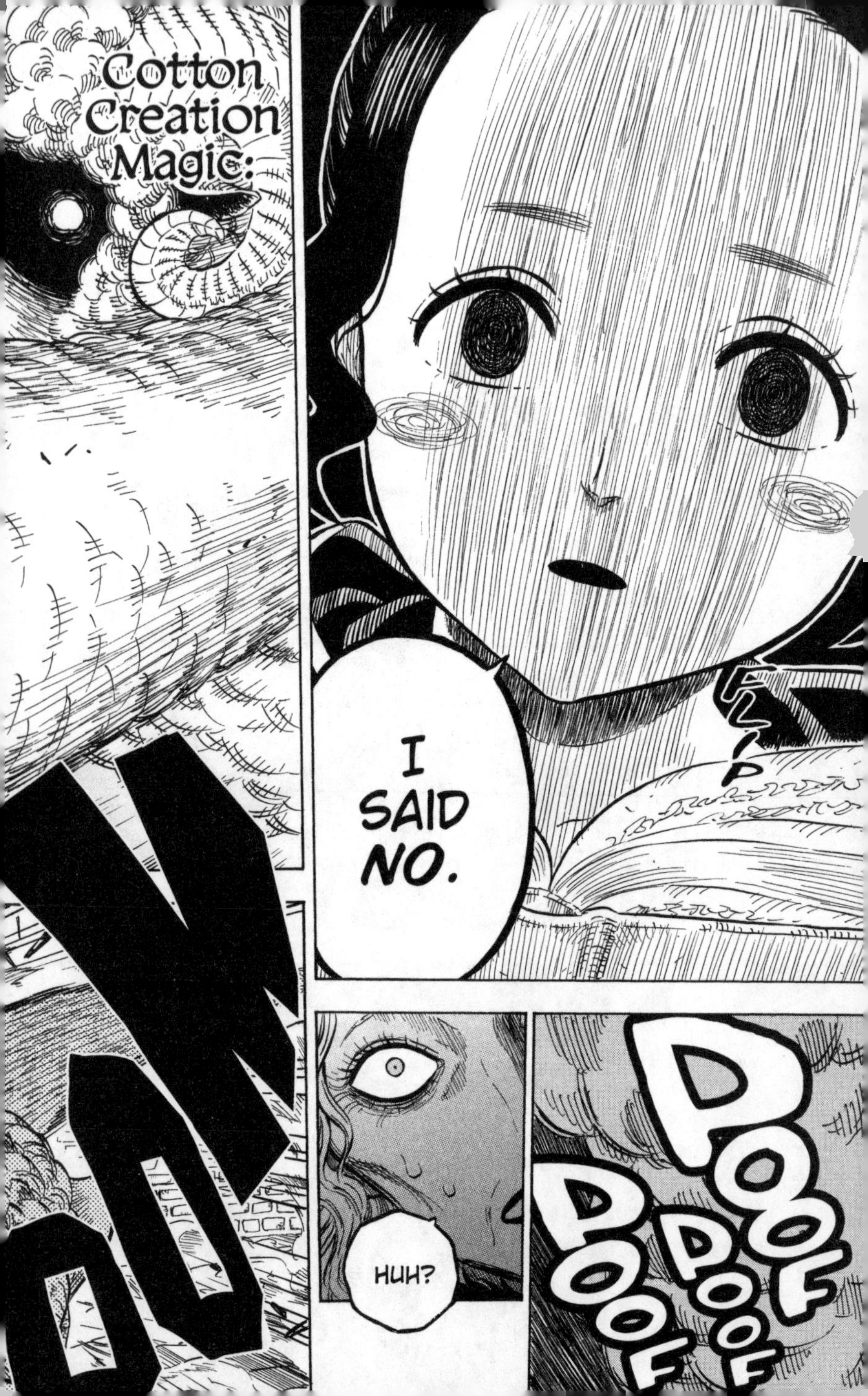
FLIP
I SAID NO.
Cotton Creation Magic:
POOF POOF POOF
HUH?

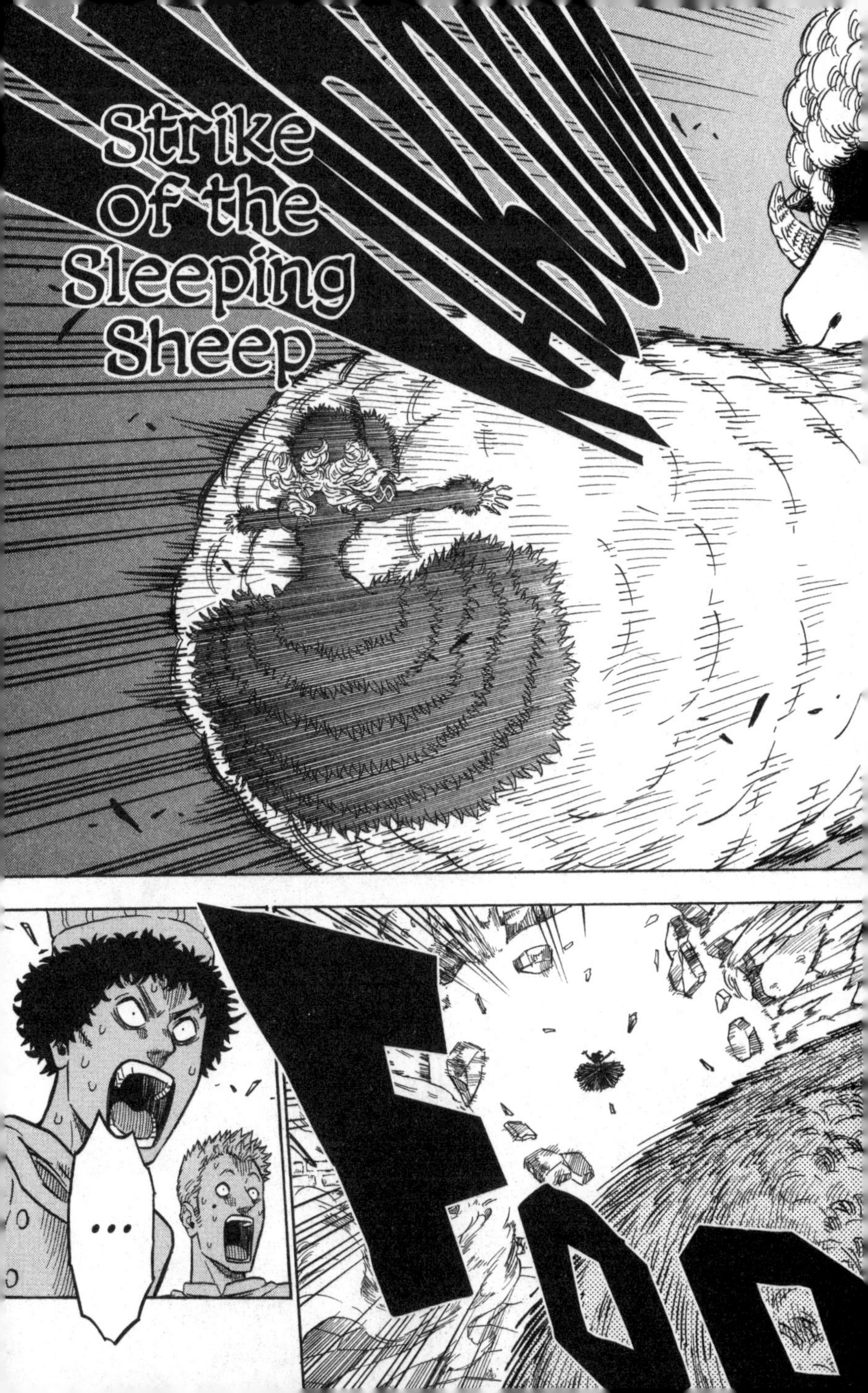
Strike of the Sleeping Sheep
...

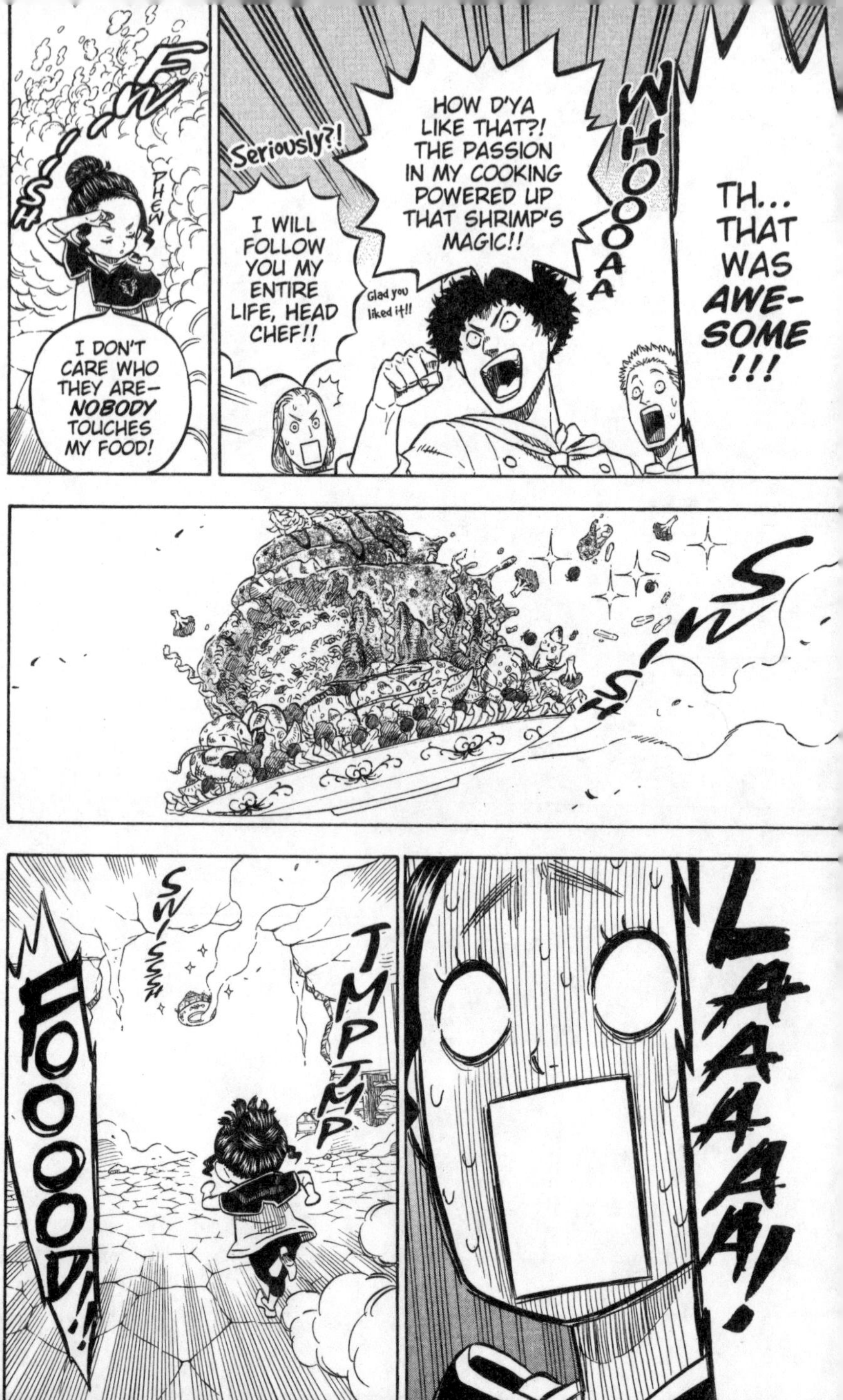
TH... THAT WAS AWESOME!!!
WHOOOOOAA
HOW D'YA LIKE THAT?! THE PASSION IN MY COOKING POWERED UP THAT SHRIMP'S MAGIC!!
Glad you liked it!!
Seriously?!
I WILL FOLLOW YOU MY ENTIRE LIFE, HEAD CHEF!!
FWISH
PHEW
I DON'T CARE WHO THEY ARE—NOBODY TOUCHES MY FOOD!
SWISH
NLAAAAAA!
SWISSSH
TMP TMP
FOOOOOD!!

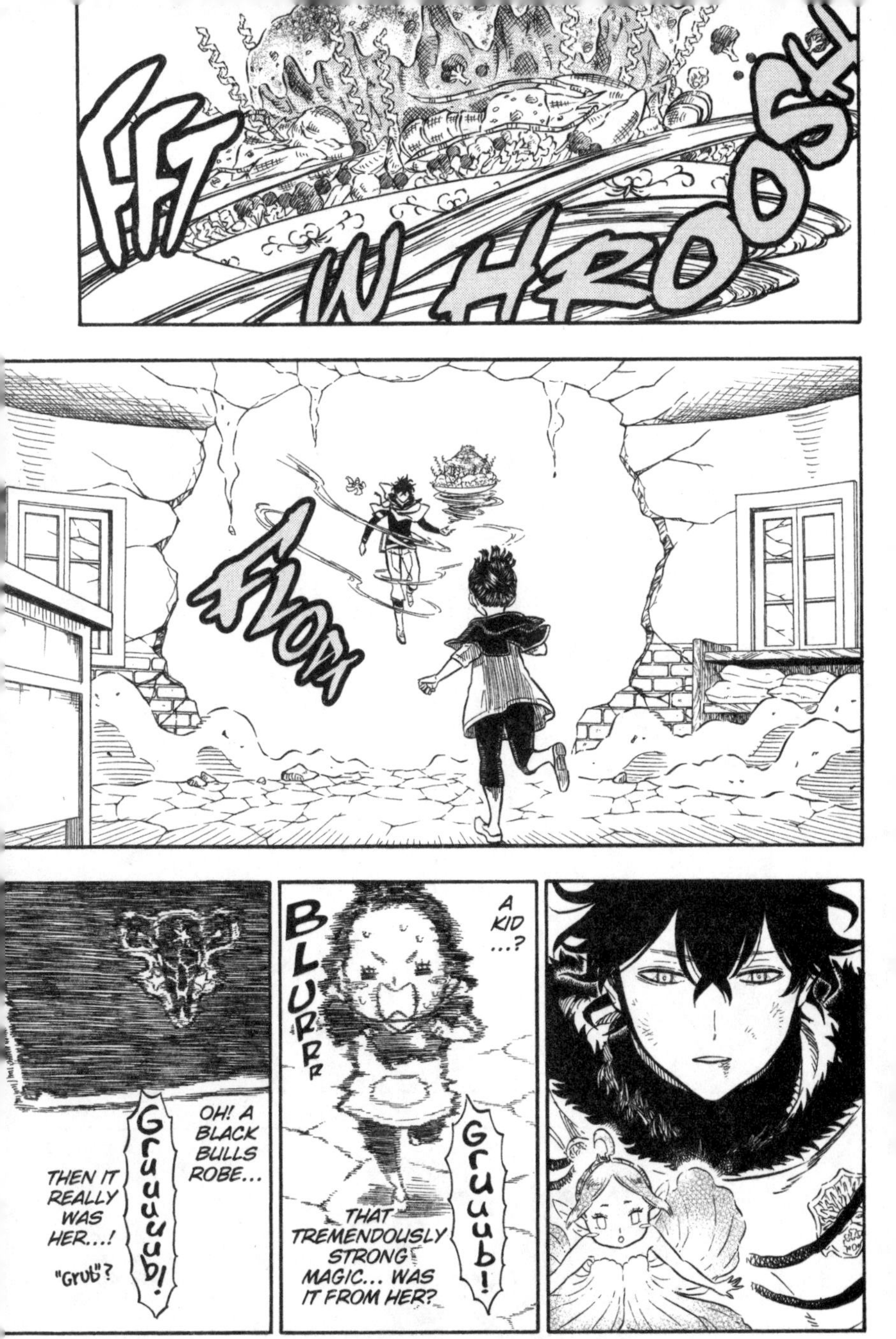
FFT
WHROOSH
FWOM
A KID...?
BLURRR
Gruuub!
THAT TREMENDOUSLY STRONG MAGIC... WAS IT FROM HER?
OH! A BLACK BULLS ROBE...
Gruuuuub!
THEN IT REALLY WAS HER...!
"Grub"?

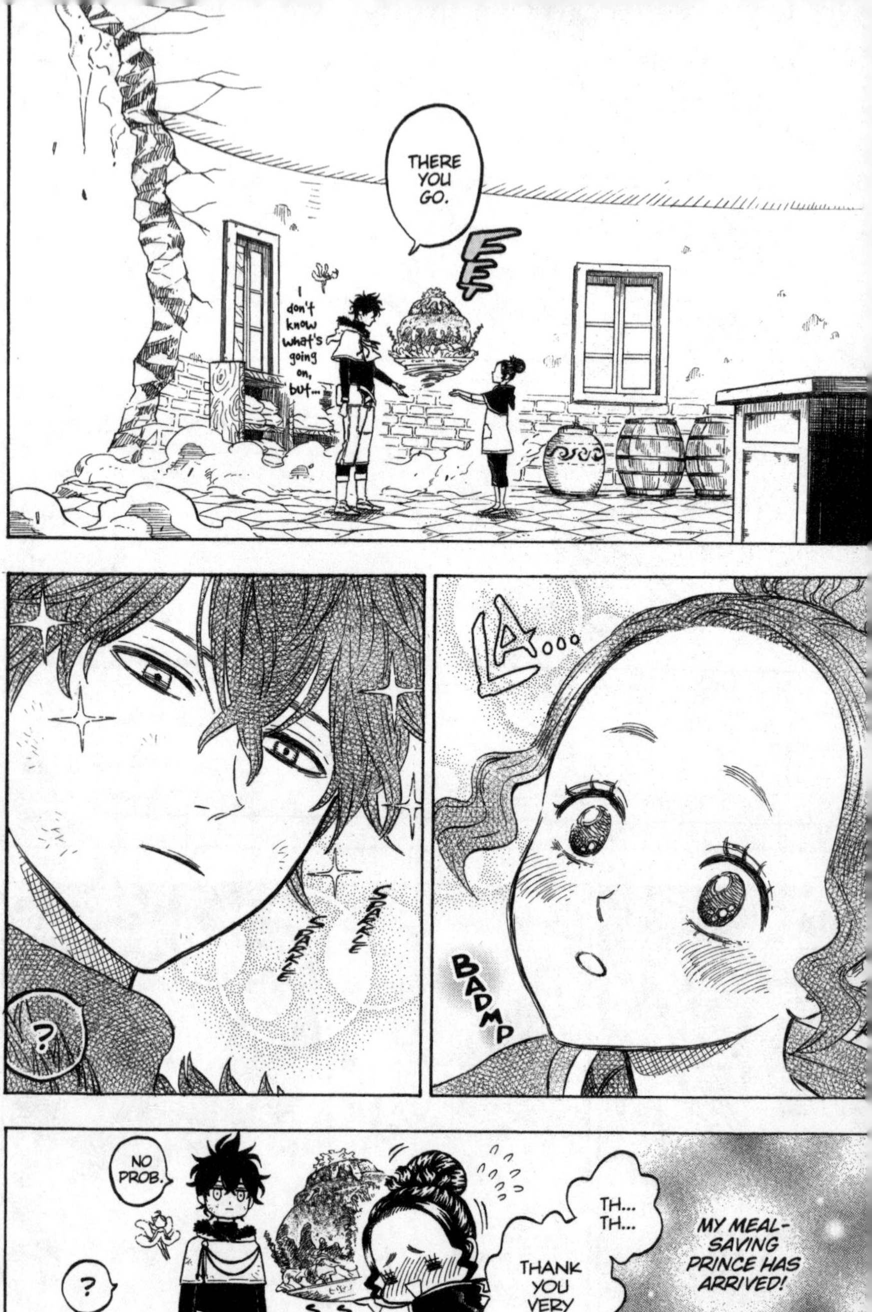
THERE YOU GO.
I don't know what's going on, but...
LA...
BADMP
SPARKLE SPARKLE
?
MY MEAL-SAVING PRINCE HAS ARRIVED!
TH... TH...
THANK YOU VERY MUCH!
NO PROB.
?

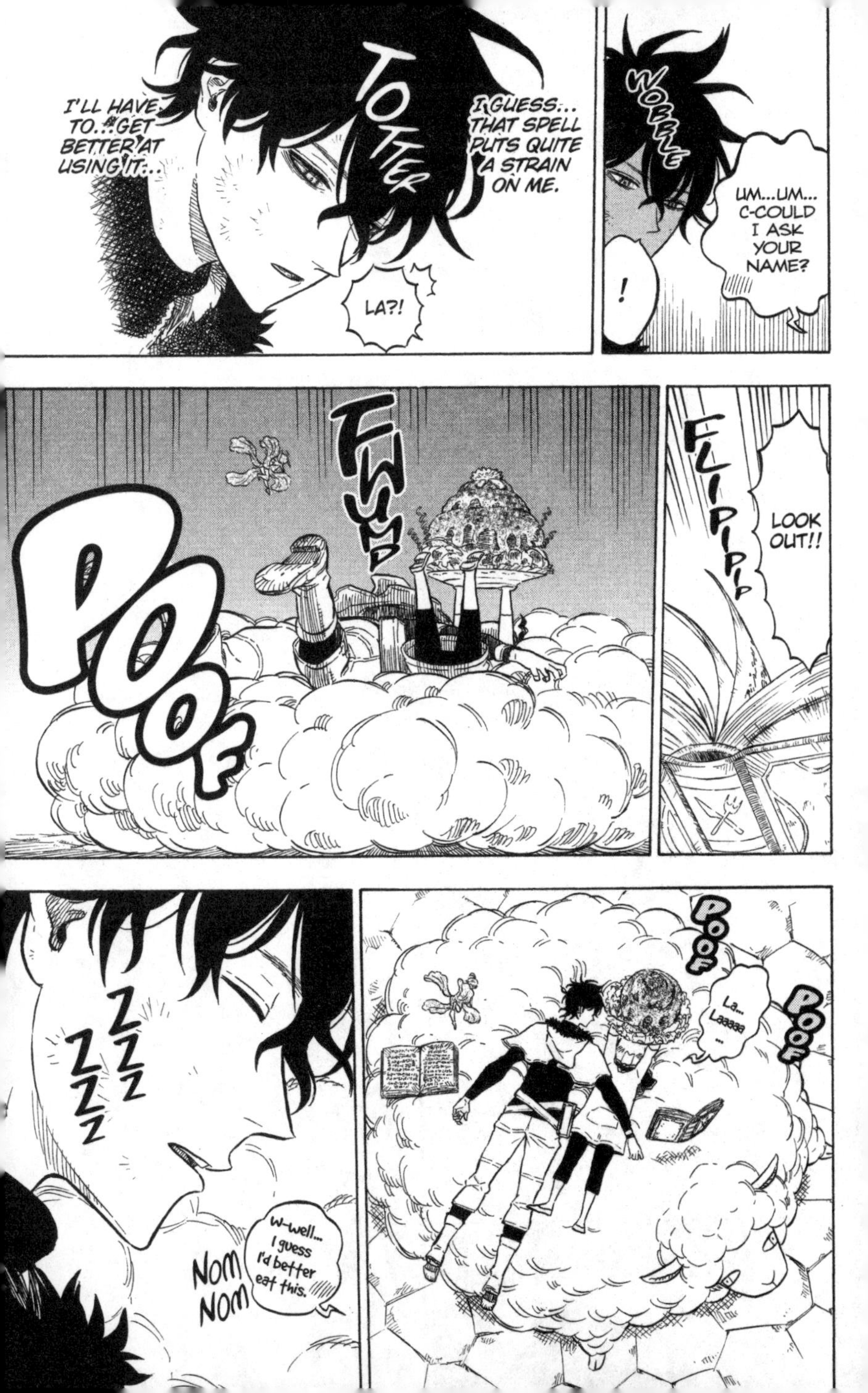
WOBBLE
UM...UM... C-COULD I ASK YOUR NAME?
!
TOTTER
I GUESS... THAT SPELL PUTS QUITE A STRAIN ON ME.
I'LL HAVE TO... GET BETTER AT USING IT...
LA?!
FLIPIPIPIP
LOOK OUT!!
FWUMP
POOOF
POOF
POOF
La... Laaaaa ...
ZZZ
ZZZ
W-well... I guess I'd better eat this.
NOM NOM

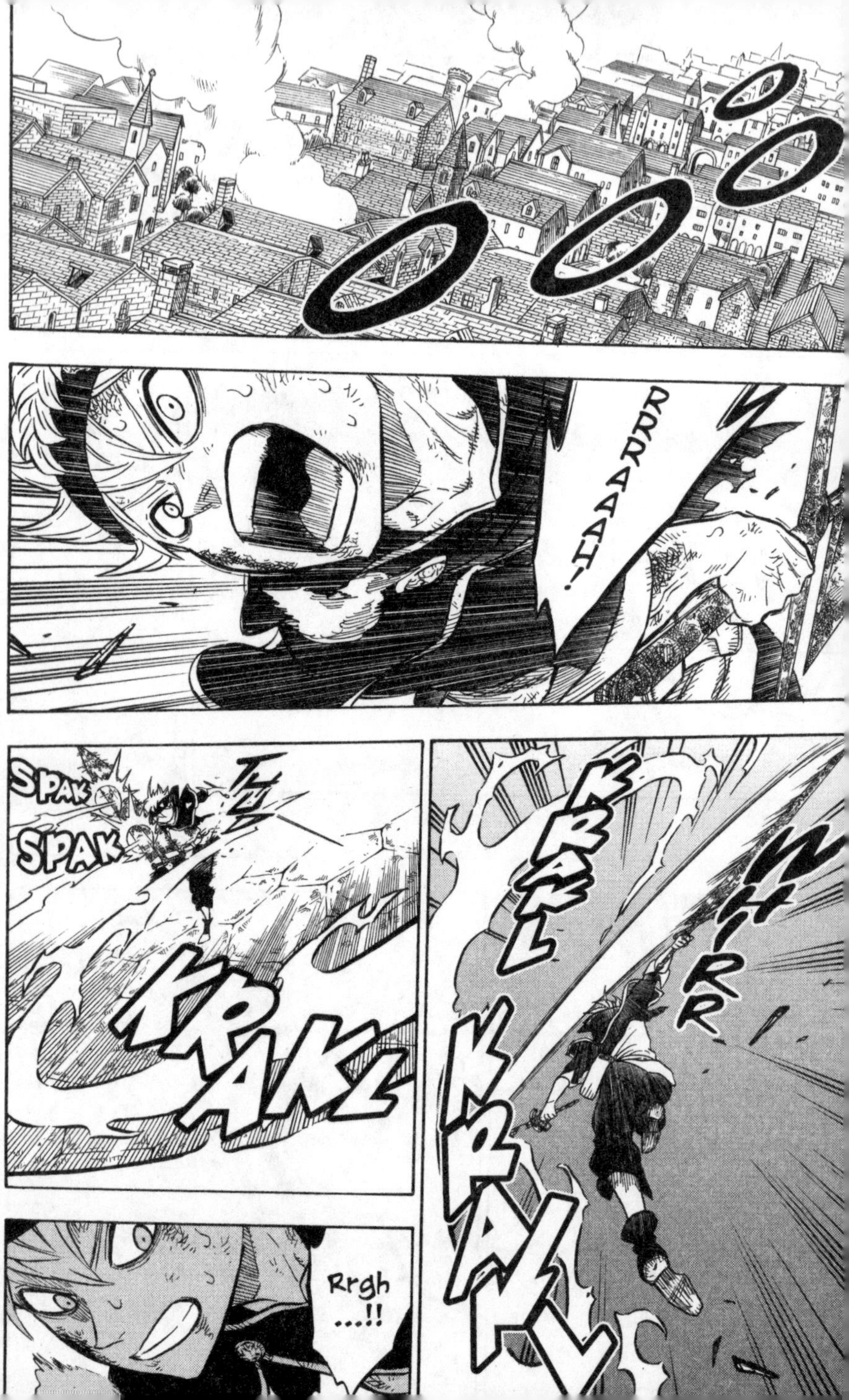

OOOO
RRRAAAAH!
WHIRRR
KRAKL
KRAKL
SPAK
SPAK
KRAKL
Rrgh
...!!

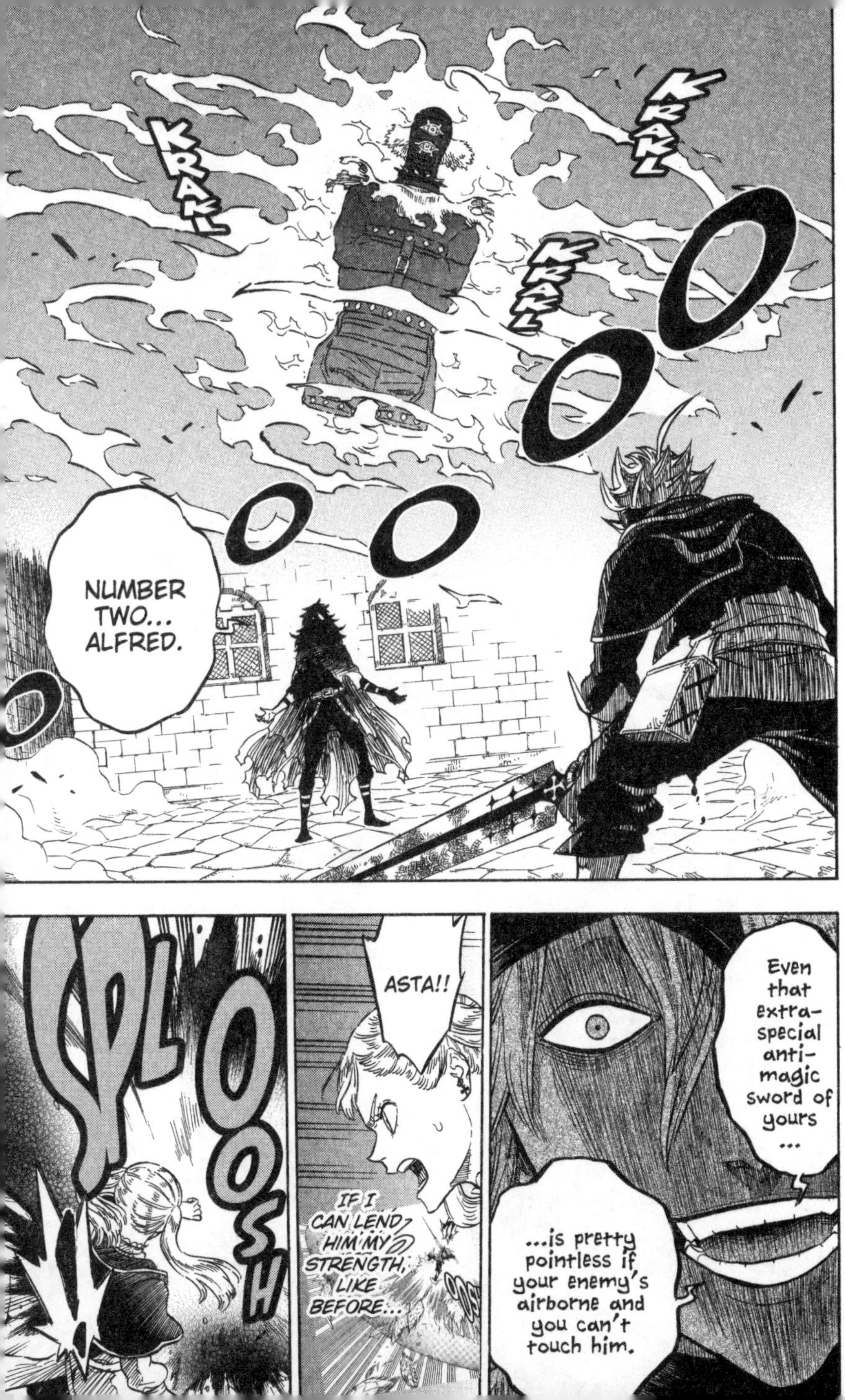
KRAKL
KRAKL
KRAKL
NUMBER TWO... ALFRED.
Even that extra-special anti-magic sword of yours...
...is pretty pointless if your enemy's airborne and you can't touch him.
ASTA!!
IF I CAN LEND HIM MY STRENGTH, LIKE BEFORE...
SPLOOOSH

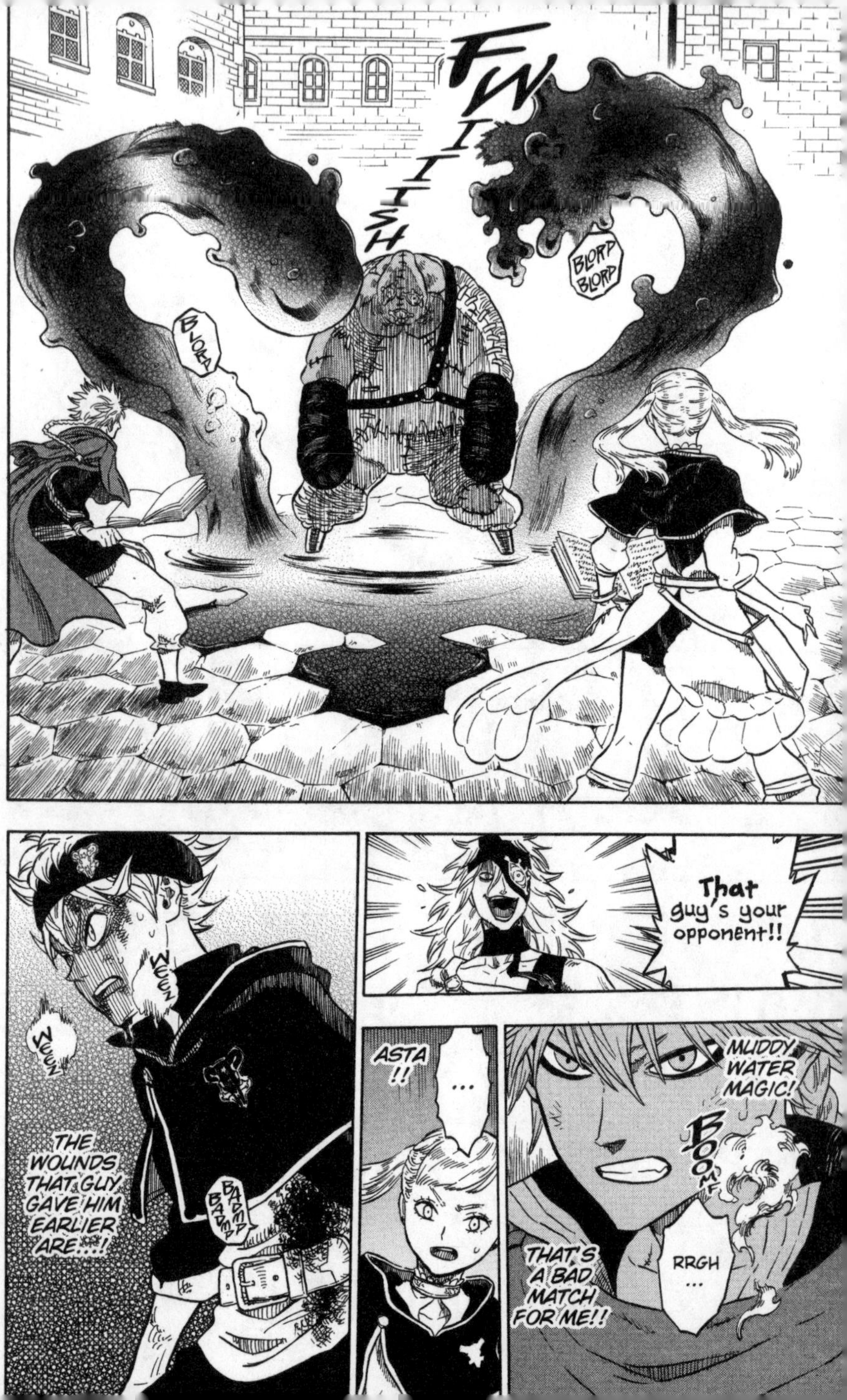
BLORP BLORP
FWIIIISH
BLORP
That guy's your opponent!!
MUDDY WATER MAGIC!
BOOMF
RRGH ...
THAT'S A BAD MATCH FOR ME!!
ASTA!!
...
WEEZ
WEEZ
THE WOUNDS THAT GUY GAVE HIM EARLIER ARE...!
BADMP BADMP

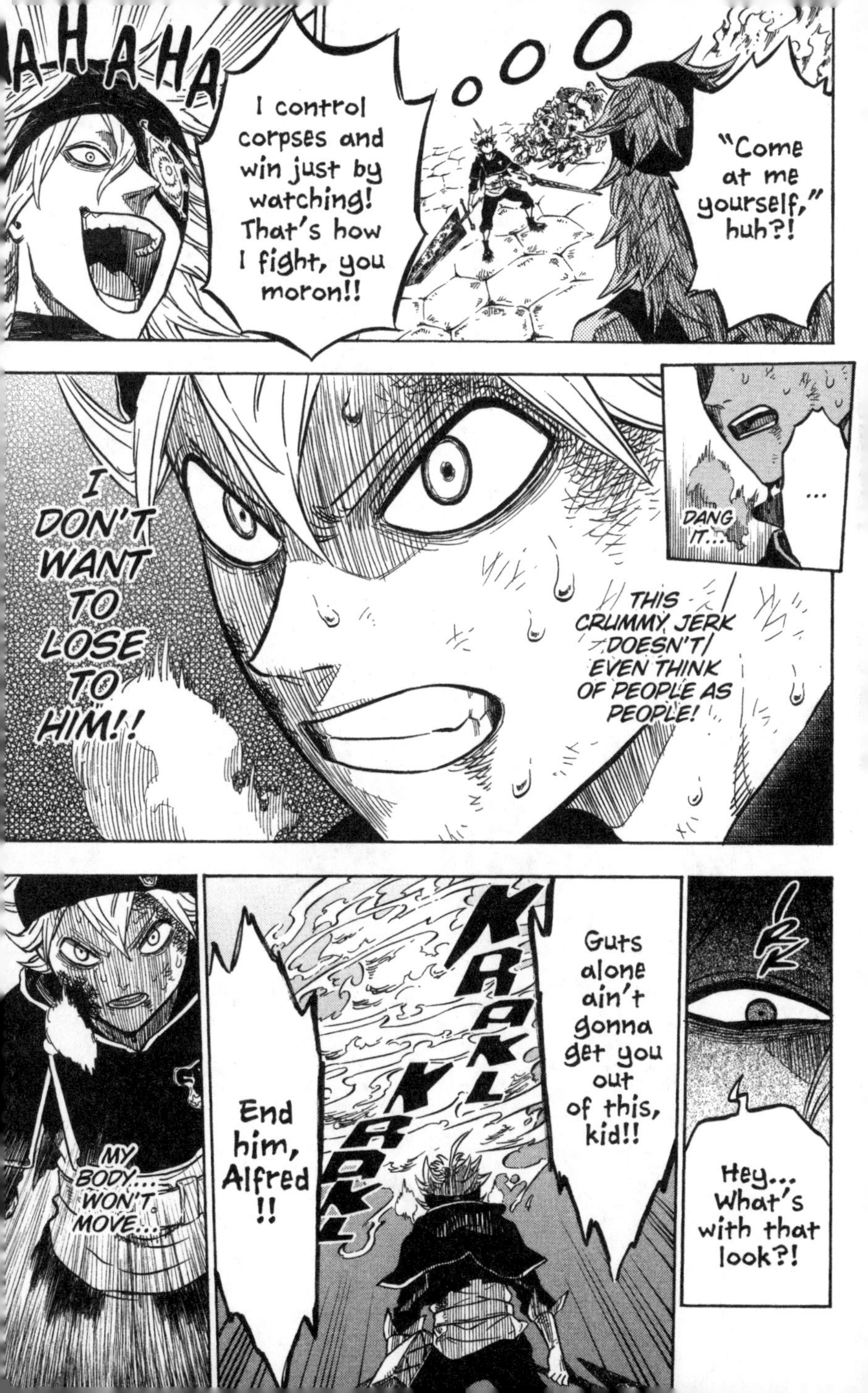
"Come at me yourself," huh?!
AHAHAHA
I control corpses and win just by watching! That's how I fight, you moron!!
OOO
...
DANG IT...
THIS CRUMMY JERK DOESN'T EVEN THINK OF PEOPLE AS PEOPLE!
I DON'T WANT TO LOSE TO HIM!!
KRK
Hey... What's with that look?!
Guts alone ain't gonna get you out of this, kid!!
KRAKL
KRAKL
End him, Alfred!!
MY BODY... WON'T MOVE...

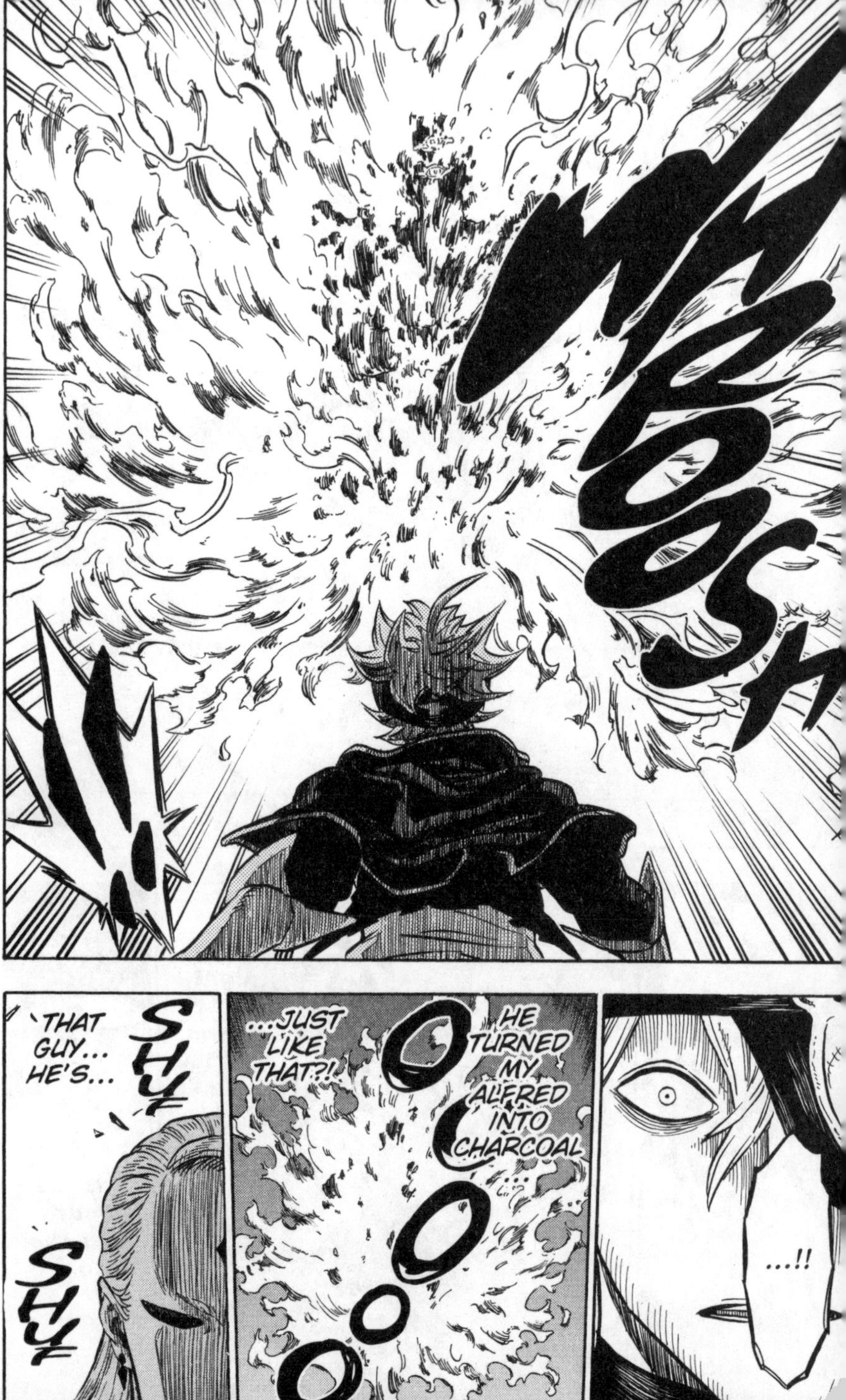
WHOOOSH
!!
...!!
HE TURNED MY ALFRED INTO CHARCOAL...
...JUST LIKE THAT?!
THAT GUY... HE'S...
SHUF
SHUF

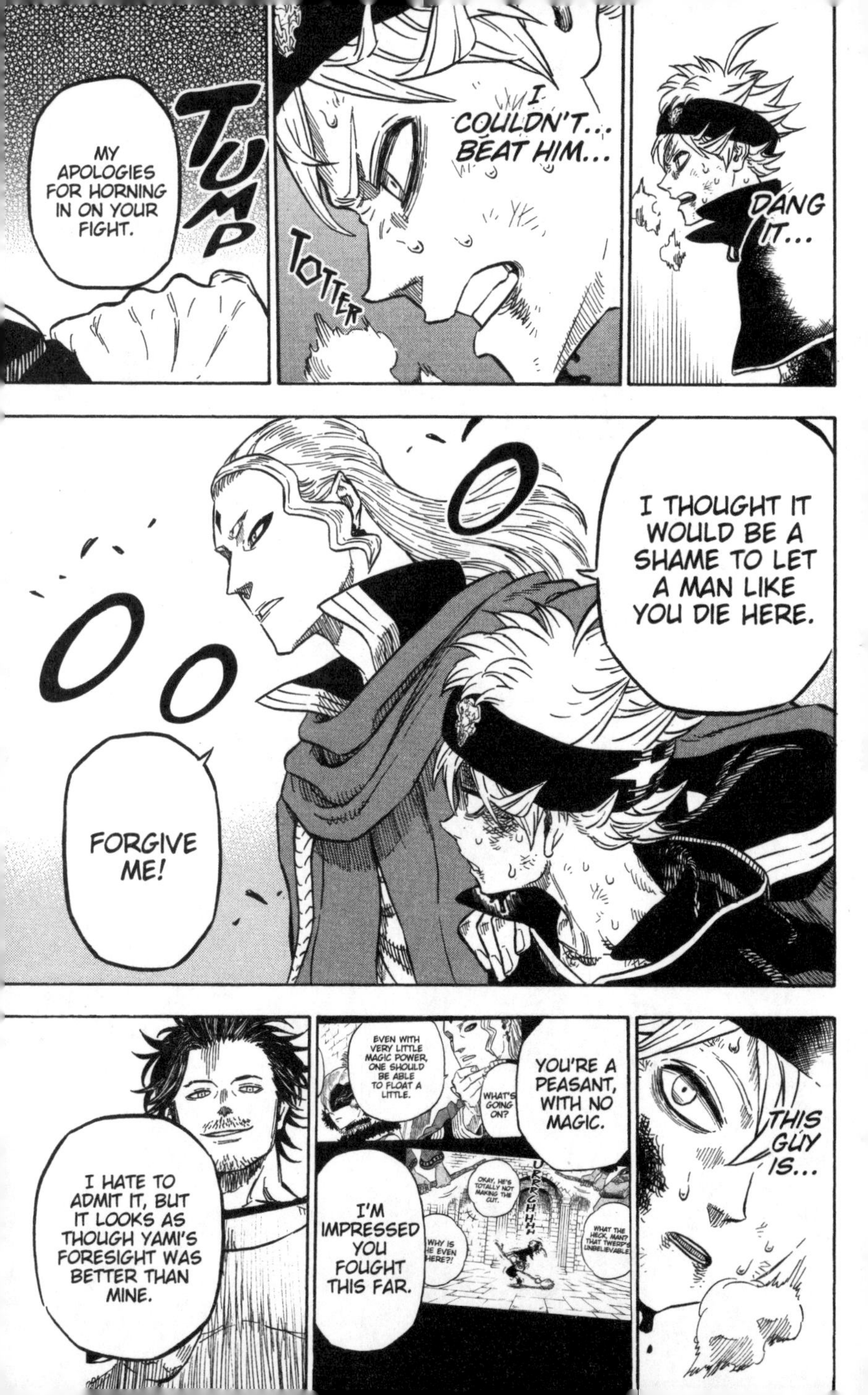
DANG IT...
I COULDN'T... BEAT HIM...
TOTTER
TUMP
MY APOLOGIES FOR HORNING IN ON YOUR FIGHT.
I THOUGHT IT WOULD BE A SHAME TO LET A MAN LIKE YOU DIE HERE.
FORGIVE ME!
THIS GUY IS...
YOU'RE A PEASANT, WITH NO MAGIC.
WHAT'S GOING ON?
EVEN WITH VERY LITTLE MAGIC POWER, ONE SHOULD BE ABLE TO FLOAT A LITTLE.
OKAY, HE'S TOTALLY NOT MAKING THE CUT.
WHAT THE HECK, MAN? THAT TWERP'S UNBELIEVABLE!
WHY IS HE EVEN HERE?!
I'M IMPRESSED YOU FOUGHT THIS FAR.
I HATE TO ADMIT IT, BUT IT LOOKS AS THOUGH YAMI'S FORESIGHT WAS BETTER THAN MINE.

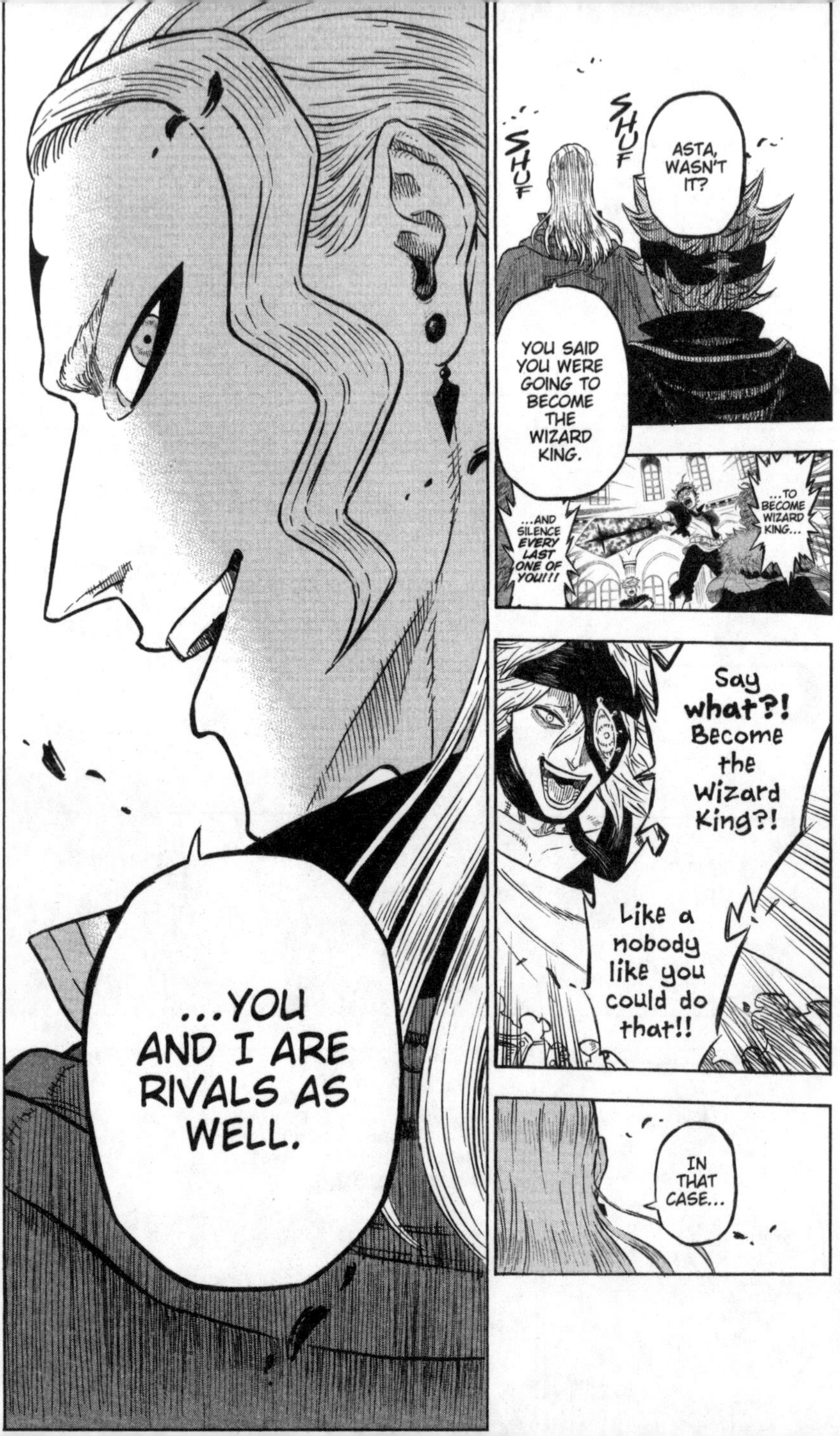
SHUF
SHUF
ASTA, WASN'T IT?
YOU SAID YOU WERE GOING TO BECOME THE WIZARD KING.
...TO BECOME WIZARD KING...
...AND SILENCE EVERY LAST ONE OF YOU!!!
Say what?! Become the Wizard King?!
Like a nobody like you could do that!!
IN THAT CASE...
...YOU AND I ARE RIVALS AS WELL.

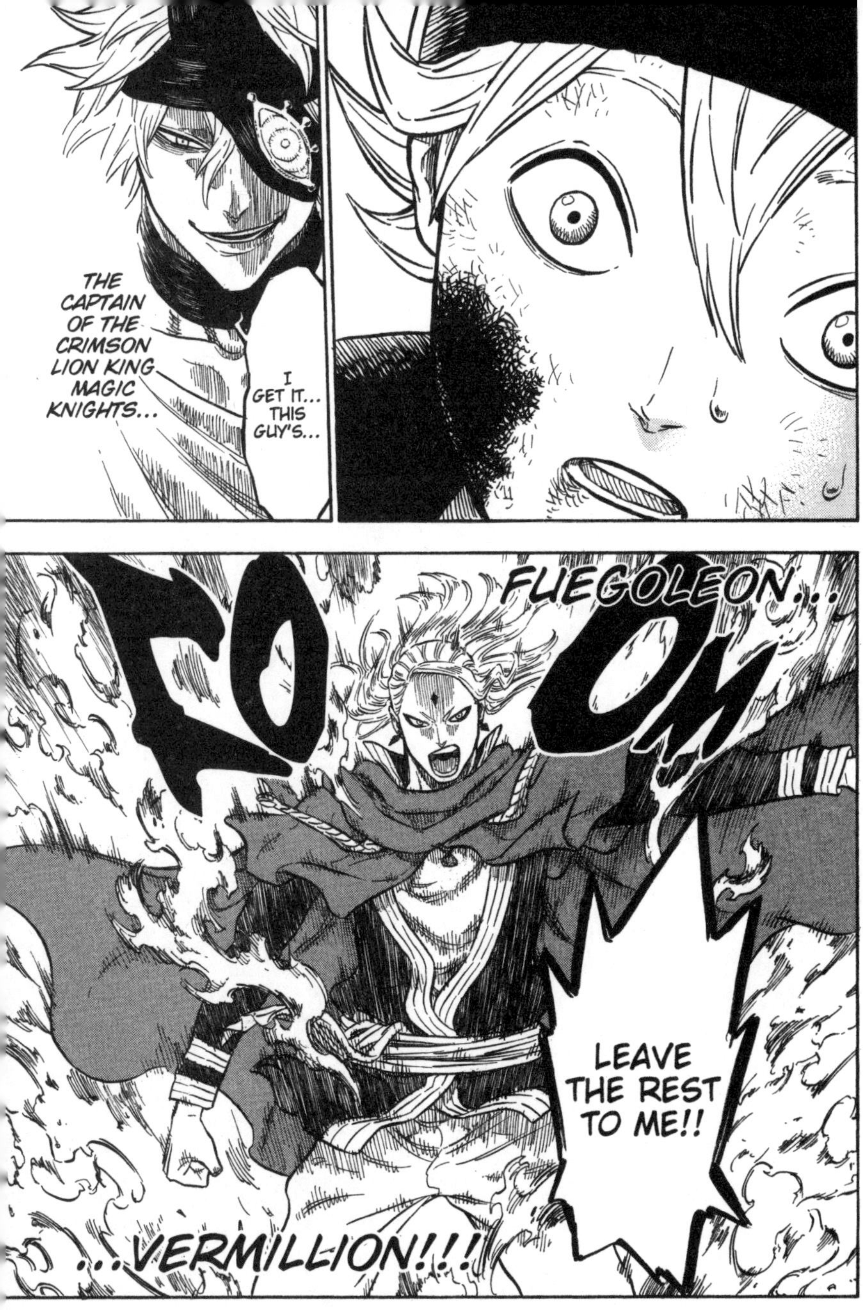
I GET IT... THIS GUY'S...
THE CAPTAIN OF THE CRIMSON LION KING MAGIC KNIGHTS...
FUEGOLEON...
FOOM
LEAVE THE REST TO ME!!
...VERMILLION!!!

Charmy
Pappitson

Age: 19
Height: 142 cm
Birthday: June 3
Sign: Gemini
Blood Type: A
Likes: Food

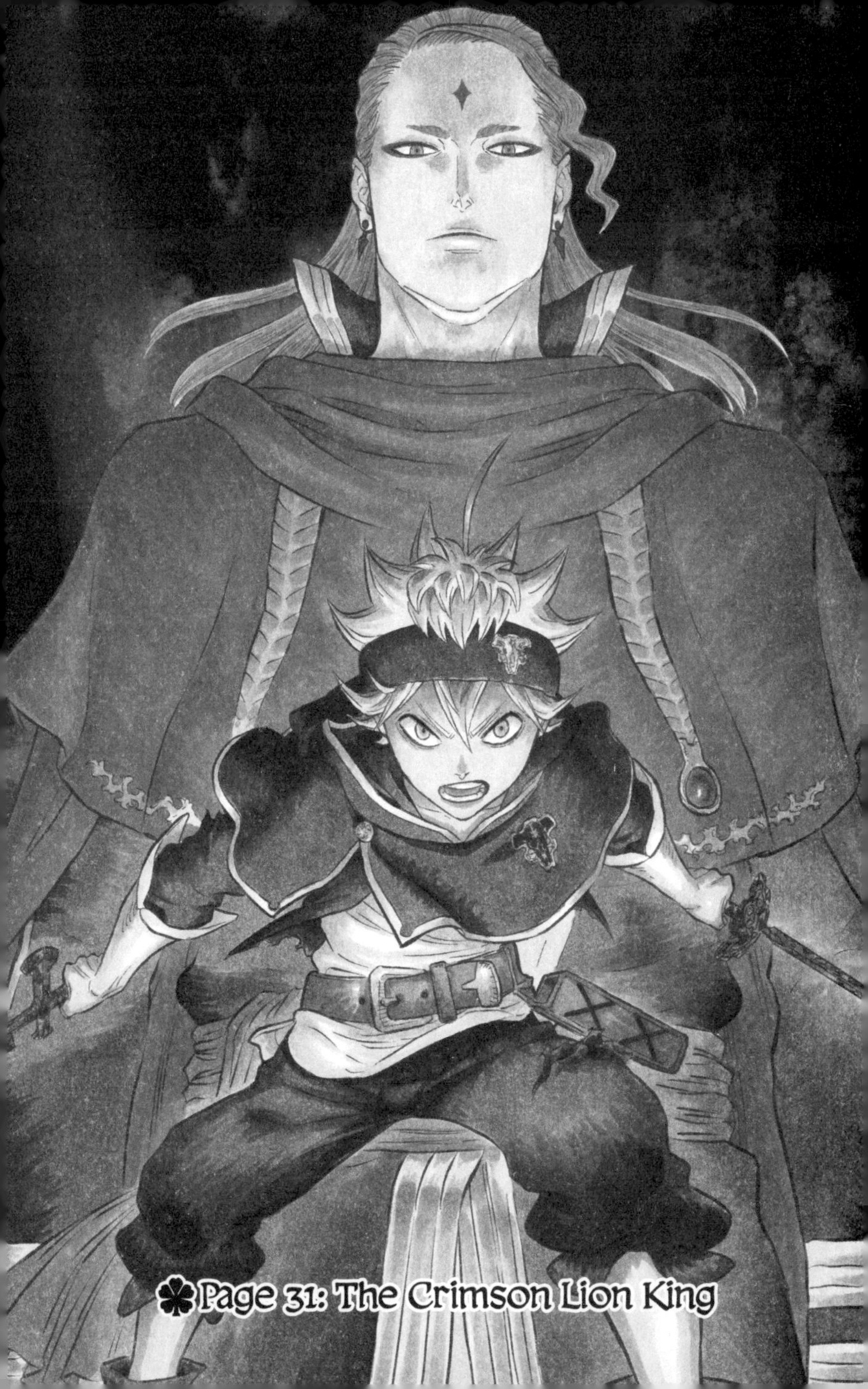
Page 31: The Crimson Lion King

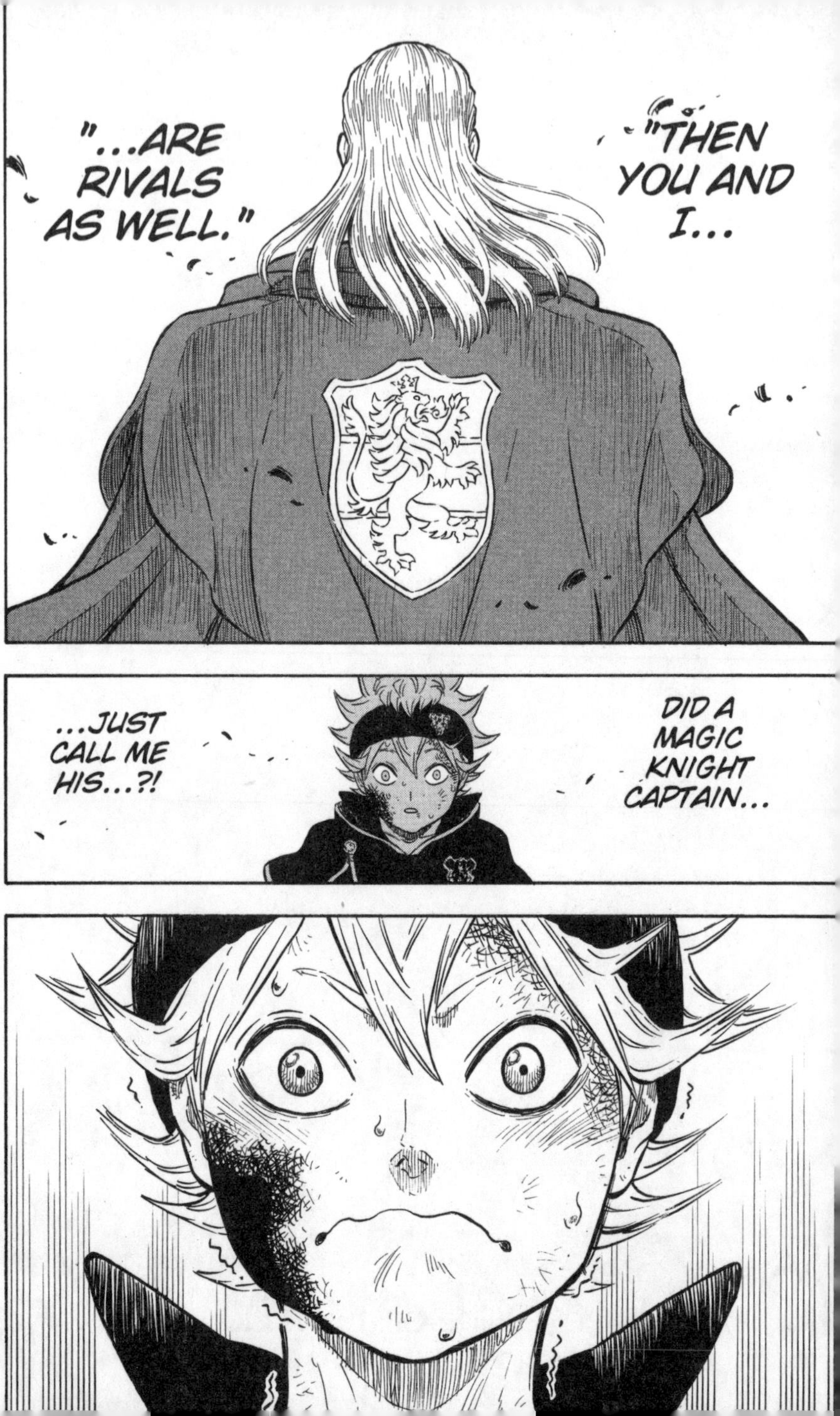
"THEN YOU AND I...
"...ARE RIVALS AS WELL."
DID A MAGIC KNIGHT CAPTAIN...
...JUST CALL ME HIS...?!

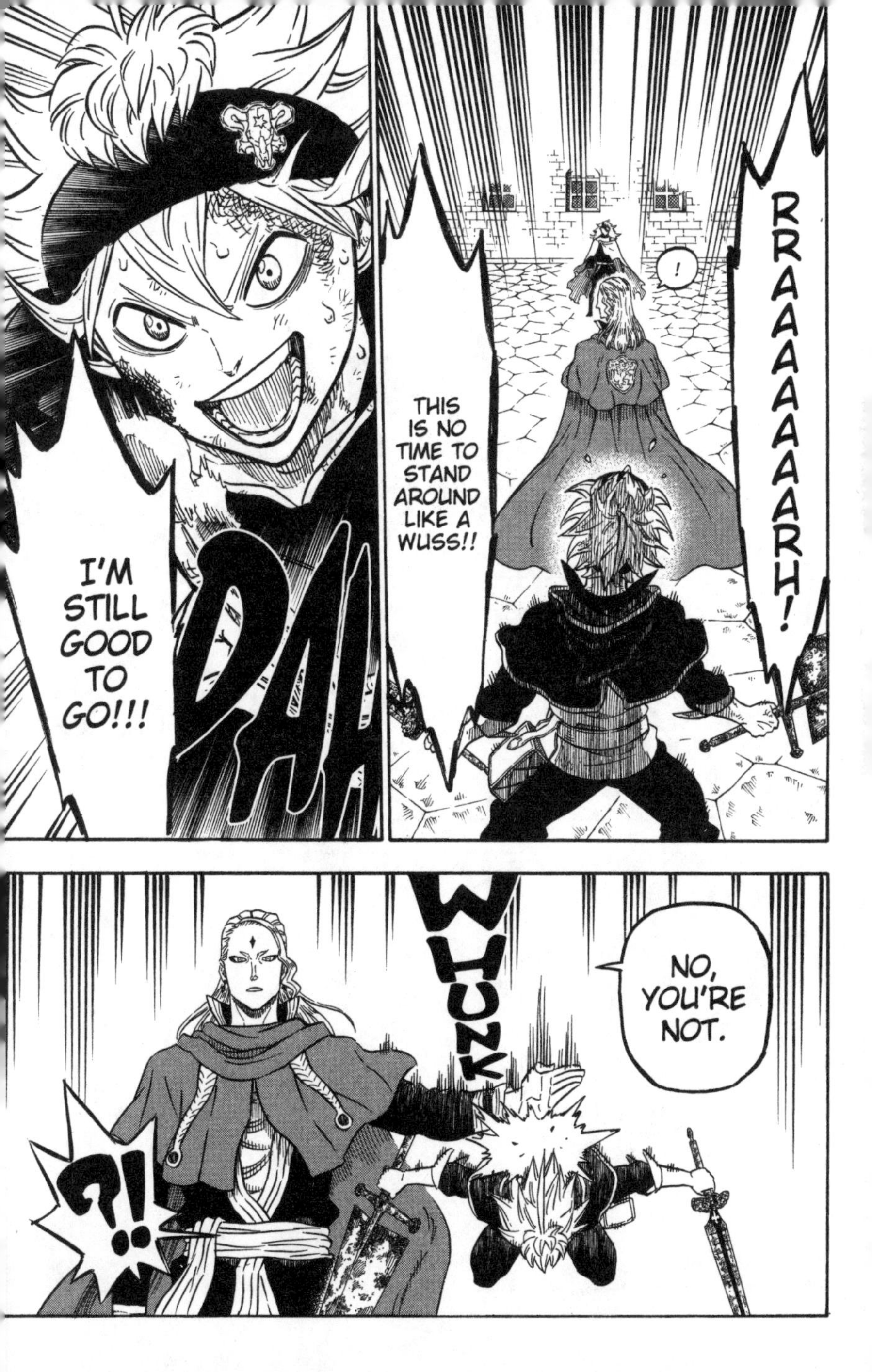
RRAAAAAAAAARH!
!
THIS IS NO TIME TO STAND AROUND LIKE A WUSS!!
I'M STILL GOOD TO GO!!!
NO, YOU'RE NOT.
WHUNK
?!!

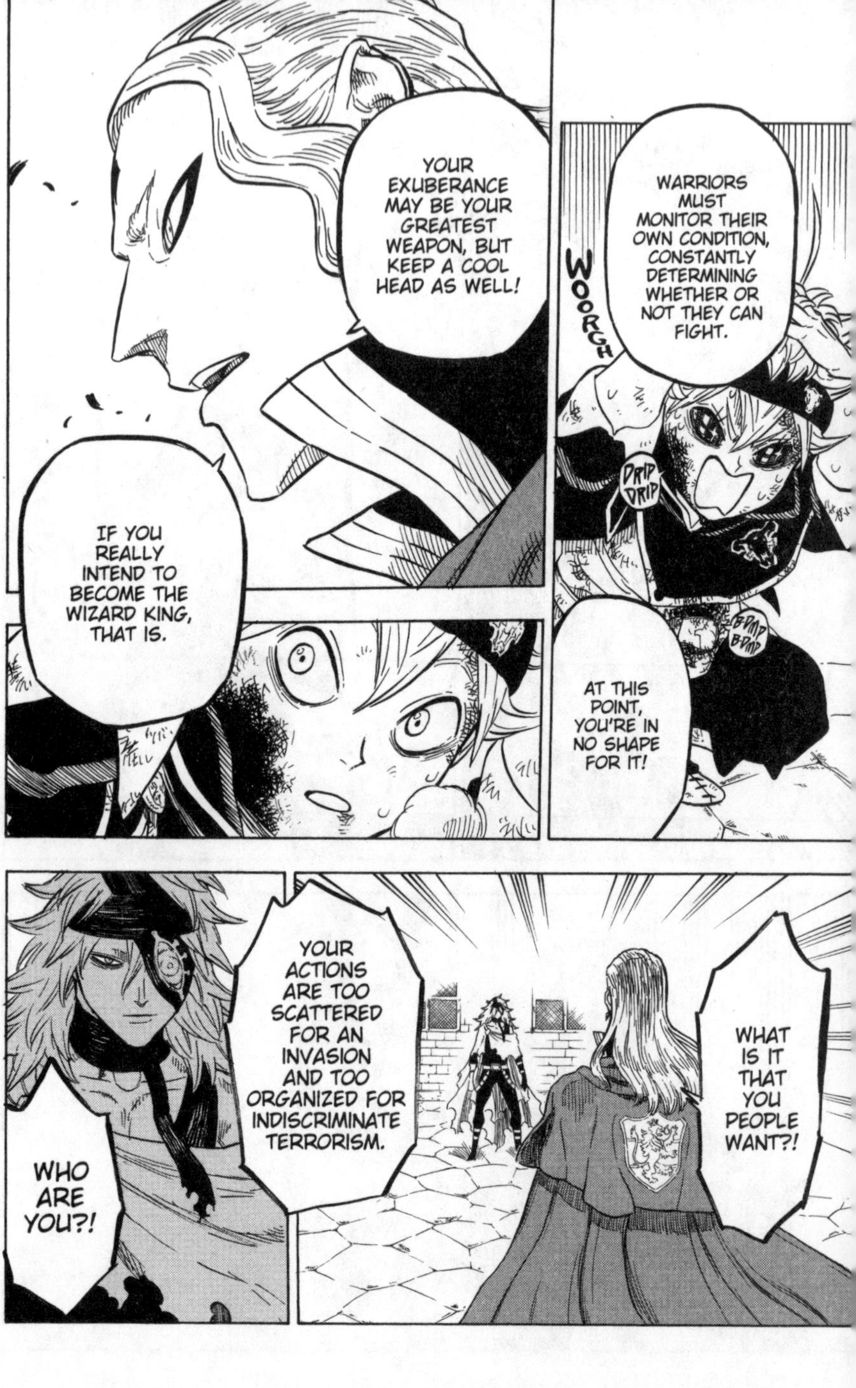
WOORGH
WARRIORS MUST MONITOR THEIR OWN CONDITION, CONSTANTLY DETERMINING WHETHER OR NOT THEY CAN FIGHT.
DRIP DRIP
B-DMP B-DMP
AT THIS POINT, YOU'RE IN NO SHAPE FOR IT!
YOUR EXUBERANCE MAY BE YOUR GREATEST WEAPON, BUT KEEP A COOL HEAD AS WELL!
IF YOU REALLY INTEND TO BECOME THE WIZARD KING, THAT IS.
WHAT IS IT THAT YOU PEOPLE WANT?!
YOUR ACTIONS ARE TOO SCATTERED FOR AN INVASION AND TOO ORGANIZED FOR INDISCRIMINATE TERRORISM.
WHO ARE YOU?!

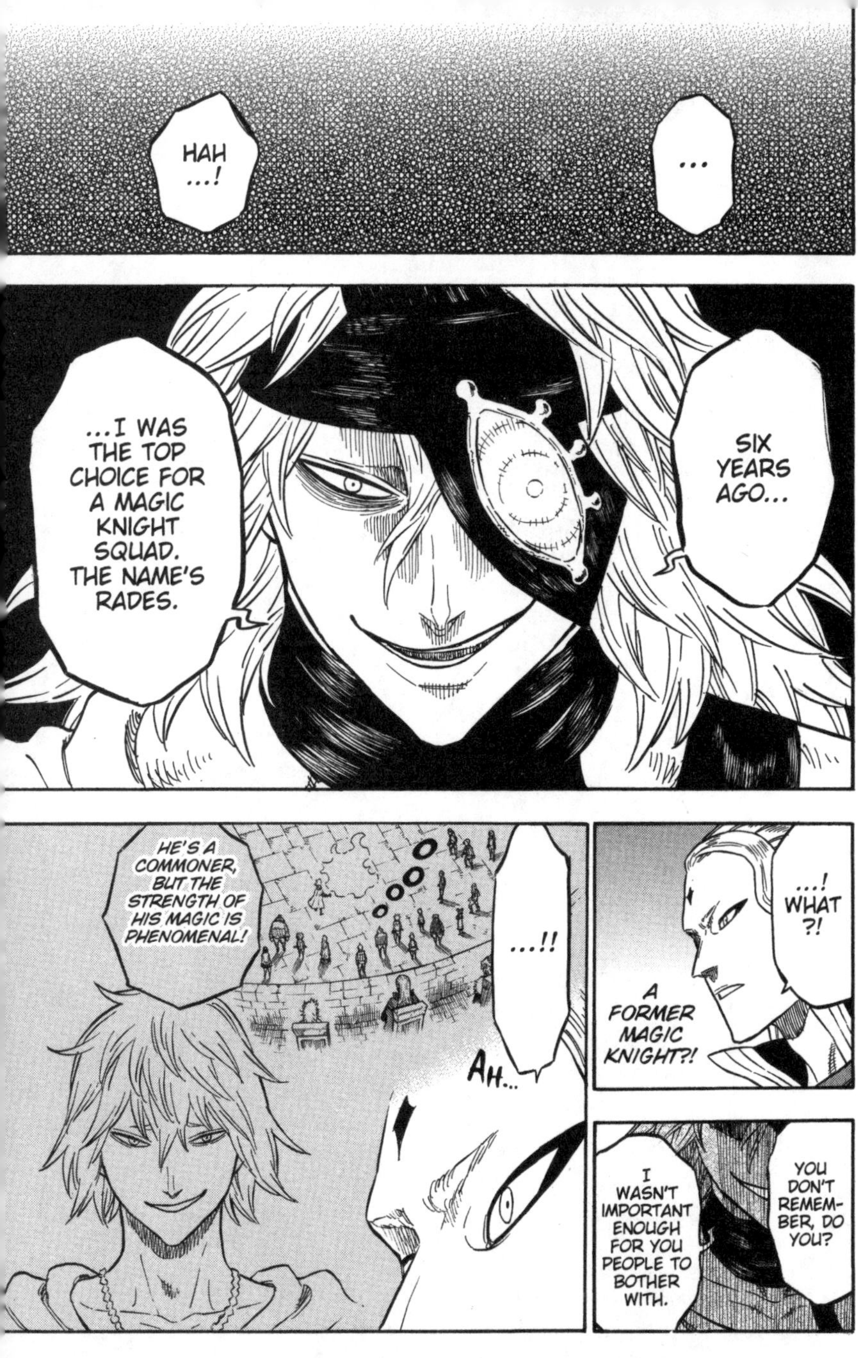
...
HAH ...!
SIX YEARS AGO...
...I WAS THE TOP CHOICE FOR A MAGIC KNIGHT SQUAD. THE NAME'S RADES.
...! WHAT ?!
A FORMER MAGIC KNIGHT?!
YOU DON'T REMEM-BER, DO YOU?
I WASN'T IMPORTANT ENOUGH FOR YOU PEOPLE TO BOTHER WITH.
...!!
HE'S A COMMONER, BUT THE STRENGTH OF HIS MAGIC IS PHENOMENAL!
AH...

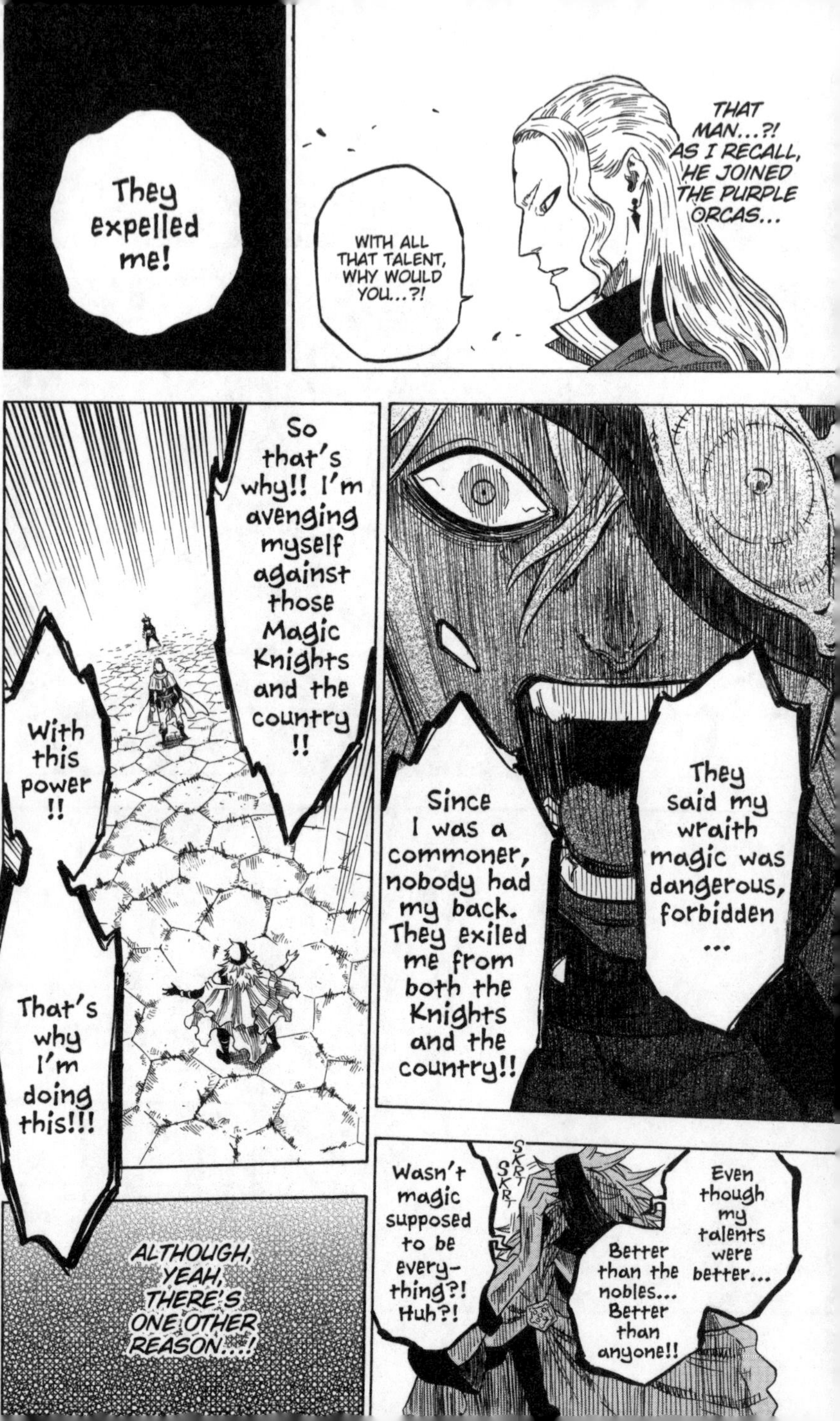
THAT MAN...?! AS I RECALL, HE JOINED THE PURPLE ORCAS...
WITH ALL THAT TALENT, WHY WOULD YOU...?!
They expelled me!
They said my wraith magic was dangerous, forbidden...
Since I was a commoner, nobody had my back. They exiled me from both the Knights and the country!!
Even though my talents were better...
Better than the nobles... Better than anyone!!
SKRT SKRT
Wasn't magic supposed to be everything?! Huh?!
So that's why!! I'm avenging myself against those Magic Knights and the country!!
With this power!!
That's why I'm doing this!!!
ALTHOUGH, YEAH, THERE'S ONE OTHER REASON...!

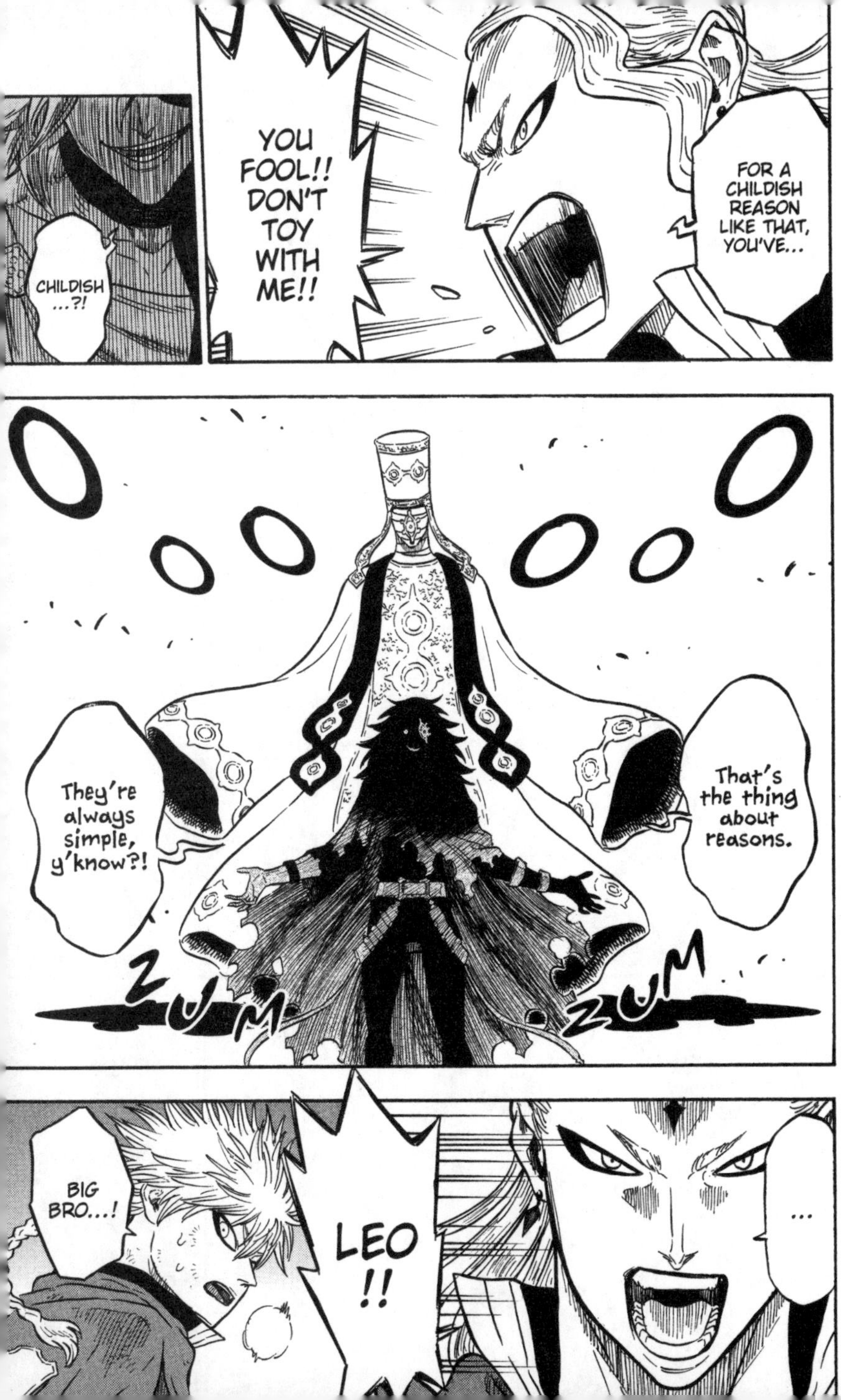
FOR A CHILDISH REASON LIKE THAT, YOU'VE...
YOU FOOL!! DON'T TOY WITH ME!!
CHILDISH...?!
That's the thing about reasons.
They're always simple, y'know?!
ZUM
ZUM
...
LEO!!
BIG BRO...!

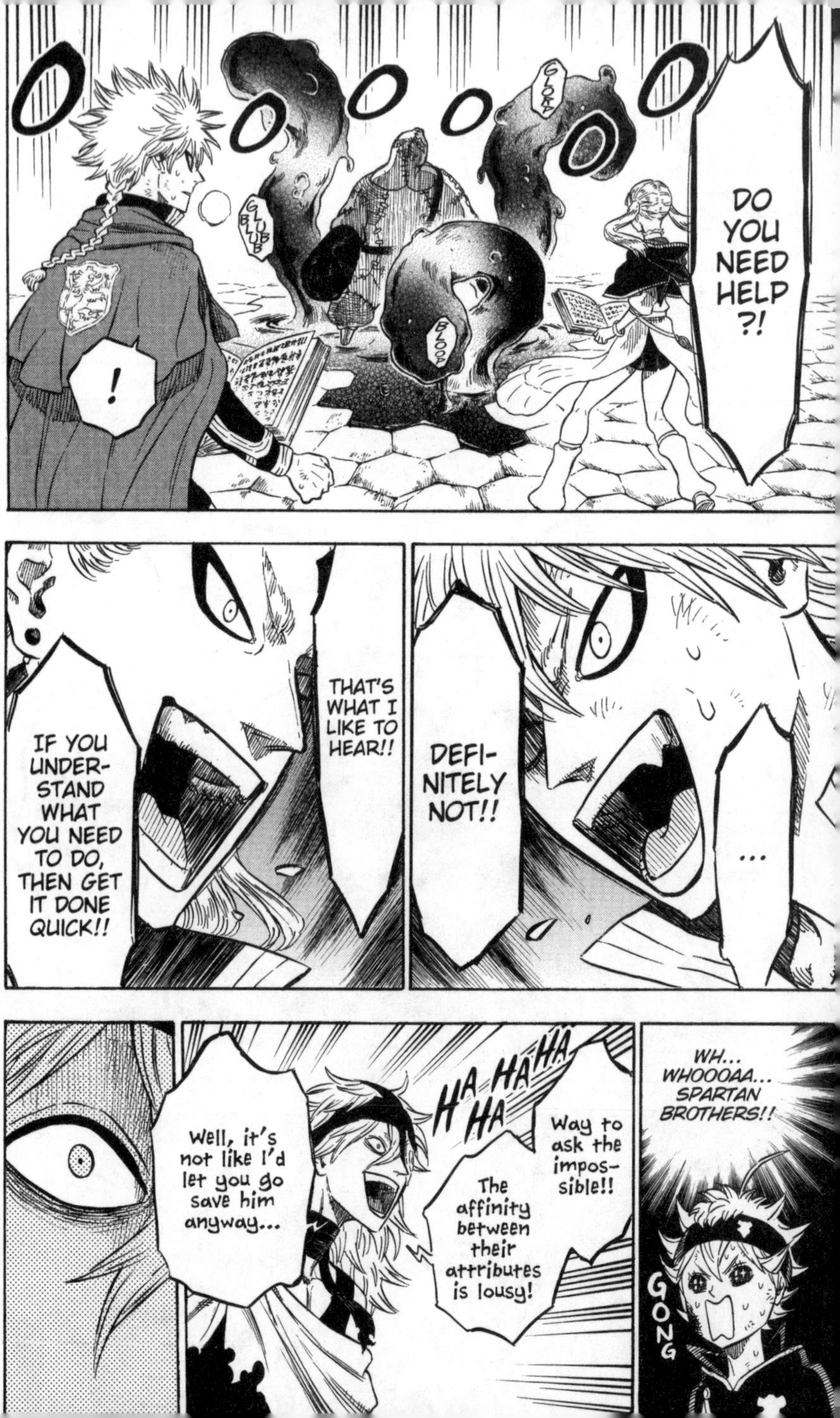
DO YOU NEED HELP?!
GLORP
GLUB BLUB
BLOOP
!
...
DEFINITELY NOT!!
THAT'S WHAT I LIKE TO HEAR!!
IF YOU UNDERSTAND WHAT YOU NEED TO DO, THEN GET IT DONE QUICK!!
WH... WHOOOAA... SPARTAN BROTHERS!!
GONG
Way to ask the impossible!!
HA HA HA HA HA
The affinity between their attributes is lousy!
Well, it's not like I'd let you go save him anyway...

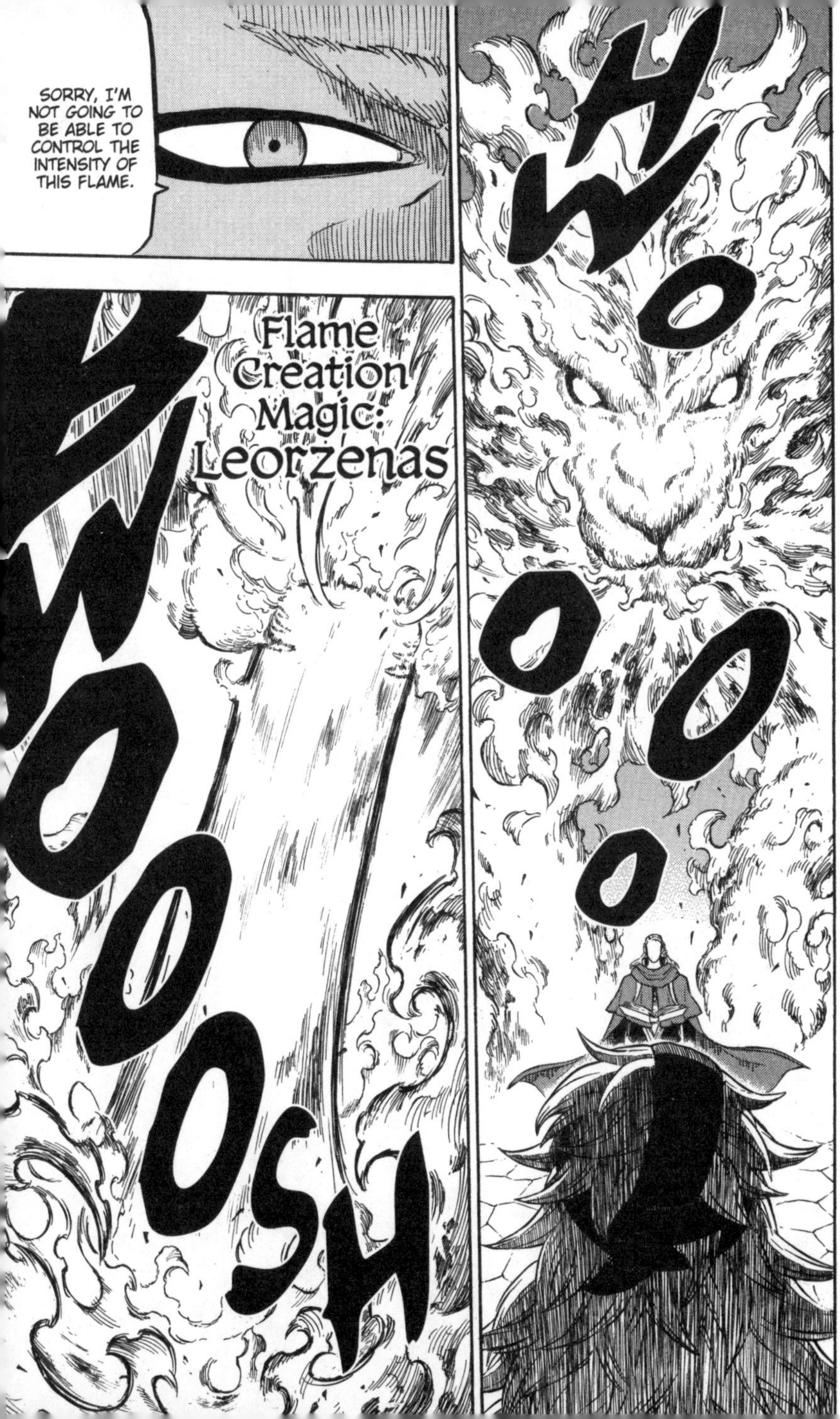
WHOOOOOO
SORRY, I'M NOT GOING TO BE ABLE TO CONTROL THE INTENSITY OF THIS FLAME.
Flame Creation Magic: Leorzenas
WHOOOOOSH

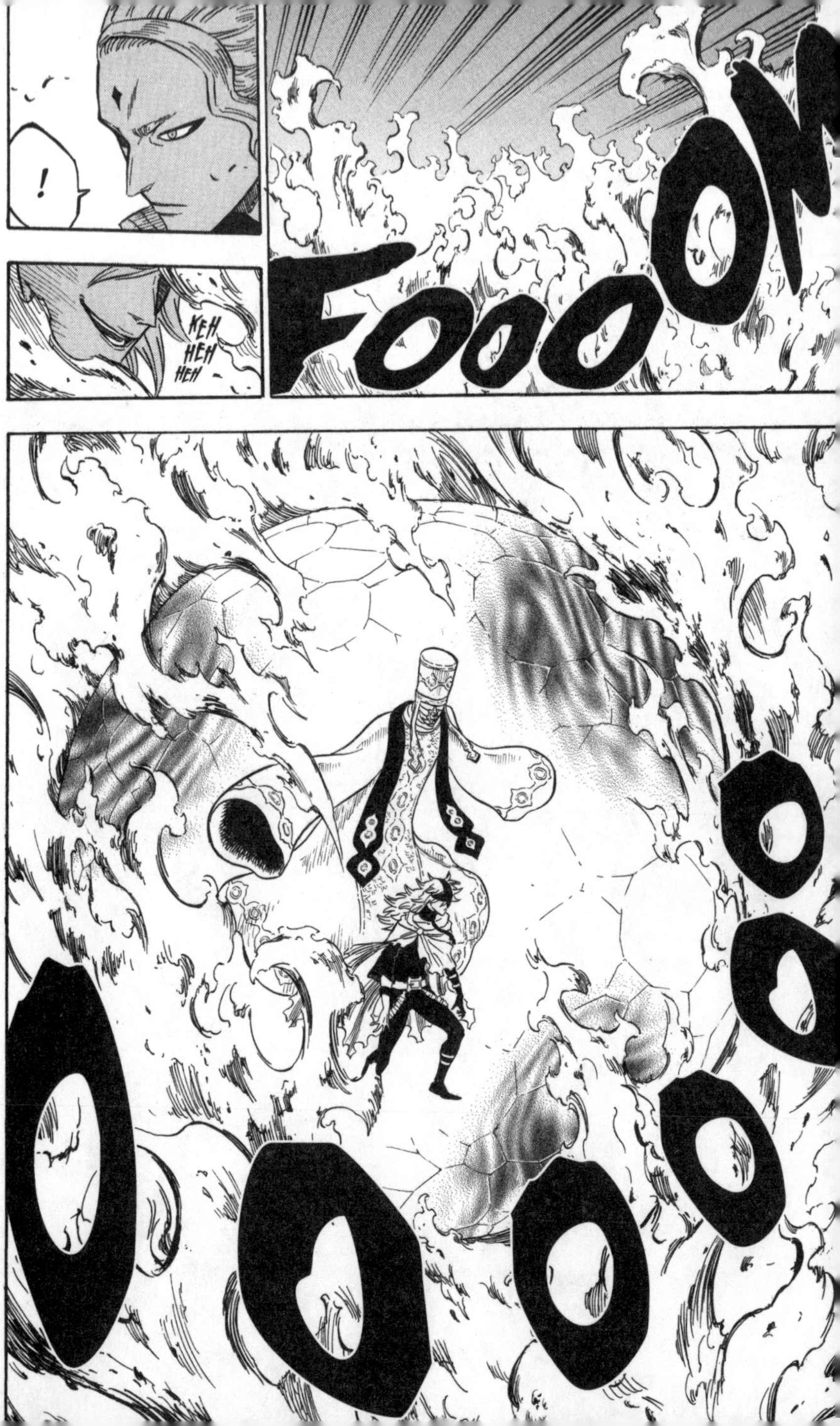
FOOOOOM
!
KEH HEH HEH
OOOOOOO

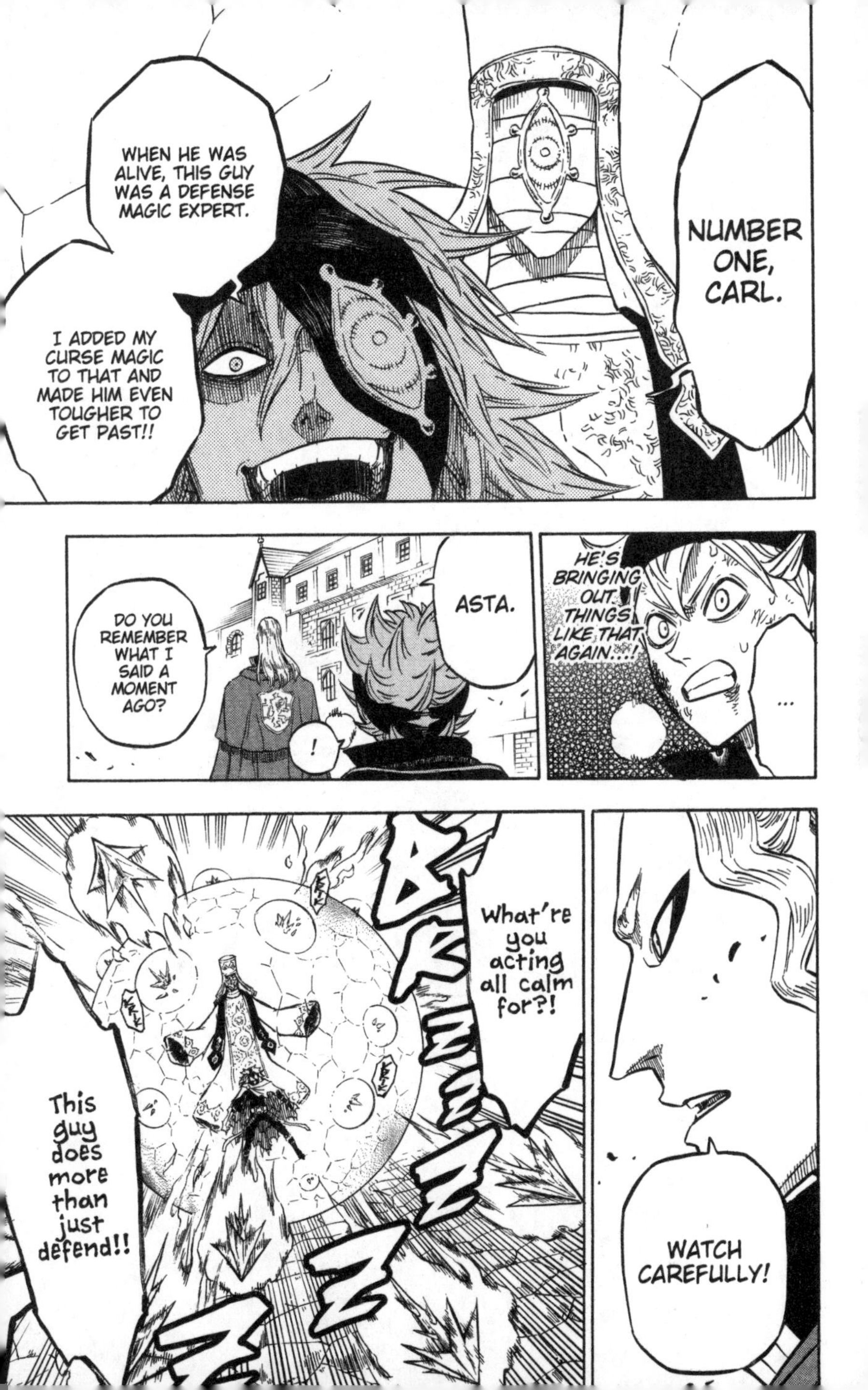
NUMBER ONE, CARL.
WHEN HE WAS ALIVE, THIS GUY WAS A DEFENSE MAGIC EXPERT.
I ADDED MY CURSE MAGIC TO THAT AND MADE HIM EVEN TOUGHER TO GET PAST!!
HE'S BRINGING OUT THINGS LIKE THAT AGAIN...!
...
ASTA.
DO YOU REMEMBER WHAT I SAID A MOMENT AGO?
!
WATCH CAREFULLY!
What're you acting all calm for?!
This guy does more than just defend!!

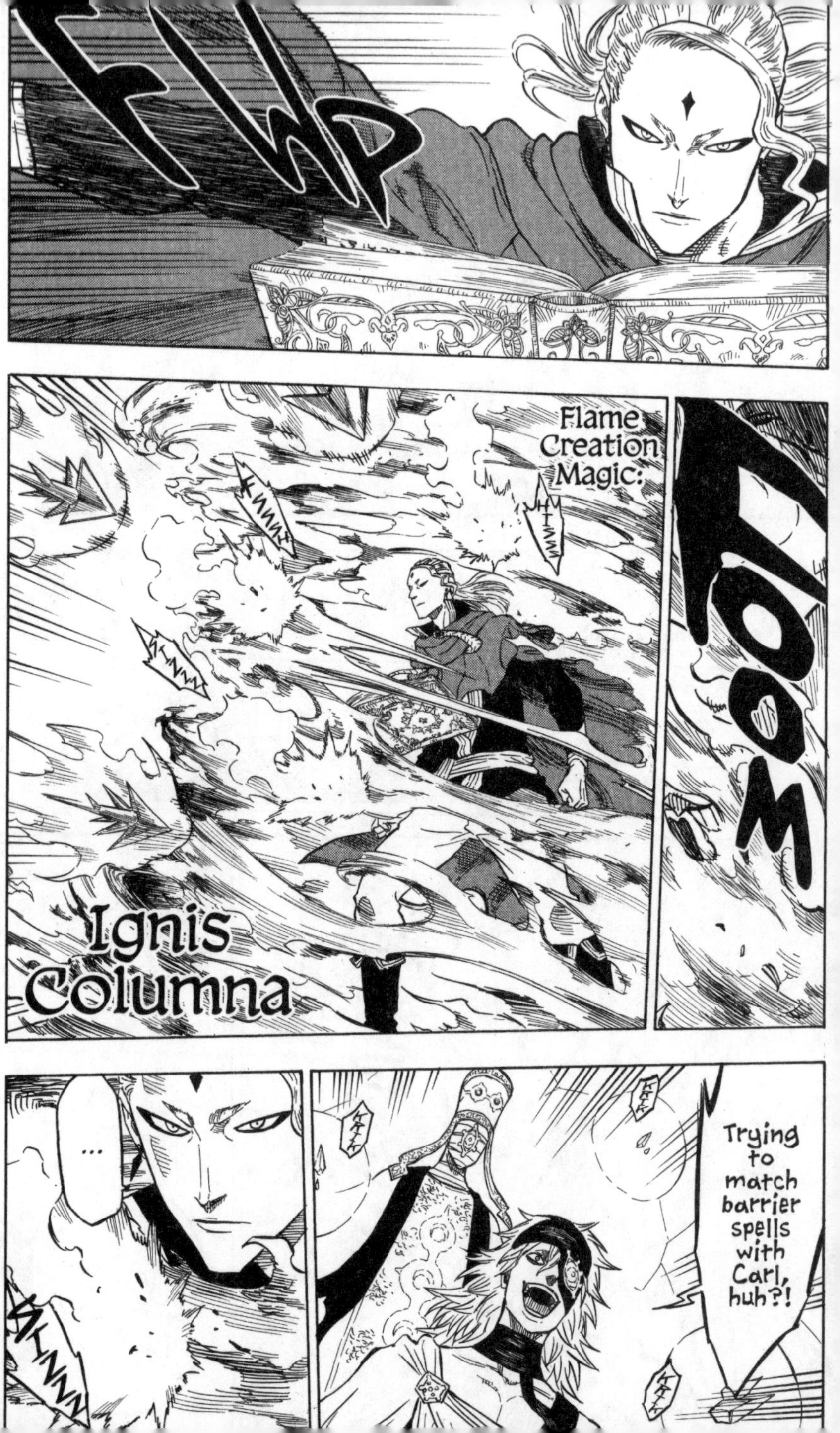
FWP
VOOM
Flame Creation Magic:
HISSS
SHINNN
Ignis Columna
Trying to match barrier spells with Carl, huh?!
...
SHINNN

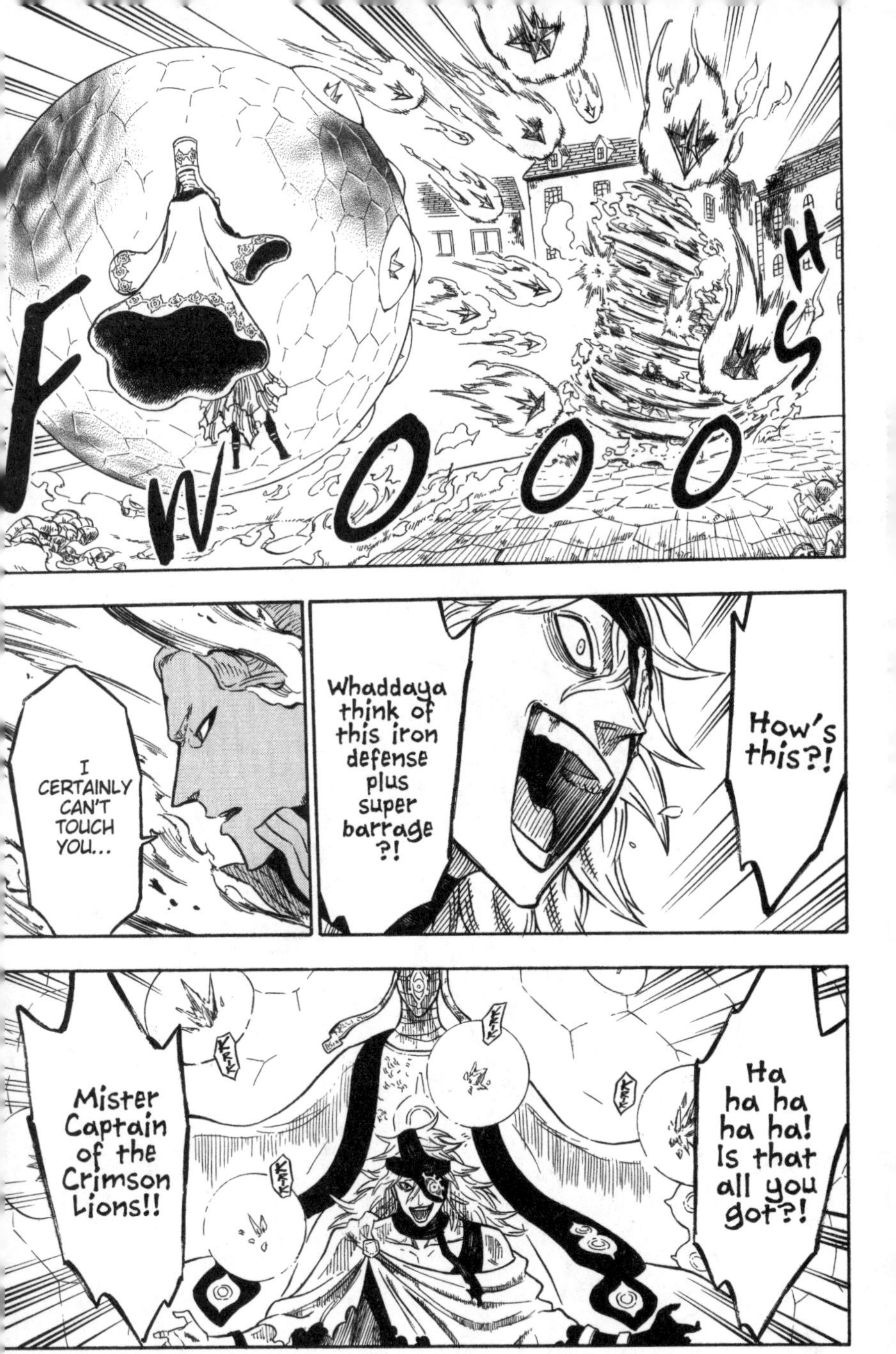
FWOOOOSH
How's this?!
Whaddaya think of this iron defense plus super barrage?!
I CERTAINLY CAN'T TOUCH YOU...
Ha ha ha ha ha! Is that all you got?!
Mister Captain of the Crimson Lions!!

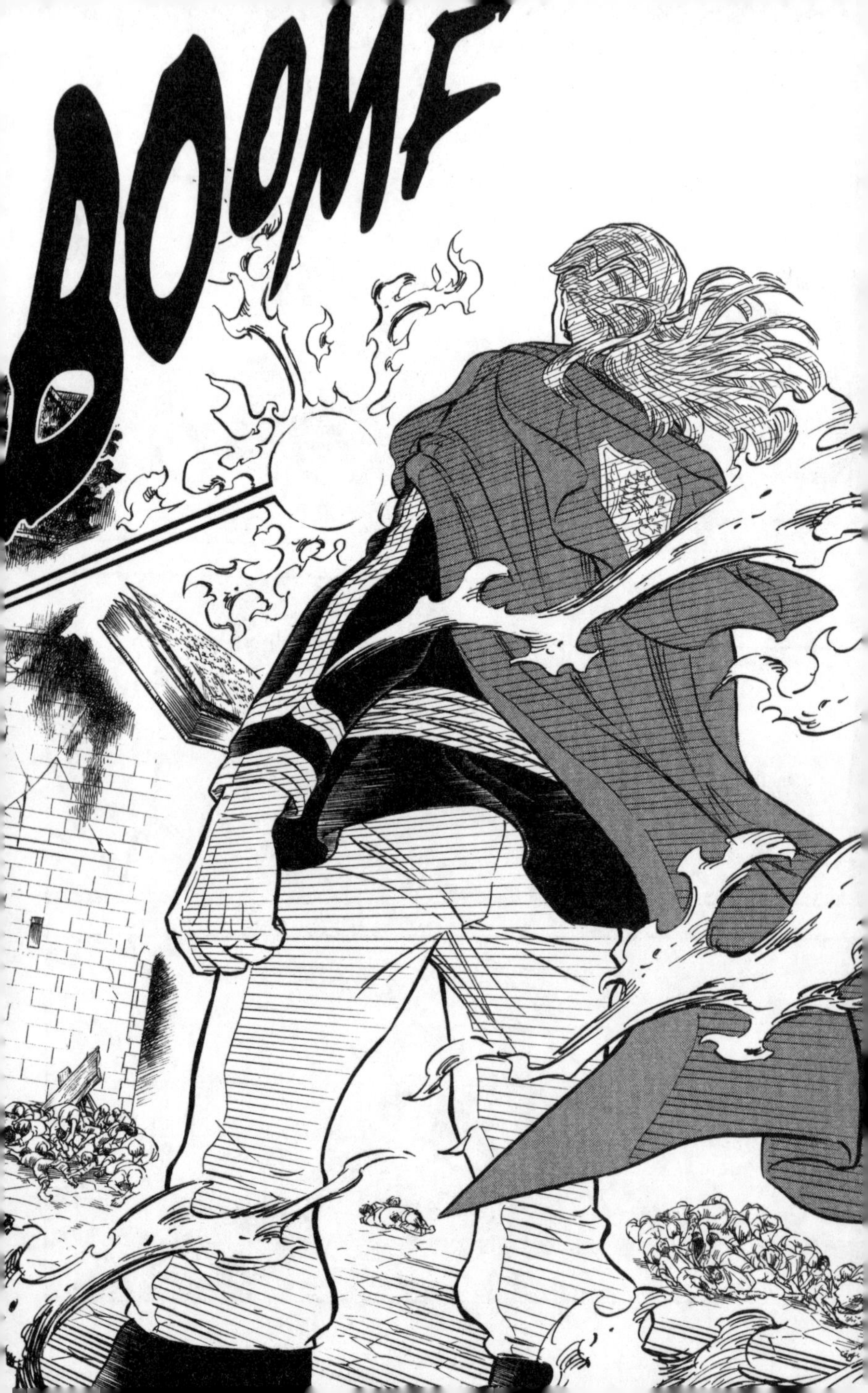
BOOMF

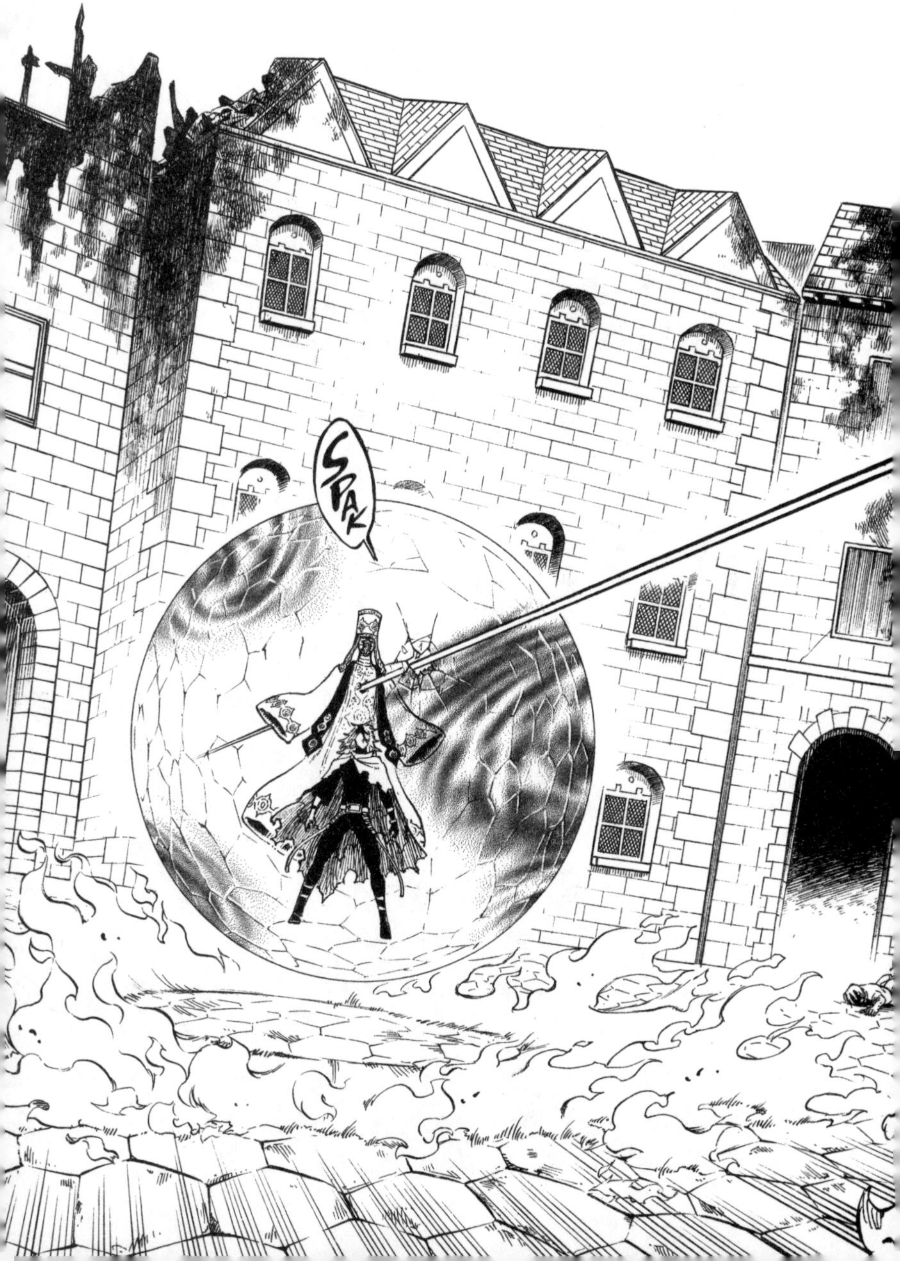
SPAK

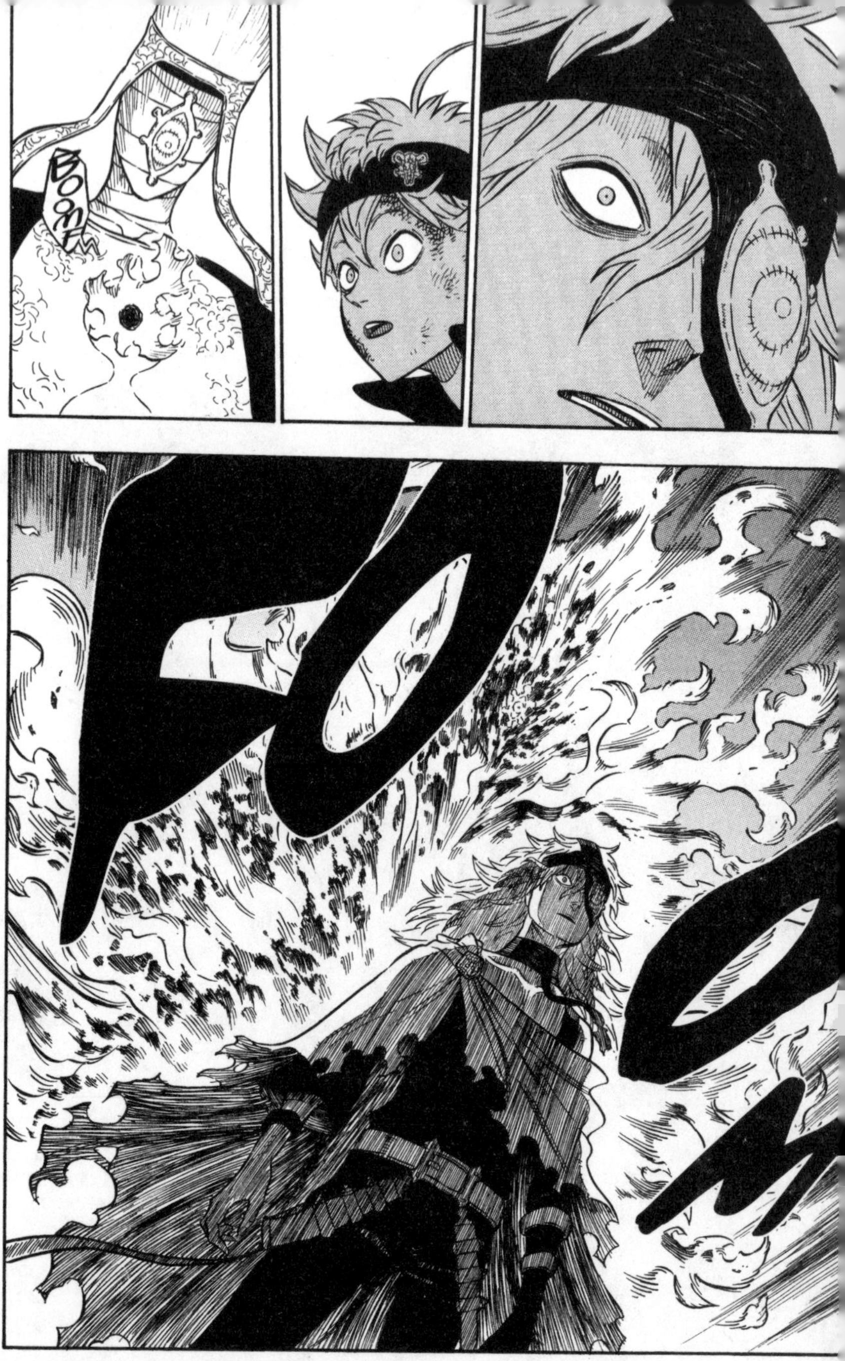
BOOM

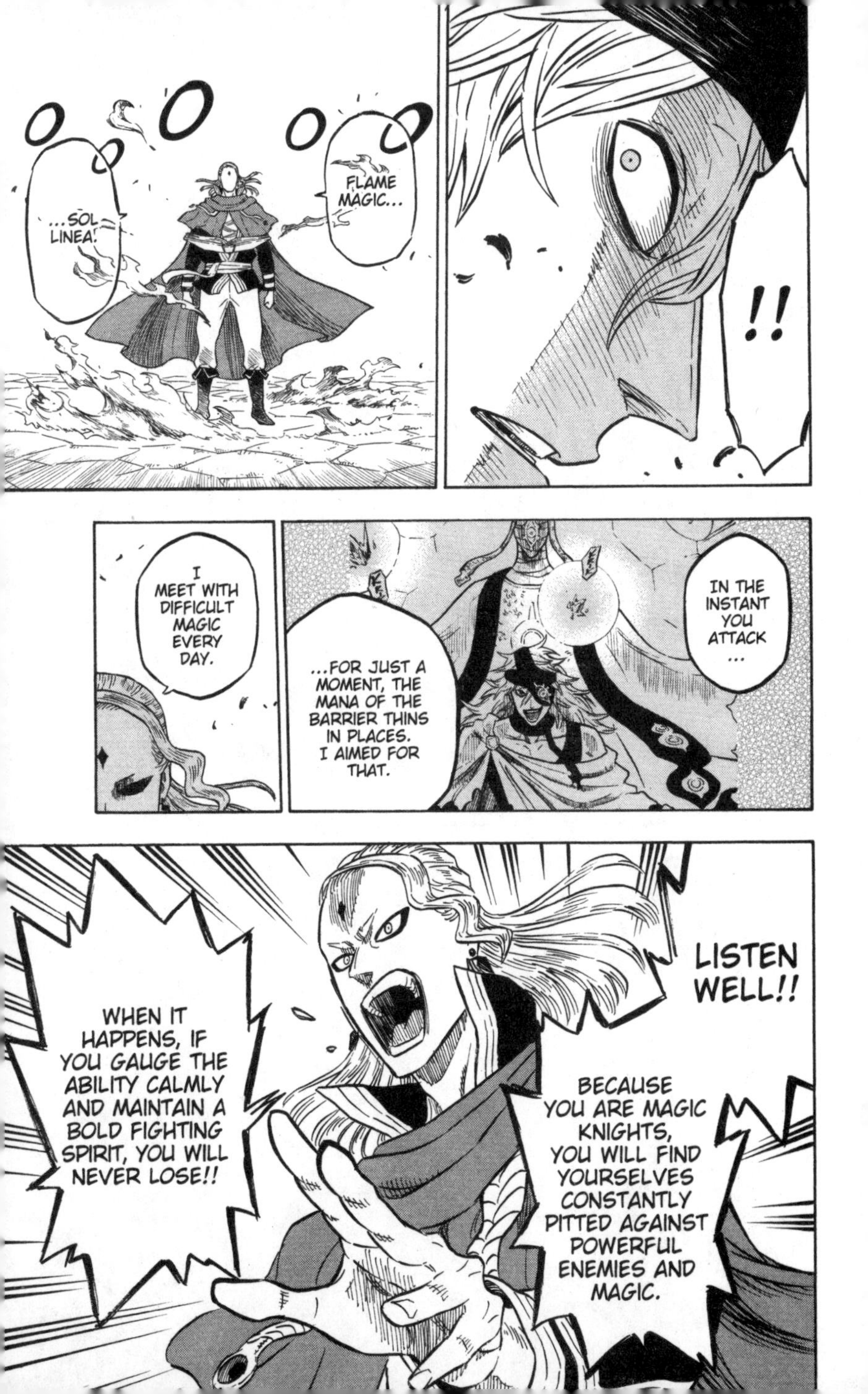
!!
FLAME MAGIC...
...SOL LINEA!
IN THE INSTANT YOU ATTACK ...
...FOR JUST A MOMENT, THE MANA OF THE BARRIER THINS IN PLACES. I AIMED FOR THAT.
I MEET WITH DIFFICULT MAGIC EVERY DAY.
LISTEN WELL!!
BECAUSE YOU ARE MAGIC KNIGHTS, YOU WILL FIND YOURSELVES CONSTANTLY PITTED AGAINST POWERFUL ENEMIES AND MAGIC.
WHEN IT HAPPENS, IF YOU GAUGE THE ABILITY CALMLY AND MAINTAIN A BOLD FIGHTING SPIRIT, YOU WILL NEVER LOSE!!

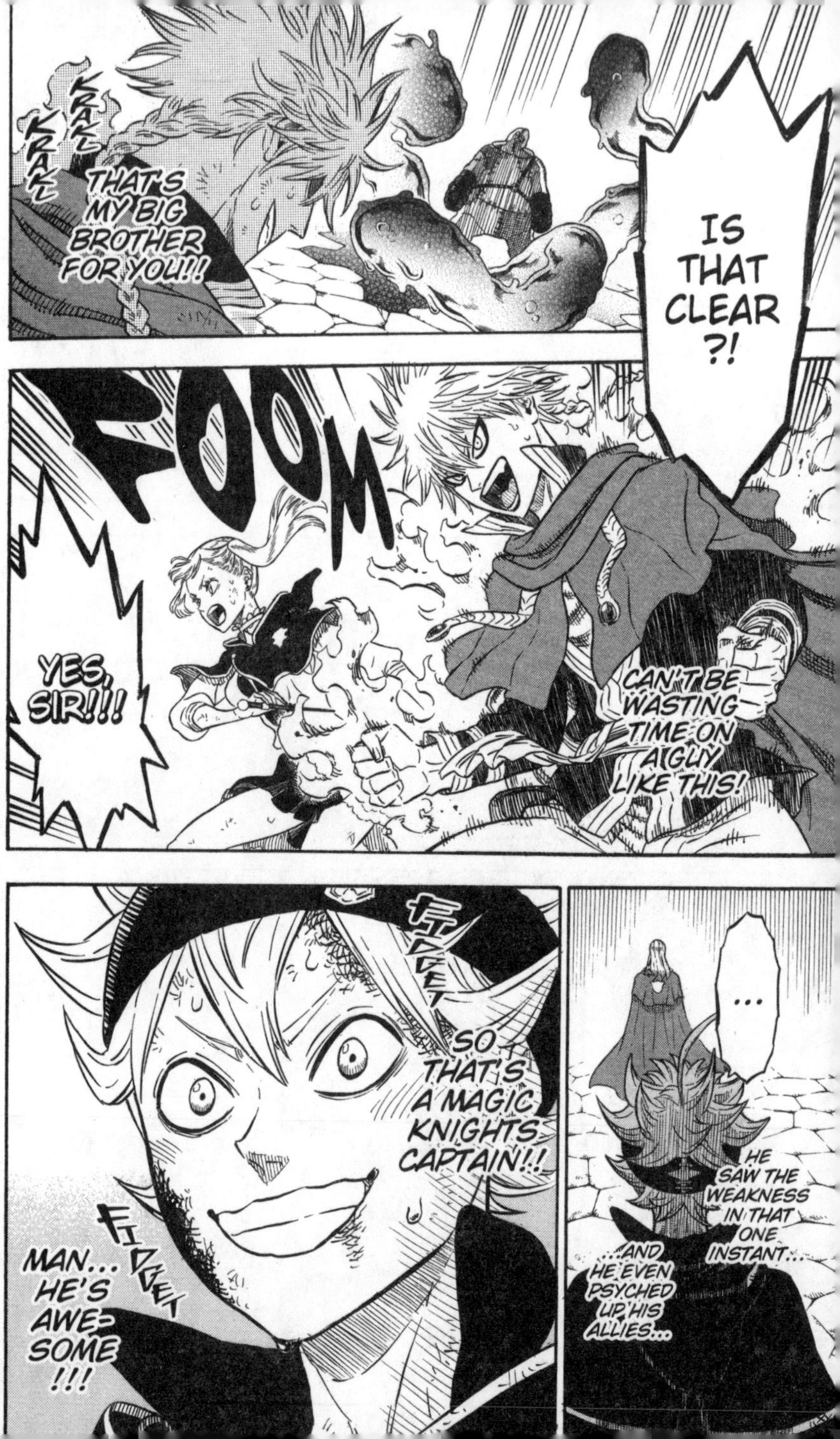

IS THAT CLEAR ?!
KRAKL KRAKL
THAT'S MY BIG BROTHER FOR YOU!!
FOOM
CAN'T BE WASTING TIME ON A GUY LIKE THIS!
YES, SIR!!!
...
HE SAW THE WEAKNESS IN THAT ONE INSTANT...
...AND HE EVEN PSYCHED UP HIS ALLIES...
FIDGET
SO THAT'S A MAGIC KNIGHTS CAPTAIN!!
FIDGET
MAN... HE'S AWE-SOME!!!

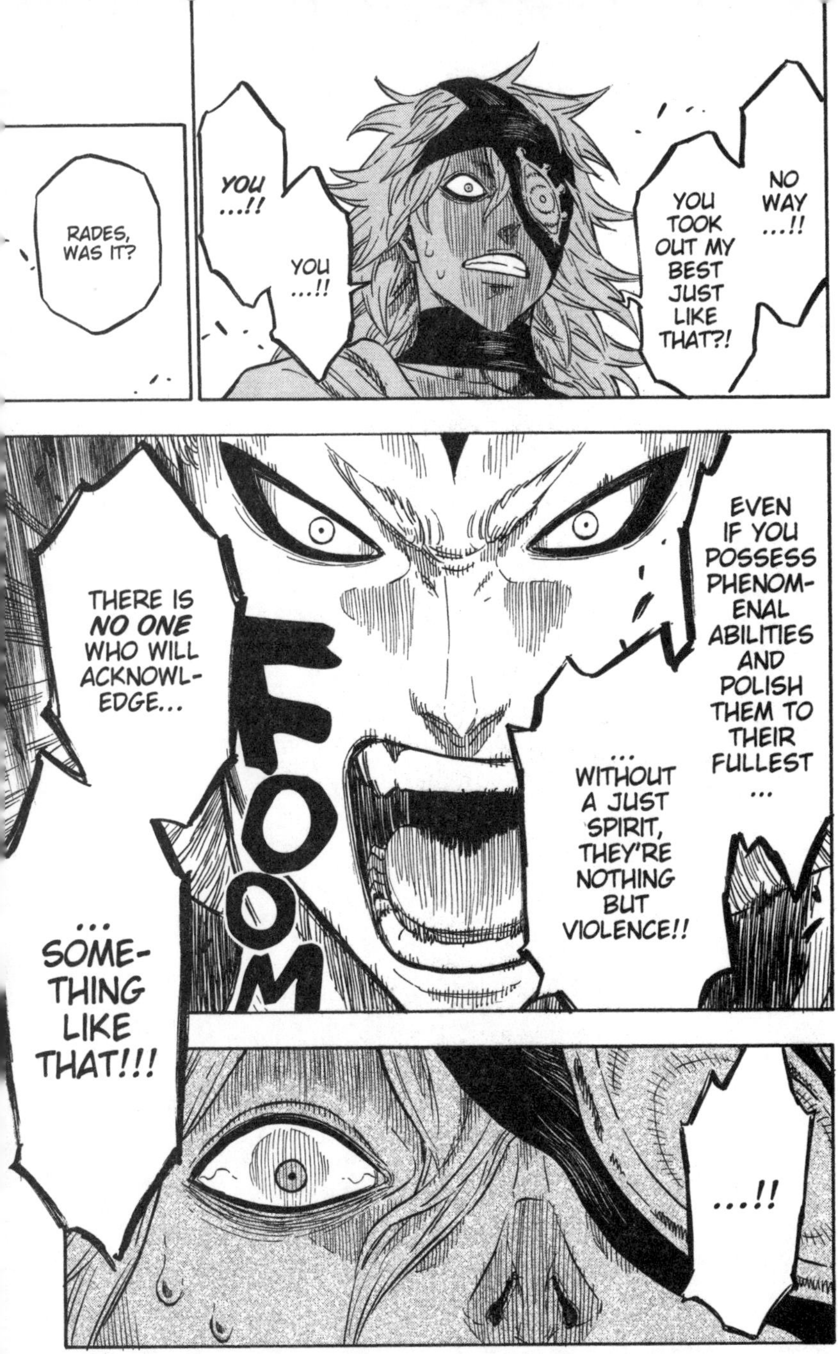
NO WAY...!!
YOU TOOK OUT MY BEST JUST LIKE THAT?!
YOU...!!
YOU...!!
RADES, WAS IT?
EVEN IF YOU POSSESS PHENOMENAL ABILITIES AND POLISH THEM TO THEIR FULLEST...
...WITHOUT A JUST SPIRIT, THEY'RE NOTHING BUT VIOLENCE!!
FOOM
THERE IS NO ONE WHO WILL ACKNOWLEDGE...
...SOMETHING LIKE THAT!!!
...!!

Fuegoleon Vermillion

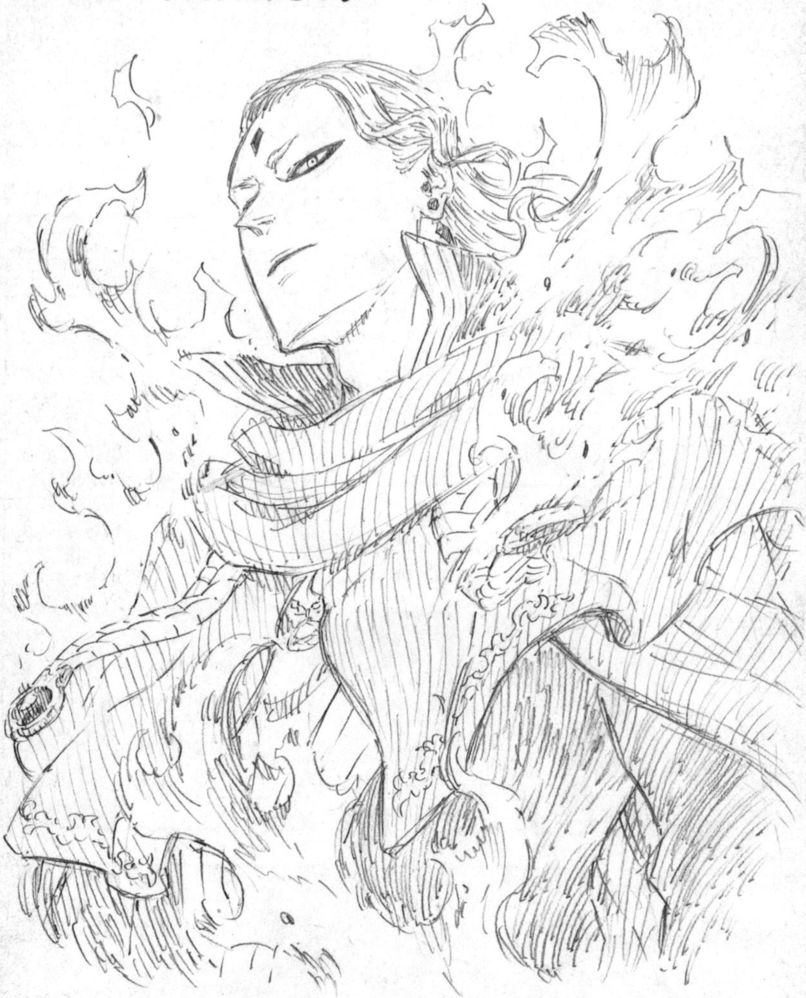

Age: 30 Height: 188 cm
Birthday: August 5 Sign: Leo Blood Type: A
Likes: People who want to improve, long soaks in large public baths

Character Profile

✤ Page 32:
The One Who Waits Deep in the Darkness

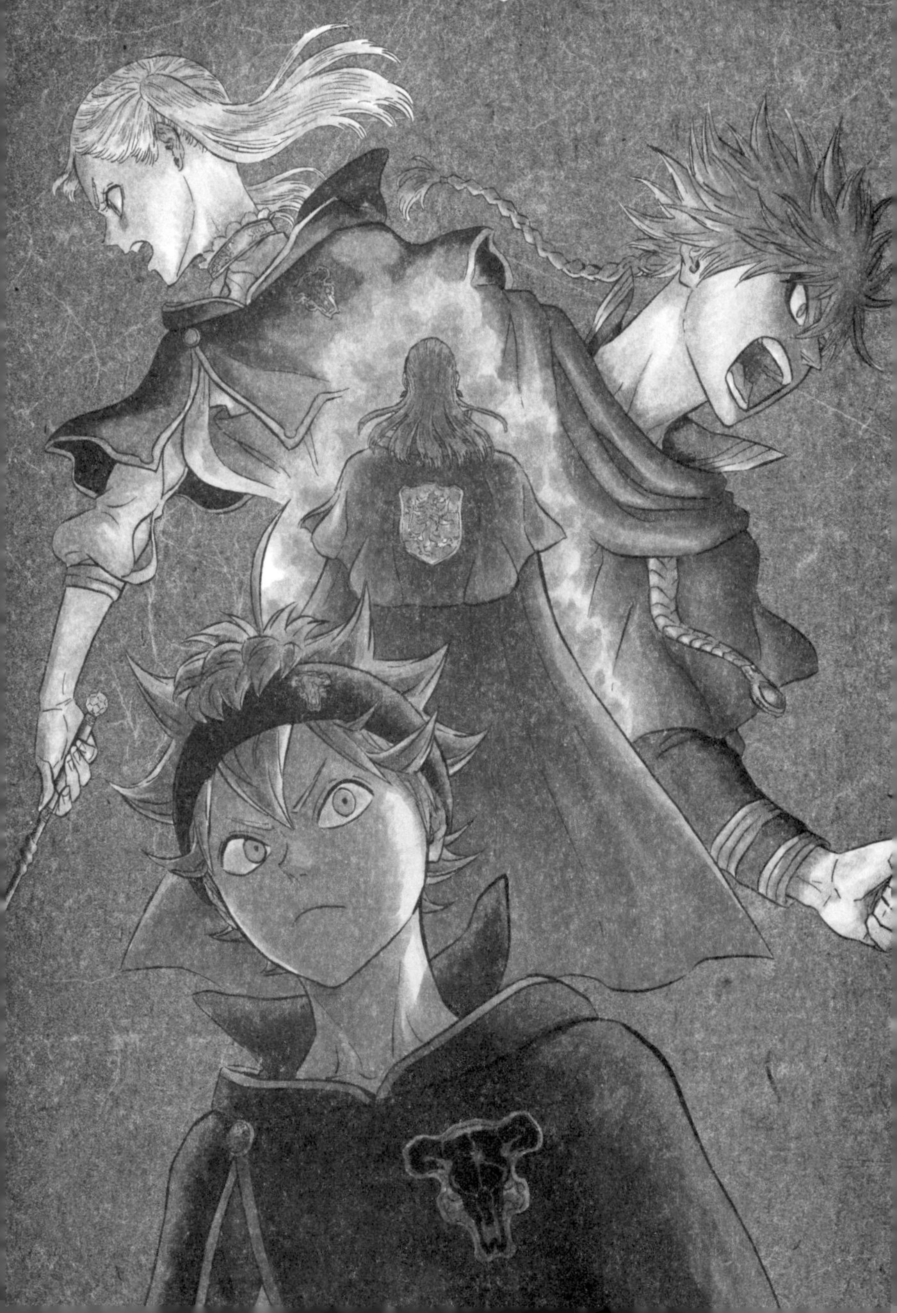

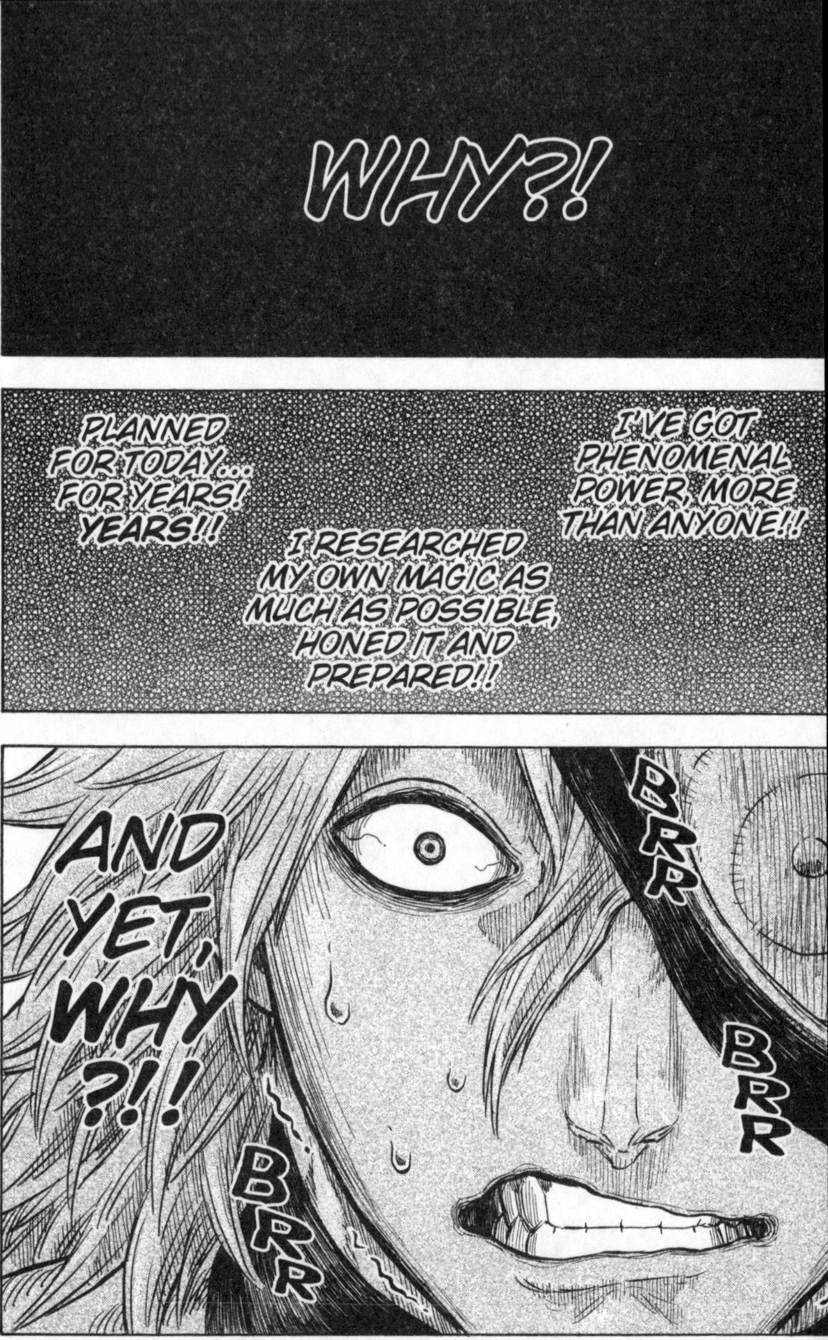
WHY?!
I'VE GOT PHENOMENAL POWER, MORE THAN ANYONE!!
I RESEARCHED MY OWN MAGIC AS MUCH AS POSSIBLE, HONED IT AND PREPARED!!
PLANNED FOR TODAY... FOR YEARS! YEARS!!
BRR
BRR
AND YET, WHY?!!
BRR

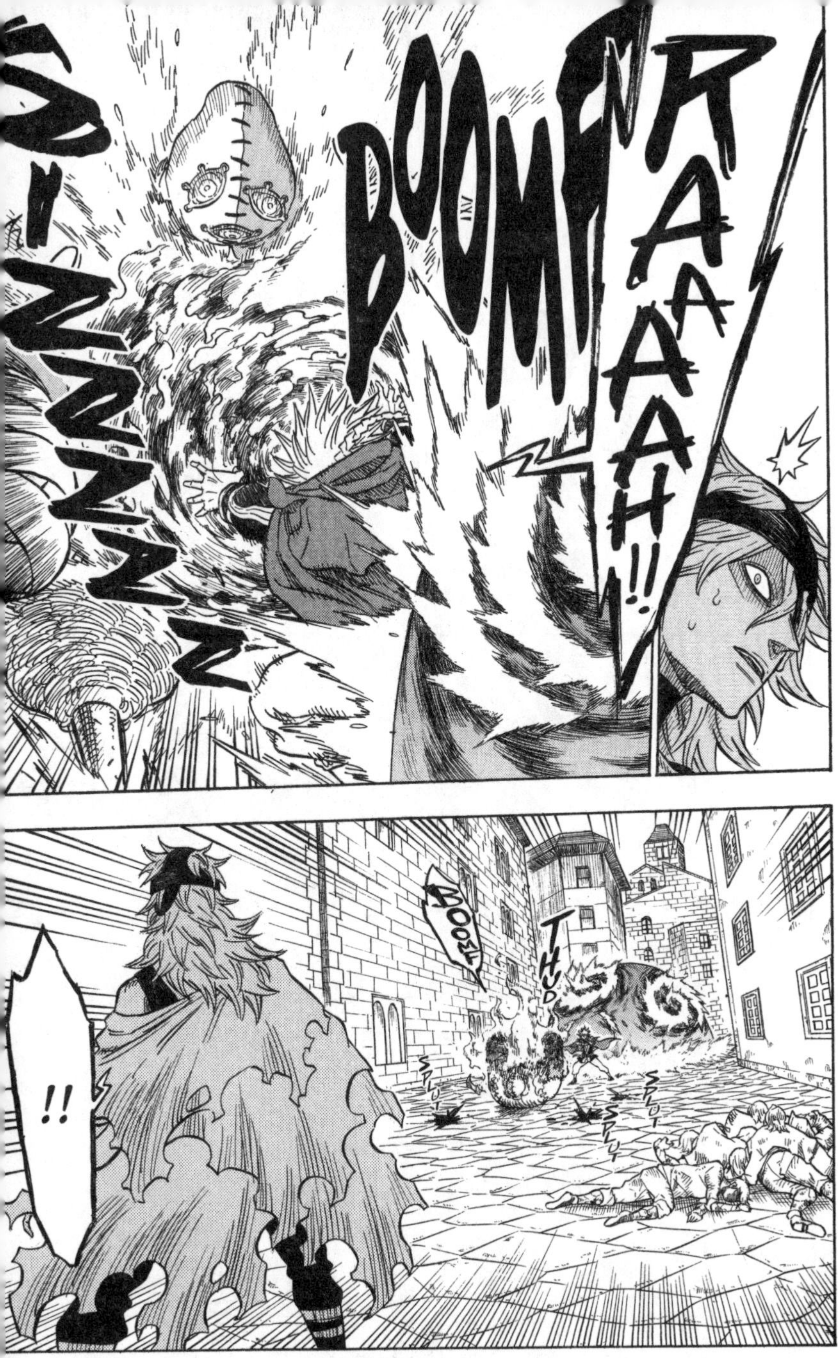
RAAAAH!!
BOOM
ZZZZZZ!!
!!
BOOM
THUD
SPLUT
SPLUT
SPLUT

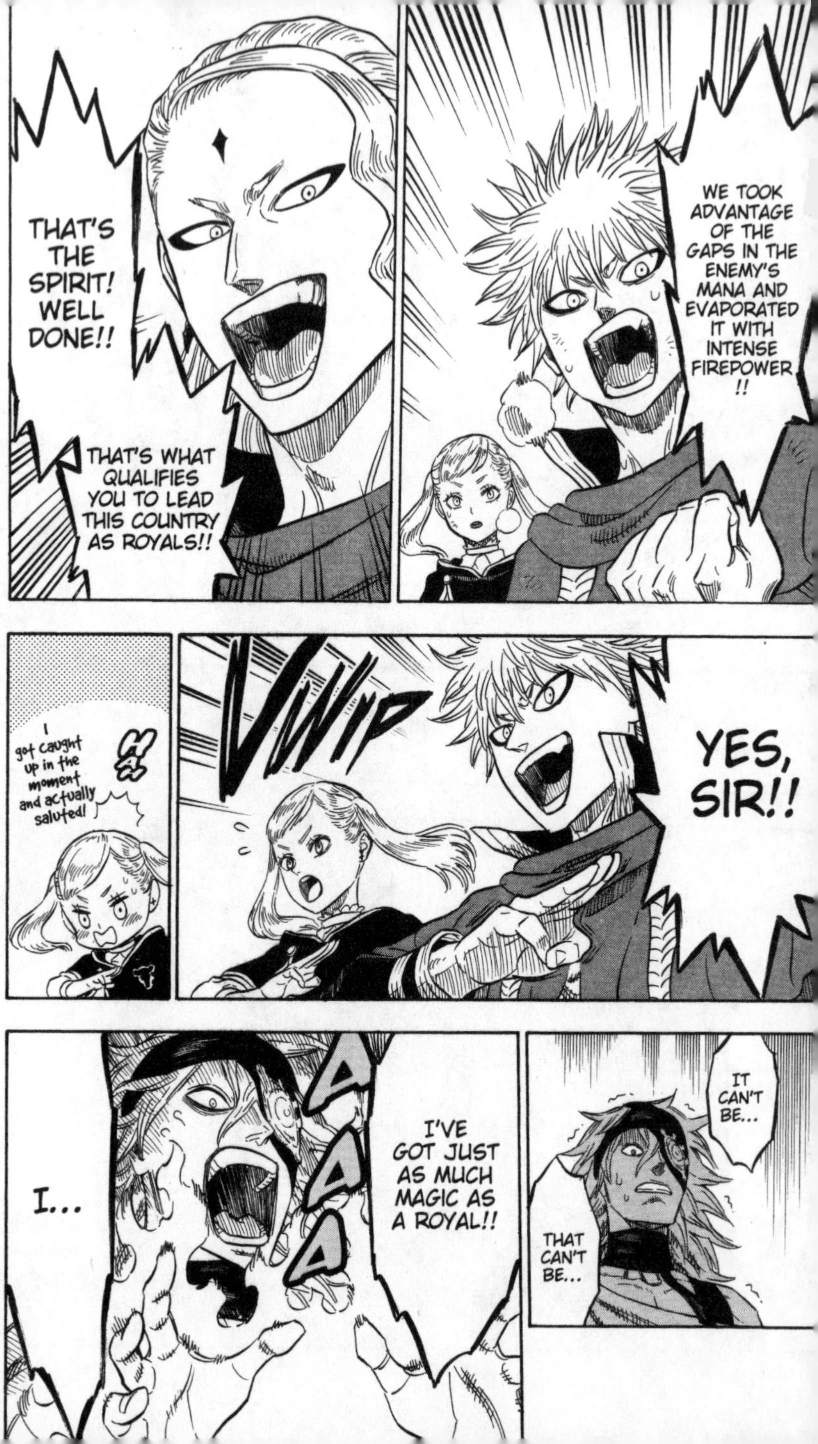
WE TOOK ADVANTAGE OF THE GAPS IN THE ENEMY'S MANA AND EVAPORATED IT WITH INTENSE FIREPOWER!!
THAT'S THE SPIRIT! WELL DONE!!
THAT'S WHAT QUALIFIES YOU TO LEAD THIS COUNTRY AS ROYALS!!
YES, SIR!!
VWIP
HA
I got caught up in the moment and actually saluted!
IT CAN'T BE...
THAT CAN'T BE...
I'VE GOT JUST AS MUCH MAGIC AS A ROYAL!!
AAAA
I...

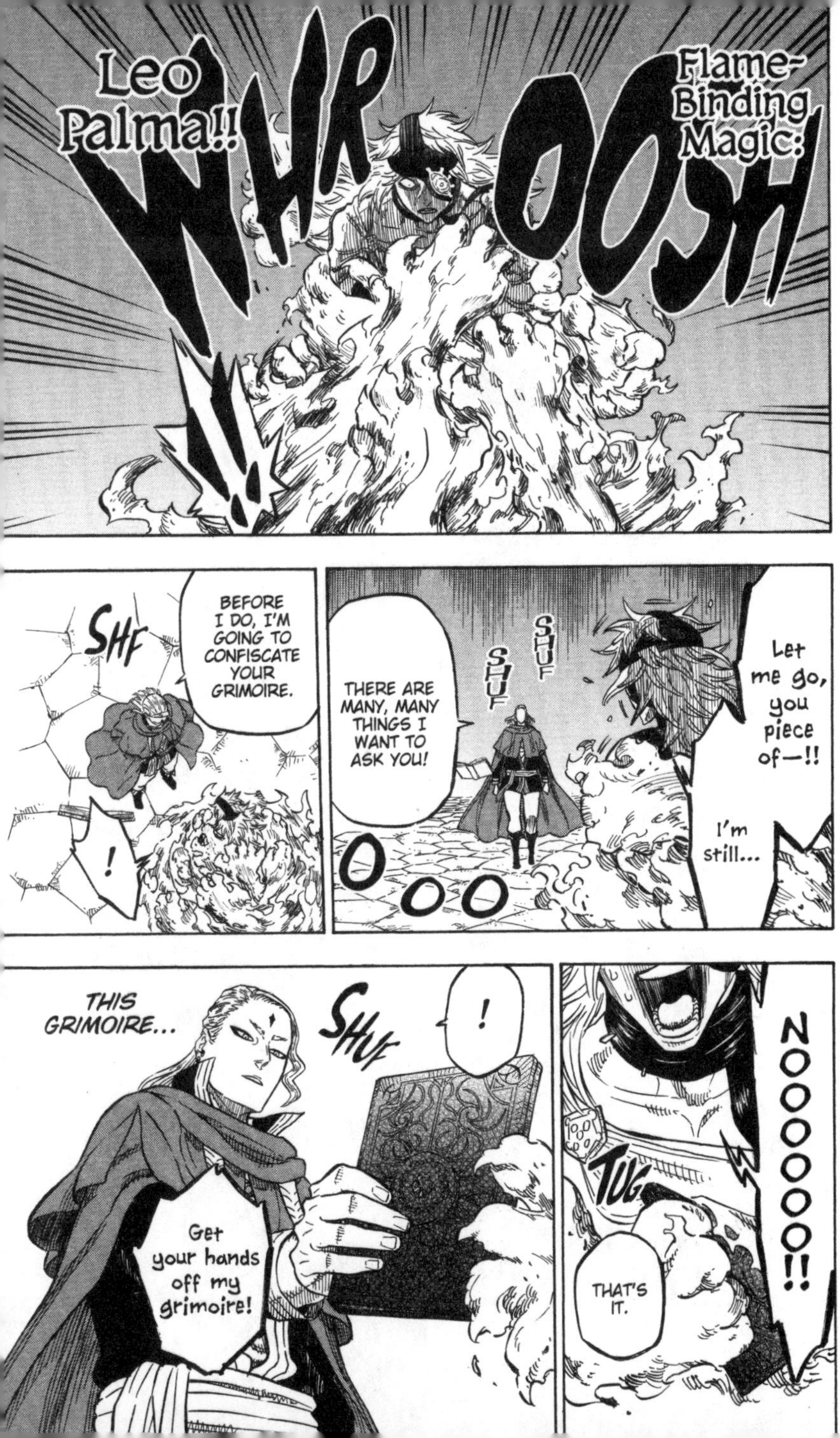
Flame-Binding Magic:
Leo Palma!!
WHROOSH
Let me go, you piece of—!!
I'm still...
SHUF
SHUF
THERE ARE MANY, MANY THINGS I WANT TO ASK YOU!
OOO
BEFORE I DO, I'M GOING TO CONFISCATE YOUR GRIMOIRE.
SHF
!
NOOOOOOO!!
TUG
THAT'S IT.
!
THIS GRIMOIRE...
SHUF
Get your hands off my grimoire!

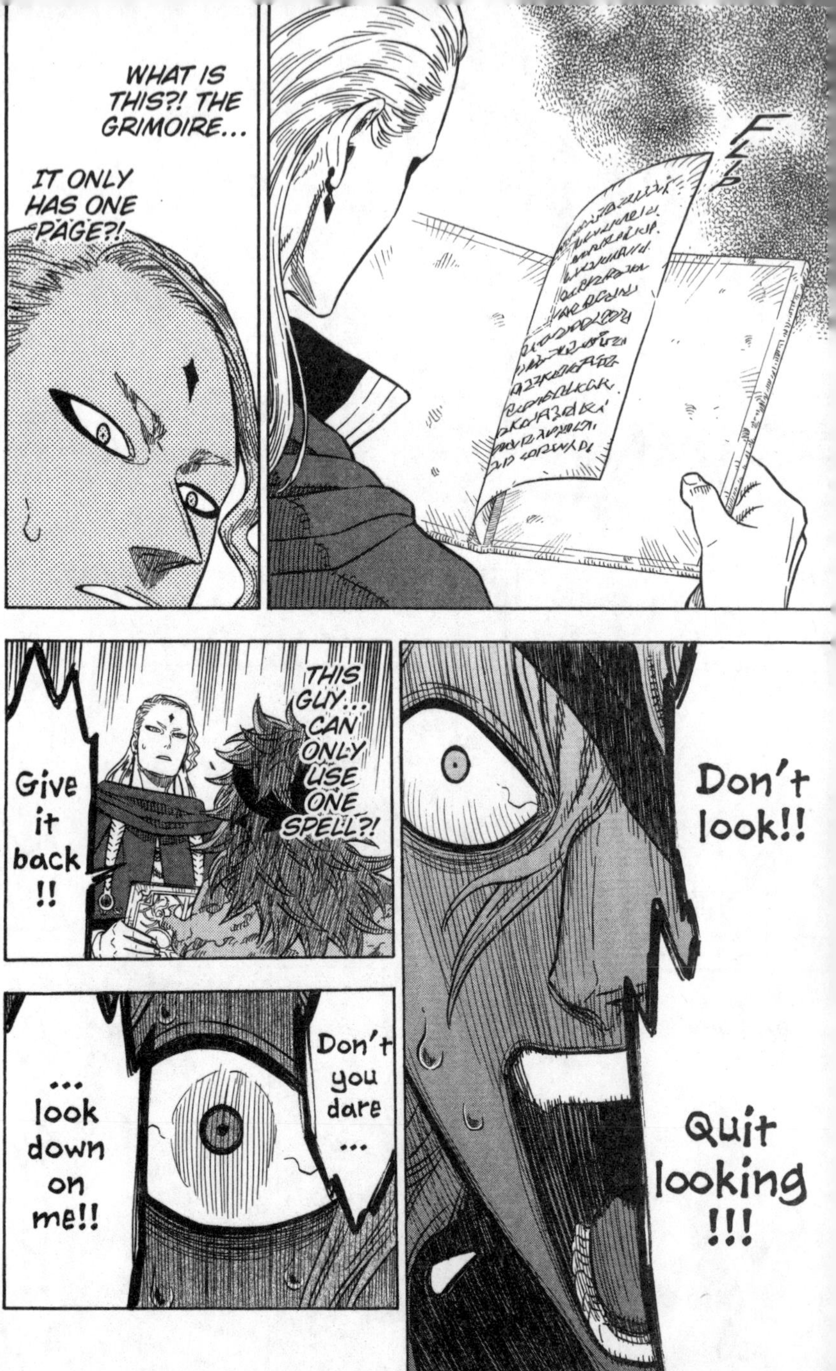
FLIP
WHAT IS THIS?! THE GRIMOIRE...
IT ONLY HAS ONE PAGE?!
Don't look!!
Quit looking!!!
THIS GUY... CAN ONLY USE ONE SPELL?!
Give it back!!
Don't you dare...
...look down on me!!

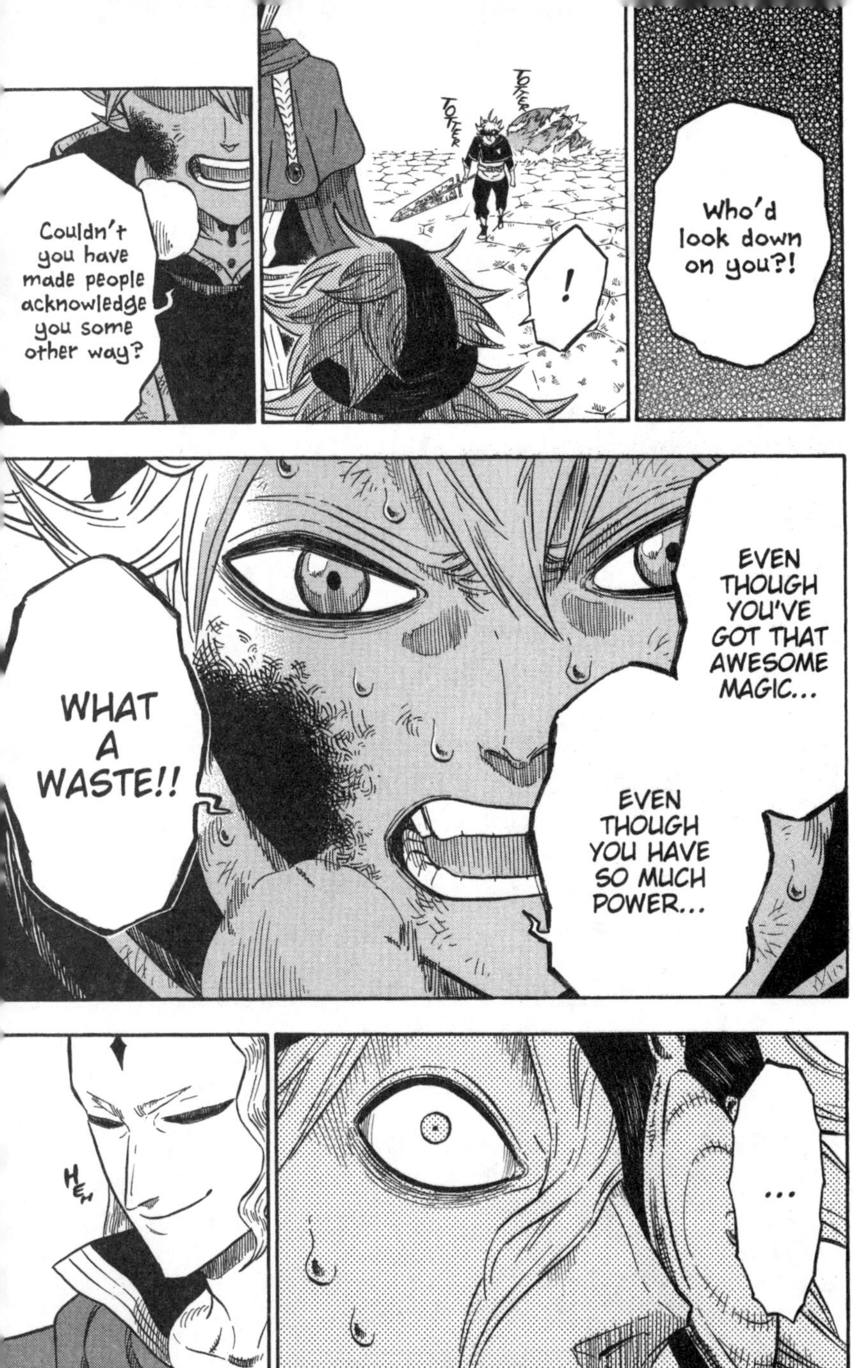
Who'd look down on you?!
TOKKER
TOKKER
!
Couldn't you have made people acknowledge you some other way?
EVEN THOUGH YOU'VE GOT THAT AWESOME MAGIC...
EVEN THOUGH YOU HAVE SO MUCH POWER...
WHAT A WASTE!!
...
HEH

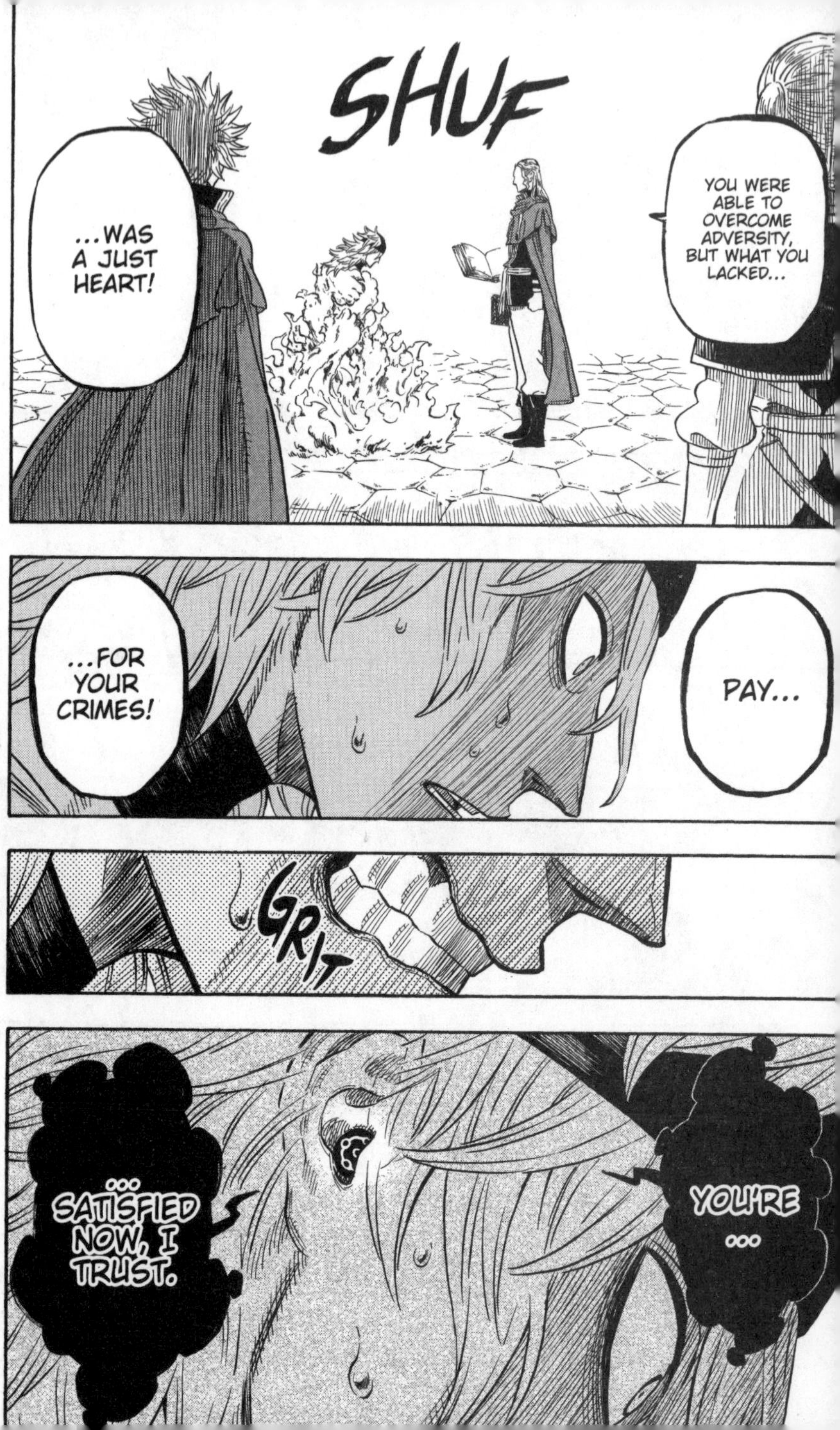
YOU WERE ABLE TO OVERCOME ADVERSITY, BUT WHAT YOU LACKED...
SHUF
...WAS A JUST HEART!
PAY...
...FOR YOUR CRIMES!
GRIT
YOU'RE ...
... SATISFIED NOW, I TRUST.

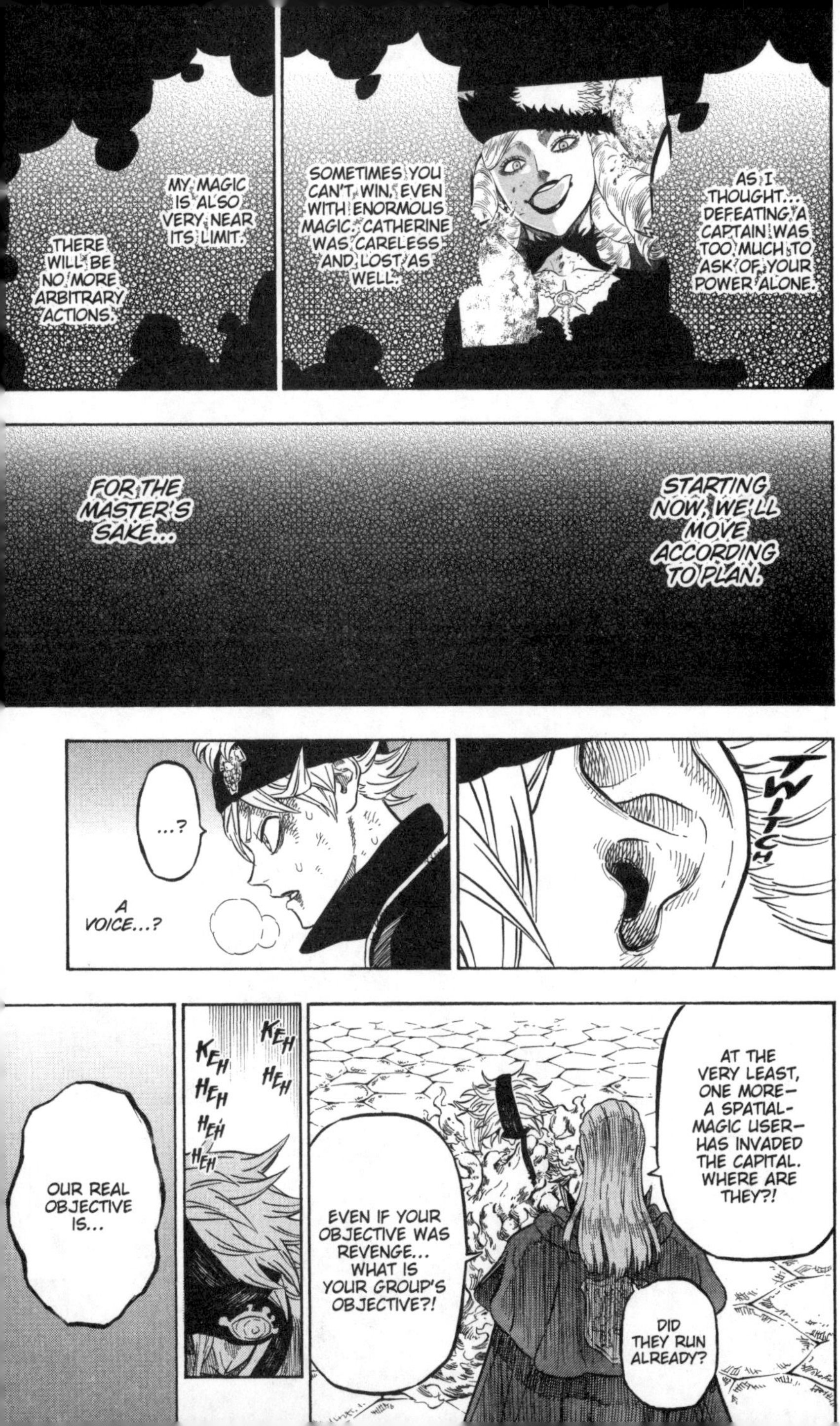
AS I THOUGHT... DEFEATING A CAPTAIN WAS TOO MUCH TO ASK OF YOUR POWER ALONE.
SOMETIMES YOU CAN'T WIN, EVEN WITH ENORMOUS MAGIC. CATHERINE WAS CARELESS AND LOST AS WELL.
MY MAGIC IS ALSO VERY NEAR ITS LIMIT.
THERE WILL BE NO MORE ARBITRARY ACTIONS.
STARTING NOW, WE'LL MOVE ACCORDING TO PLAN.
FOR THE MASTER'S SAKE...
TWITCH
...?
A VOICE...?
AT THE VERY LEAST, ONE MORE— A SPATIAL-MAGIC USER— HAS INVADED THE CAPITAL. WHERE ARE THEY?!
EVEN IF YOUR OBJECTIVE WAS REVENGE... WHAT IS YOUR GROUP'S OBJECTIVE?!
DID THEY RUN ALREADY?
KEH HEH
KEH HEH HEH HEH
OUR REAL OBJECTIVE IS...

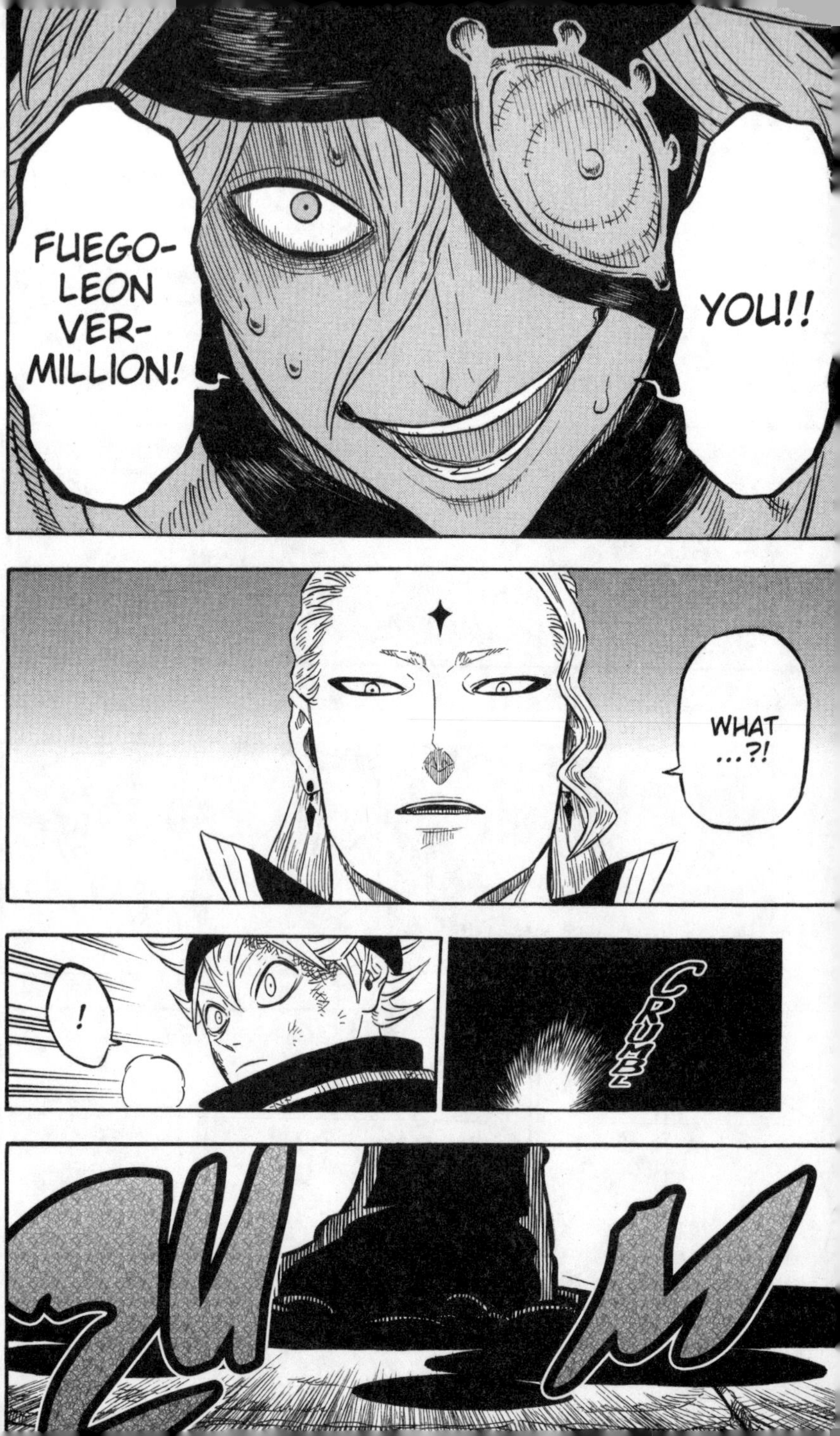
YOU!!
FUEGO-LEON VER-MILLION!
WHAT ...?!
CRUMBLE
!
ZUM

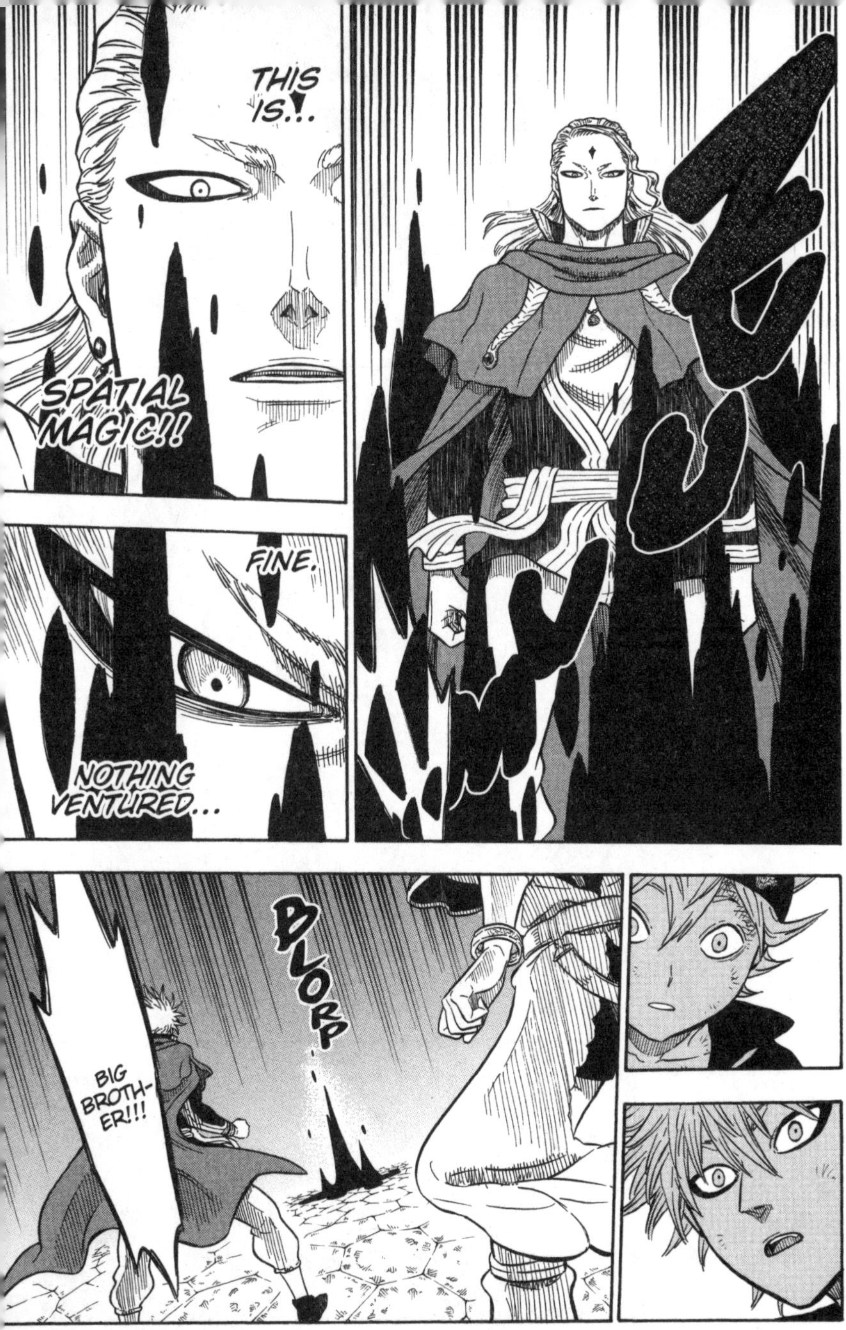
THIS IS...!
SPATIAL MAGIC!!
FINE.
NOTHING VENTURED...
BLORP
BIG BROTHER!!!

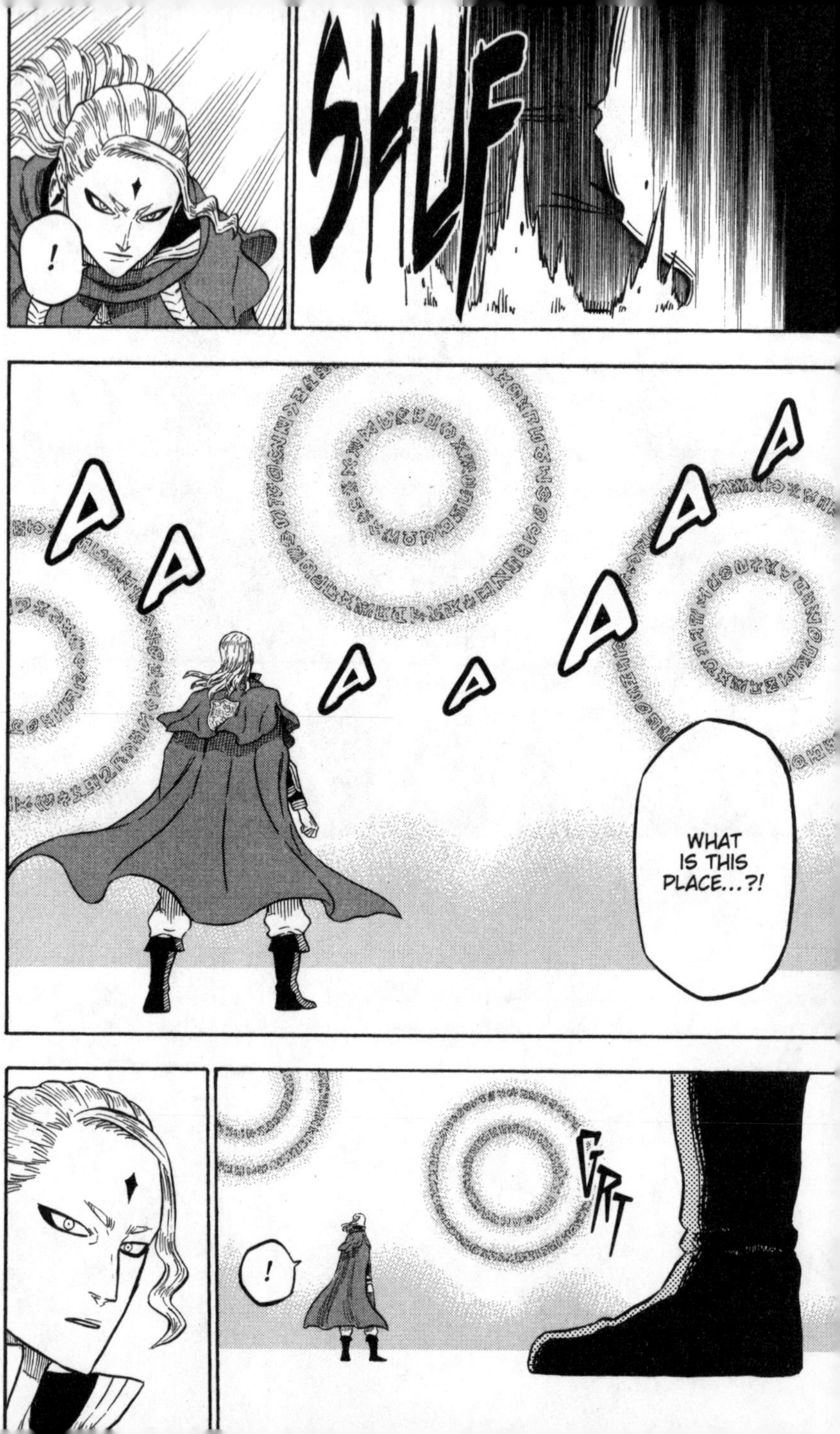
SHUF
!
AAAAAAAA
WHAT IS THIS PLACE...?!
GRT
!

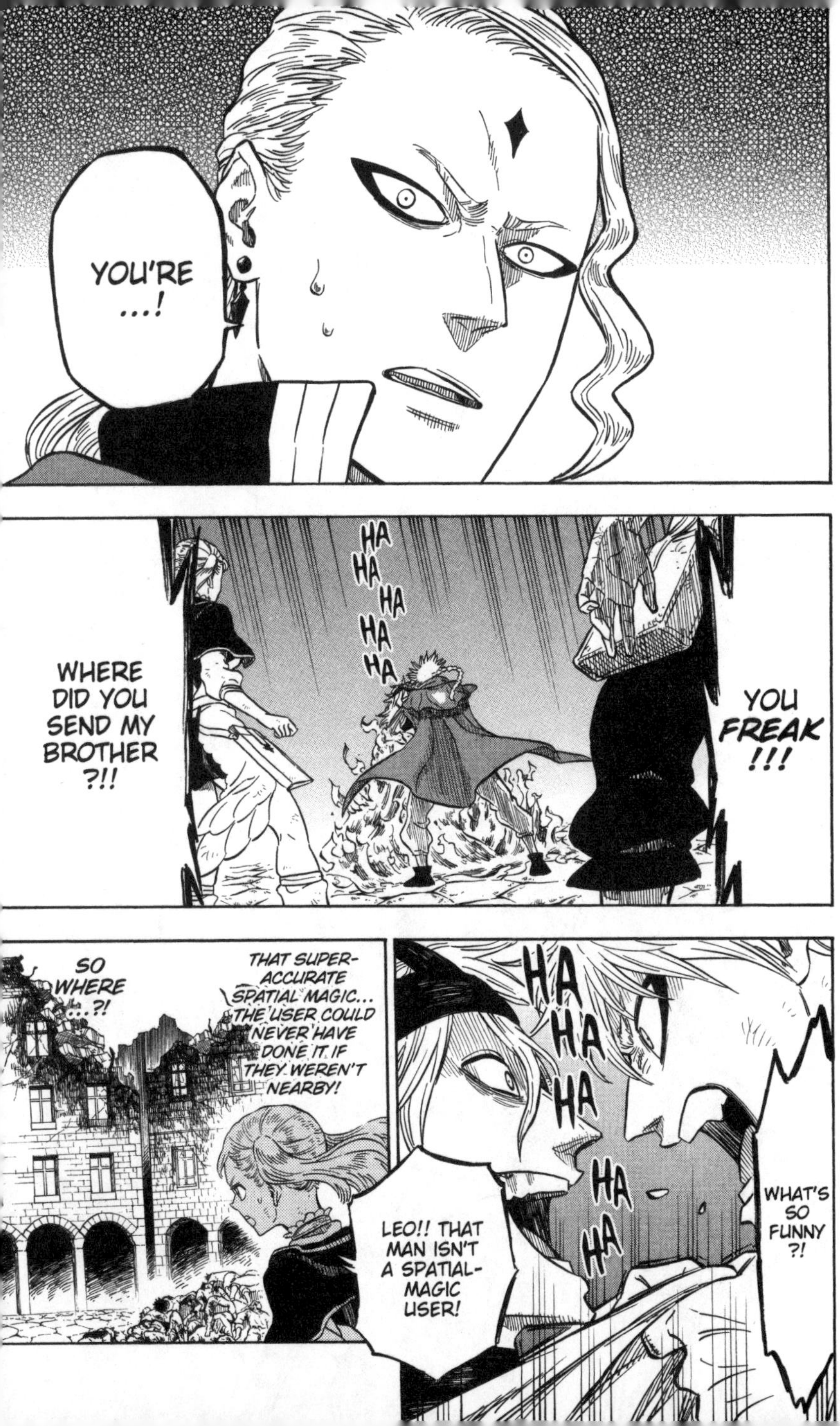
YOU'RE ...!
HA HA HA HA HA
YOU FREAK!!!
WHERE DID YOU SEND MY BROTHER?!!
HA HA HA HA HA HA
WHAT'S SO FUNNY?!
LEO!! THAT MAN ISN'T A SPATIAL-MAGIC USER!
THAT SUPER-ACCURATE SPATIAL MAGIC... THE USER COULD NEVER HAVE DONE IT IF THEY WEREN'T NEARBY!
SO WHERE...?!

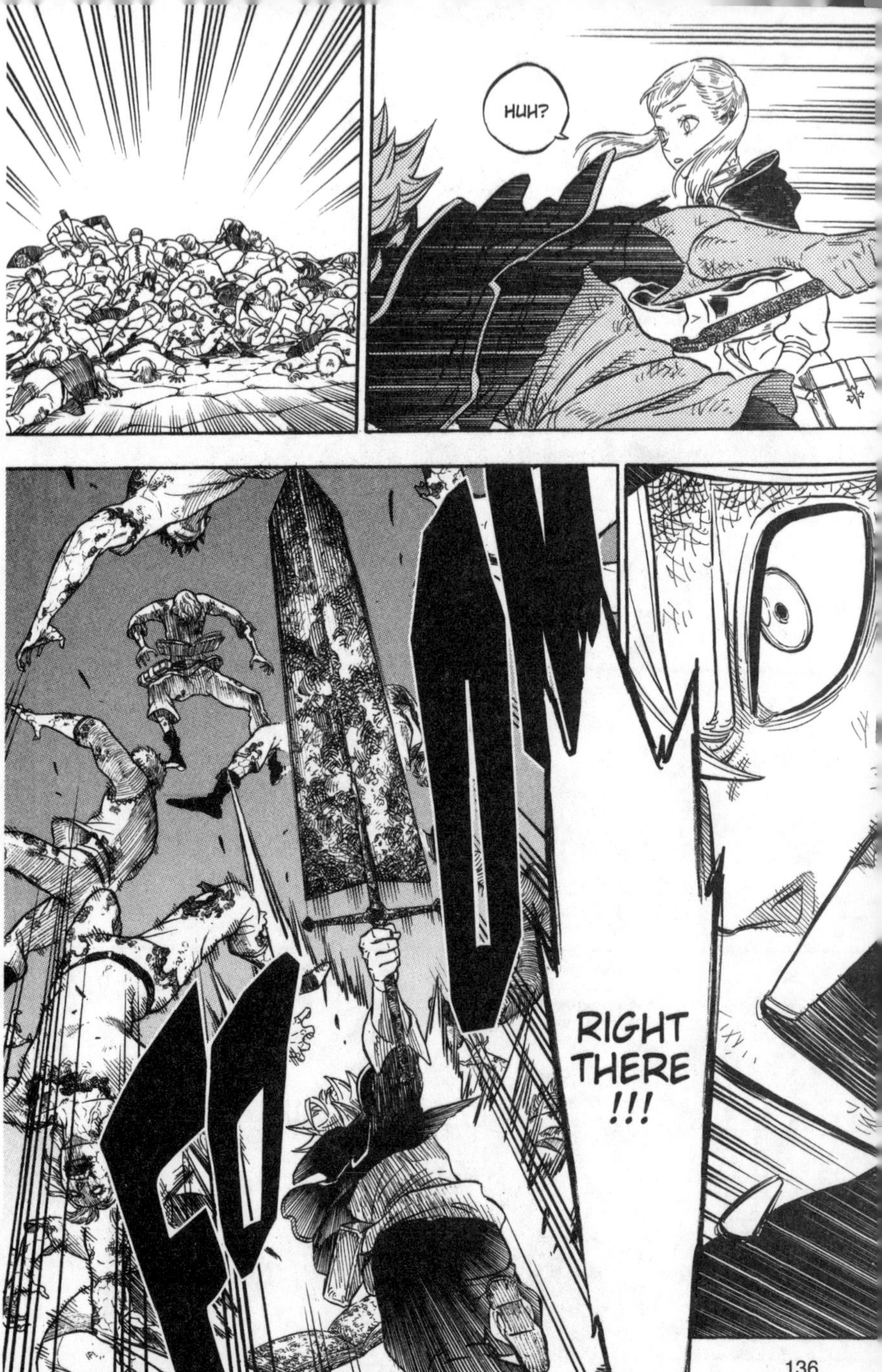
HUH?
RIGHT THERE !!!

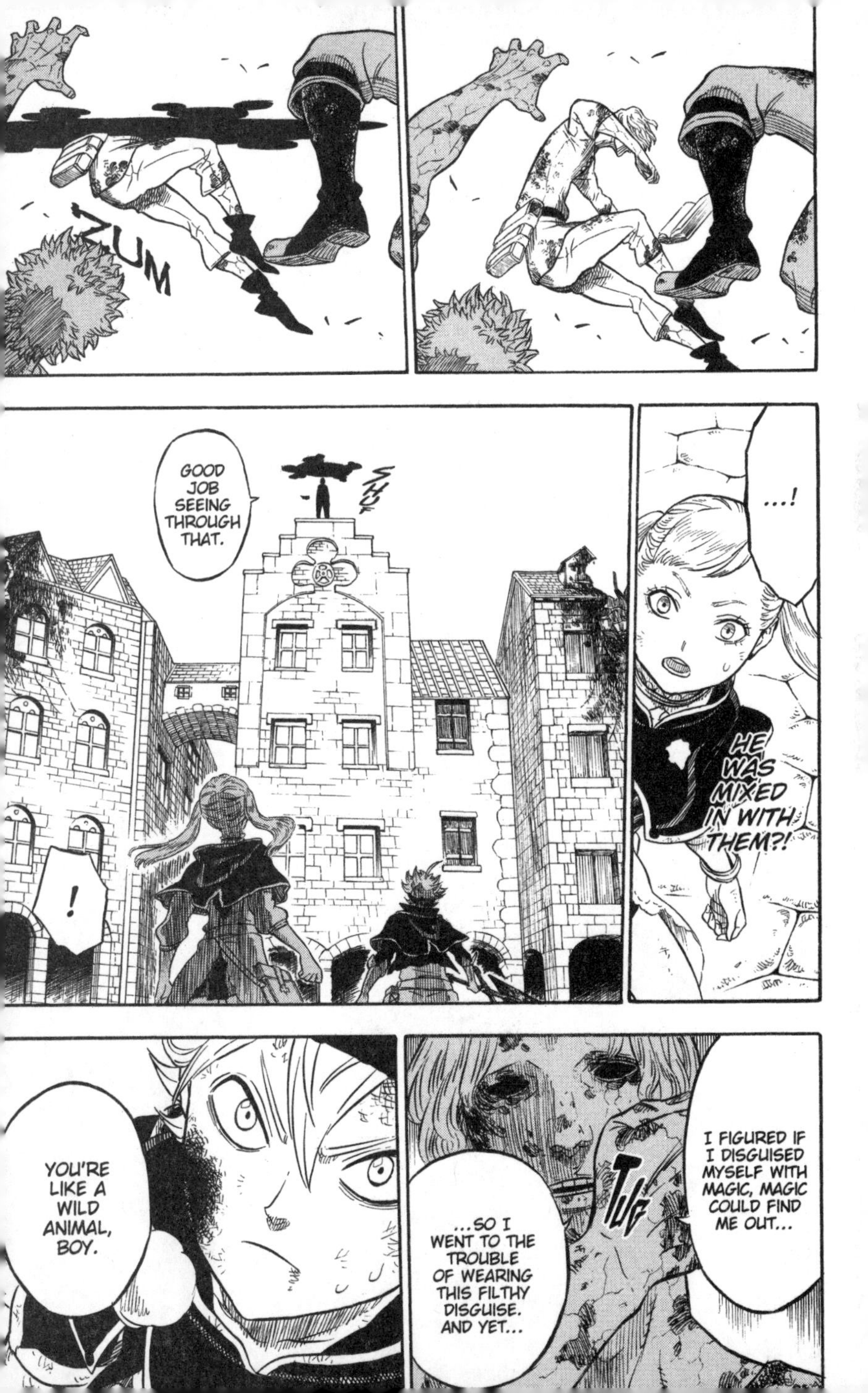
ZUM
...!
HE WAS MIXED IN WITH THEM?!
GOOD JOB SEEING THROUGH THAT.
SHUF
!
I FIGURED IF I DISGUISED MYSELF WITH MAGIC, MAGIC COULD FIND ME OUT...
TUG
...SO I WENT TO THE TROUBLE OF WEARING THIS FILTHY DISGUISE. AND YET...
YOU'RE LIKE A WILD ANIMAL, BOY.

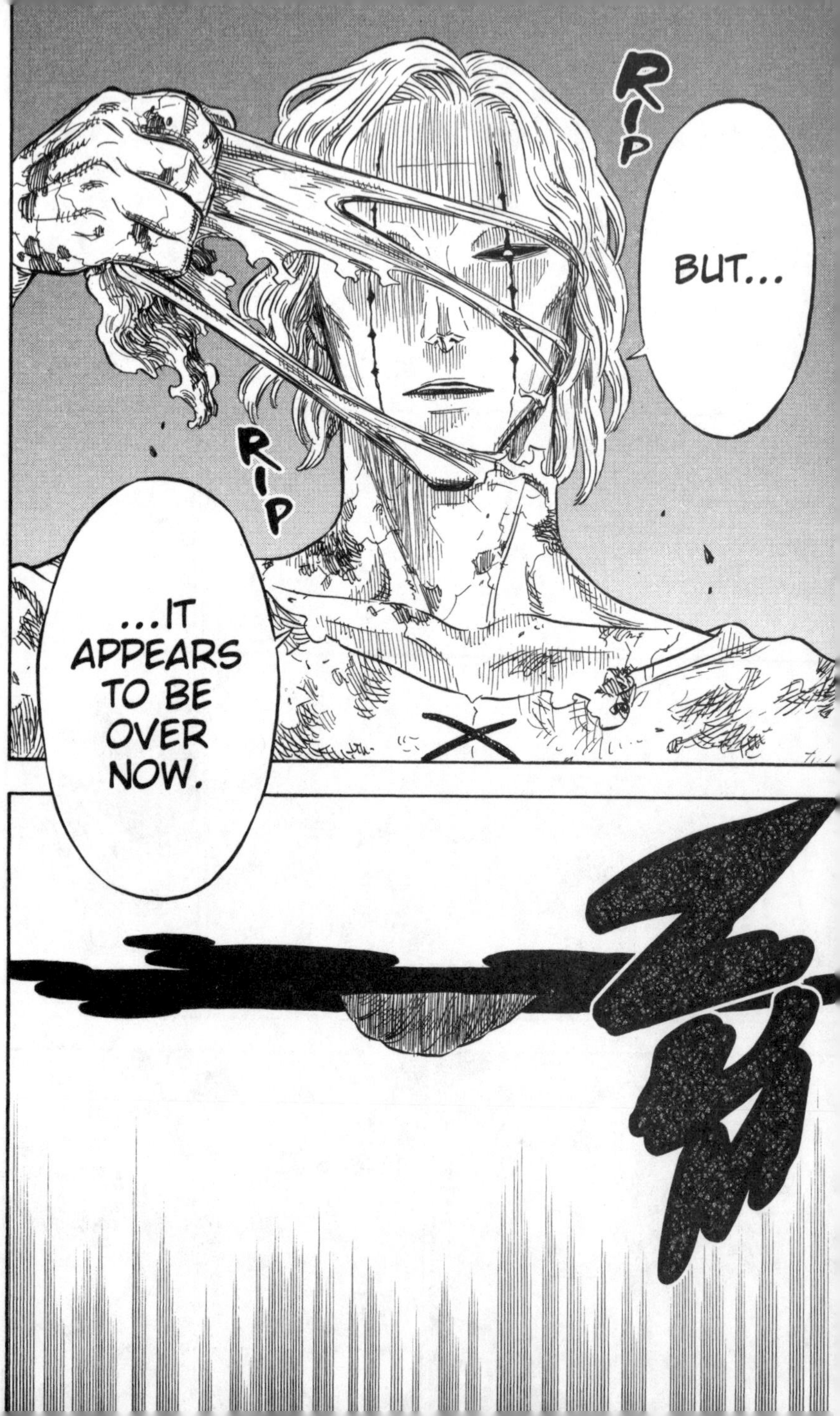
RIP
BUT...
RIP
...IT APPEARS TO BE OVER NOW.

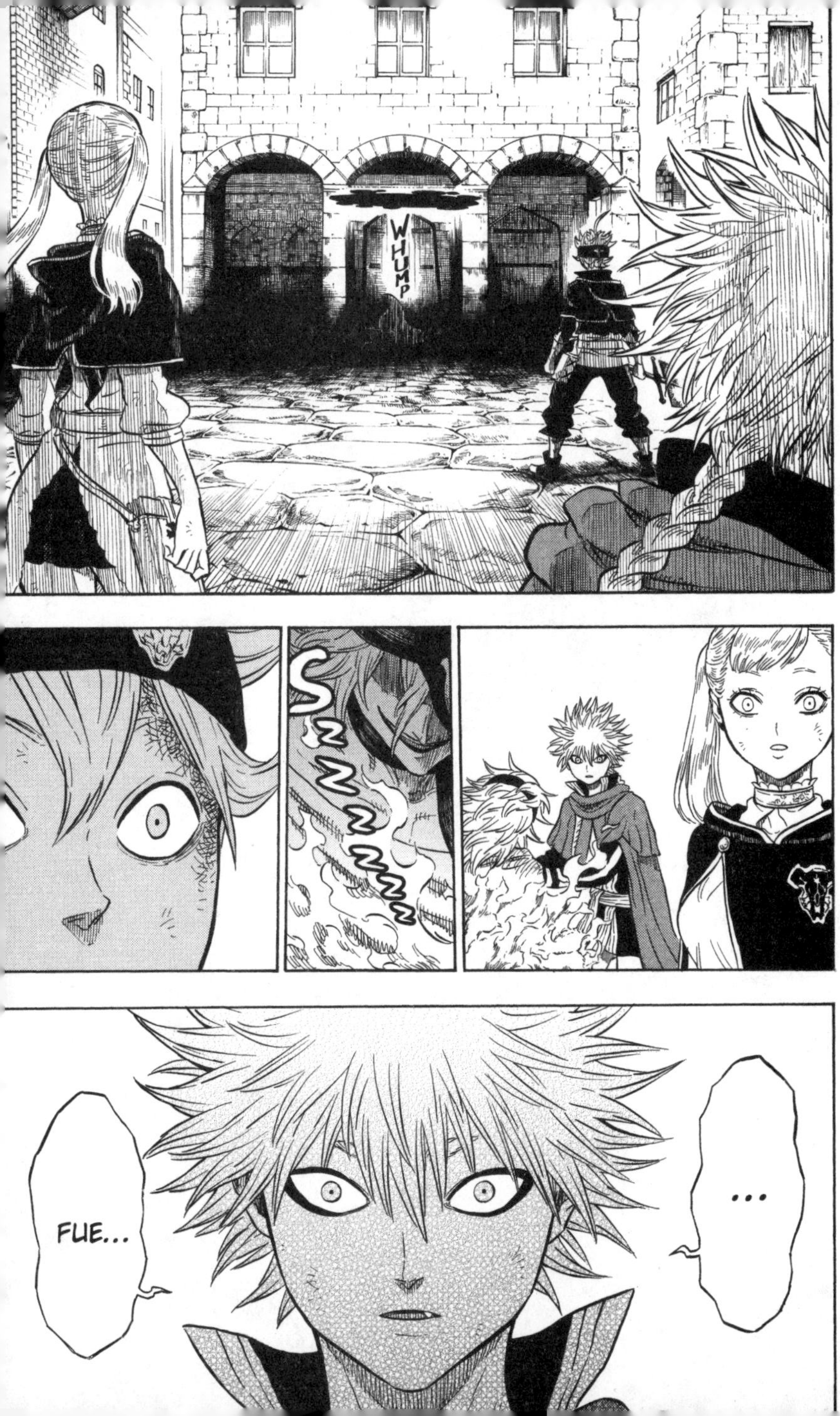
WHUMP
SZZZZZZZ
...
FUE...

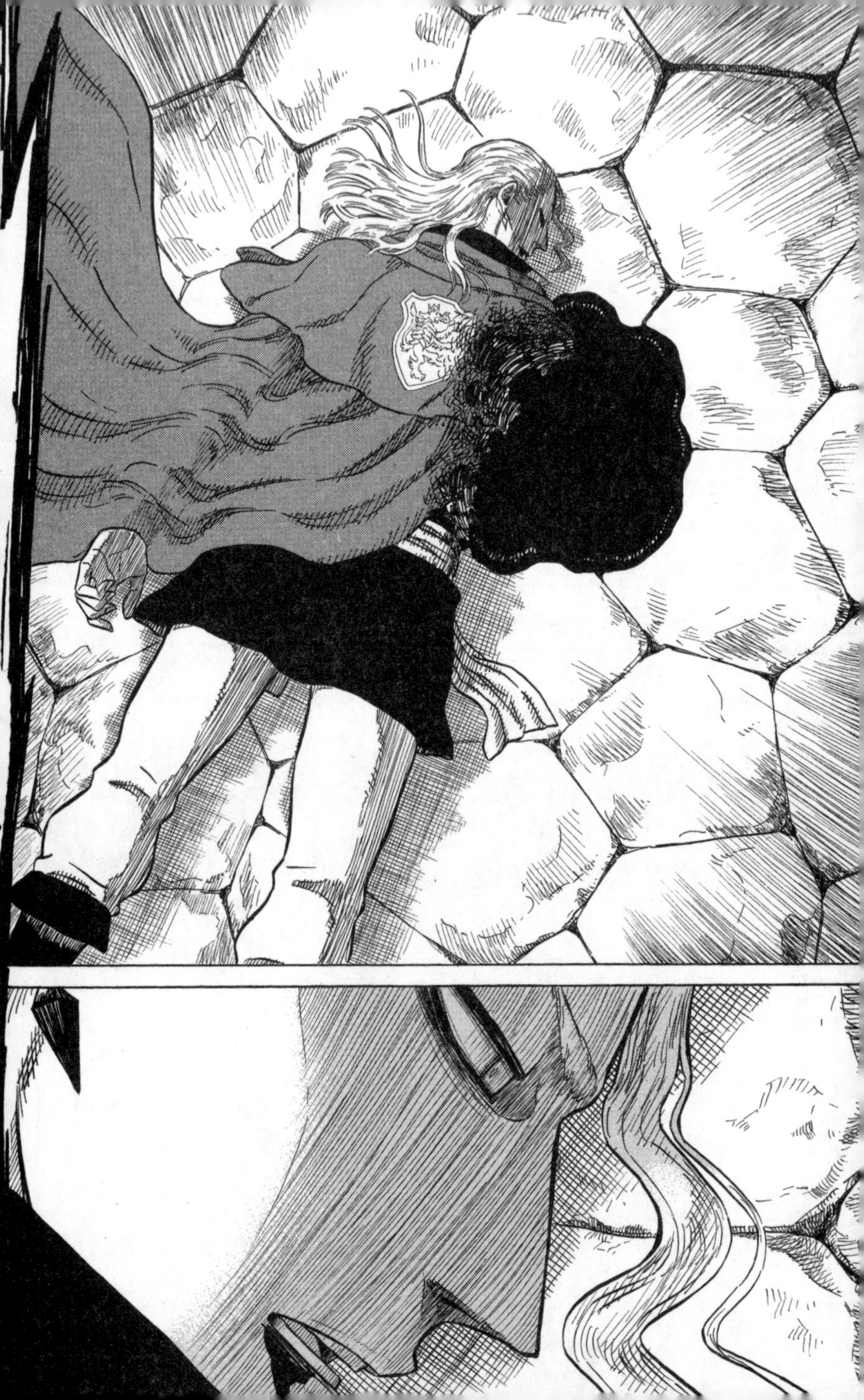

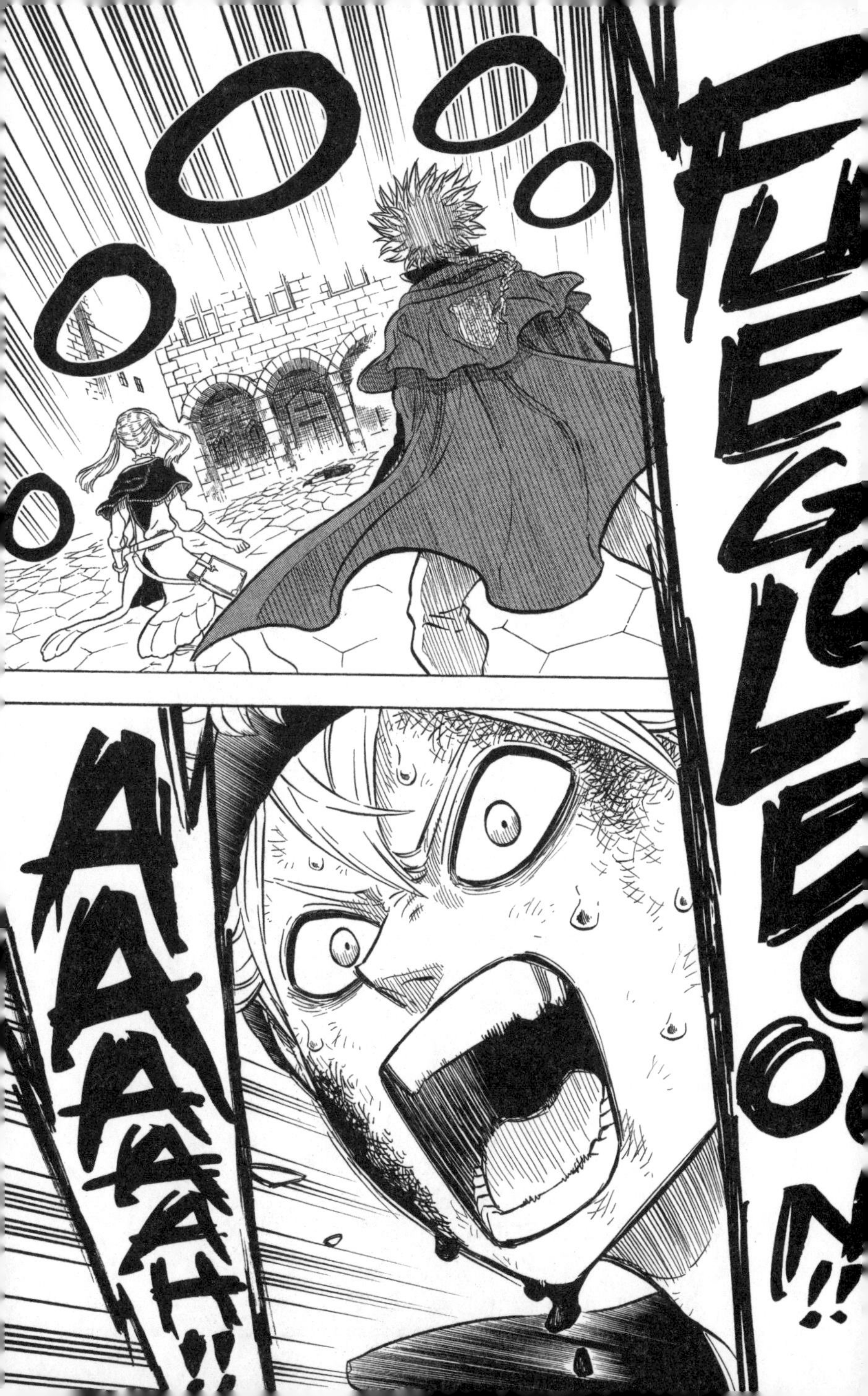

FUEGOLEOOON!!
AAAAAH!!

Leopold Vermillion

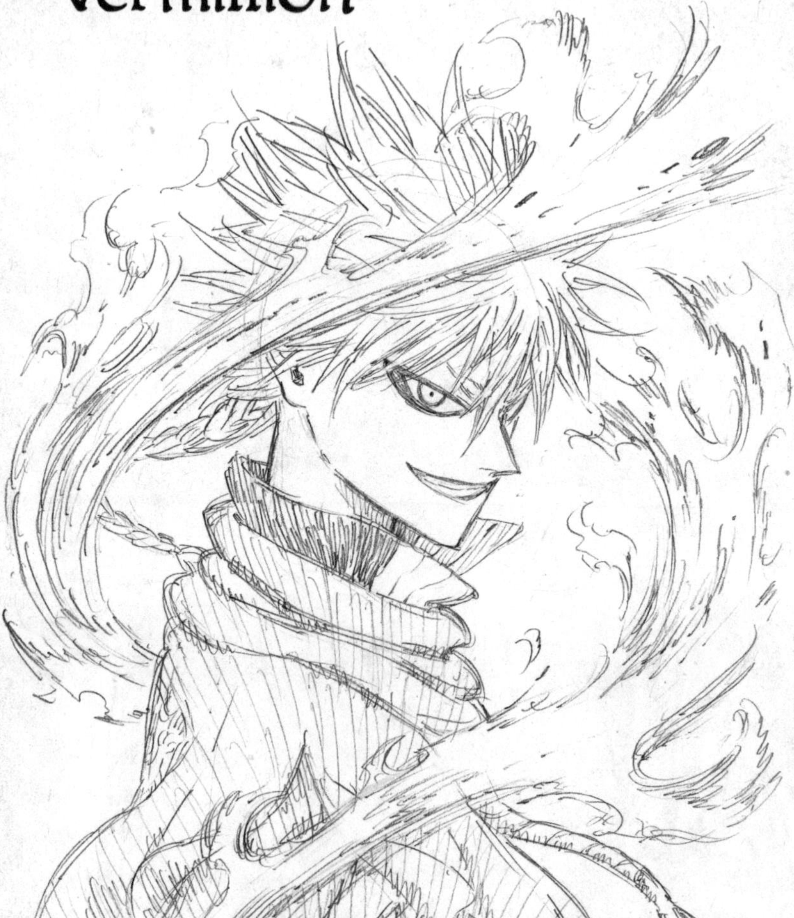

Age: 16 Height: 164 cm
Birthday: August 13 Sign: Leo Blood Type: O
Likes: Interesting guys, his big brother

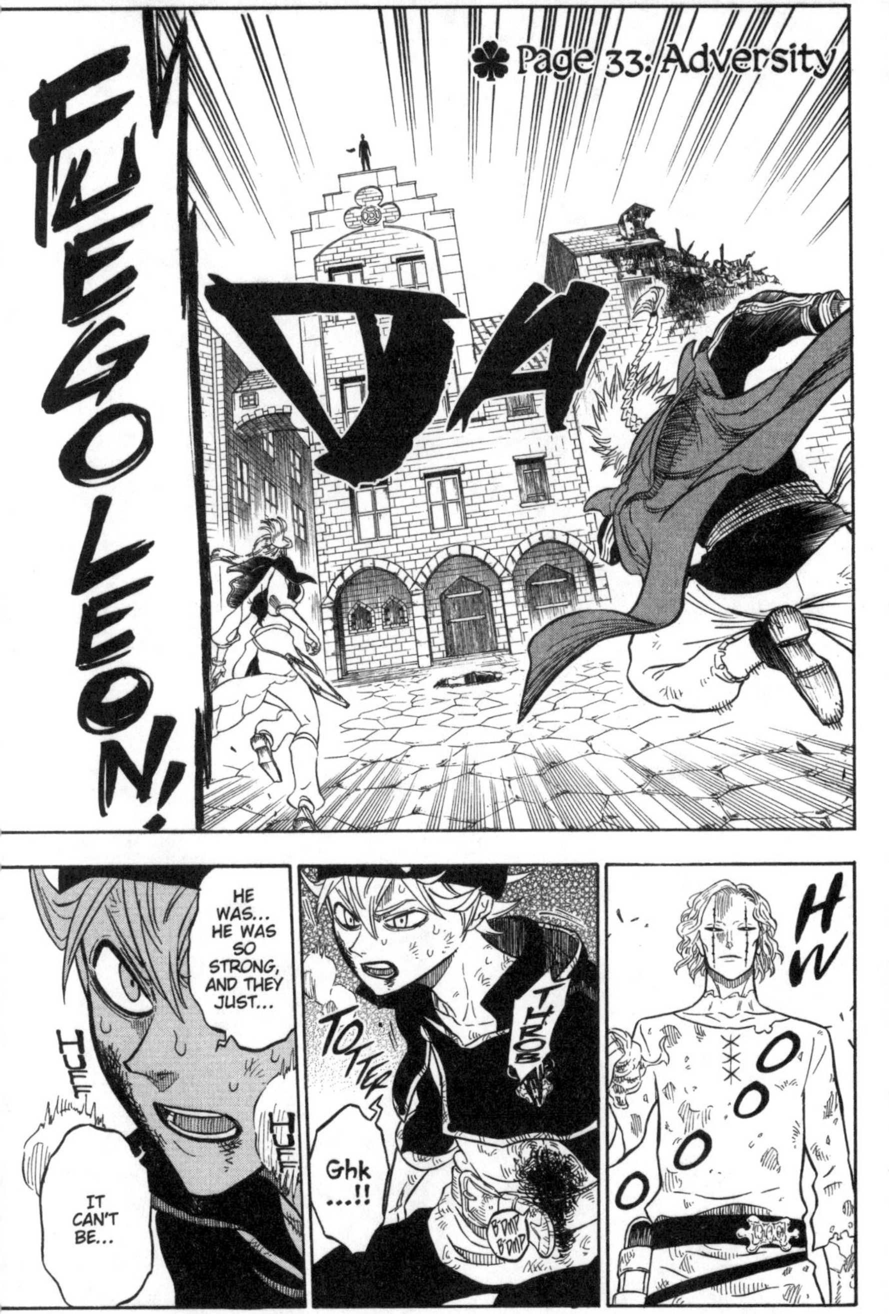
Page 33: Adversity
FUEGOLEON!
DA
HWOOOOO
THROB
TOTTER
Ghk ...!!
B'DMP B'DMP
HE WAS... HE WAS SO STRONG, AND THEY JUST...
HUFF
HUFF
IT CAN'T BE...

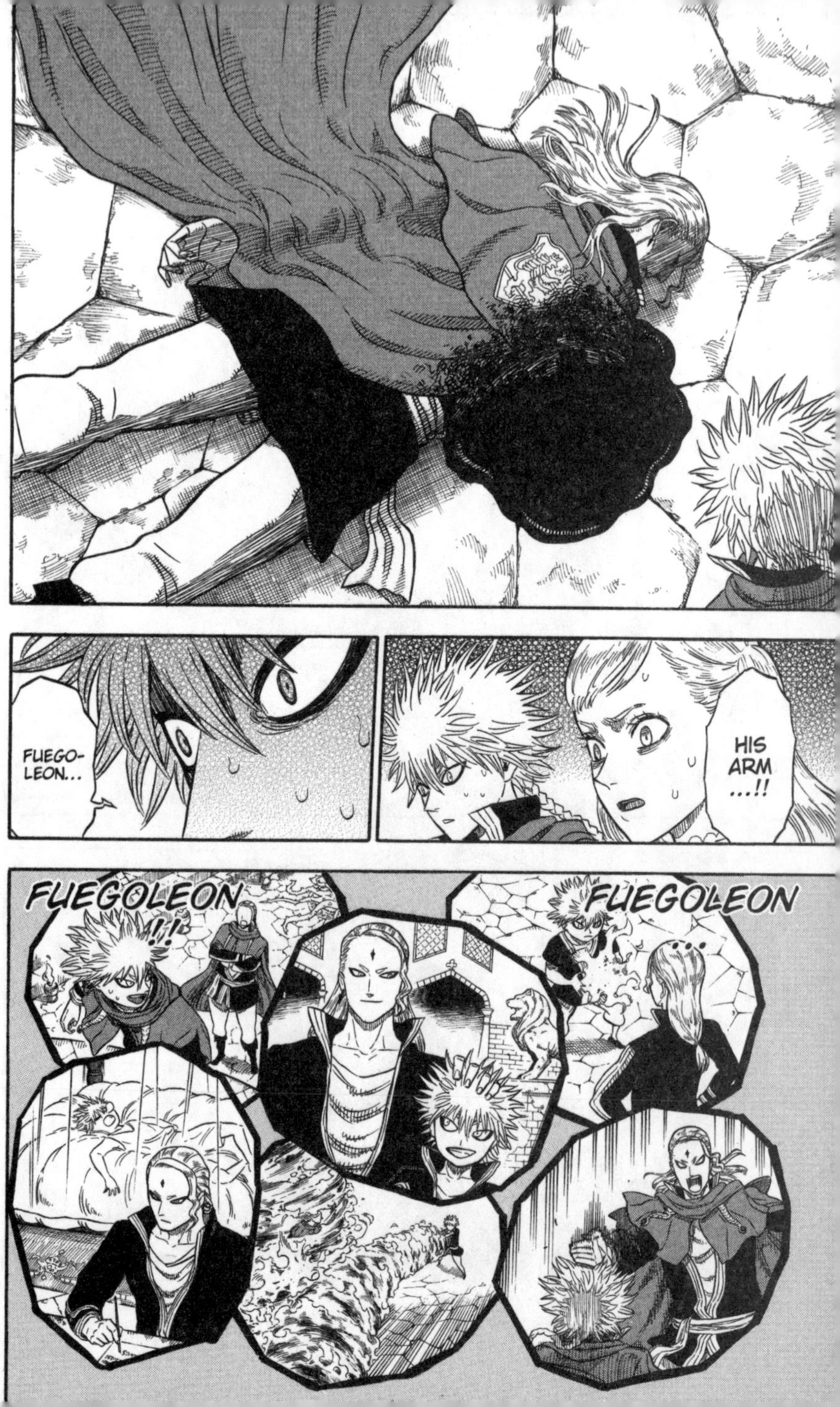
HIS ARM ...!!
FUEGO-LEON...
FUEGOLEON
...
FUEGOLEON !!

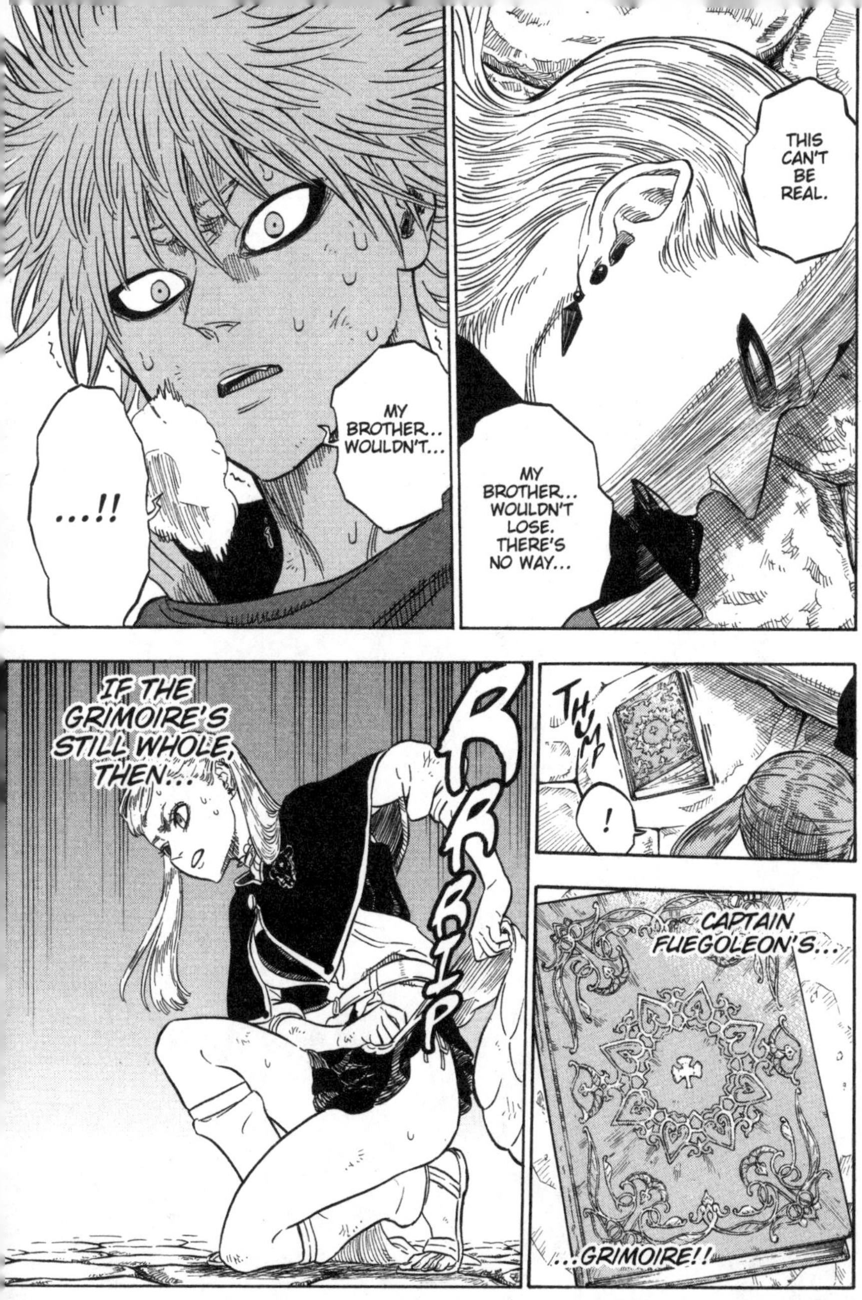
THIS CAN'T BE REAL.
MY BROTHER.. WOULDN'T LOSE. THERE'S NO WAY...
MY BROTHER... WOULDN'T...
...!!
THUMP
!
CAPTAIN FUEGOLEON'S...
...GRIMOIRE!!
RRRIP
IF THE GRIMOIRE'S STILL WHOLE, THEN...

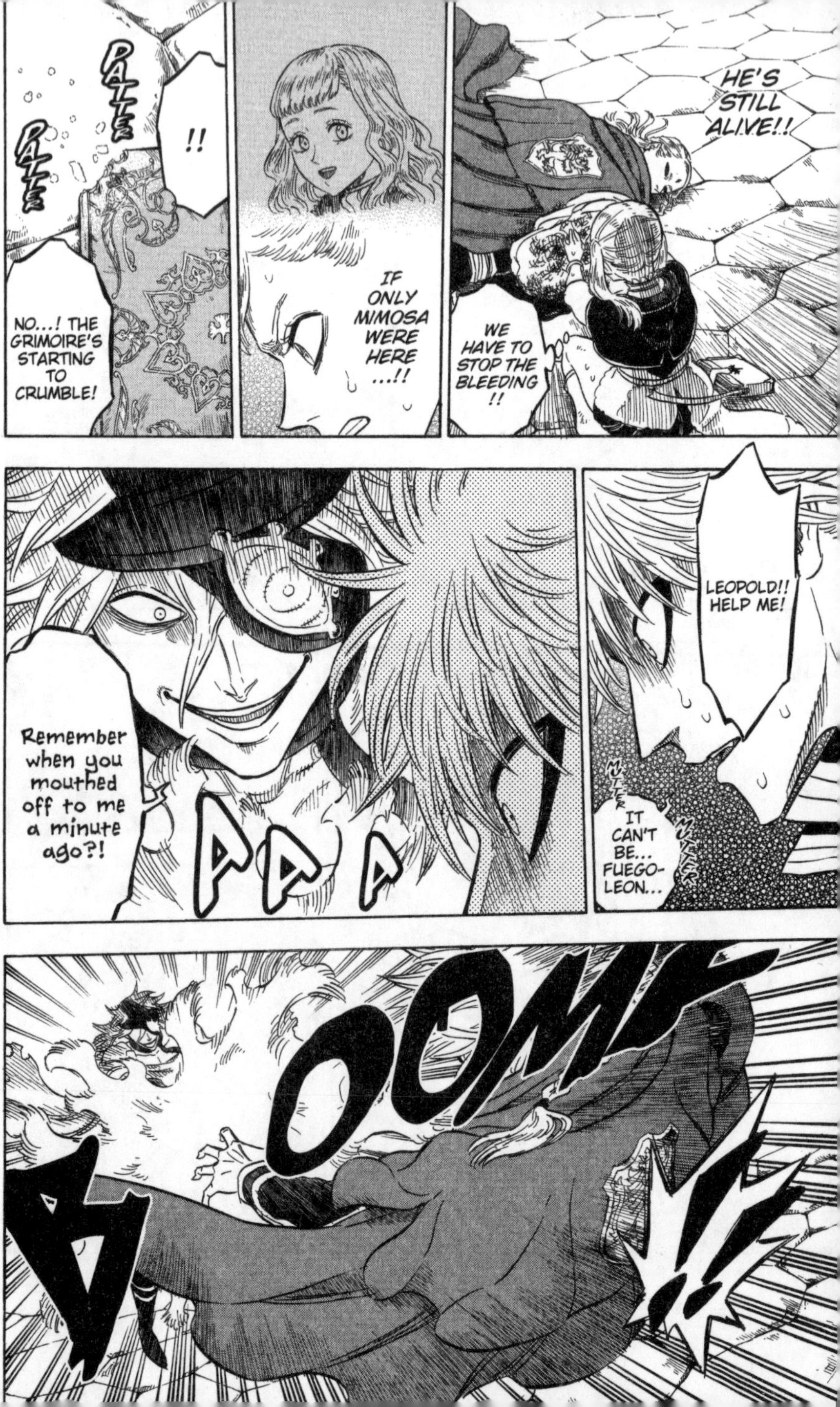
HE'S STILL ALIVE!!
WE HAVE TO STOP THE BLEEDING!!
IF ONLY MIMOSA WERE HERE...!!
!!
PATTER
PATTER
NO...! THE GRIMOIRE'S STARTING TO CRUMBLE!
LEOPOLD!! HELP ME!
MUTTER
MUTTER
IT CAN'T BE... FUEGO-LEON...
Remember when you mouthed off to me a minute ago?!
A A A
OOMF
!!

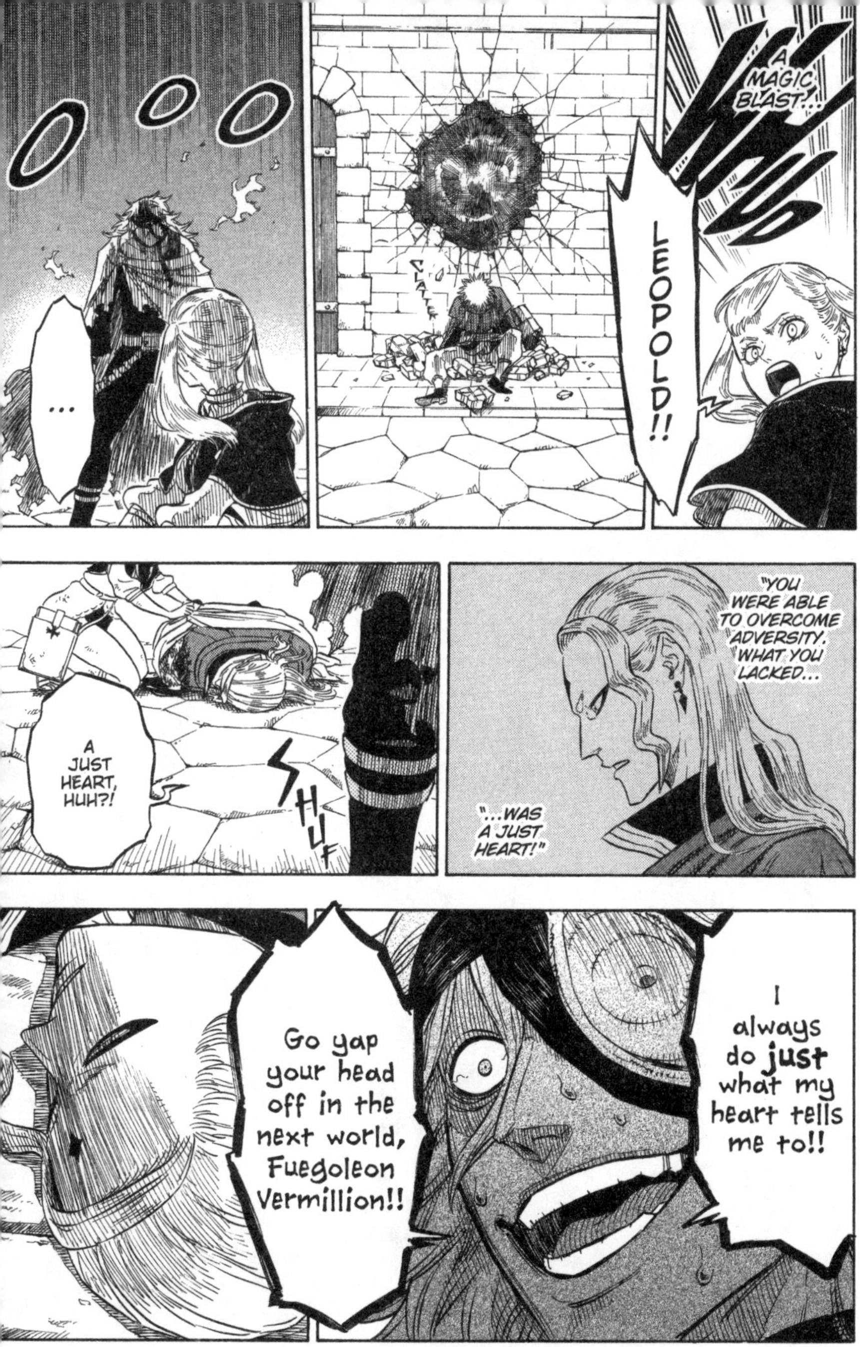

A MAGIC BLAST?!
WHUD
LEOPOLD!!
CLATTER
OOO
...
"YOU WERE ABLE TO OVERCOME ADVERSITY. WHAT YOU LACKED...
"...WAS A JUST HEART!"
SHUF
A JUST HEART, HUH?!
I always do just what my heart tells me to!!
Go yap your head off in the next world, Fuegoleon Vermillion!!

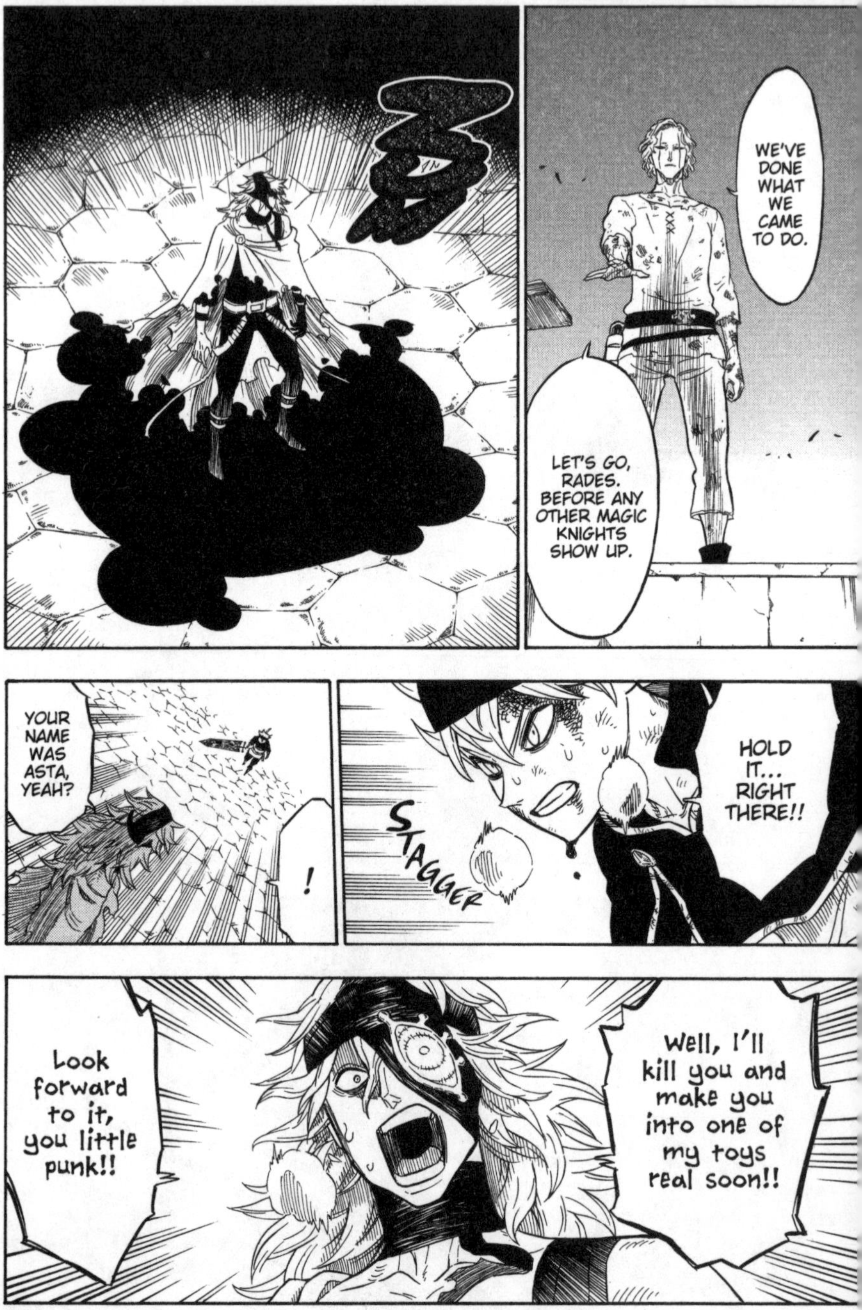
WE'VE DONE WHAT WE CAME TO DO.
LET'S GO, RADES. BEFORE ANY OTHER MAGIC KNIGHTS SHOW UP.
HOLD IT... RIGHT THERE!!
STAGGER
!
YOUR NAME WAS ASTA, YEAH?
Well, I'll kill you and make you into one of my toys real soon!!
Look forward to it, you little punk!!

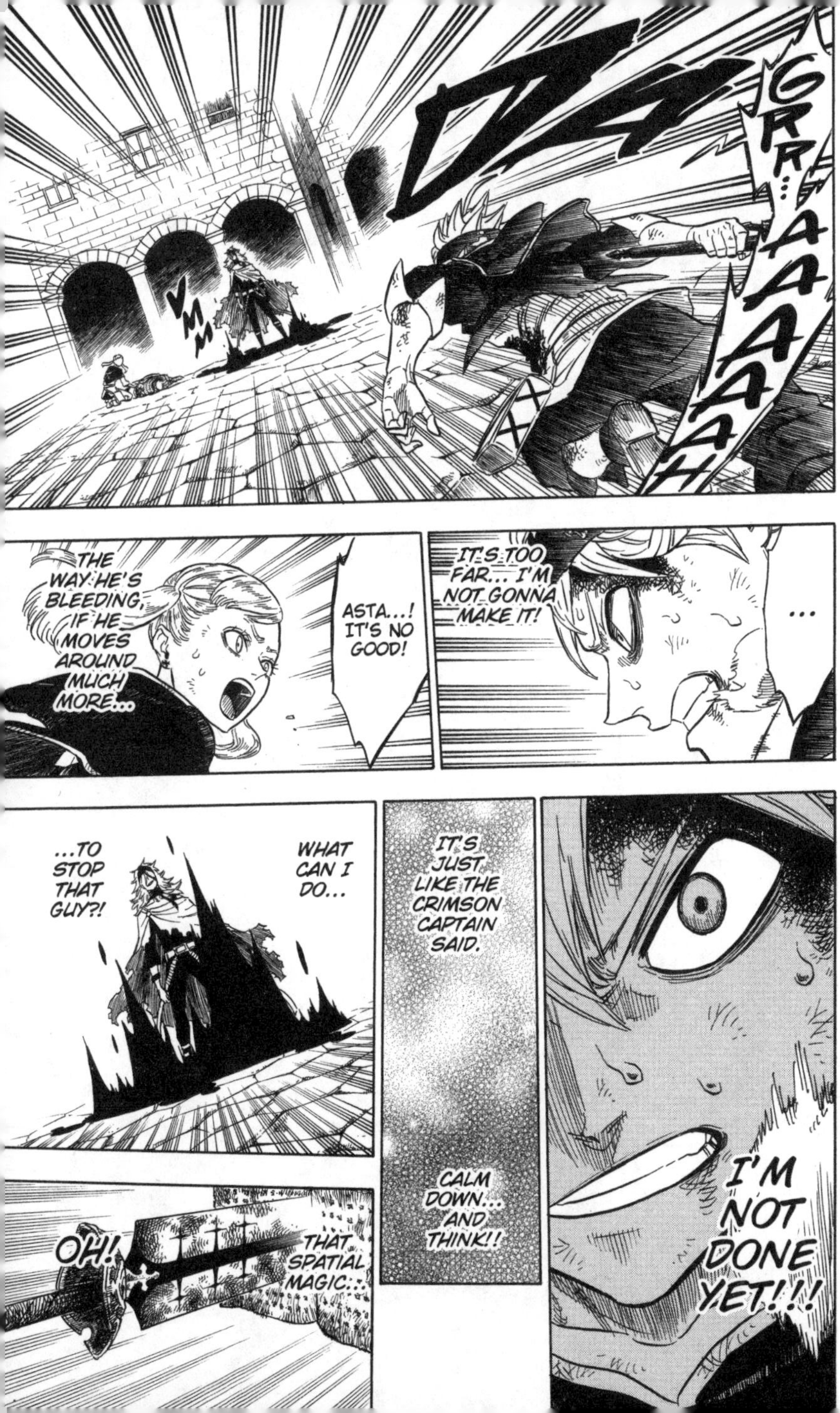
GRR...AAAAAH
DA
VMM
...
IT'S TOO FAR... I'M NOT GONNA MAKE IT!
ASTA...! IT'S NO GOOD!
THE WAY HE'S BLEEDING, IF HE MOVES AROUND MUCH MORE...
I'M NOT DONE YET!!!
IT'S JUST LIKE THE CRIMSON CAPTAIN SAID.
CALM DOWN... AND THINK!!
WHAT CAN I DO...
...TO STOP THAT GUY?!
THAT SPATIAL MAGIC...
OH!

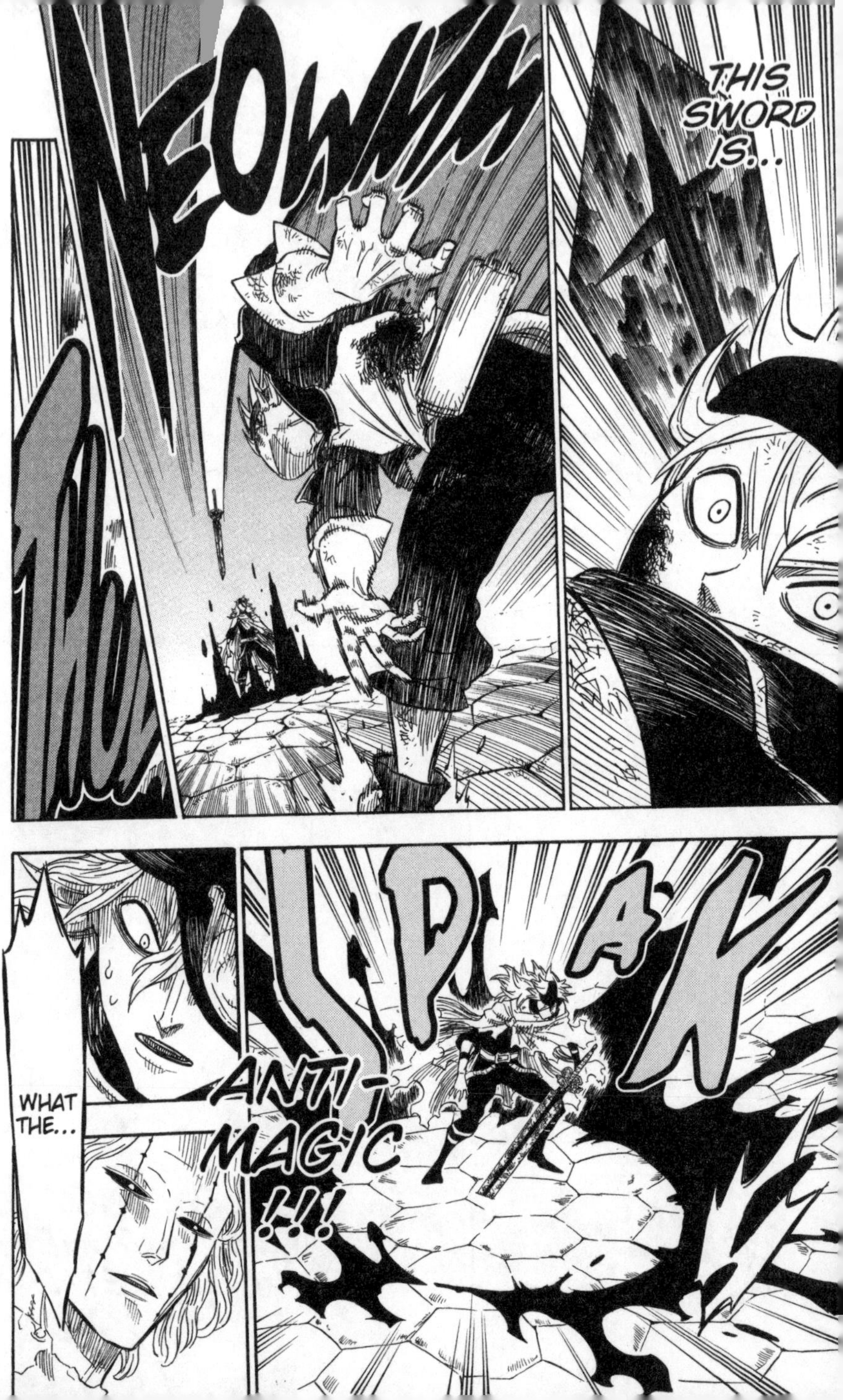
THIS SWORD IS...
ANTI-MAGIC !!!
WHAT THE...

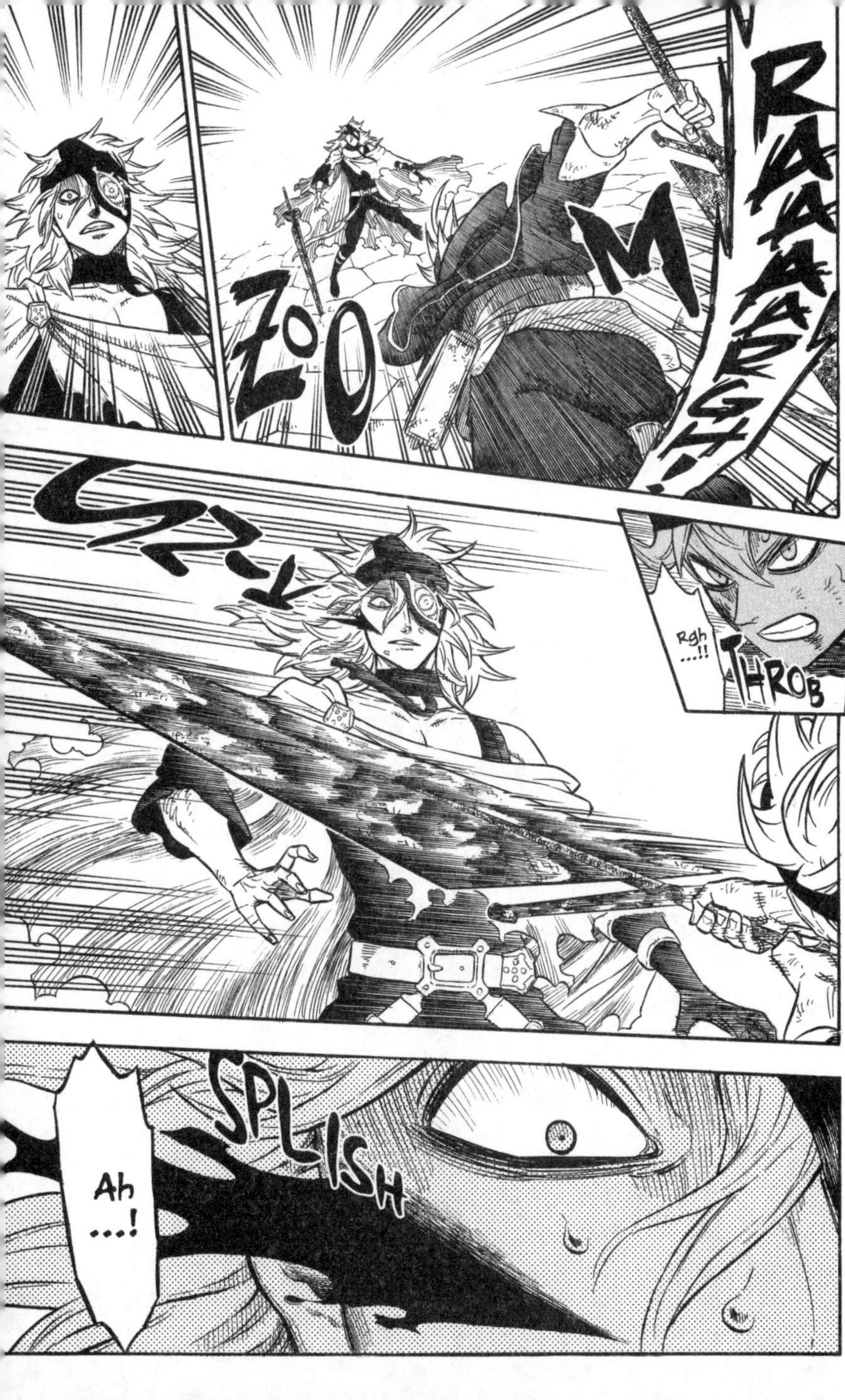
RAAAAEGH!!
ZOOM
GRIP
Rgh...!!
THROB
SPLISH
Ah...!

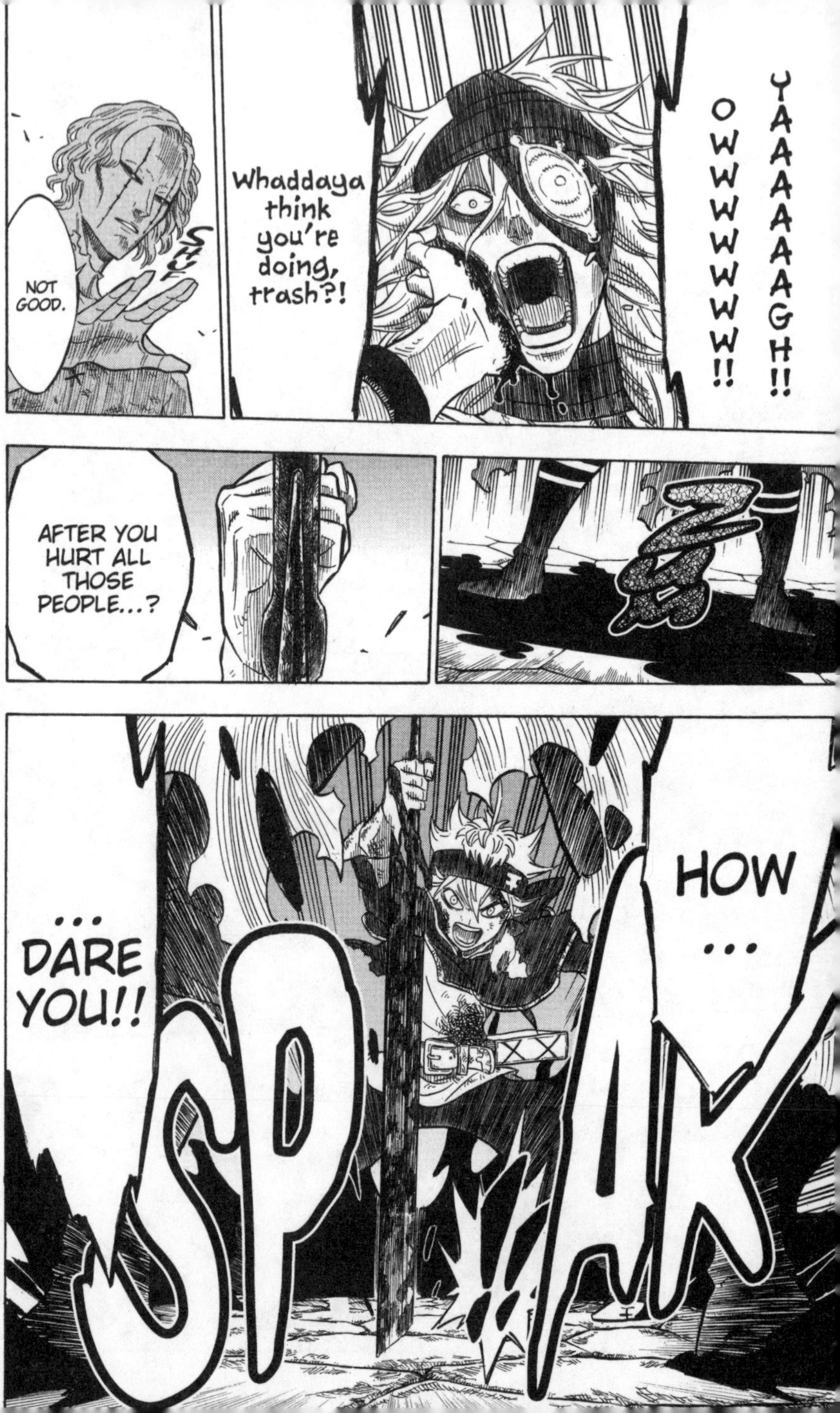
YAAAAAAGH!!
OWWWWWWW!!
Whaddaya think you're doing, trash?!
SHUF
NOT GOOD.
AFTER YOU HURT ALL THOSE PEOPLE...?
HOW...
...DARE YOU!!
SPAK

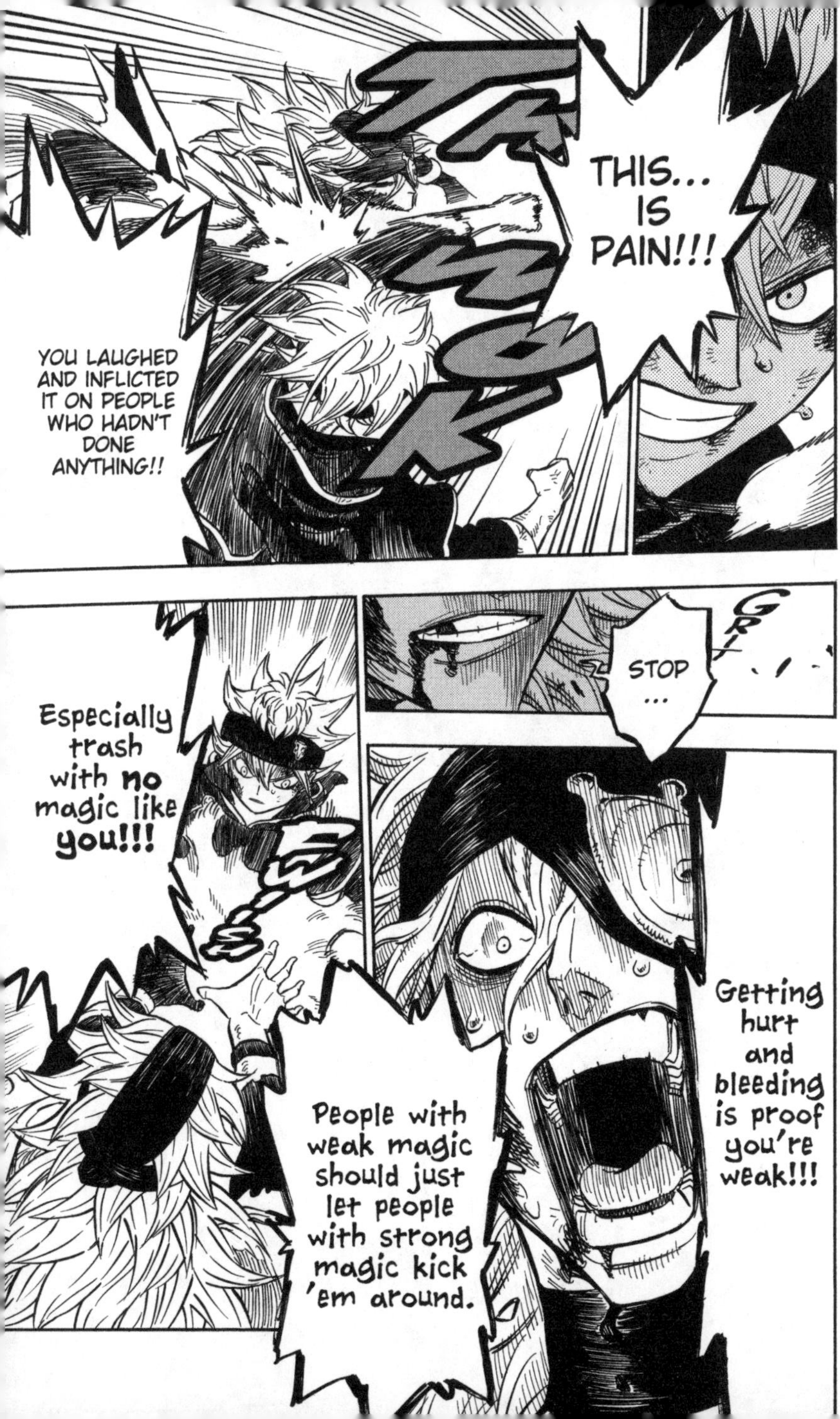
THIS... IS PAIN!!!
YOU LAUGHED AND INFLICTED IT ON PEOPLE WHO HADN'T DONE ANYTHING!!
STOP ...
Getting hurt and bleeding is proof you're weak!!!
People with weak magic should just let people with strong magic kick 'em around.
Especially trash with no magic like you!!!

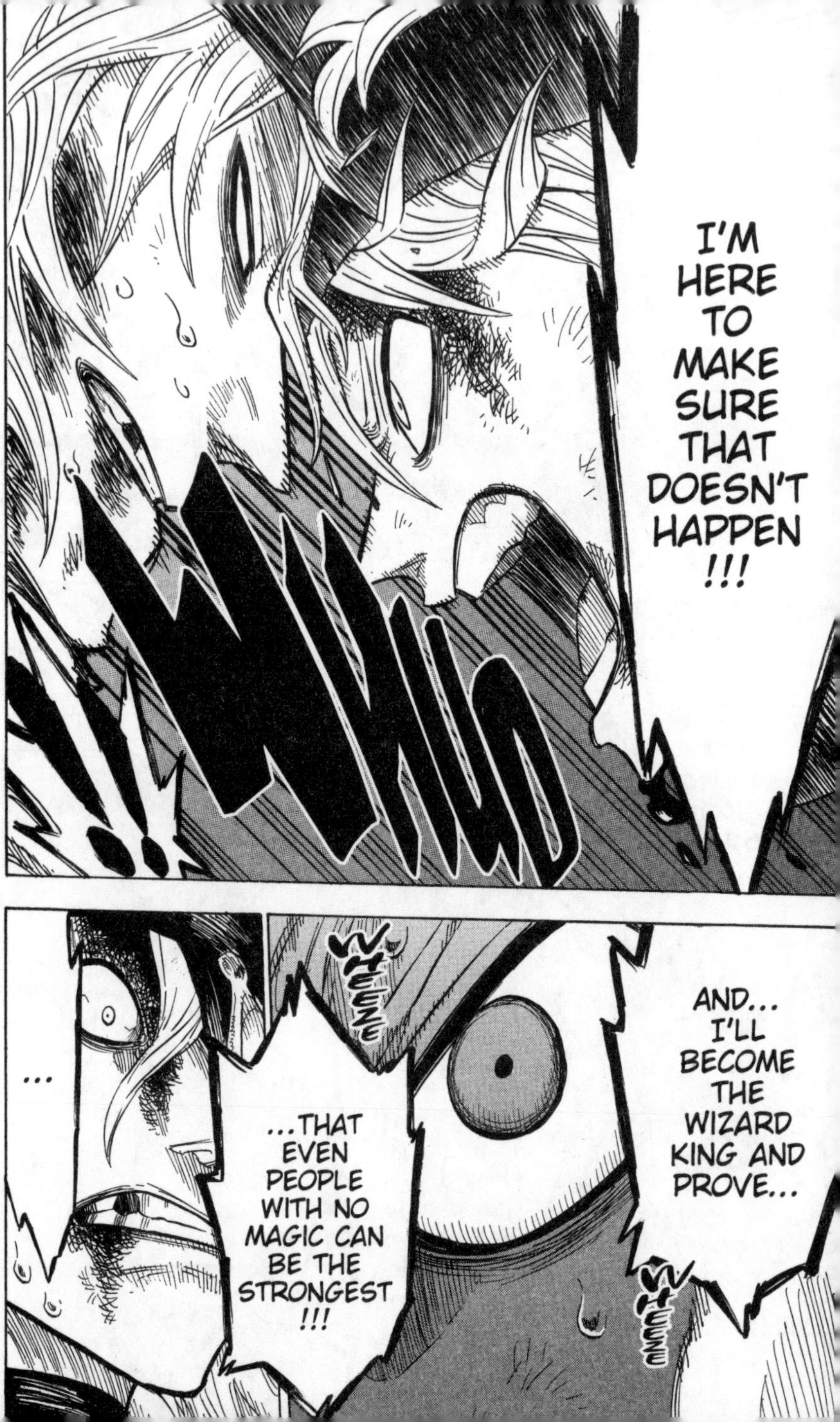
I'M HERE TO MAKE SURE THAT DOESN'T HAPPEN!!!
AND... I'LL BECOME THE WIZARD KING AND PROVE...
WHEEZE
WHEEZE
...THAT EVEN PEOPLE WITH NO MAGIC CAN BE THE STRONGEST!!!
...

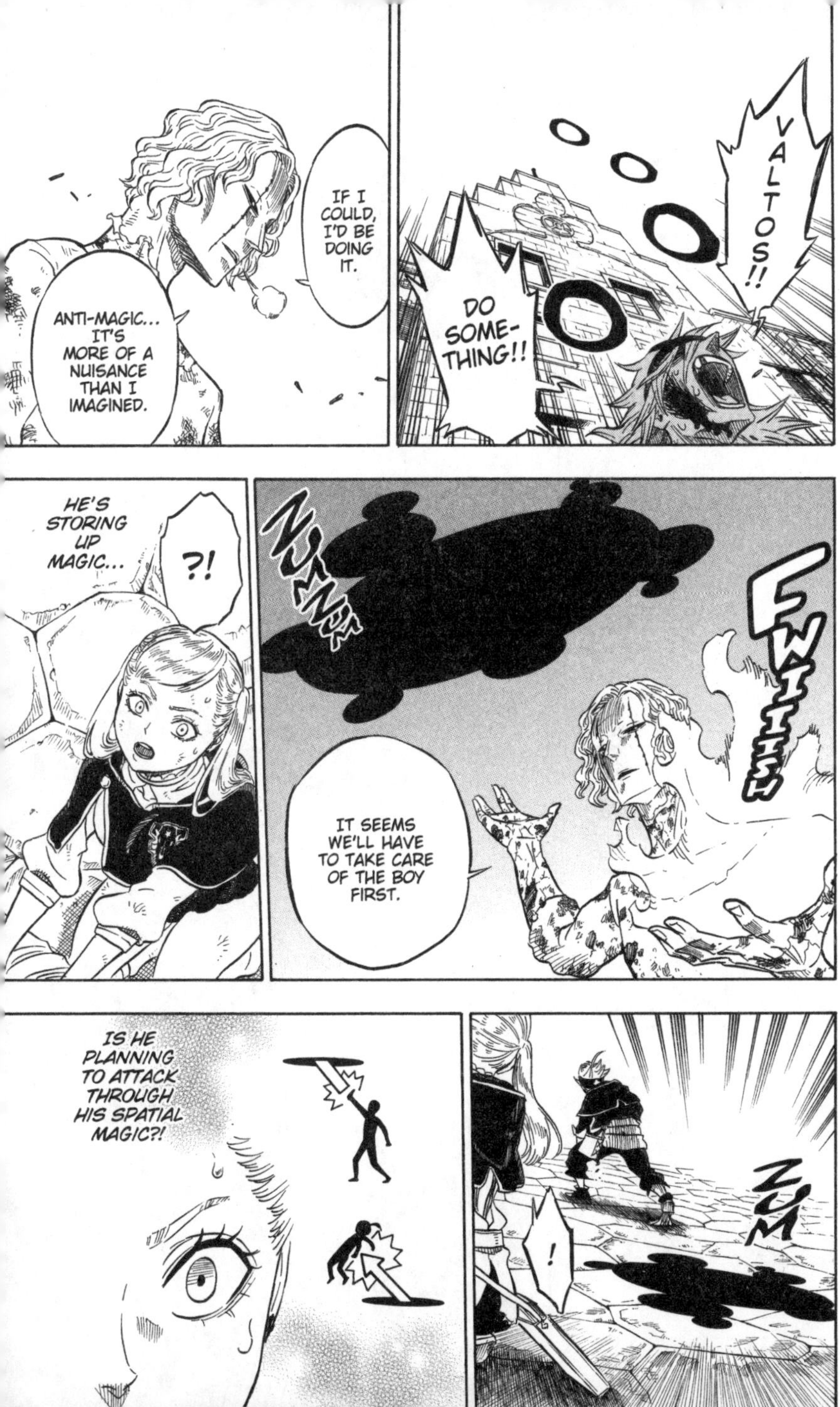
VALTOS!!
OOOO
DO SOME-THING!!
IF I COULD, I'D BE DOING IT.
ANTI-MAGIC... IT'S MORE OF A NUISANCE THAN I IMAGINED.
FWIIISH
IT SEEMS WE'LL HAVE TO TAKE CARE OF THE BOY FIRST.
?!
HE'S STORING UP MAGIC...
ZUM
!
IS HE PLANNING TO ATTACK THROUGH HIS SPATIAL MAGIC?!

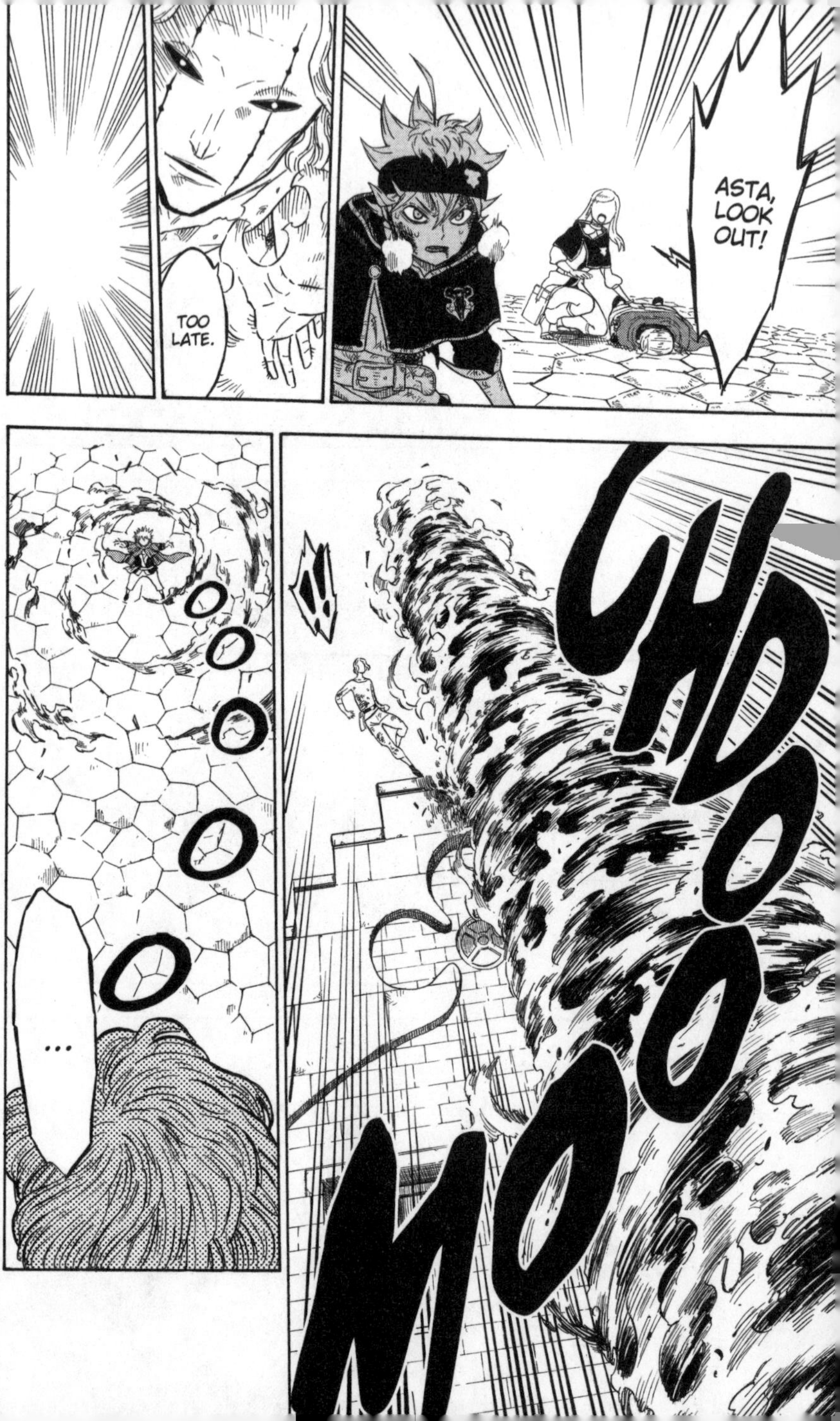
ASTA, LOOK OUT!
TOO LATE.
...

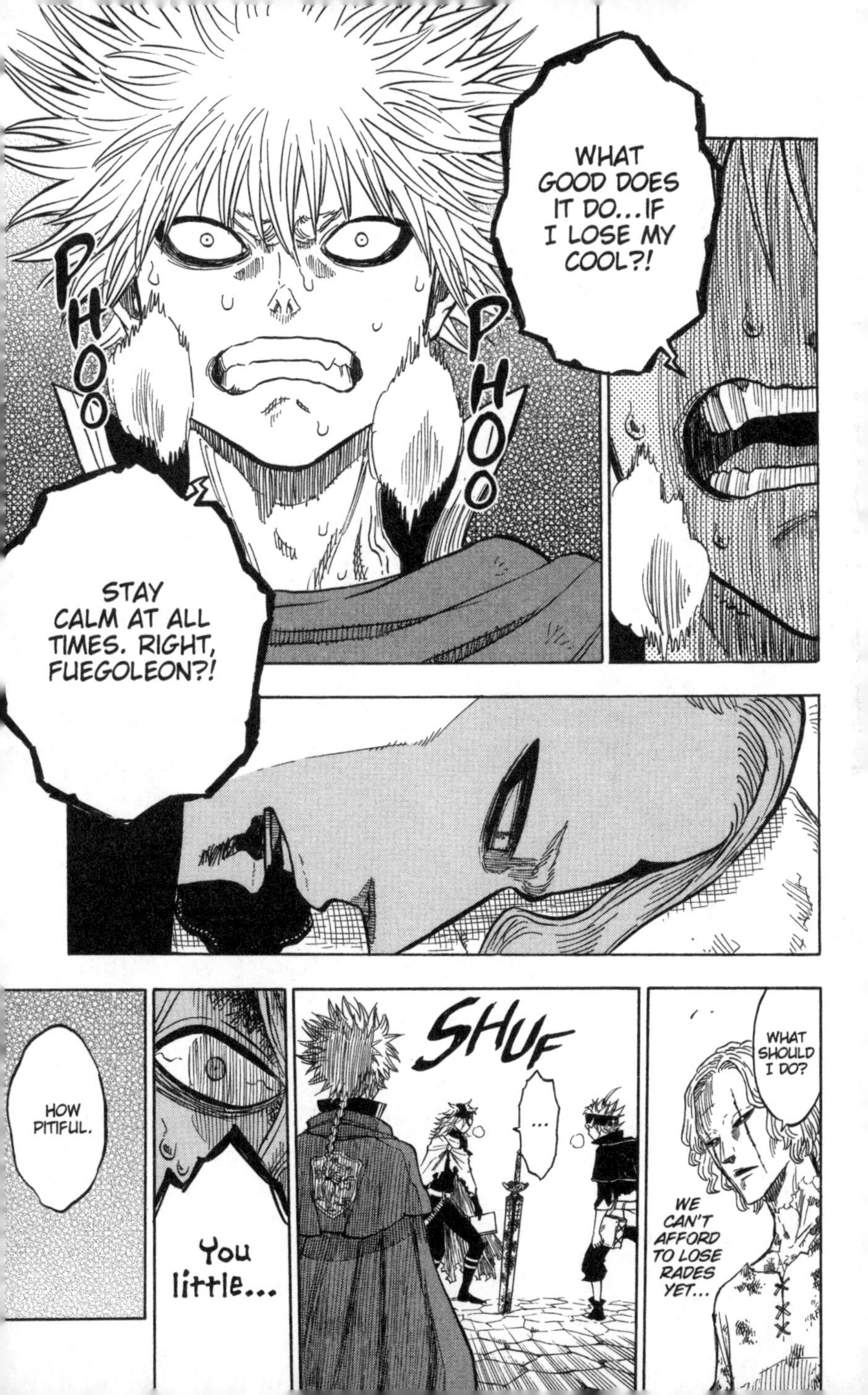
WHAT GOOD DOES IT DO...IF I LOSE MY COOL?!
PHOO
PHOO
STAY CALM AT ALL TIMES. RIGHT, FUEGOLEON?!
WHAT SHOULD I DO?
WE CAN'T AFFORD TO LOSE RADES YET...
SHUF
...
You little...
HOW PITIFUL.

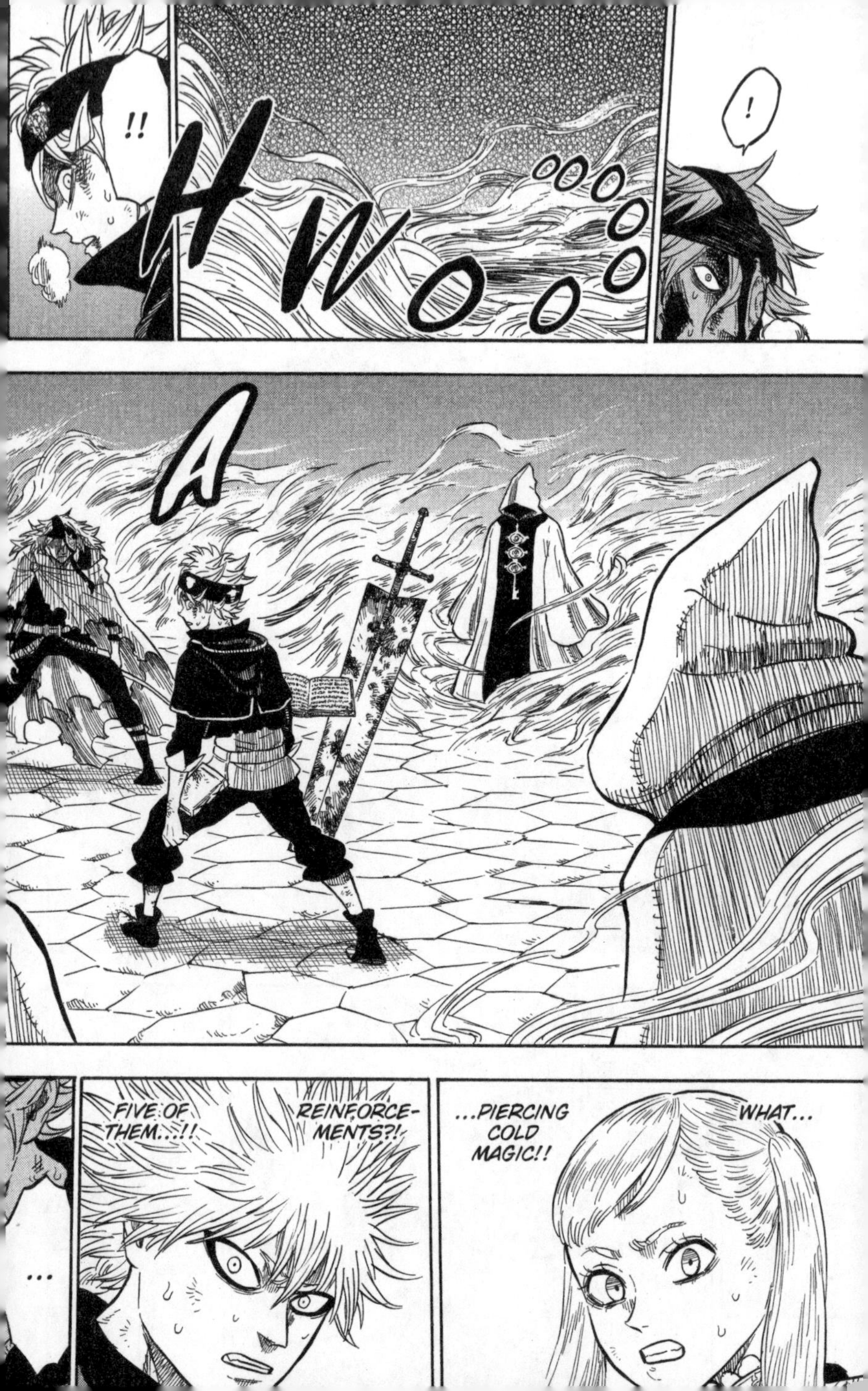
!
HWOOOOOOOO
!!
A
WHAT...
...PIERCING COLD MAGIC!!
REINFORCE-MENTS?!
FIVE OF THEM...!!
...

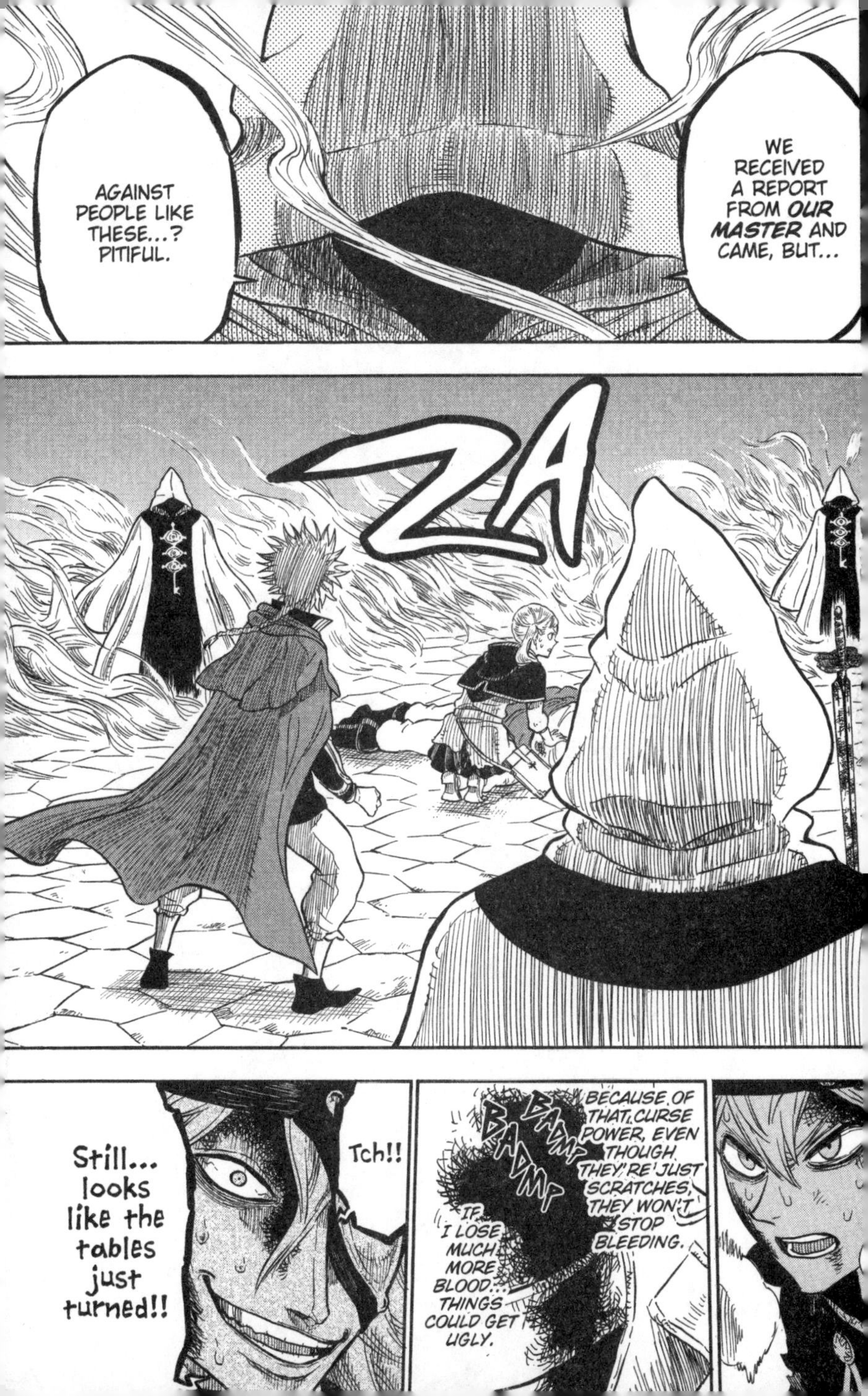
WE RECEIVED A REPORT FROM OUR MASTER AND CAME, BUT...
AGAINST PEOPLE LIKE THESE...? PITIFUL.
ZA
BADMP BADMP
BECAUSE OF THAT CURSE POWER, EVEN THOUGH THEY'RE JUST SCRATCHES, THEY WON'T STOP BLEEDING.
IF I LOSE MUCH MORE BLOOD... THINGS COULD GET UGLY.
Tch!!
Still... looks like the tables just turned!!

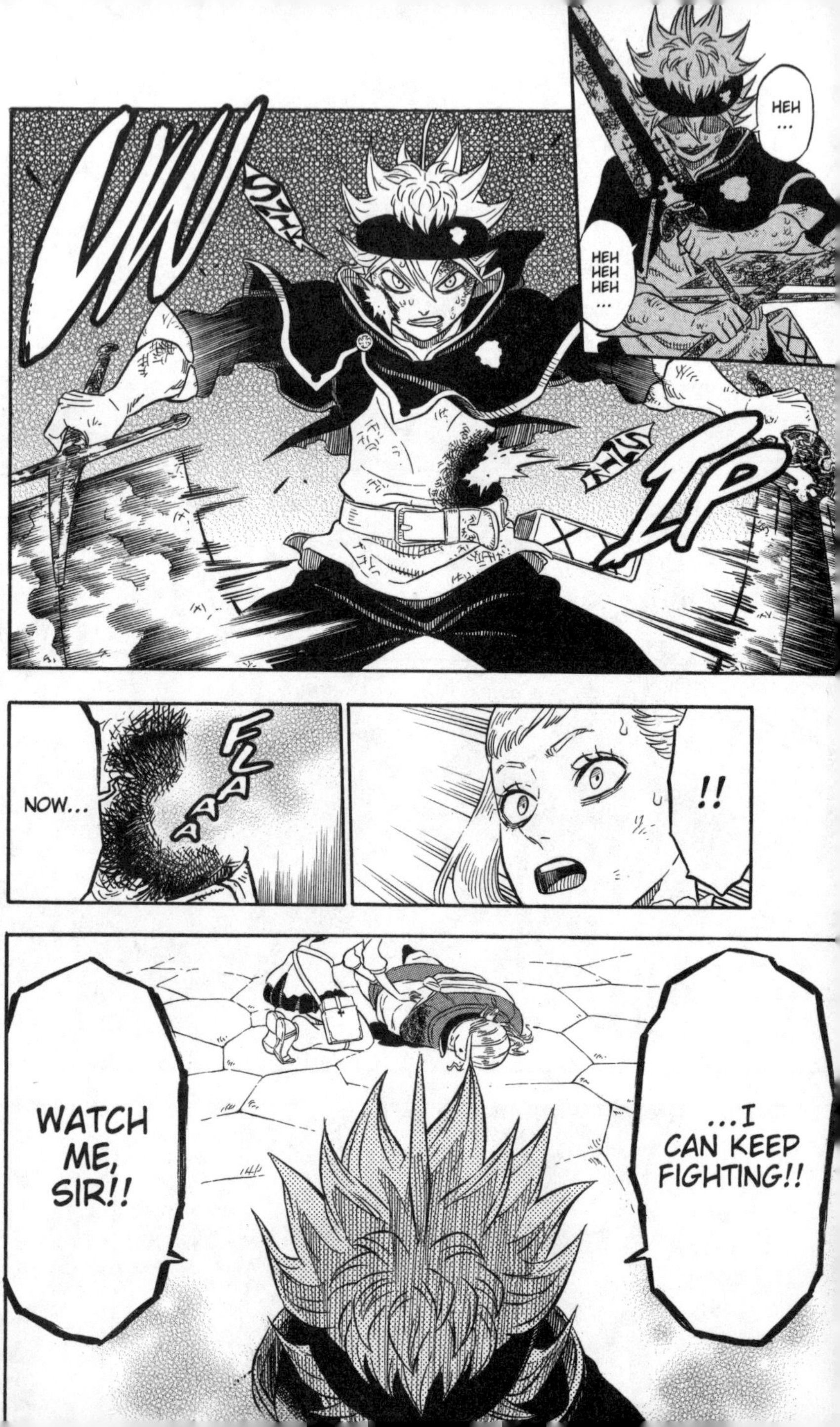
HEH ...
HEH HEH HEH ...
!!
NOW...
...I CAN KEEP FIGHTING!!
WATCH ME, SIR!!

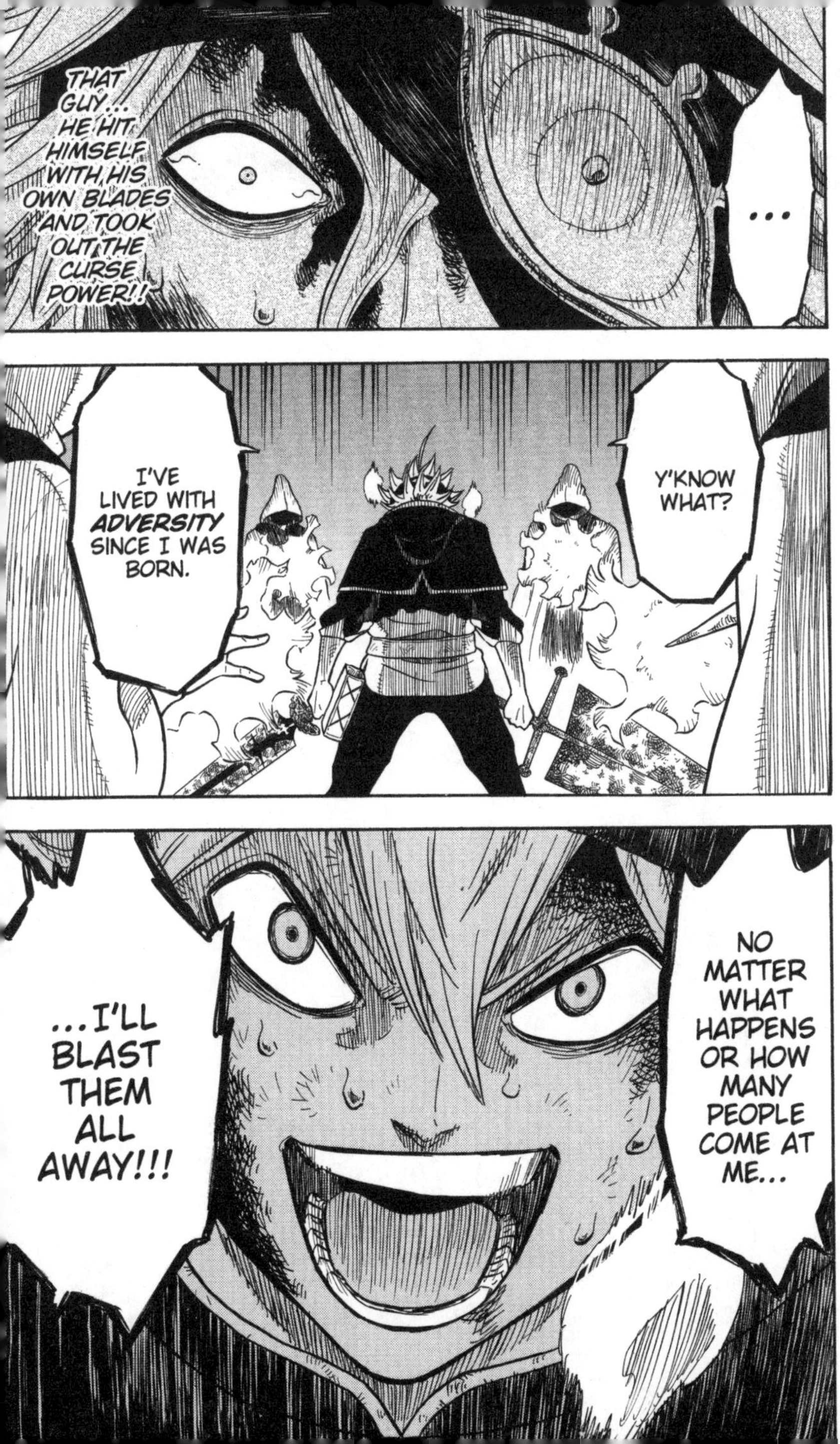
...
THAT GUY... HE HIT HIMSELF WITH HIS OWN BLADES AND TOOK OUT THE CURSE POWER!!
Y'KNOW WHAT?
I'VE LIVED WITH ADVERSITY SINCE I WAS BORN.
NO MATTER WHAT HAPPENS OR HOW MANY PEOPLE COME AT ME...
...I'LL BLAST THEM ALL AWAY!!!

The Blank Page Brigade

This volume's topic: What lines in the manga made the biggest impression on you?
(A reader submitted this topic!)

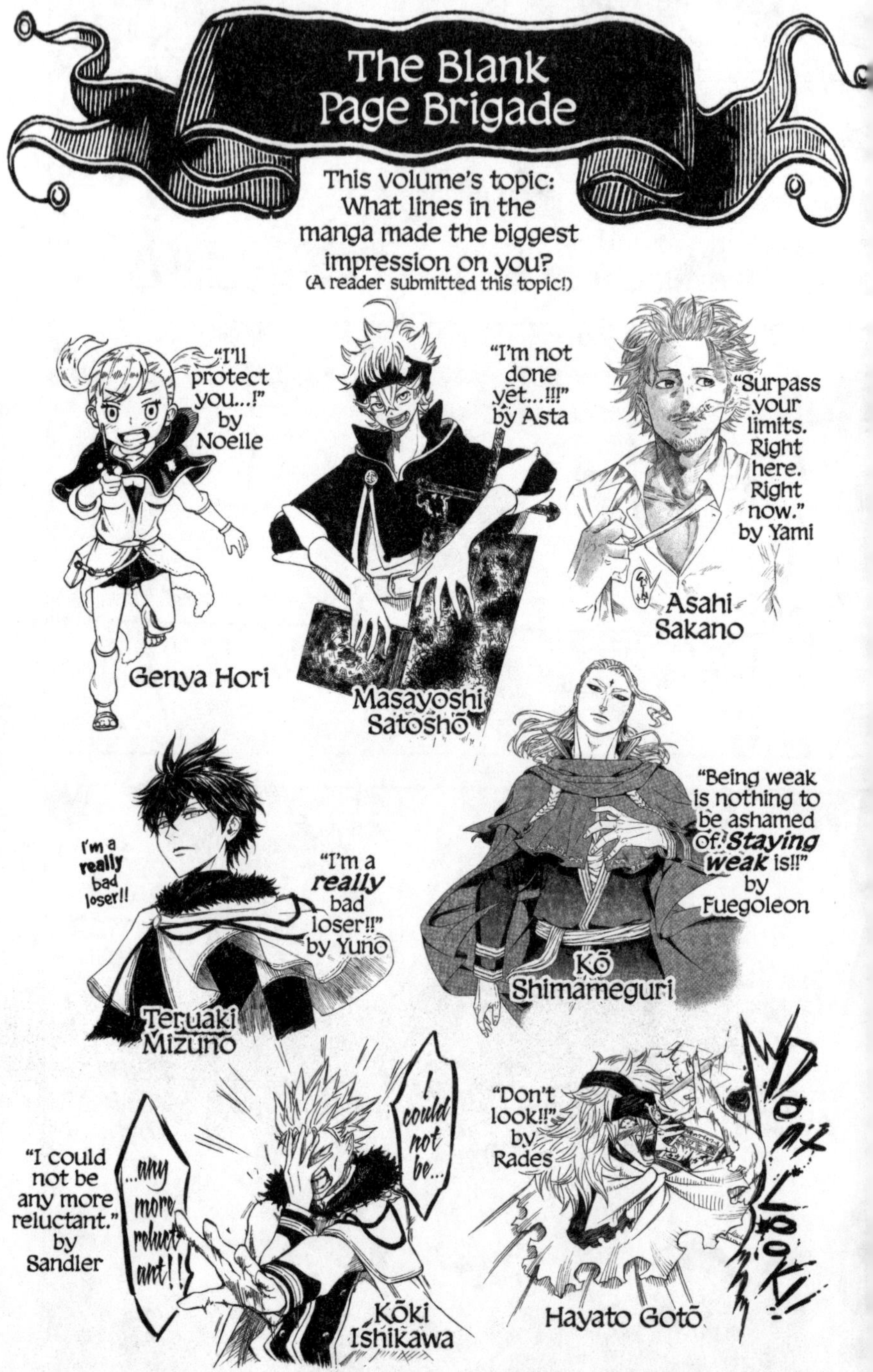

"Surpass your limits. Right here. Right now." by Yami
Asahi Sakano
"I'm not done yet...!!!" by Asta
Masayoshi Satoshō
"I'll protect you...!" by Noelle
Genya Hori
"Being weak is nothing to be ashamed of. **Staying weak** is!!" by Fuegoleon
Kō Shimameguri
"I'm a *really* bad loser!!" by Yuno
I'm a really bad loser!!
Teruaki Mizuno
"Don't look!!" by Rades
DON'T LOOK!!
Hayato Gotō
"I could not be any more reluctant." by Sandler
I could not be...
...any more reluctant!!
Kōki Ishikawa

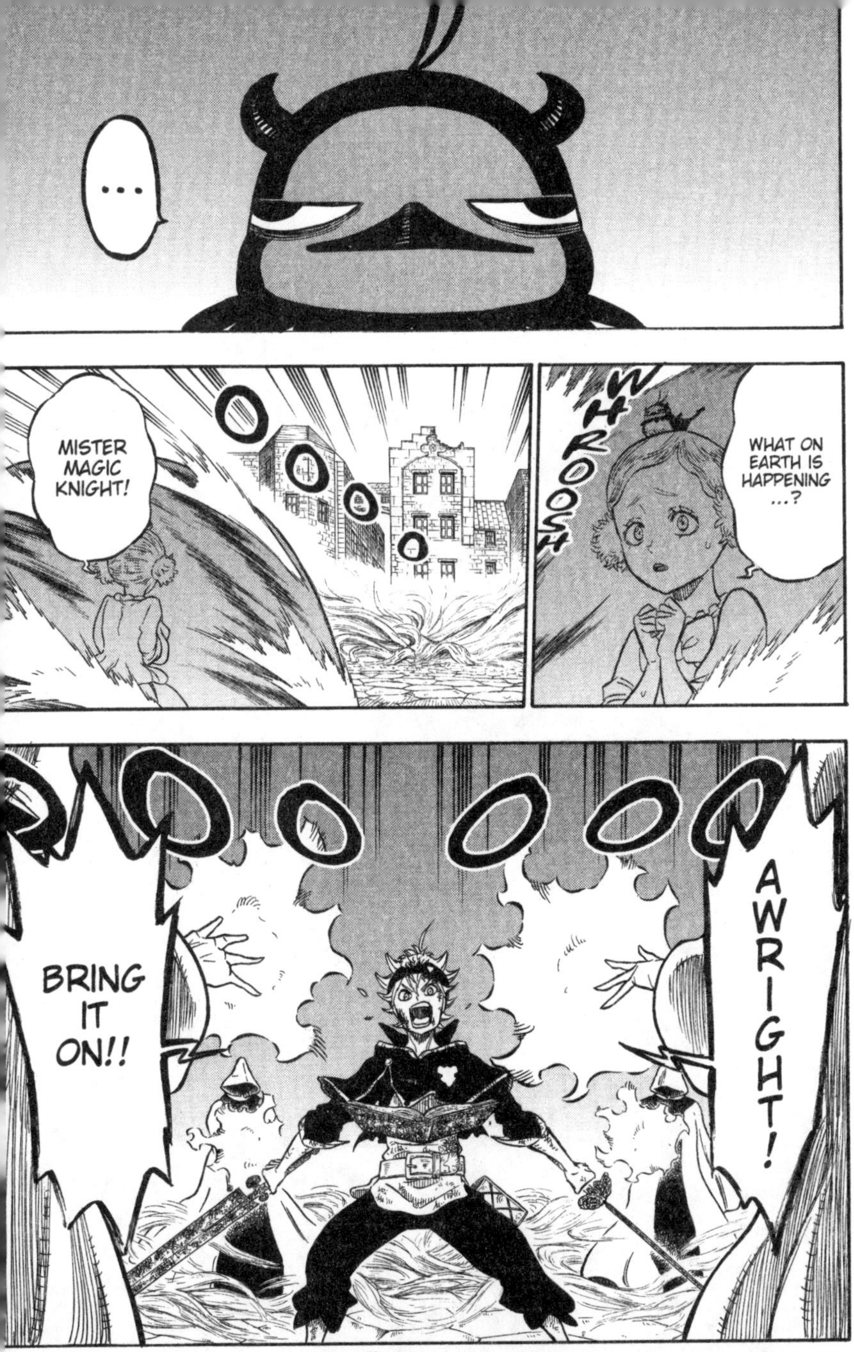
...
WHROOOSH
WHAT ON EARTH IS HAPPENING ...?
MISTER MAGIC KNIGHT!
AWRIGHT!
BRING IT ON!!

Page 34: Wounded Beasts

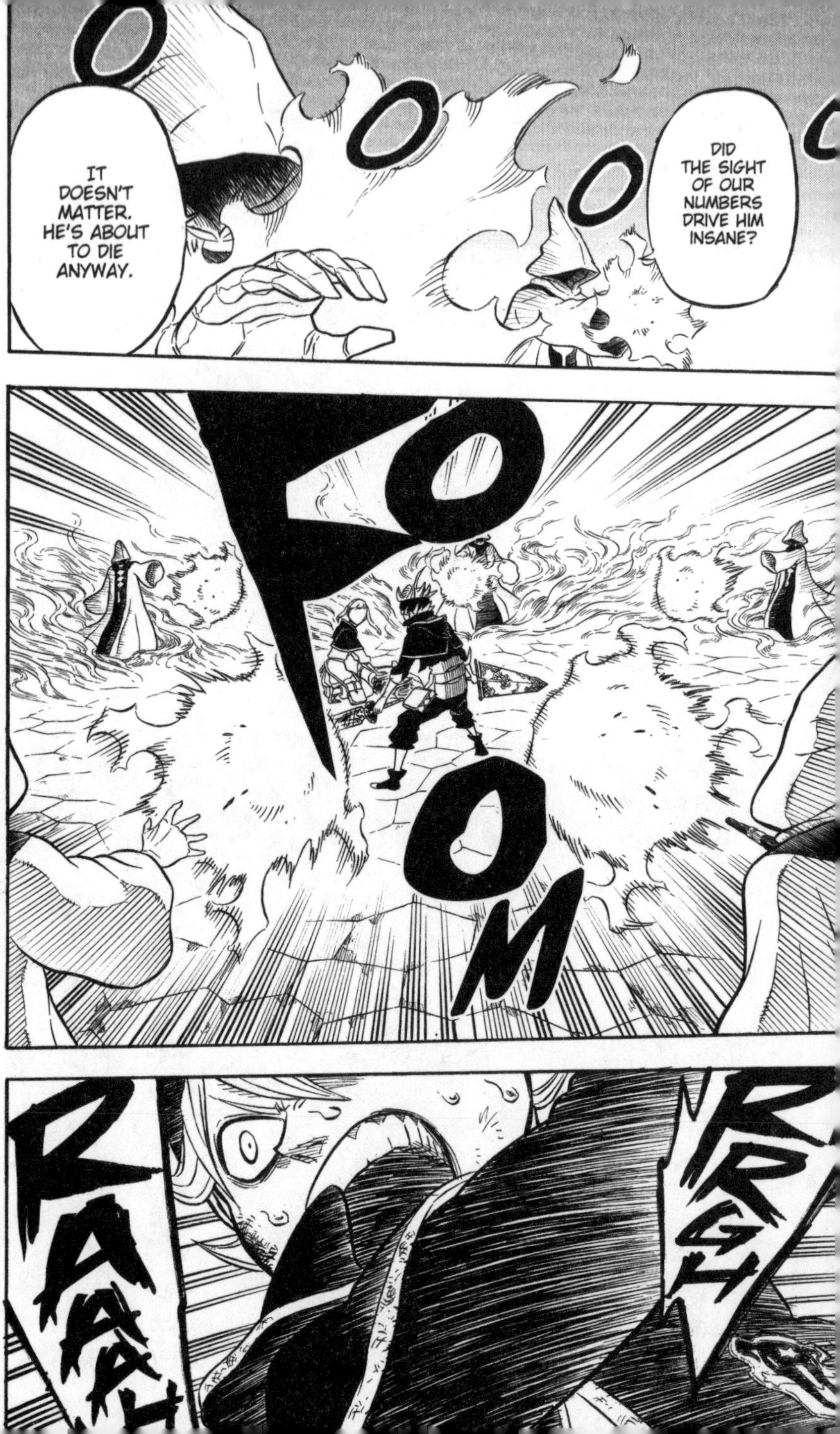
DID THE SIGHT OF OUR NUMBERS DRIVE HIM INSANE?
IT DOESN'T MATTER. HE'S ABOUT TO DIE ANYWAY.
FOOM
NRRRGH
RAAAAH

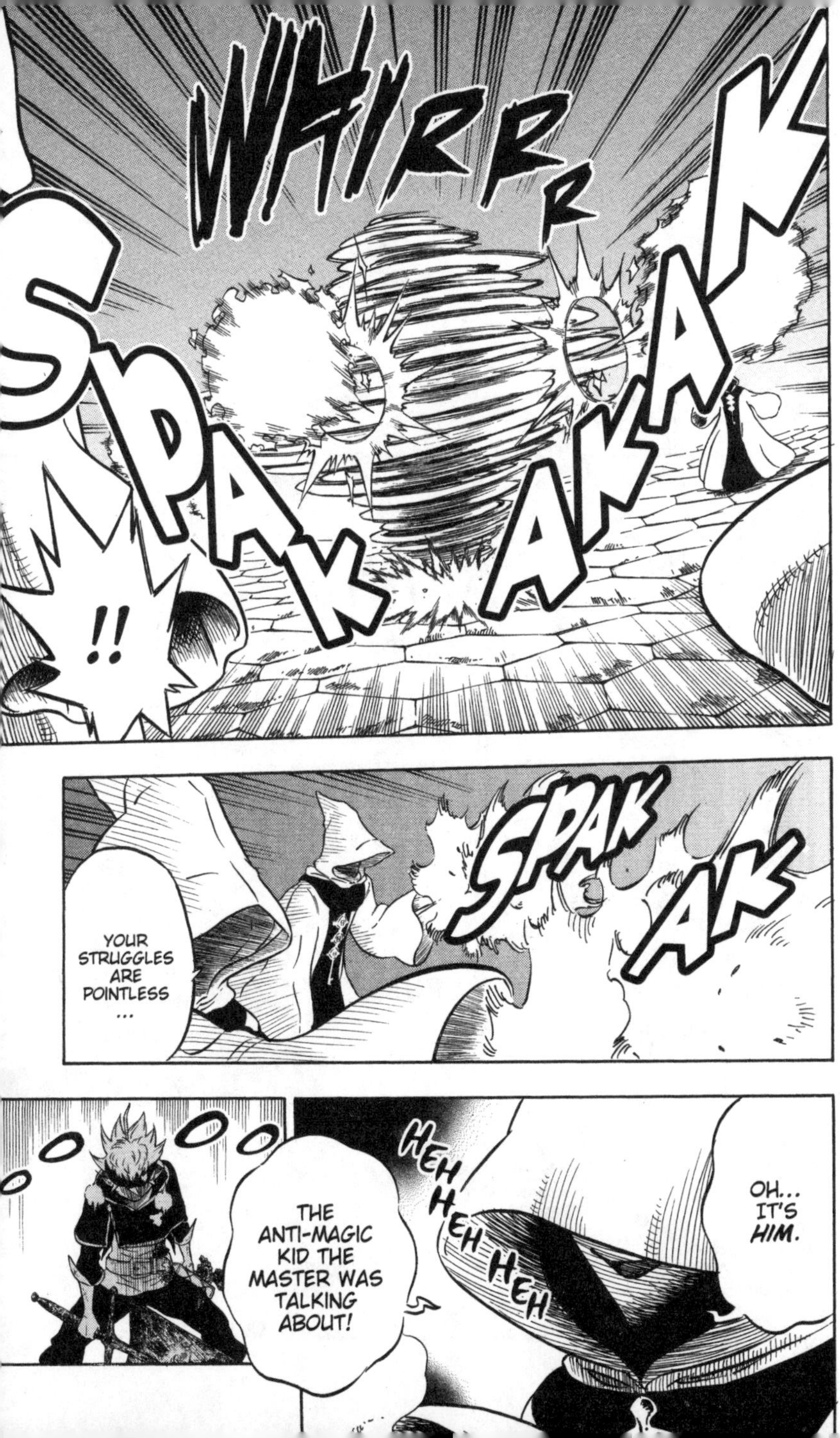
WHIRRRR
SPAKAKAK
!!
SPAK AK
YOUR STRUGGLES ARE POINTLESS...
OH... IT'S *HIM*.
HEH HEH HEH
THE ANTI-MAGIC KID THE MASTER WAS TALKING ABOUT!

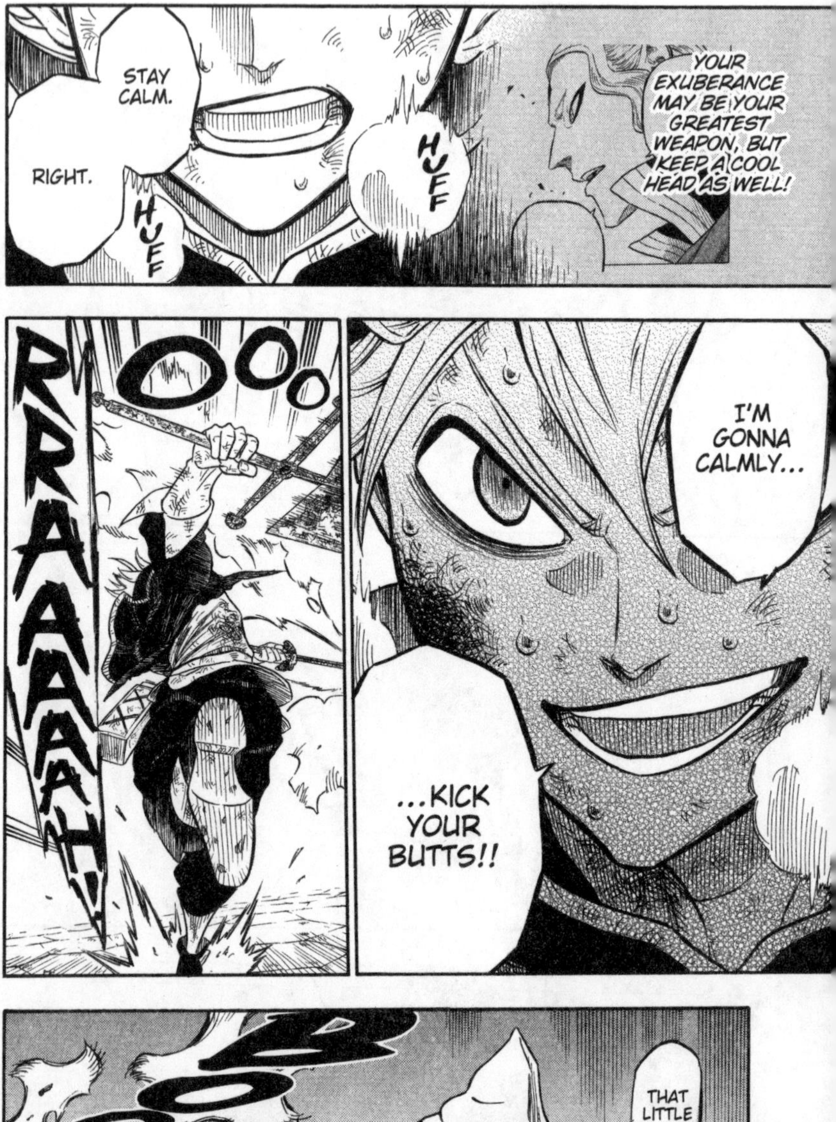
YOUR EXUBERANCE MAY BE YOUR GREATEST WEAPON, BUT KEEP A COOL HEAD AS WELL!
HUFF
STAY CALM.
RIGHT.
HUFF
I'M GONNA CALMLY...
...KICK YOUR BUTTS!!
OOO
RRAAAAAAH!!
THAT LITTLE ...!
BOOMF

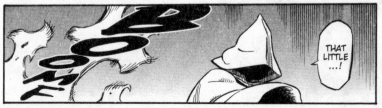

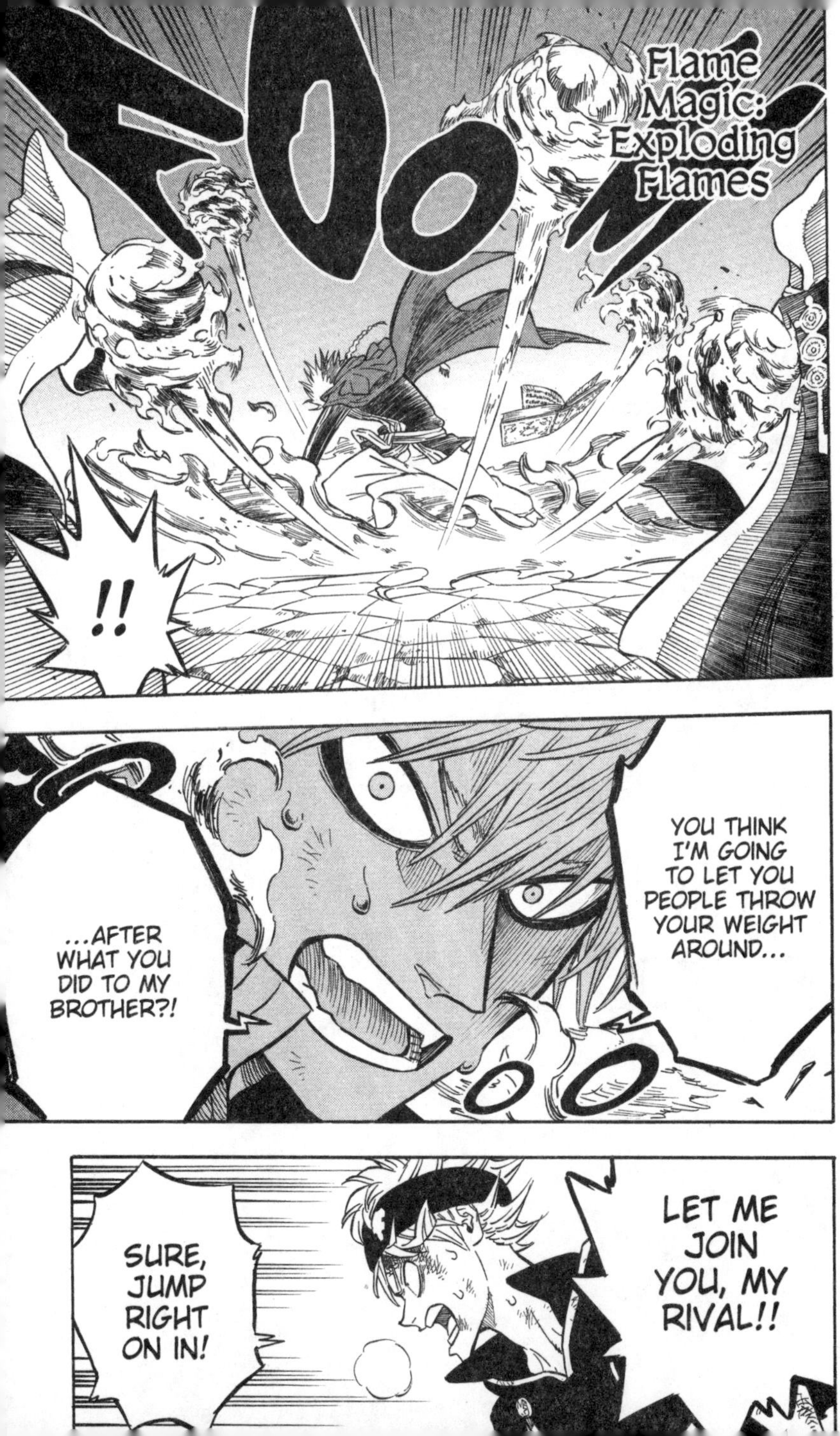
Flame Magic: Exploding Flames
FOOM
!!
YOU THINK I'M GOING TO LET YOU PEOPLE THROW YOUR WEIGHT AROUND...
...AFTER WHAT YOU DID TO MY BROTHER?!
LET ME JOIN YOU, MY RIVAL!!
SURE, JUMP RIGHT ON IN!

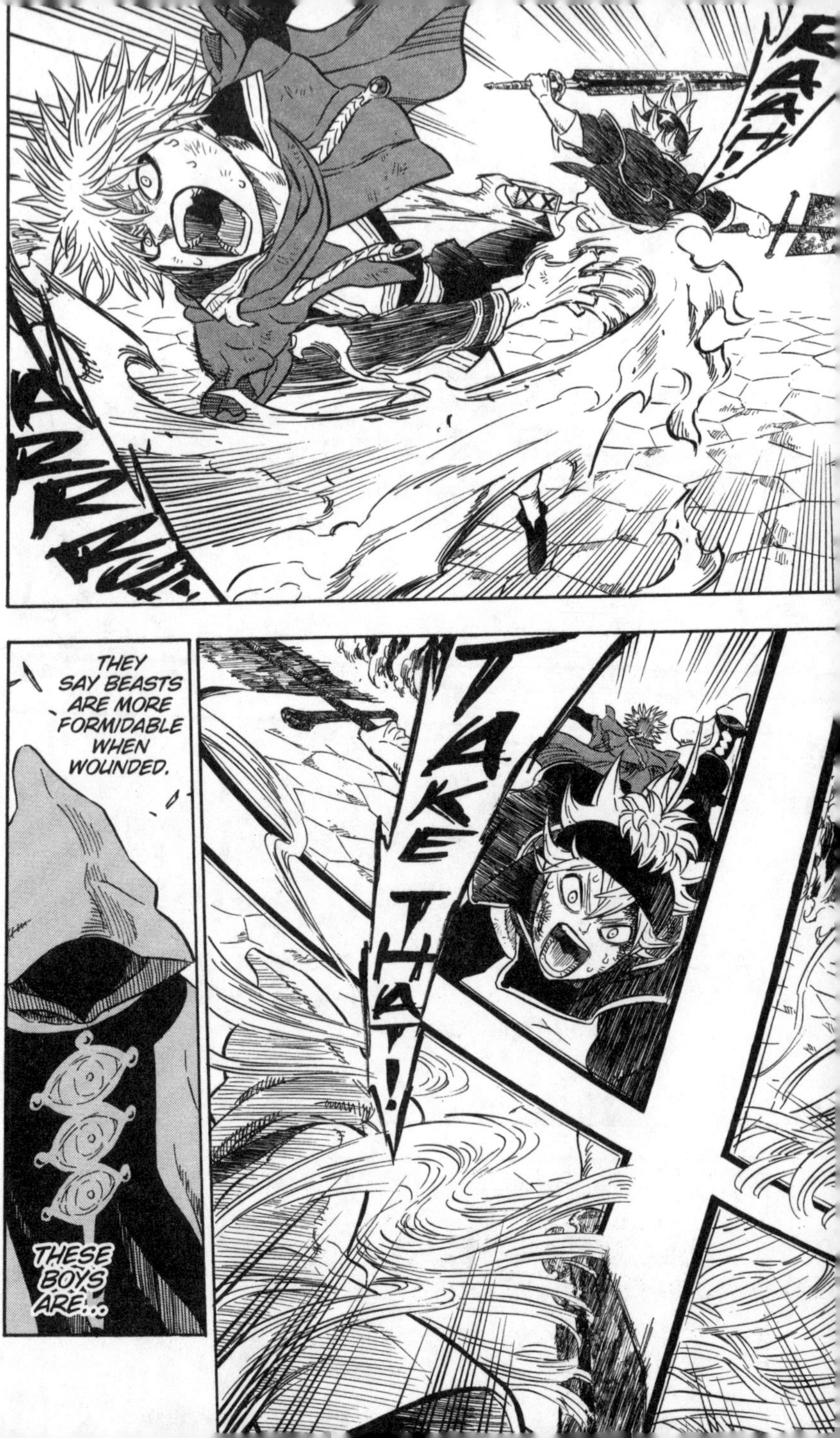
RAAH!!
TAKE THAT!!
THEY SAY BEASTS ARE MORE FORMIDABLE WHEN WOUNDED.
THESE BOYS ARE...

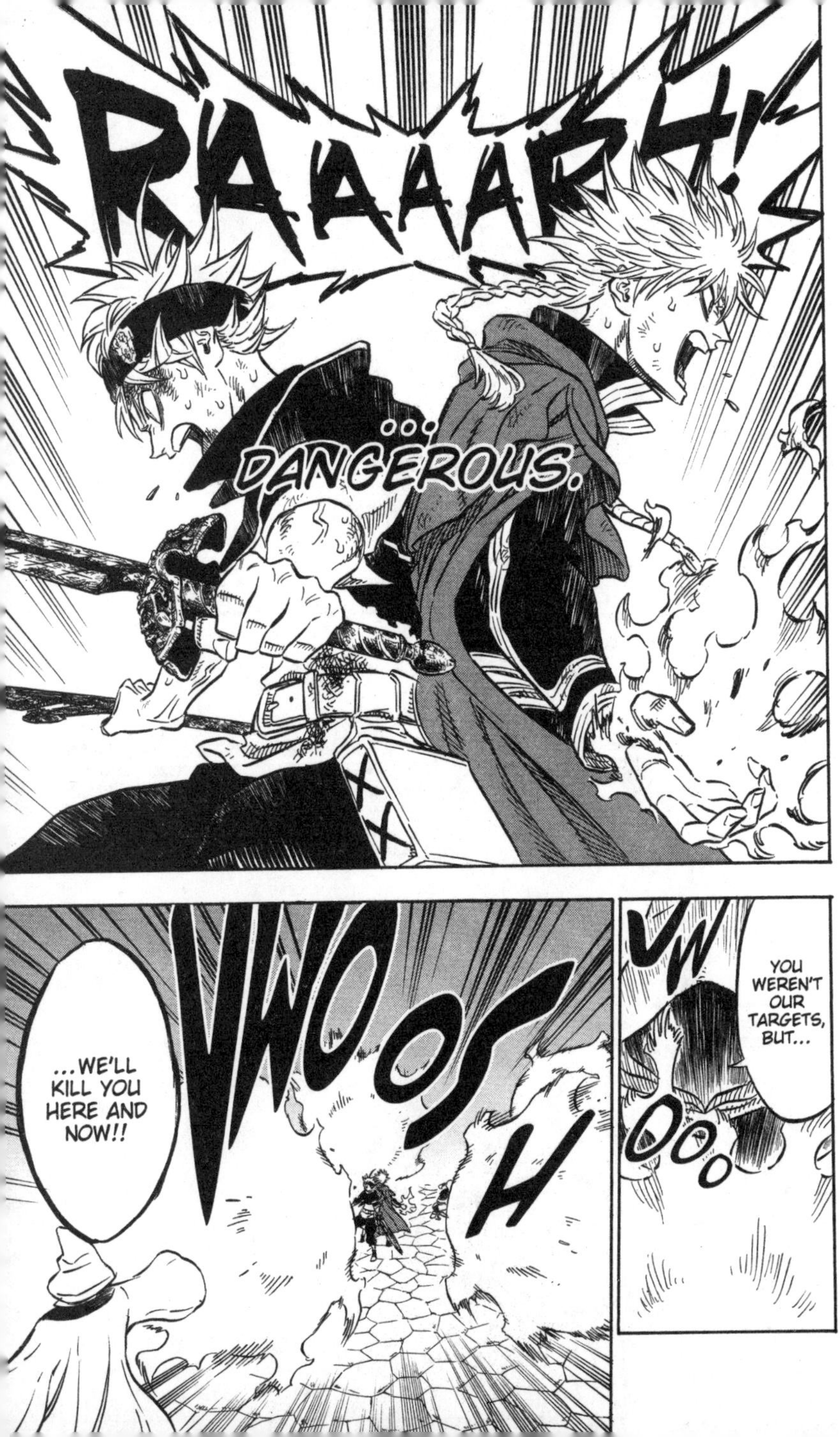
RAAAARGH!
...DANGEROUS.
YOU WEREN'T OUR TARGETS, BUT...
VWOOOSH
...WE'LL KILL YOU HERE AND NOW!!

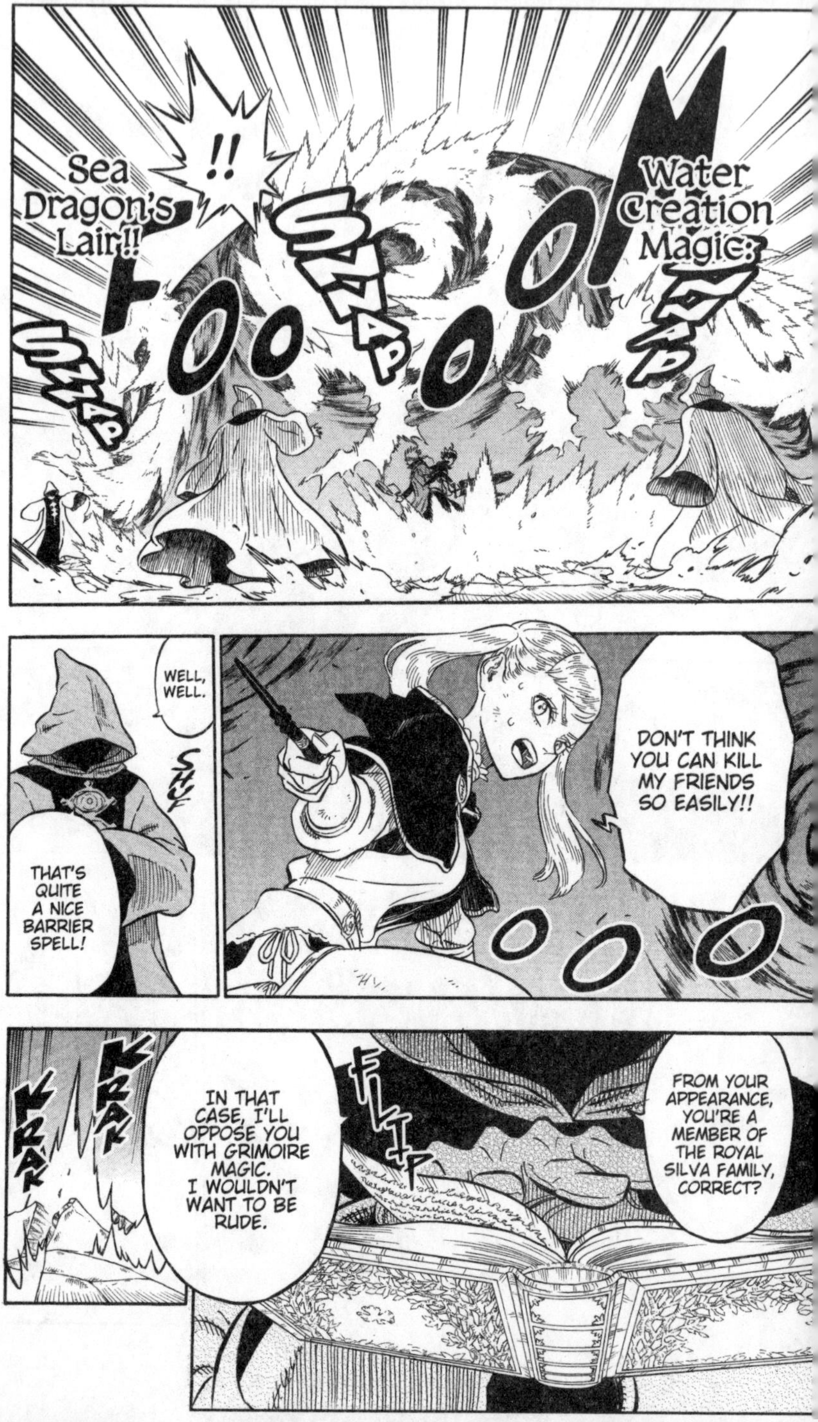
Water Creation Magic:
!!
SWAP
Sea Dragon's Lair!!
SWAP
WELL, WELL.
DON'T THINK YOU CAN KILL MY FRIENDS SO EASILY!!
THAT'S QUITE A NICE BARRIER SPELL!
FROM YOUR APPEARANCE, YOU'RE A MEMBER OF THE ROYAL SILVA FAMILY, CORRECT?
FLIP
IN THAT CASE, I'LL OPPOSE YOU WITH GRIMOIRE MAGIC. I WOULDN'T WANT TO BE RUDE.
KRAK
KRAK

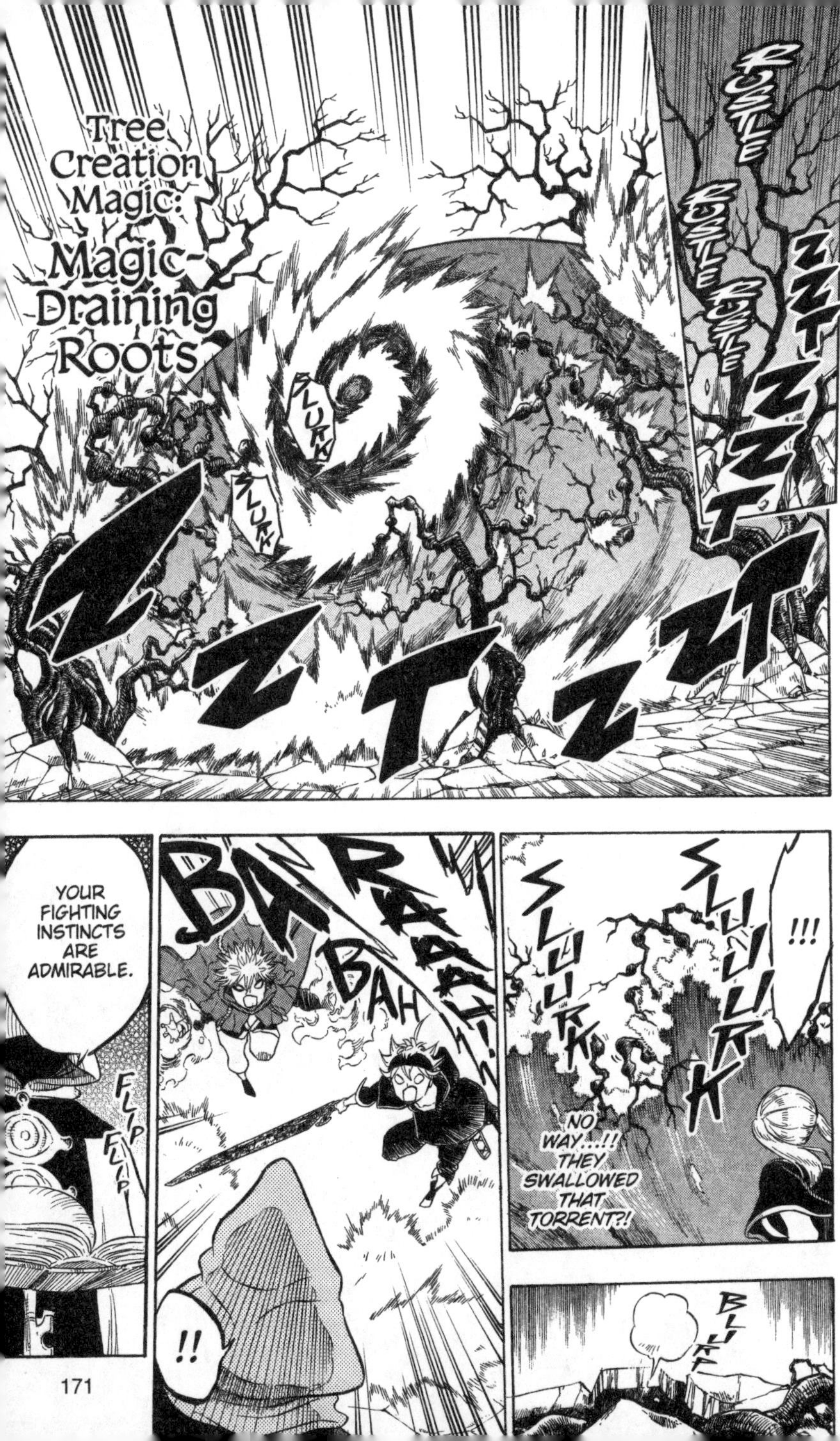
RUSTLE RUSTLE RUSTLE
ZZZT
Tree Creation Magic: Magic-Draining Roots
SLURK
SLURK
SLUURK SLUURK
!!!
NO WAY...!! THEY SWALLOWED THAT TORRENT?!
BLURF
BARRAAAH!
BAH
!!
YOUR FIGHTING INSTINCTS ARE ADMIRABLE.
FLIP FLIP

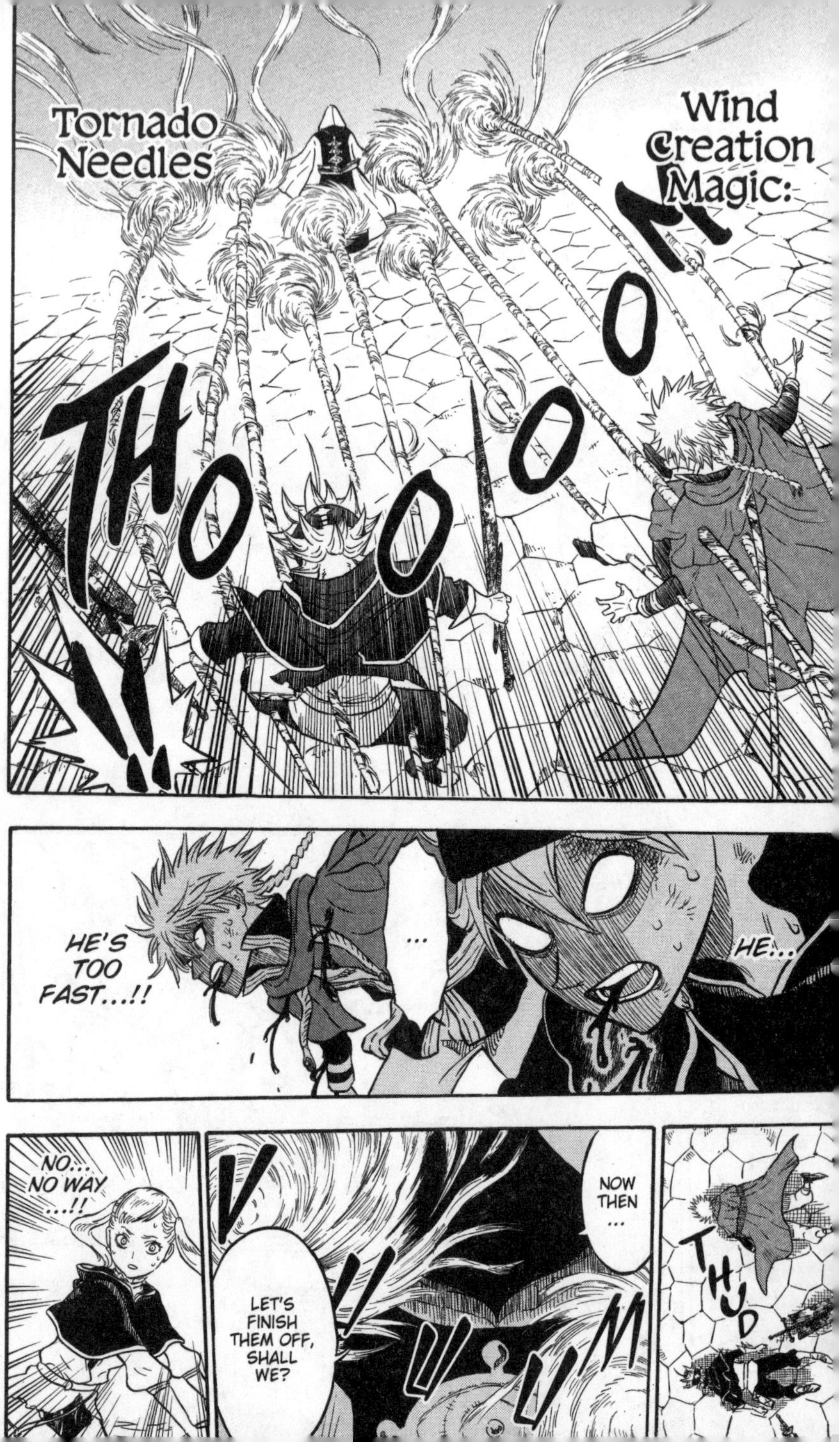
Wind Creation Magic:
Tornado Needles
HE...
...
HE'S TOO FAST...!!
THUD
NOW THEN...
LET'S FINISH THEM OFF, SHALL WE?
NO... NO WAY ...!!

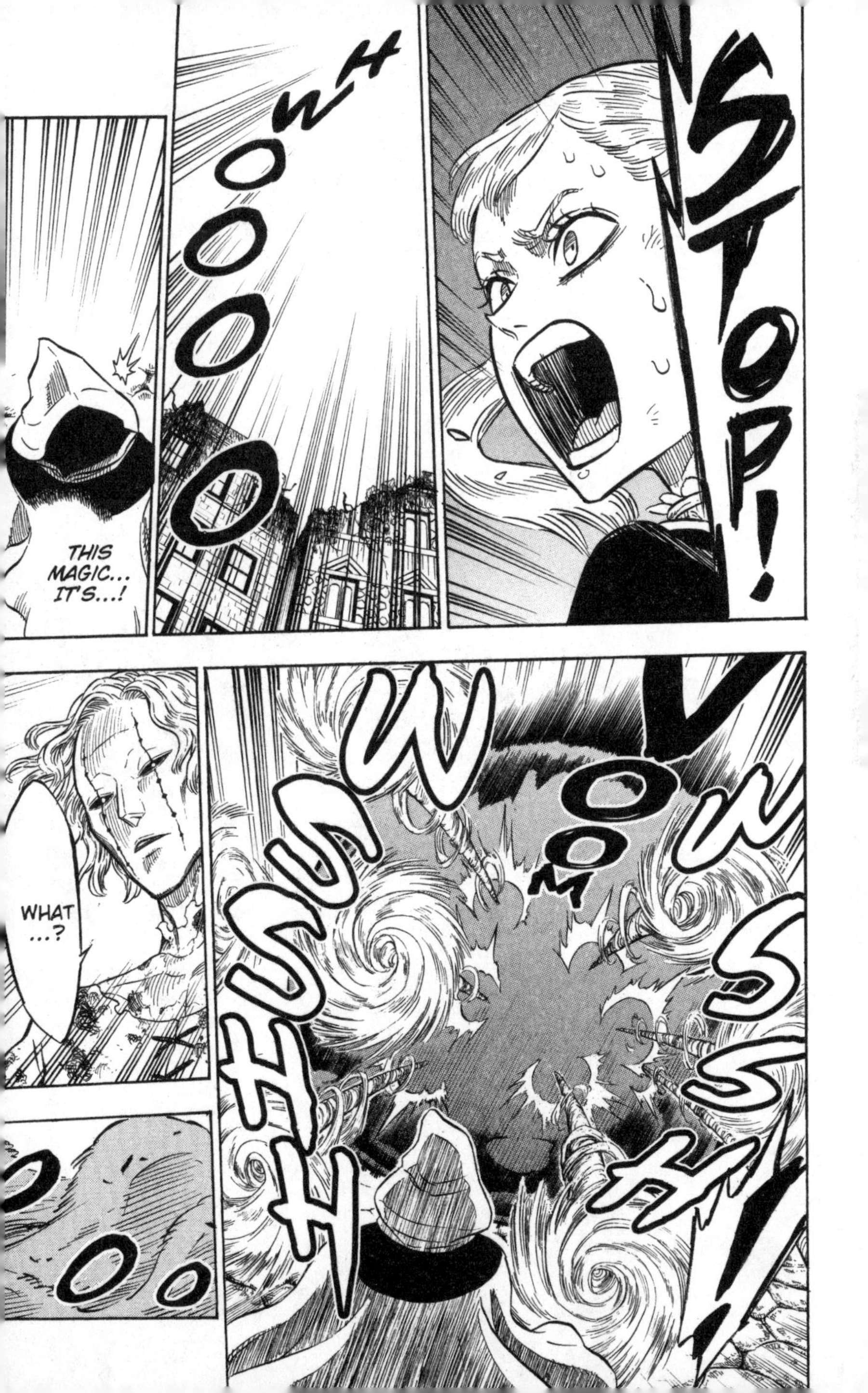
STOP!
THIS MAGIC... IT'S...!
WHAT ...?

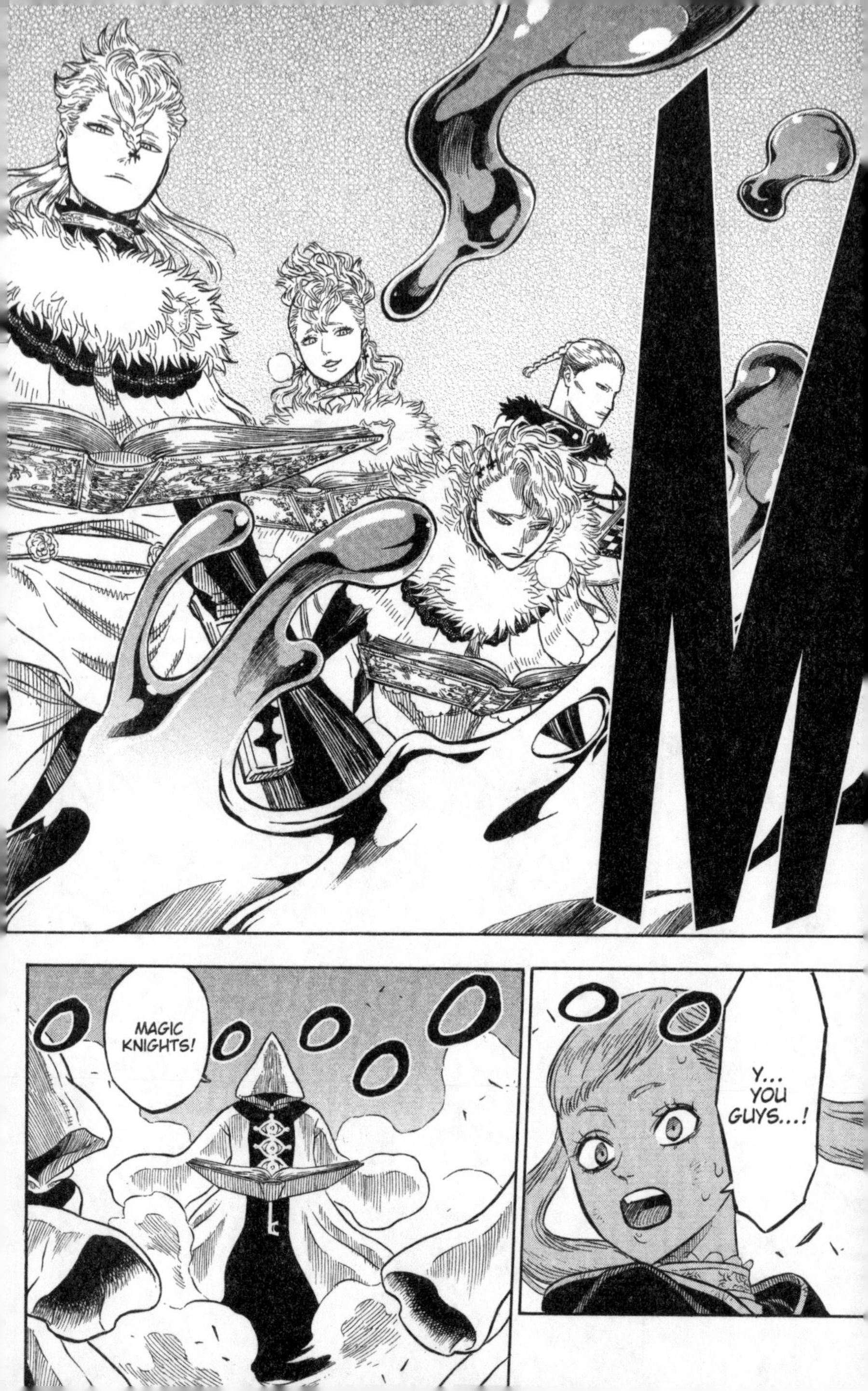
Y... YOU GUYS...!
MAGIC KNIGHTS!

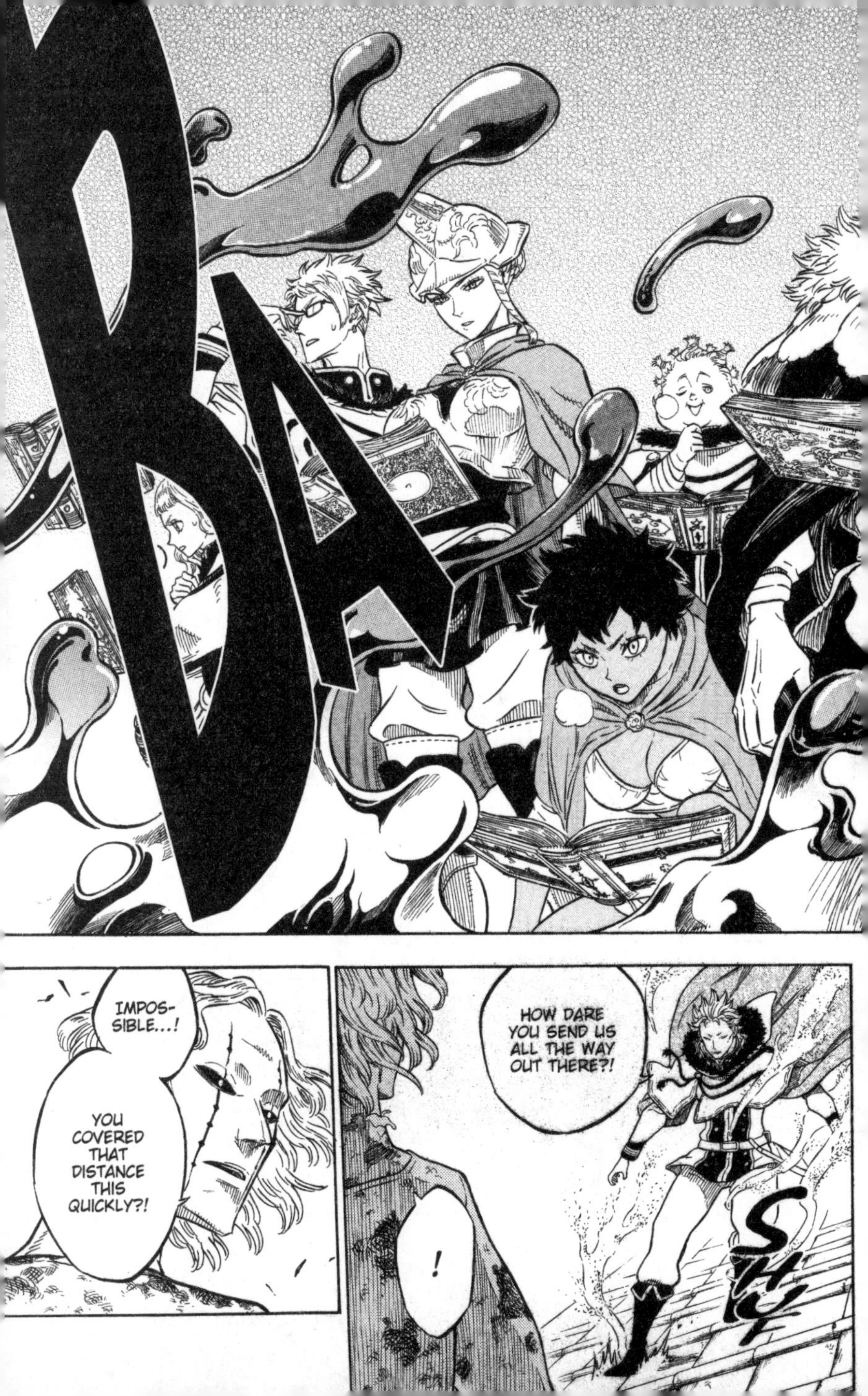
BA
HOW DARE YOU SEND US ALL THE WAY OUT THERE?!
!
IMPOS-SIBLE...!
YOU COVERED THAT DISTANCE THIS QUICKLY?!

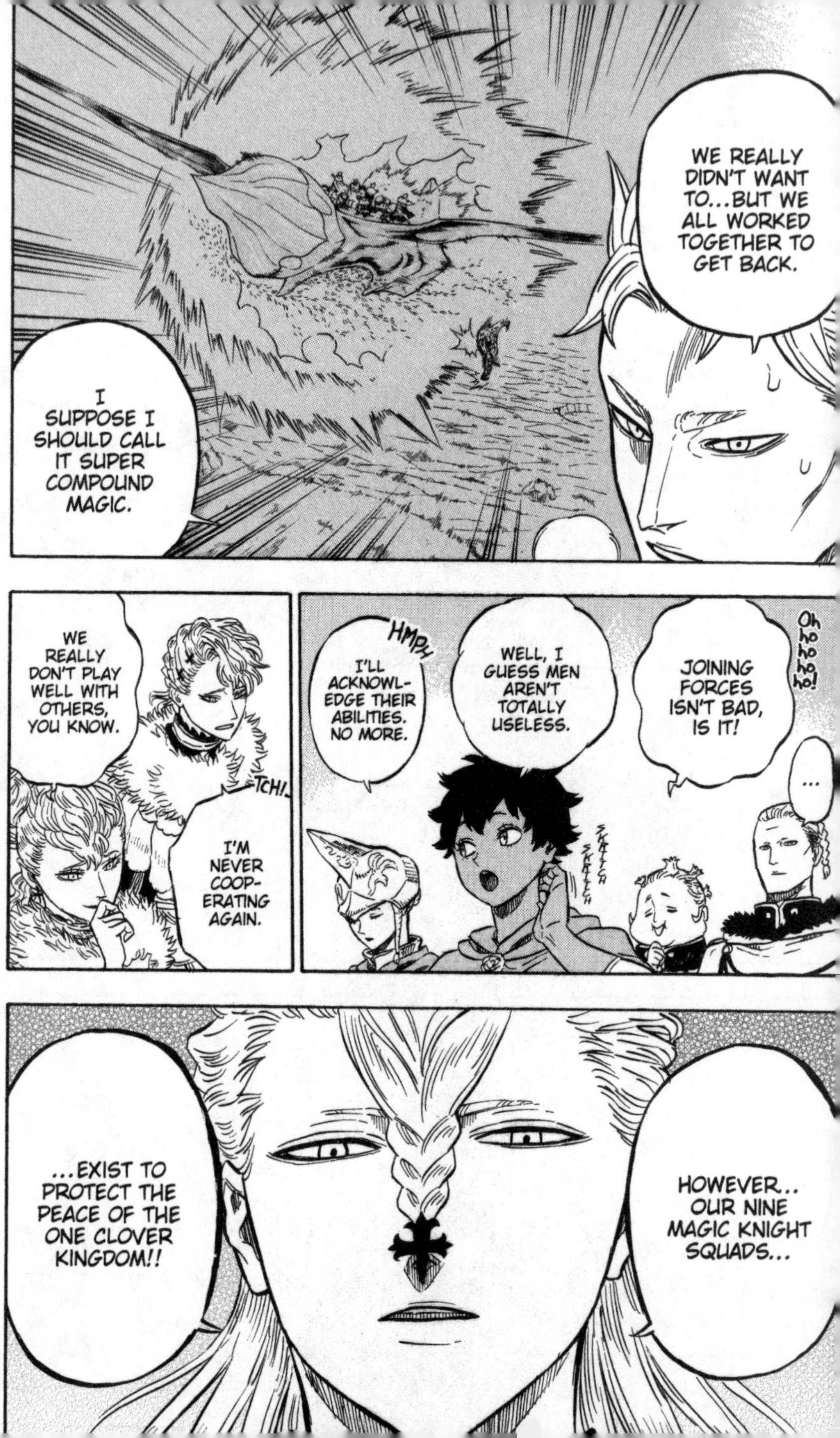
WE REALLY DIDN'T WANT TO...BUT WE ALL WORKED TOGETHER TO GET BACK.
I SUPPOSE I SHOULD CALL IT SUPER COMPOUND MAGIC.
Oh ho ho ho ho!
JOINING FORCES ISN'T BAD, IS IT!
...
WELL, I GUESS MEN AREN'T TOTALLY USELESS.
SKRITCH SKRITCH
HMPH
I'LL ACKNOWL-EDGE THEIR ABILITIES. NO MORE.
WE REALLY DON'T PLAY WELL WITH OTHERS, YOU KNOW.
TCH!
I'M NEVER COOP-ERATING AGAIN.
HOWEVER... OUR NINE MAGIC KNIGHT SQUADS...
...EXIST TO PROTECT THE PEACE OF THE ONE CLOVER KINGDOM!!

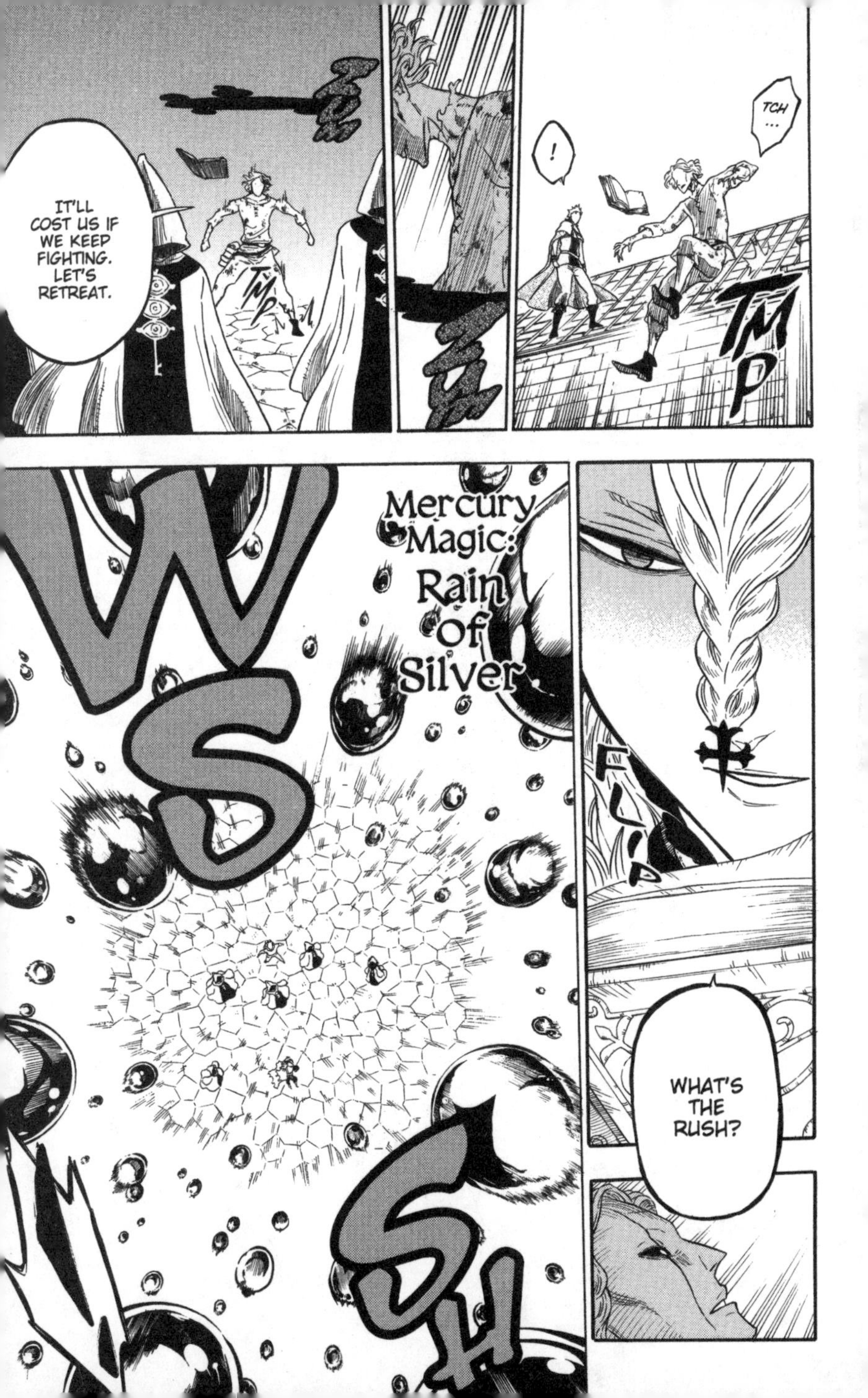
TCH ...
!
TMP
IT'LL COST US IF WE KEEP FIGHTING. LET'S RETREAT.
TMP
FLIP
WHAT'S THE RUSH?
Mercury Magic: Rain of Silver
WS
SH

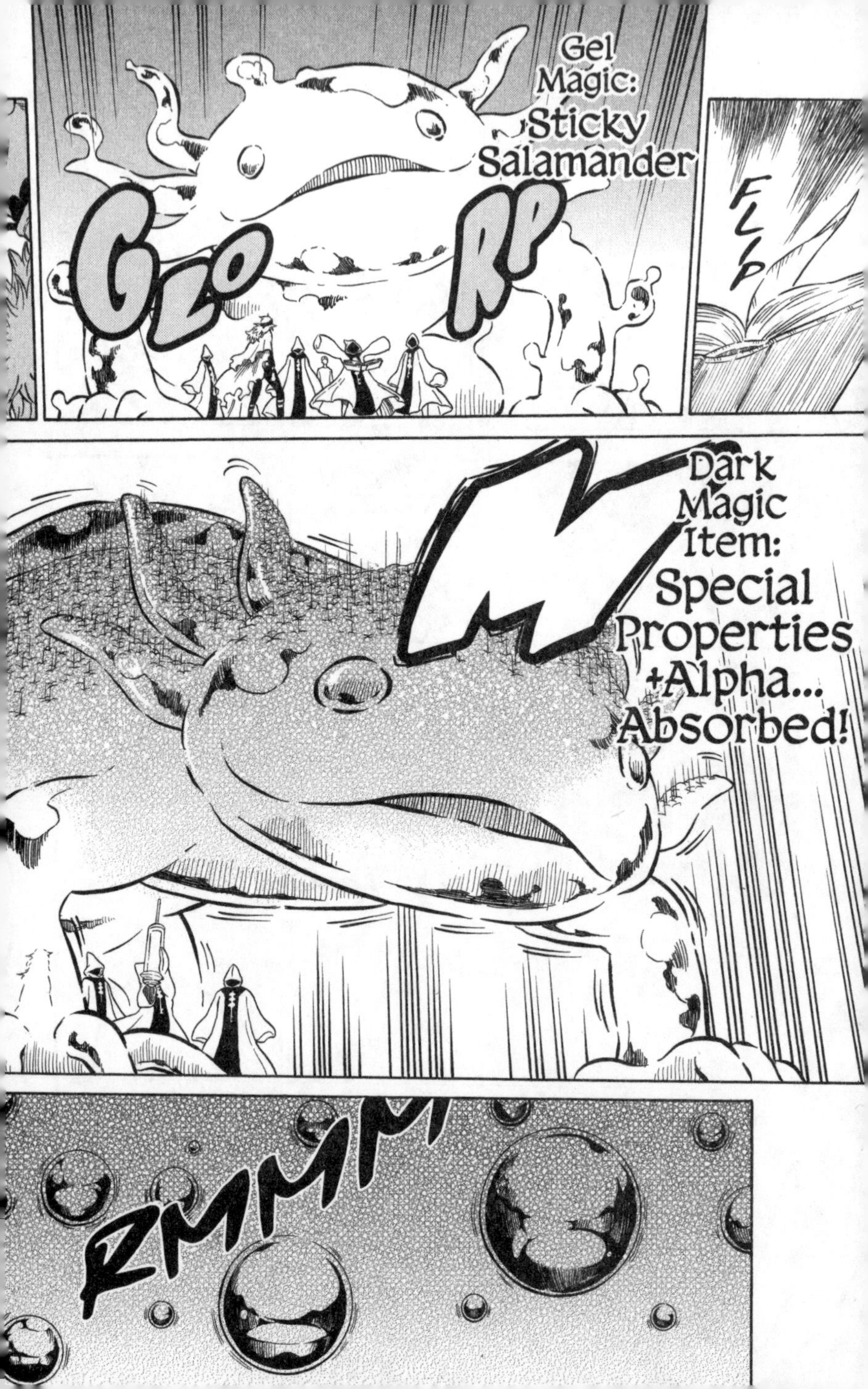
FLIP
Gel Magic: Sticky Salamander
GLORP
Dark Magic Item: Special Properties +Alpha... Absorbed!
RMMMM

SHDF

WHAT...

AND THEN...

MY RAIN WILL GO RIGHT THROUGH A SPELL LIKE THAT.

BAH

...IS THAT MAGIC ITEM?!

GATOOMP

GLIP

R

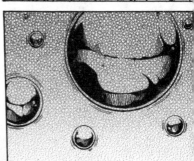

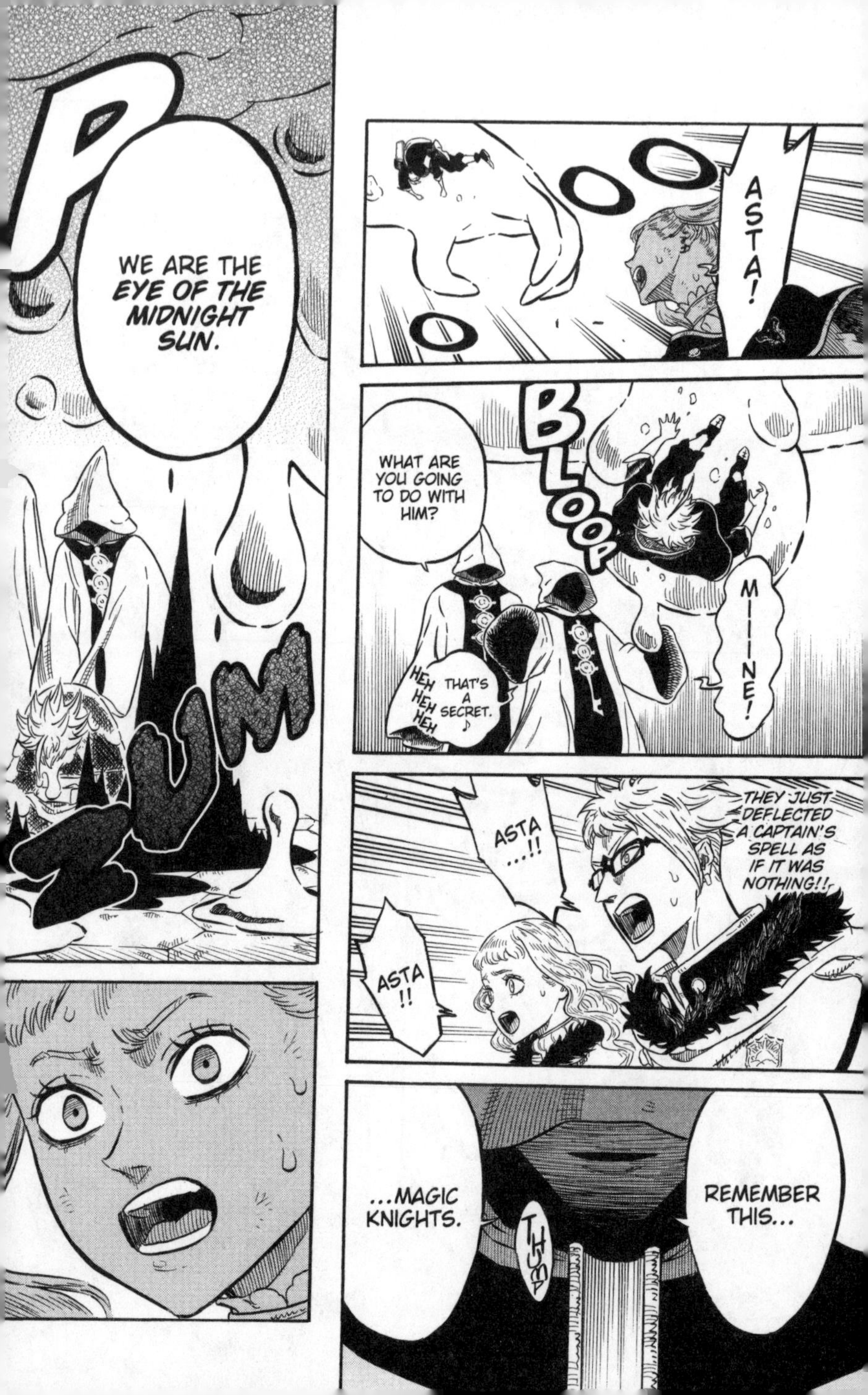
ASTA!
POOO
BLOOP
MIIINE!
WHAT ARE YOU GOING TO DO WITH HIM?
THAT'S A SECRET. ♪
HEH HEH HEH
THEY JUST DEFLECTED A CAPTAIN'S SPELL AS IF IT WAS NOTHING!!
ASTA...!!
ASTA!!
REMEMBER THIS...
THUMP
...MAGIC KNIGHTS.
P
WE ARE THE EYE OF THE MIDNIGHT SUN.
ZUM

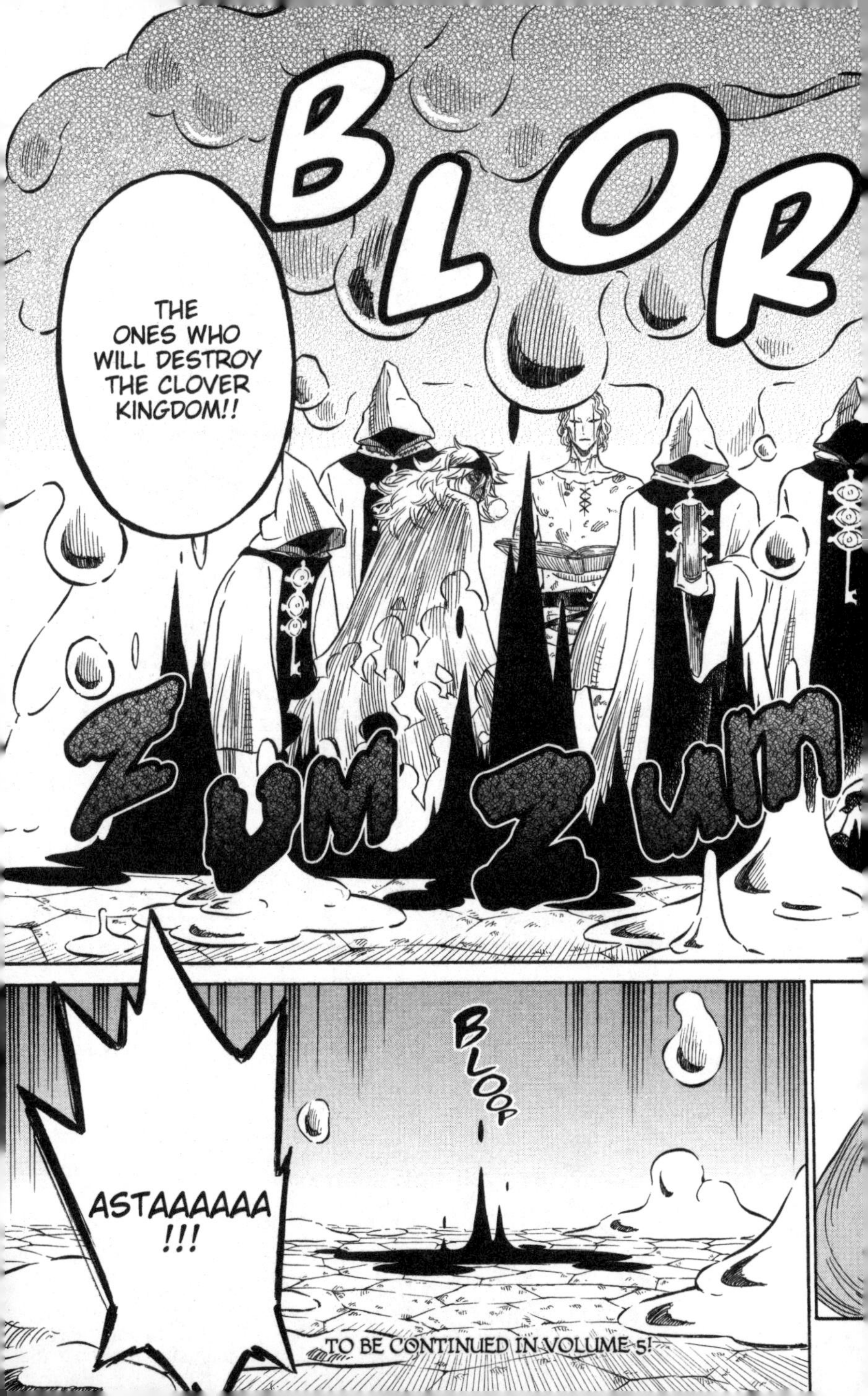
BLOR
THE ONES WHO WILL DESTROY THE CLOVER KINGDOM!!
ZUM ZUM
BLOOP
ASTAAAAAA !!!
TO BE CONTINUED IN VOLUME 5!

Special project to celebrate the vol. 4 release!!

Special Support Manga from Yuto Tsukuda: "Memories with Tabacchan"

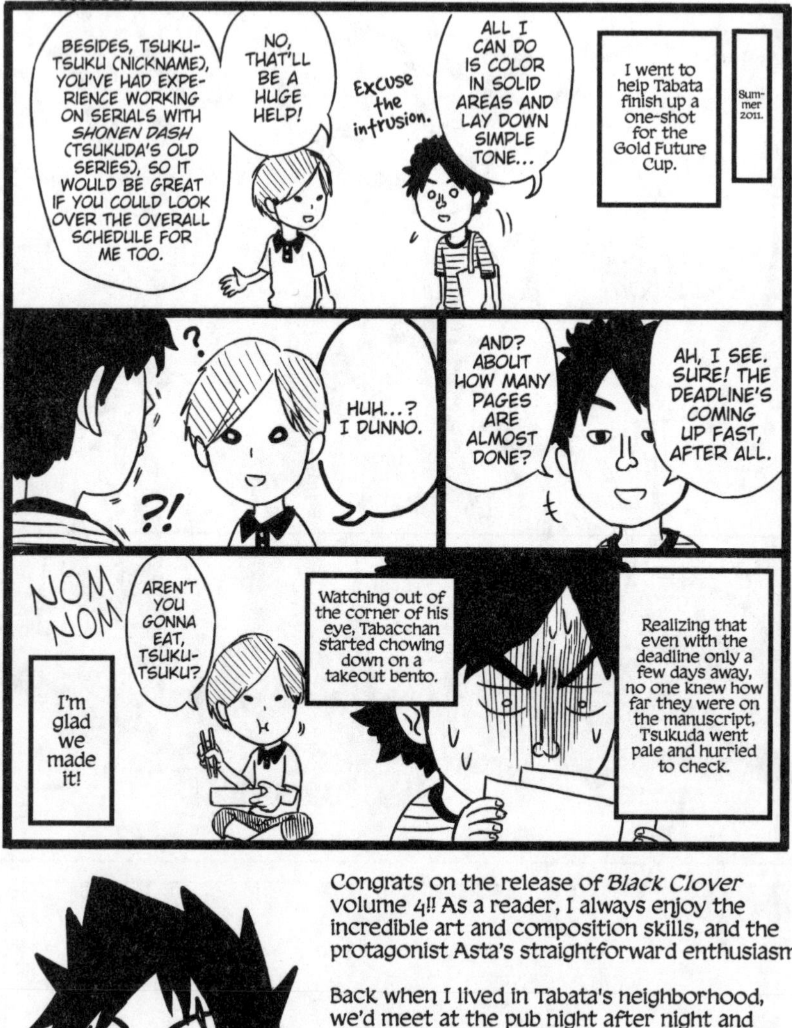
Summer 2011.
I went to help Tabata finish up a one-shot for the Gold Future Cup.
ALL I CAN DO IS COLOR IN SOLID AREAS AND LAY DOWN SIMPLE TONE...
Excuse the intrusion.
NO, THAT'LL BE A HUGE HELP!
BESIDES, TSUKU-TSUKU (NICKNAME), YOU'VE HAD EXPE-RIENCE WORKING ON SERIALS WITH *SHONEN DASH* (TSUKUDA'S OLD SERIES), SO IT WOULD BE GREAT IF YOU COULD LOOK OVER THE OVERALL SCHEDULE FOR ME TOO.
AH, I SEE. SURE! THE DEADLINE'S COMING UP FAST, AFTER ALL.
AND? ABOUT HOW MANY PAGES ARE ALMOST DONE?
?
HUH...? I DUNNO.
?!
Realizing that even with the deadline only a few days away, no one knew how far they were on the manuscript, Tsukuda went pale and hurried to check.
Watching out of the corner of his eye, Tabacchan started chowing down on a takeout bento.
AREN'T YOU GONNA EAT, TSUKU-TSUKU?
NOM NOM
I'm glad we made it!

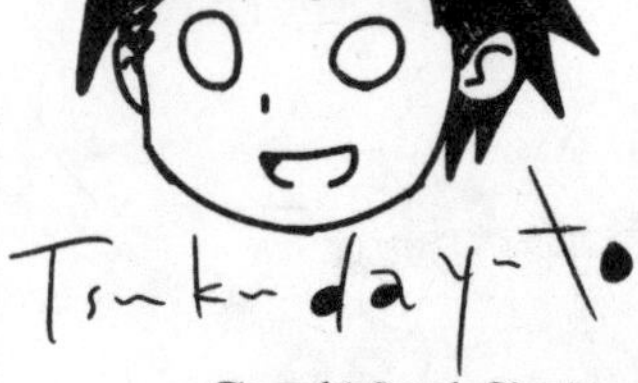
Tsukuda Yuto

Congrats on the release of *Black Clover* volume 4!! As a reader, I always enjoy the incredible art and composition skills, and the protagonist Asta's straightforward enthusiasm.

Back when I lived in Tabata's neighborhood, we'd meet at the pub night after night and talk about manga for hours on end. Those are terrific memories. Now we both have manga running in the same magazine, and I feel like, "We did it! Go, us!"

Let's both keep giving it our best!!

Food Wars!: Shokugeki no Soma, written by Yuto Tsukuda, currently runs in *Weekly Shonen Jump* and is available as graphic novels!

This volume's topic: What lines in the manga made the biggest impression on you?
Comics Editor Tomiyama
"So that means... You're a real man, ain'tcha!" by Magna
Captain Tabata
"My magic is never giving up!!!" by Asta
Wife Zenas !!!
"I said *no*." by Charmy
FWOOSH
©
Editor Zenas !!!
"..." by Nero
FWOOSH
Editor Katayama

AFTERWORD

This time, Tsukuda Sensei a.k.a., my friend Tsuku-Tsuku, drew a support manga for me! Woohoo! Thank yoooooou!!

We're from the same part of the country, and he's close to my age. Since he was a nice person with a good head on his shoulders, I had him hang out with me a lot. Heh heh heh.

He's a really nice guy who gave a flawless speech as the representative of my friends at my wedding.

He's really enthusiastic about manga, and at the pub, although I always said insubstantial stuff, the things he said were really useful, and I always used them as reference. Heh heh heh.

I'm seriously moved that I get to work hard in the same magazine with a guy like that!
"We did it! Go, us!"
Come by the studio to work on roughs again, okay?

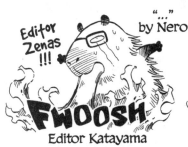

Special Bonus Materials

Presenting early sketches of the Silva siblings and more! You can see the process of trial and error they went through before they were completed. By the way, who's the character with a striking resemblance to *that* person...??

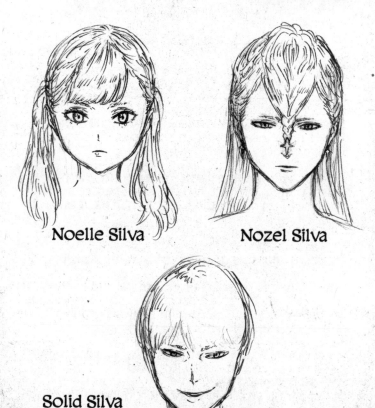

Noelle Silva

Nozel Silva

Solid Silva

C'mon.

???

Hamon Caseus

Lotus Whomalt

Shiren Tium

A KILLER COMEDY FROM *WEEKLY SHONEN JUMP*

ASSASSINATION CLASSROOM

STORY AND ART BY
YUSEI MATSUI

Ever caught yourself screaming, "I could just kill that teacher"? What would it take to justify such antisocial behavior and weeks of detention? Especially if he's the best teacher you've ever had? Giving you an "F" on a quiz? Mispronouncing your name during roll call...*again*? How about blowing up the moon and threatening to do the same to Mother Earth—unless you take him out first?! Plus a reward of a cool 100 million from the Ministry of Defense!

Okay, now that you're committed... How are you going to pull this off? What does your pathetic class of misfits have in their arsenal to combat Teach's alien technology, bizarre powers and...*tentacles*?!

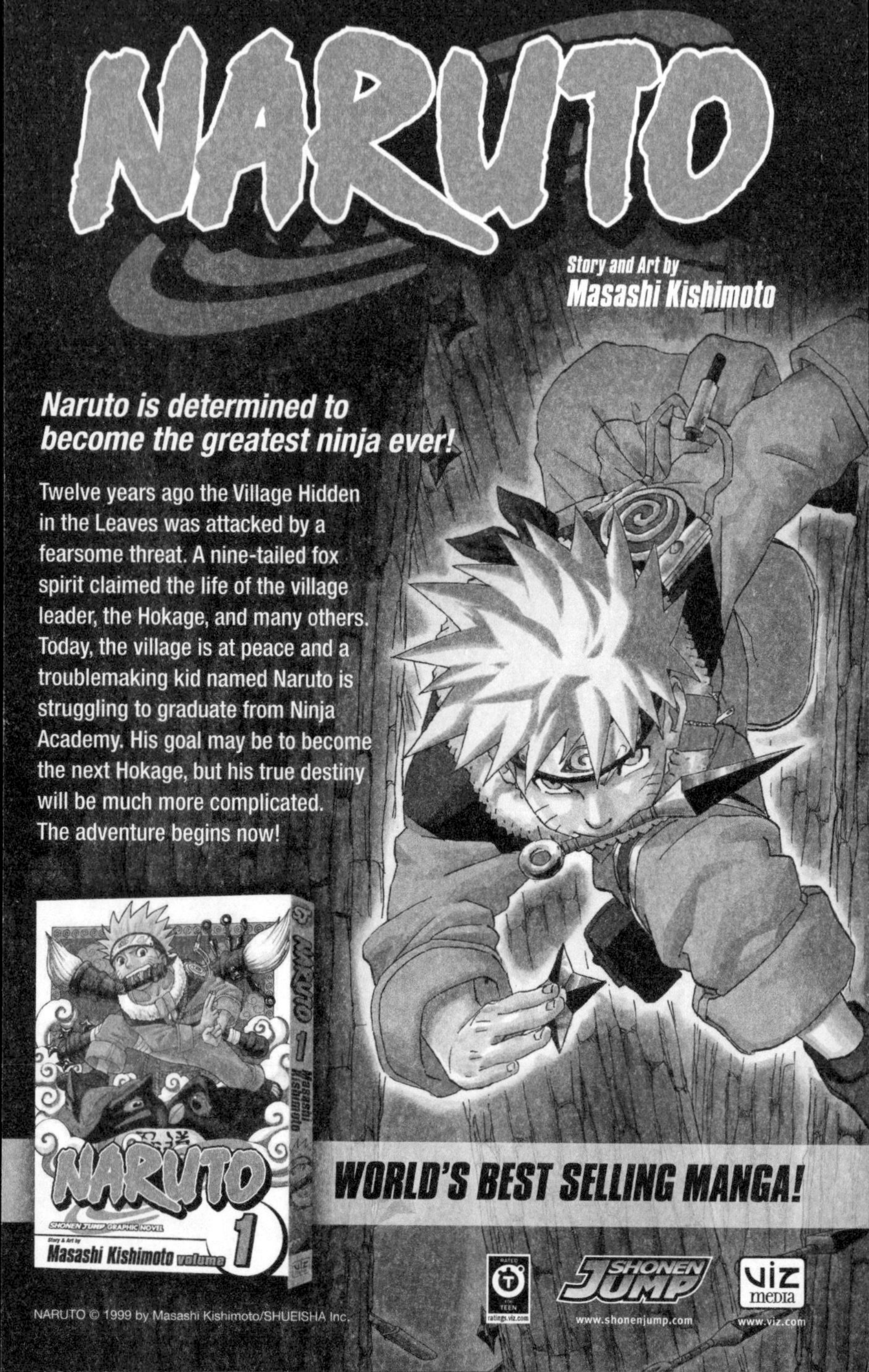
NARUTO
Story and Art by
Masashi Kishimoto
Naruto is determined to become the greatest ninja ever!
Twelve years ago the Village Hidden in the Leaves was attacked by a fearsome threat. A nine-tailed fox spirit claimed the life of the village leader, the Hokage, and many others. Today, the village is at peace and a troublemaking kid named Naruto is struggling to graduate from Ninja Academy. His goal may be to become the next Hokage, but his true destiny will be much more complicated. The adventure begins now!
NARUTO
SHONEN JUMP GRAPHIC NOVEL
Story & Art by
Masashi Kishimoto volume 1
WORLD'S BEST SELLING MANGA!
RATED T TEEN
ratings.viz.com
SHONEN JUMP
www.shonenjump.com
viz media
www.viz.com
NARUTO © 1999 by Masashi Kishimoto/SHUEISHA Inc.

Stop

YOU'RE READING THE WRONG WAY!

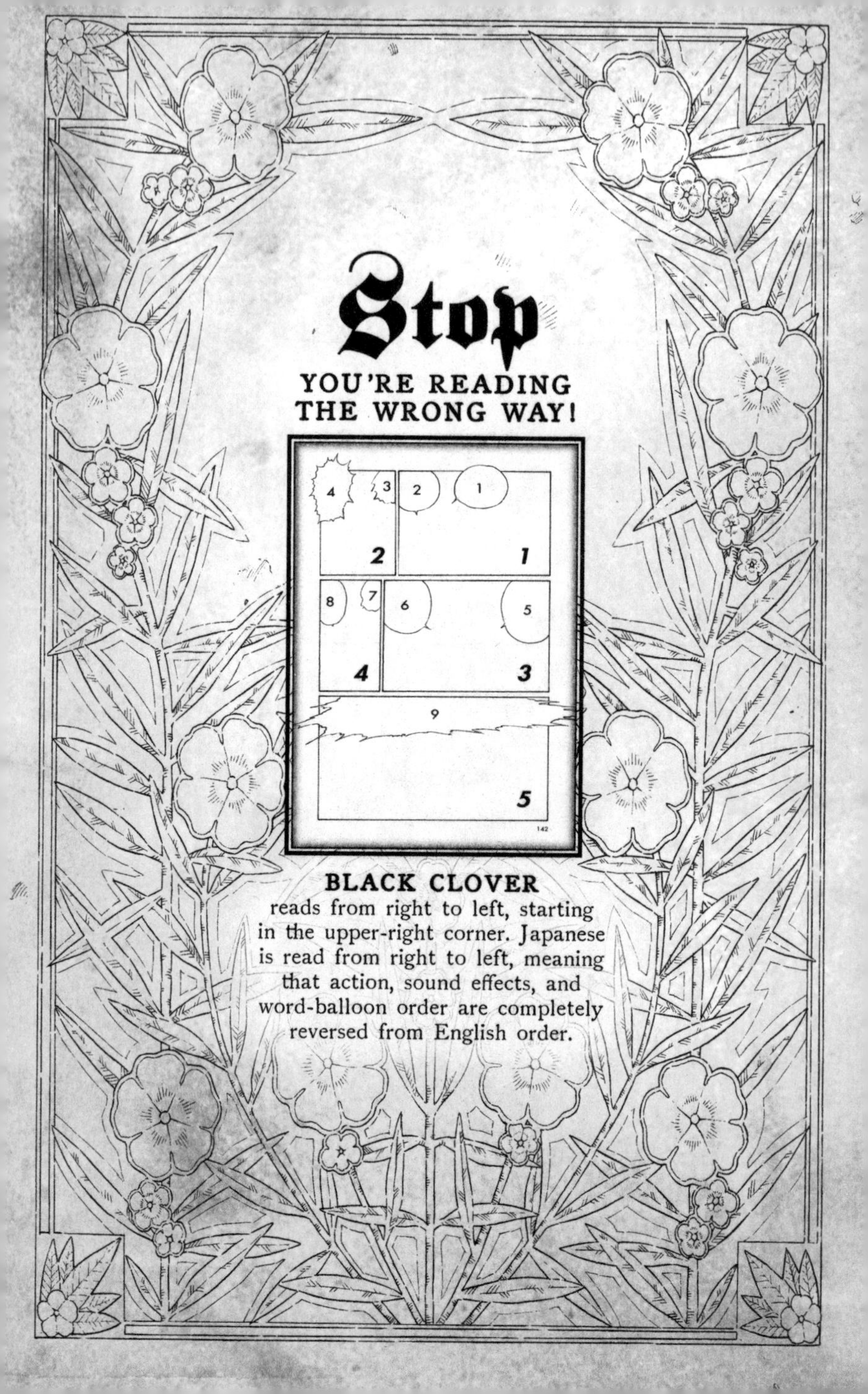
1
2
3
4
5
6
7
8
9
1
2
3
4
5
142

BLACK CLOVER
reads from right to left, starting in the upper-right corner. Japanese is read from right to left, meaning that action, sound effects, and word-balloon order are completely reversed from English order.